World War II
in Numbers

World War II in Numbers

An Infographic Guide to the Conflict, Its Conduct, and Its Casualties

Published by Firefly Books Ltd. 2013

First printing

Publisher Cataloging-in-Publication Data (U.S.)

Doyle, Peter.
World War II in numbers : an infographic guide to World War II / Peter Doyle ; Lindsey Johns.
[224] p. : col. ill., col. photos., maps ; cm.
Includes index.
Summary: The story of the World War II illustrated through graphs. Information is groups into six chapters: people and personnel, on the ground, in the air, at sea, campaigns and conflict, and total war.
ISBN-13: 978-1-77085-195-5
1. World War, 1939-1945 – Miscellanea. I. Johns, Lindsey. II. Title.
940.53 dc23 D744.D6954 2013

Library and Archives Canada Cataloguing in Publication

Doyle, Peter, 1960–
World War II in numbers : an infographic guide to World War II / Peter Doyle ; illustrated by Lindsey Johns.
Includes index.
ISBN 978-1-77085-195-5
1. World War, 1939-1945. I. Title. II. Title: World War 2 in numbers. III. Title: World War Two in numbers.
D743.D69 2013 940.53 C2013-901086-6

Published in the United States by
Firefly Books (U.S.) Inc.
P.O. Box 1338, Ellicott Station
Buffalo, New York 14205

Published in Canada by
Firefly Books Ltd.
50 Staples Avenue, Unit 1
Richmond Hill, Ontario L4B 0A7

Printed in China

Cover and interior design: Lindsey Johns
Quid Publishing
Level 4, Sheridan House
114 Western Road
Hove BN3 1DD
England

The enemy is still proud and powerful. He is hard to get at. He still possesses enormous armies, vast resources, and invaluable strategic territories... No one can tell what new complications and perils might arise in four or five more years of war. And it is in the dragging-out of the war at enormous expense, until the democracies are tired or bored or split that the main hopes of Germany and Japan must reside.

Sir Winston S. Churchill, Washington DC,
May 19th, 1943

Contents

Introduction

World War II, 1939–1945, was a truly global war; gradually sucking into a maelstrom the majority of the world's nations, and certainly the world's strongest powers, it became the greatest conflict in world history. Yet, in many ways, it arose from the aftermath of World War I. In 1918 world frontiers were redrawn and old empires dismantled, while the Treaty of Versailles, signed in 1919, condemned Germany to bankruptcy. The 1920s saw the rise of the dangerously maverick figure Adolf Hitler, who aligned German politics with the state control instigated by the Italian leader Benito Mussolini, and moved the country quickly to a point of military readiness in the late 1930s that was in direct contravention of the Versailles treaty.

Adolf Hitler looks out over gathered supporters during a parade, c.1930.

The Western Allies, weakened by the earlier war and reluctant to start another, stood meekly by. In the East, Josef Stalin, leader of the Soviet Union, viewed Hitler with caution, and colluded with him until his own country was drawn into the fight in 1941. With Hitler wishing to avenge Germany's humiliation, he was prepared to push his demands to breaking point, and testing the policy of appeasement practiced by both Britain and France, he would drive the world to the brink.

The war would be fought on four continents, with at least 25 combatant nations. With such distances, the war was driven by its logistical capabilities—on land, the availability of fuel and the extension of supply lines would become paramount. At sea, the world's navies fought extended campaigns, in the protection of civilian supply routes, or in direct ship-to-ship (or aircraft-to-ship) actions. In the skies, air superiority would be all, and new battles would be fought. Aircraft were flying higher, faster, and longer; missiles, unmanned aircraft, jets—all would appear in this technological war. And tank warfare would be developed to its greatest degree.

In the East, Japan had also grown into a power that viewed expansion as a means to its greater development and thought nothing of military conquest to achieve this. The Sino–Japanese war of 1937–1945 was a conflict indicative of Japanese ambition: the control of the Pacific. The Japanese were swift to join the Axis powers, bringing the United States into the fray at Pearl Harbor in December 1941, and changing the direction and future of the war. Hitler's ambitions to conquer the Soviet Empire through the largest invasion in history, Operation Barbarossa, was also pivotal. It would ultimately lead to the dismantling of the Nazi state, and the creation of the Cold War, which would bring the world even closer to the brink of destruction in later generations.

World War II was a total war. Across the world, economies were linked directly to the needs of the war machine. Industries were geared completely to the production of munitions, and naval engagements became battles to guarantee supply and to break blockades like never before. New and more terrible weapons would be married to new and incredible innovations; battle wounds would be treated with penicillin, aviators would fly in jet aircraft before the war was done. And civilians were no longer capable of standing back from the fight.

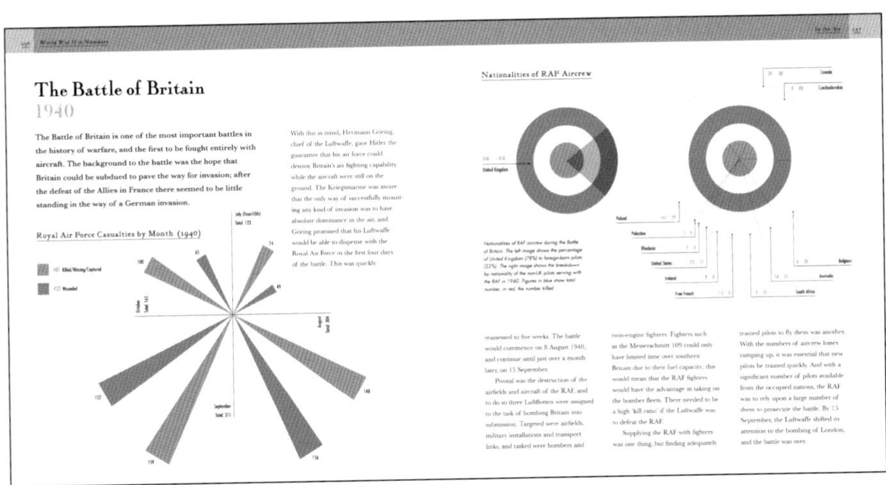

The Battle of Britain

1940

The Battle of Britain is one of the most important battles in the history of warfare, and the first to be fought entirely with aircraft. The background to the battle was the hope that Britain could be subdued to pave the way for invasion; after the defeat of the Allies in France there seemed to be little standing in the way of a German invasion.

With this in mind, Hermann Göring, chief of the Luftwaffe, gave Hitler the guarantee that his air force could destroy Britain's air fighting capability while the aircraft were still on the ground. The Kriegsmarine was aware that the only way of successfully mounting any kind of invasion was to have absolute dominance in the air, and Göring promised that his Luftwaffe would be able to dispense with the Royal Air Force in the first four days of the battle. This was quickly reassessed to five weeks. The battle would commence on 8 August 1940, and continue until just over a month later, on 15 September.

Pivotal was the destruction of the airfields and aircraft of the RAF, and to do so three Luftflotten were assigned to the task of bombing Britain into submission. Targeted were airfields, military installations and transport links, and tasked were bombers and twin-engine fighters. Fighters such as the Messerschmitt 109 could only have limited time over southern Britain due to their fuel capacity; this would mean that the RAF fighters would have the advantage in taking on the bomber fleets. There needed to be a high 'kill ratio' if the Luftwaffe was to defeat the RAF.

Supplying the RAF with fighters was one thing, but finding adequately trained pilots to fly them was another. With the numbers of aircrew losses ramping up, it was essential that new pilots be trained quickly. And with a significant number of pilots available from the occupied nations, the RAF was to rely upon a large number of them to prosecute the battle. By 15 September, the Luftwaffe shifted its attention to the bombing of London, and the battle was over.

Royal Air Force Casualties by Month (1940)

Nationalities of RAF Aircrew

Nationalities of RAF aircrew during the Battle of Britain. The left image shows the percentage of United Kingdom (78%) to foreign-born pilots (22%). The right image shows the breakdown by nationality of the non-UK pilots serving with the RAF in 1940. Figures in blue show total number, in red, the number killed.

This book features a variety of infographics, as the example above shows. They tie in to the text on the page to deliver the data from World War II in a clear and visually stimulating way. Each infographic includes a key, and an explanatory caption where necessary.

As had been predicted by pre-war theorists, aerial armadas would wreak havoc over major cities; bomb tonnages would grow and new ways of razing cities to the ground would be invented, from firestorms to atomic weapons. This would be the only conflict in history where nuclear weapons would be used in action; a reminder of the awesome and terrible power that nations of the world could levy against each other if not kept in check. All in all, some 100 million people worldwide served in a military capacity; their actions would see 73 million people, combatants, and civilians alike, killed. Among these would be the indescribable and breathtaking slaughter of innocents, the murder of the Jews by the Nazis, two out of every three in Nazi-occupied territory; and the terror of the Japanese in China.

The war in Europe ended with much of the continent in ruins, the Nazi state destroyed and dismantled, its territory carved up into eastern and western blocs that would last through to the end of the Cold War in 1990, with the fall of the Berlin Wall. In Japan, the combatant nation with the highest rates of battlefield fatalities, the armed forces were committed to last-ditch defence, the home islands were destroyed through bombing, conventional at first, then through the deployment of atomic weapons, and the country was brought to its knees by the time the war was finally over on August 15th, 1945.

Chapter One

PREPARATION FOR WAR

With Adolf Hitler rising to Chancellor of Germany in 1933, war was inevitable, his approach undeniably belligerent. In 1939, Britain still had the largest navy in the world, and while France remained the strongest military power, both nations were swept aside in 1940. Alone, Britain called upon the United States for help, and "Lend-Lease" was the result. In the Far East, Japan's thirst for military expansion was all too evident—particularly for those Western nations with remnants of empire, or spheres of interest.

Populations and Powers

World War II was the greatest conflict in world history. The vast majority of countries fell into four categories: the Axis, a belligerent military alliance of Nazi Germany, Italy, and Japan; the Allies, a wider military alliance that had its roots in World War I; the neutral countries—many of which would be occupied, joining the Allies in their struggles; and those nations occupied without recourse to direct military engagement. Those nations with the biggest populations (and economic wealth) could field the greatest military forces in the long term.

AXIS

The Axis was the alliance created from the anti-communist pact signed by Germany and Japan in 1936; the Italians joined a year later. With Mussolini and Adolf Hitler closely aligned in their fascist ideology, a military alliance was forged between them on May 22nd, 1939: the "Pact of Steel" or "Rome–Berlin Axis." Imperial Japan reaffirmed its commitment on September 27th, 1940, and other countries joined as the war progressed: Bulgaria in April 1940; Romania and Hungary in November 1940; and Finland, not technically a member of the Axis, became embroiled after its war with the USSR in 1939, known as the "Winter War."

The main countries involved in the conflict and their populations (in millions) in 1940.

AXIS

Country	1940
Bulgaria	6.5
Finland (1939–1944)	3.7
Germany (and Austria)	70.7
Hungary (1939–1945)	9.3
Italy (1940–1943)	43.8
Japan (1941–1945)	71.3
Romania (1940–1944)	15.9
Totals	**222.1**

ALLIES

Country	1940
Australia (1939–1945)	7.1
Belgium (1940–1945)	8.4
Brazil (1942–1945)	41.1
Canada (1939–1945)	11.4
China (1937–1945)	520.1
Denmark (1940–1945)	3.8
France (1939–1945)	39.0
India (1939–1945)	316.0
Lebanon (1945)	1.2
Mexico (1942–1945)	19.8
Netherlands (1940–1945)	8.8
New Zealand (1939–1945)	1.6
Norway (1940–1945)	3.0
Poland (1939–1945)	26.9
South Africa (1939–1945)	10.3
USSR (1941–1945)	110.1
UK (1939–1945)	48.2
US (1941–1945)	132.2
Yugoslavia (1941–1945)	15.8
Totals	**1,324.8**

ALLIES

Following the German annexation of Czechoslovakia in 1938, Britain and France guaranteed the borders of Poland. When the Poles were attacked on September 1st, 1939, the Allies had little choice but to act, declaring war two days later. The dominion governments of Australia, Canada, India, and New Zealand joined soon after. Countries that had once declared neutrality became Allies: Belgium, Denmark, Netherlands, and Norway. Overwhelmed, they continued to contribute to the war effort. For the US and the USSR, joining the Allies was a result of military intervention by Axis powers, the Western Allies joining China in opposing the Japanese.

PAN-AMERICAN UNION

The Pan-American Union countries were neutral until the Imperial Japanese Navy attacked the US at Pearl Harbor in 1941. The union had signed a mutual defence pact in 1940 in light of the worsening international situation; most contributed economically, while Brazil and Mexico committed forces. Only Uruguay remained neutral.

OCCUPIED STATES

Though many occupied nations became part of the Allies, a large number were simply overrun and embroiled in the war. Czechoslovakia was first to fall, and was divided; Slovakia became a supporter of the Axis. Situations in the Balkan and Baltic states were similarly complex. The Philippines, under US control, fell to the Japanese in 1941 and remained so until liberation in 1944.

NEUTRAL STATES

Of the countries that declared neutrality in 1939, many fell to Germany in 1940. Remaining were the fascist state of Spain, which sent volunteers to the German armed forces, Portugal and Sweden, which stayed neutral but permitted German forces to cross its borders during the invasion of Norway. Switzerland and the smaller European states also maintained their neutrality.

PAN-AMERICAN UNION

Country	1940
Argentina (1945)	14.2
Chile (1945)	5.0
Colombia	9.1
Costa Rica	0.6
Cuba	4.3
Dominican Republic	1.7
El Salvador	1.6
Guatemala	2.2
Haiti	2.8
Honduras	1.1
Nicaragua	0.8
Panama	0.6
Paraguay	1.0
Venezuela	3.7
Totals	**48.7**

OCCUPIED COUNTRIES

Country	1940
Albania	1.1
Czechoslovakia	11.2
Estonia	1.1
Ethiopia	17.7
Greece	7.3
Luxembourg	0.3
Philippines	16.4
Poland	26.9
Totals	**82.0**

NEUTRAL COUNTRIES

Country	1940
Andorra	0.006
Ireland	3.0
Liechtenstein	0.01
Portugal	7.8
Spain	25.9
Sweden	6.4
Switzerland	4.2
Uruguay	2.0
Vatican City	0.001
Totals	**49.317**

Approximate Country GDPs in 1940

Gross Domestic Product (GDP) is a means of estimating the overall size of an economy. Ultimately, the country—or alliance of states—with the highest GDP will have the greatest war-winning capability in the long term. Figures are early war, showing potential for war-winning of the Axis, Allies, and neutral/occupied states, and are in millions of dollars. Question marks indicate that figures are unknown.

AXIS

Country	1940
Bulgaria	41,578
Finland	11,909
Germany	377,284
Hungary	24,391
Italy	155,424
Japan	209,728
Romania	19,375

ALLIES

Country	1940
Australia	43,422
Belgium	38,072
Brazil	51,382
Canada	55,167
China	288,653
Denmark	19,606
France	165,729
India	265,455
Lebanon	?
Mexico	37,767
Netherlands	42,898
New Zealand	10,308
Norway	12,005
Poland	67,788
South Africa	?
UK	330,638
US	929,737
USSR	420,091

PAN-AMERICAN UNION

Country	1940
Argentina	58,963
Chile	16,364
Colombia	17,386
Cuba	5,516
Dominican Republic	?
El Salvador	1,811
Guatemala	6,033
Haiti	?
Honduras	1,334
Nicaragua	1,139
Panama	?
Paraguay	1,947
Venezuela	15,307

OCCUPIED

Country	1940
Albania	~905
Czechoslovakia	24,391
Estonia	?
Ethiopia	?
Greece	16,183
Luxembourg	?
Philippines	24,993

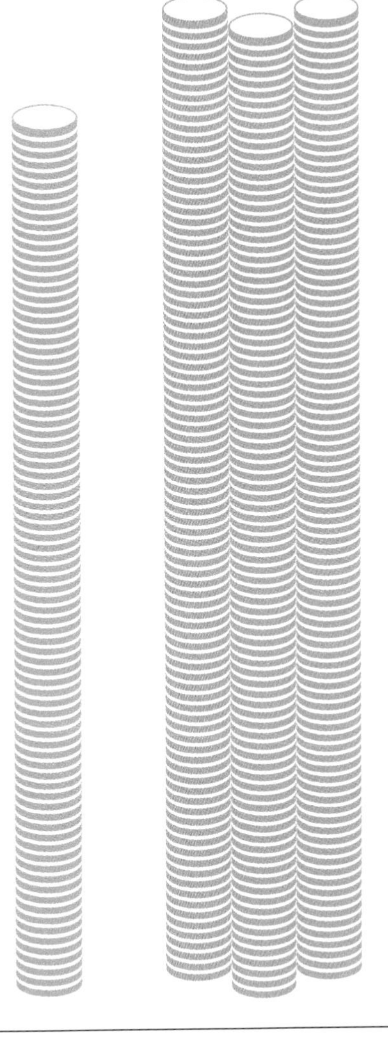

AXIS	ALLIES	PAN-AMERICAN UNION	OCCUPIED
840,000,000	2,790,000,000	125,800,000	66,472,000
(840 billion)	(2.79 trillion)		

Approximate Totals

Totals for each block, with each coin representing ten million dollars for 1940; figures in brackets are for 1945.

Military Strengths of the Allies
1939

After World War I, most of the Allied nations had scaled down their military machines, and in many cases military matériel was obsolete. Rearmament was essential if they were to survive.

UNITED KINGDOM

The strength of the UK lay, as it had for centuries, with its navy. By far the most powerful navy in the world, given the UK's commitments across the globe, the Royal Navy was essential in delivering its military might. With most effort expended in developing the navy, the army was second in line. Though Britain had led the world in the development of tank warfare, it was woefully ill-equipped for a new conflict in 1939, and its infantry divisions could only call upon a cadre of regulars; the remainder would be Saturday-night soldiers of the Territorial Army, and the newly called-up Militia Men—hastily conscripted men who had reached the age of 21 in 1939. Britain's air force was in a state of re-equipping with fast fighters, but it had some way to go.

FRANCE

Suffering a loss of 5 million men in World War I, the French armed forces, though impressive on paper, were focused on defence. The French Army was strong, with 900,000 regular troops and a large number of reservists, and with some of the most impressive tanks fielded in 1939–1940, but the development of the Maginot Line had instilled a defensive mentality that would have been alien in 1914–1917. The French had a large standing navy, and an air force with some good aircraft.

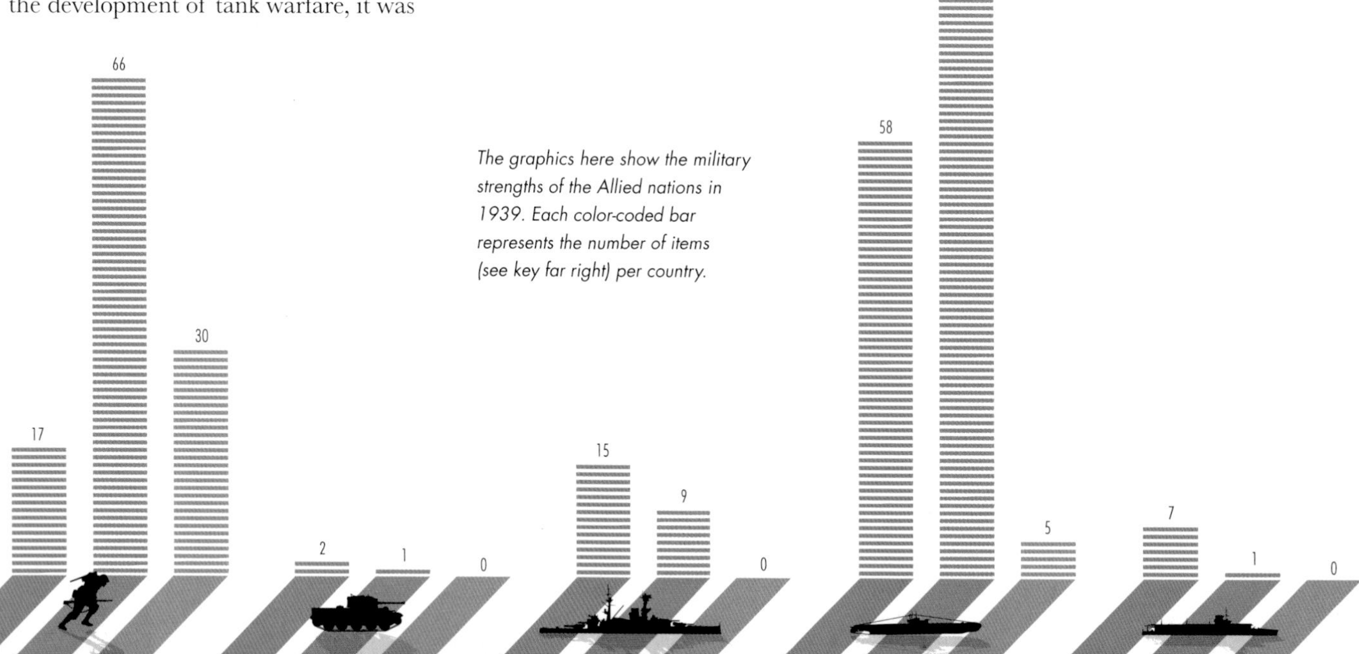

The graphics here show the military strengths of the Allied nations in 1939. Each color-coded bar represents the number of items (see key far right) per country.

UK

FRANCE

POLAND

POLAND

When Poland was attacked in 1939 its forces were largely unmechanized and dependent upon traditional horse power—in the delivery of troops and in its elite cavalry. With a relatively small army, limited aerial power and an almost nonexistent navy, Poland was not in a good state to prevent invasion—especially, as it turned out, invasion on two fronts. When the USSR launched its offensive, Poland's fate was sealed.

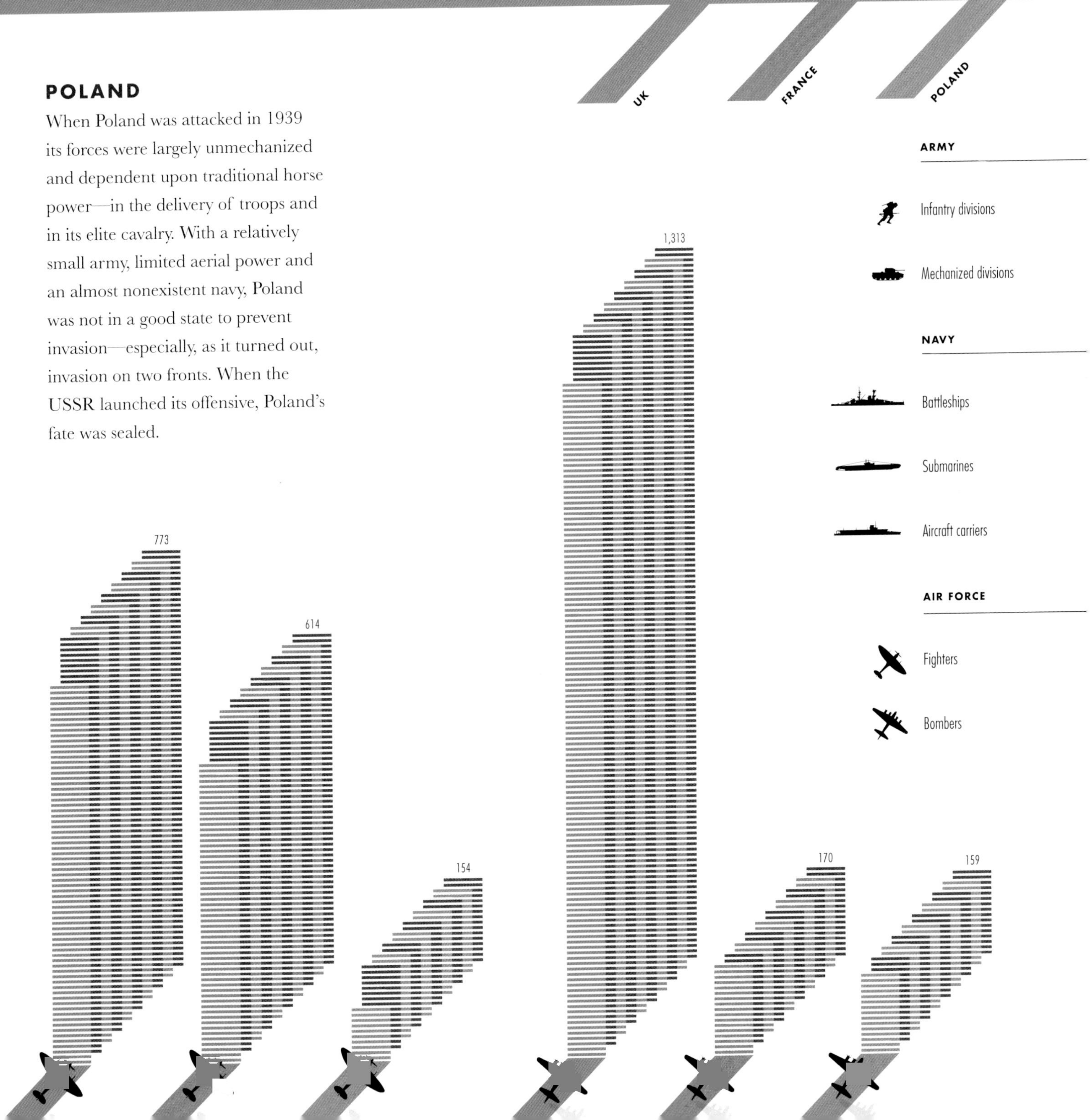

ARMY

Infantry divisions

Mechanized divisions

NAVY

Battleships

Submarines

Aircraft carriers

AIR FORCE

Fighters

Bombers

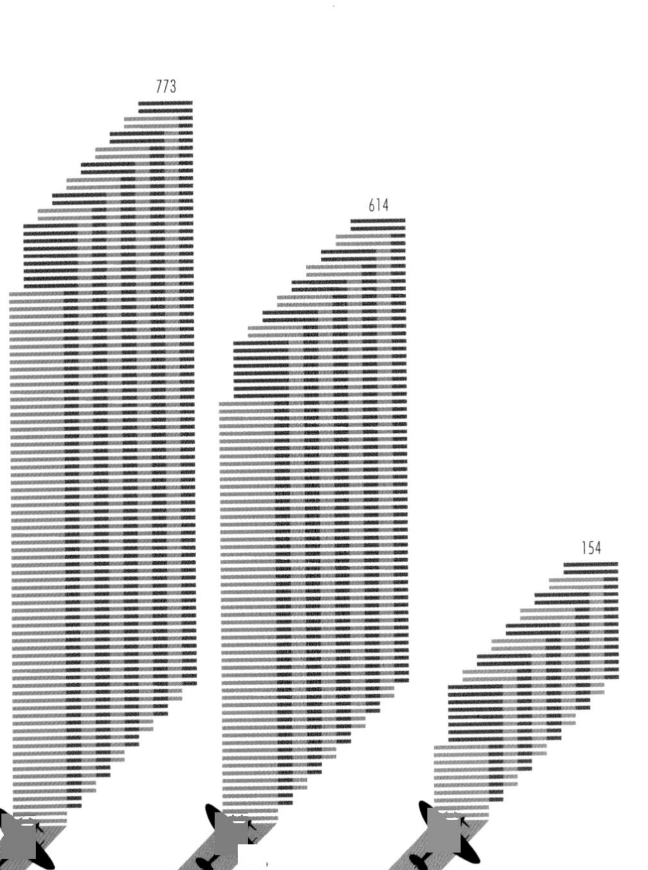

1,313

170

159

Military Strengths of the Axis
1939

With Hitler planning for war from 1935, enlarging the armed forces and rearming them to the highest standards was paramount. The Italian forces were equipped with largely obsolete equipment, so there would be a disparity between them.

GERMANY

Germany was limited to an army of no more than 100,000 men by the Treaty of Versailles, although this was no bar to Hitler's ambitions—he introduced conscription in 1935, with intakes of 300,000 men a year into the armed forces. Germany's rearmament in the wake of the Nazis coming to power meant the creation of an army that would be dependent upon the doctrine of lightning war, or blitzkrieg, yet that would still see the widespread use of horses. Each armored division contained 328 tanks. There was strength in the German air force, too; since the Luftwaffe had been conceived in 1933, it had become the mightiest aerial force—one that was tried and tested in the Spanish Civil War of 1936. It was no wonder that the Nazi authorities felt that it was possible to defeat the Allies through a combination of aerial power and mechanized might. The lessons of the Great War had also been learned at sea: Nazi Germany had a large number of U-boats, and expansion of the surface fleet was slated for 1942.

The graphics here show the military strengths of the Axis nations in 1939. Each color-coded bar represents the number of items (see key far right) per country.

86

40

14

2

3

4

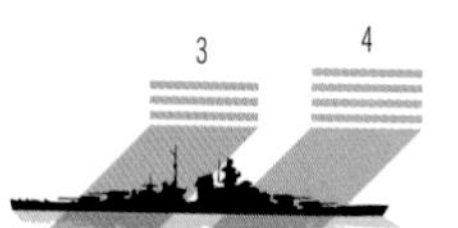

170

115

0

0

ITALY

Italy had a strong navy, much of which was deployed in the Mediterranean—"Musso's Lake"—and it was seen as a major threat to Allied intervention here. On paper, Mussolini's air force and army was also impressive; they had served in the expansionist campaigns in Ethiopia and Eritrea in 1936. Here they achieved success against limited opposition, but both were relatively ill-equipped, with outdated biplanes and inadequate armor.

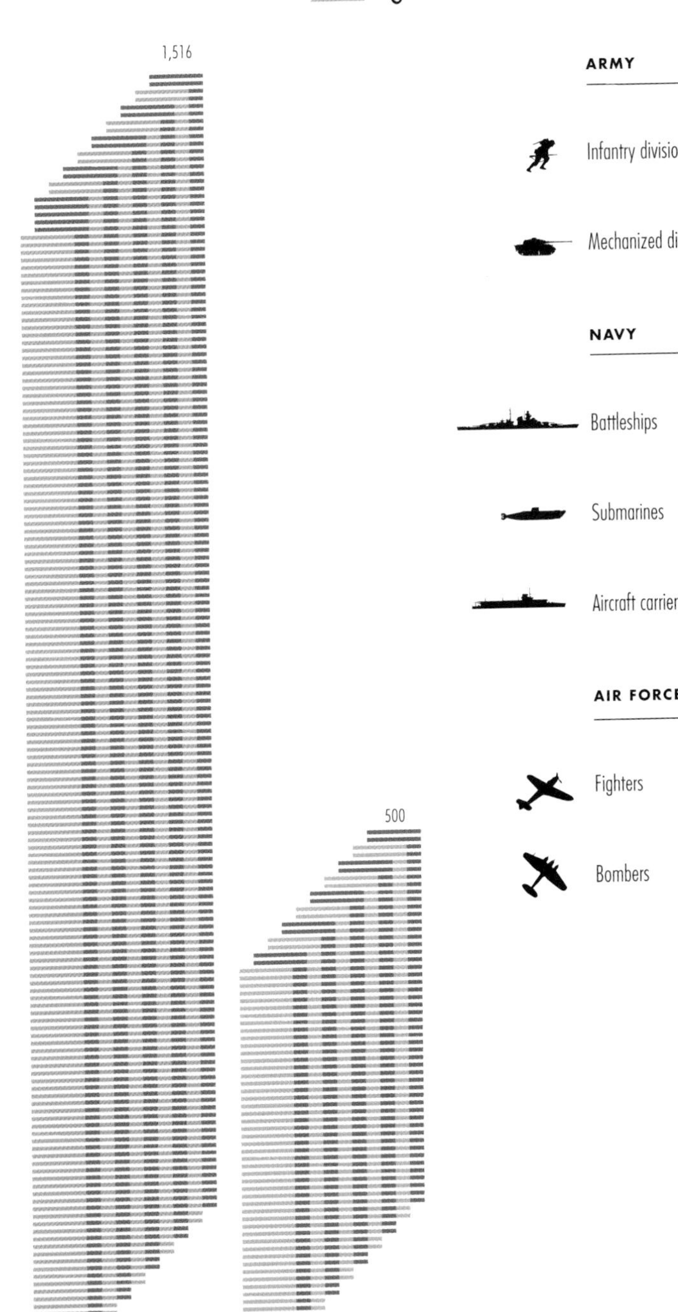

Fleets of Major World Powers 1939

In 1939, comparison of the world's fleets was considered to be one of the most important indicators of military strength—and of military prestige. With the British and Americans operating in the Atlantic and Pacific, it was Hitler's ambition to build up his fleet of capital ships to challenge them—especially as the building of battleships was precluded by the Treaty of Versailles. In the Pacific, the strength of the Japanese fleet was a direct threat to the Americans, while in the Mediterranean, the Italians and French were directly opposed.

THE BRITISH

By far and away, the British had the strongest fleet in the world in 1939. Though its battleships and battle-cruisers were old, five King George V–class ships and a number of aircraft carriers were under construction, and its fleet of cruisers was in respectable shape. Over half of the navy's destroyers were modern and well equipped, although sonar, the principal system for detecting submarines,

HMS Hood, *a fast battlecruiser that was considered "the Pride of the British Navy." The* Hood *was lost in May 1941 while in pursuit of the* Bismarck.

The US Navy exercises its Pacific Fleet near Hawaii in September 1940.

was of limited use against surfaced German U-boats. The navy's dedicated air force, the Fleet Air Arm (FAA), was armed with largely obsolescent aircraft, which nevertheless were operational for much of World War II. What was expected, however, was that Britain would only have to fight against threats to the homeland (rather than in the Pacific, for example), with its primary objectives being defence of the coasts, protection of trade routes, and suppression of submarine warfare.

THE UNITED STATES

The US Navy was similarly strong. Its focus was the prime threat provided by the Japanese in the Pacific, as it had been since the early 1920s. As the world situation worsened, the US engaged in a serious program of expansion in 1940, which involved a ship-building program of 1,324,999 tons (1,202,019 tonnes). The aim was to enable the US Navy to operate in both the Atlantic and the Pacific oceans.

JAPAN

The Imperial Japanese Navy considered the US Navy its foremost rival, and embarked on a campaign to develop a naval power that would match that of the US. But the Japanese were torn between battleship or carrier elites, and effectively neglected their submarines and other ships capable of maintaining trade support of the homeland. This would cost them dearly in the latter part of the war; reliant on imports, they were almost starved into submission.

FRANCE AND ITALY

The French and Italian navies, similar in size and scope, considered each other major threats, particularly as Mussolini claimed the Mediterranean as his own. Both fleets would suffer at the hands of the British as the war progressed, with the French fleet attacked by the British to prevent it falling into the hands of the Nazis.

The table overleaf (pp 22–23) shows the fleets of each of the major world powers in 1939, broken down into number of vessels per country. The figures have been color-coded from light to dark to indicate comparative strength—for example, the US was the country with the most destroyers (dark blue), whereas Germany had the fewest (light blue).

Fleets of Major World Powers

Key to color gradation: 0, < 5, 5–10, 11–20, 21–30, 31–40, 41–50, 51–60, 61–70, 71–80, 81–90, 91–100, 101–150, > 150, > 200

	UK AND COMMONWEALTH	FRANCE
Battleships	15	5
Battlecruisers	3	1
Pocket battleships	0	0
Cruisers	62	18
Aircraft carriers	7	1
Seaplane carriers	2	1
Destroyers	159	58
Torpedo boats	11	13
Submarines	54	76
Monitors and coast defence ships	3	0
Minelayers	1	1
Sloops and escort vessels	38	25
Gunboats and patrol vessels	27	10
Minesweepers	38	8

GERMANY	ITALY	JAPAN	US
2	4	9	15
2	0	0	0
3	0	0	0
6	21	39	32
0	0	5	5
0	0	3	0
17	48	84	209
16	69	38	0
57	104	58	87
0	1	1	0
0	0	10	8
8	32	0	0
0	2	10	20
29	39	12	0

Soviet Forces in Europe
1939–1940

Prior to Operation Barbarossa, the German invasion of the USSR, Stalin attempted to maintain an uneasy peace with his belligerent neighbor. Knowing that Hitler might well have designs on the western part of the USSR, and with both Leningrad and Moscow close to the USSR's western border, Stalin sought to create and maintain a buffer by two aggressive campaigns, with the Non-Aggression Pact designed to prevent all-out war with Germany.

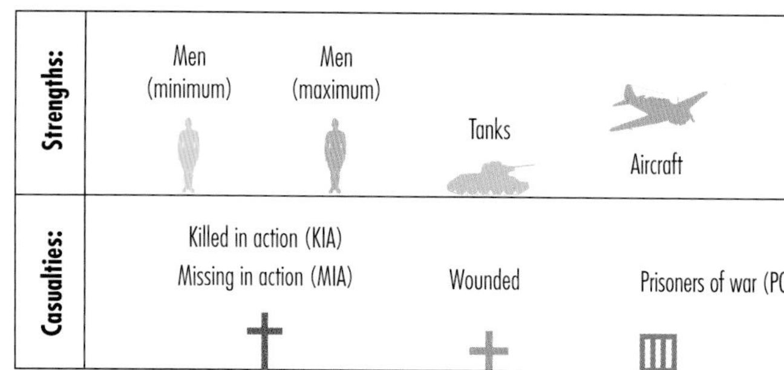

Casualties and Strengths During the Invasion of Poland

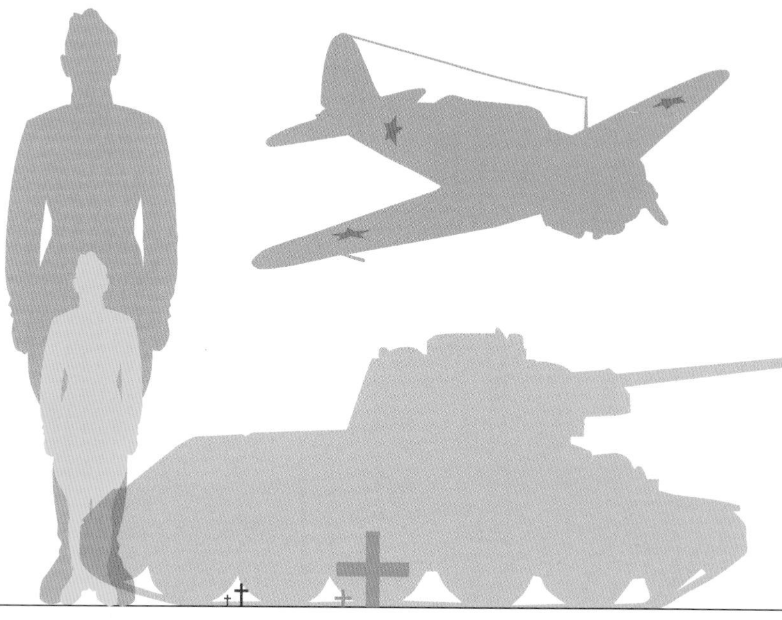

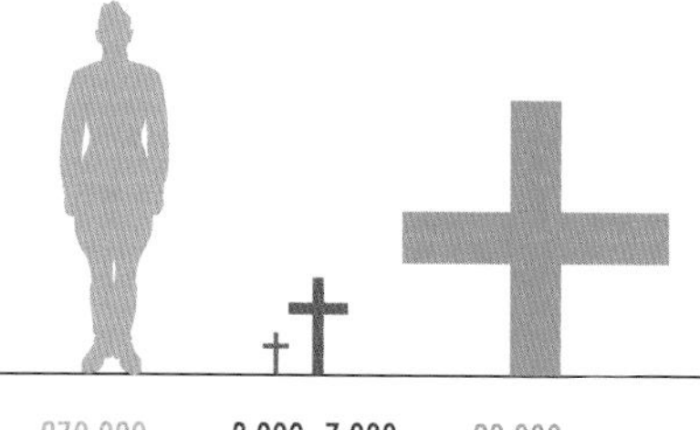

466,516–800,000	1,475–3,000	2,383–10,000	4,736	3,300
USSR				

270,000	3,000–7,000	~20,000
POLAND		

THE INVASION OF POLAND

The Soviet invasion of Poland was a direct result of the signing of a Non-Aggression Pact with Nazi Germany on August 23rd, 1939, which secretly agreed the division of Poland, Romania, and the Balkan states between the USSR and Germany; for the USSR this meant that there would be a significant "buffer zone" between an aggressive Germany and its territory in the west. Germany's invasion of Poland on September 1st, 1939 triggered a response, and, on September 17th, the USSR invaded from the east, thereby effectively extinguishing Poland, and again pushing the borders of the USSR away from the vulnerable cities of the west.

WINTER WAR WITH FINLAND

The Winter War with Finland (November 30th, 1939–March 13th, 1940) grew out of the USSR's desire to obtain land on the Baltic, and create a zone of safety around Leningrad. The Finns were less than happy about this, and so ensued the Winter War that would see the Finns aligned as cobelligerents with the Axis—this despite the fact that the Western Allies, France and the UK, were on the verge of supporting them with weapons and other military hardware.

Casualties and Strengths During the Winter War with Finland

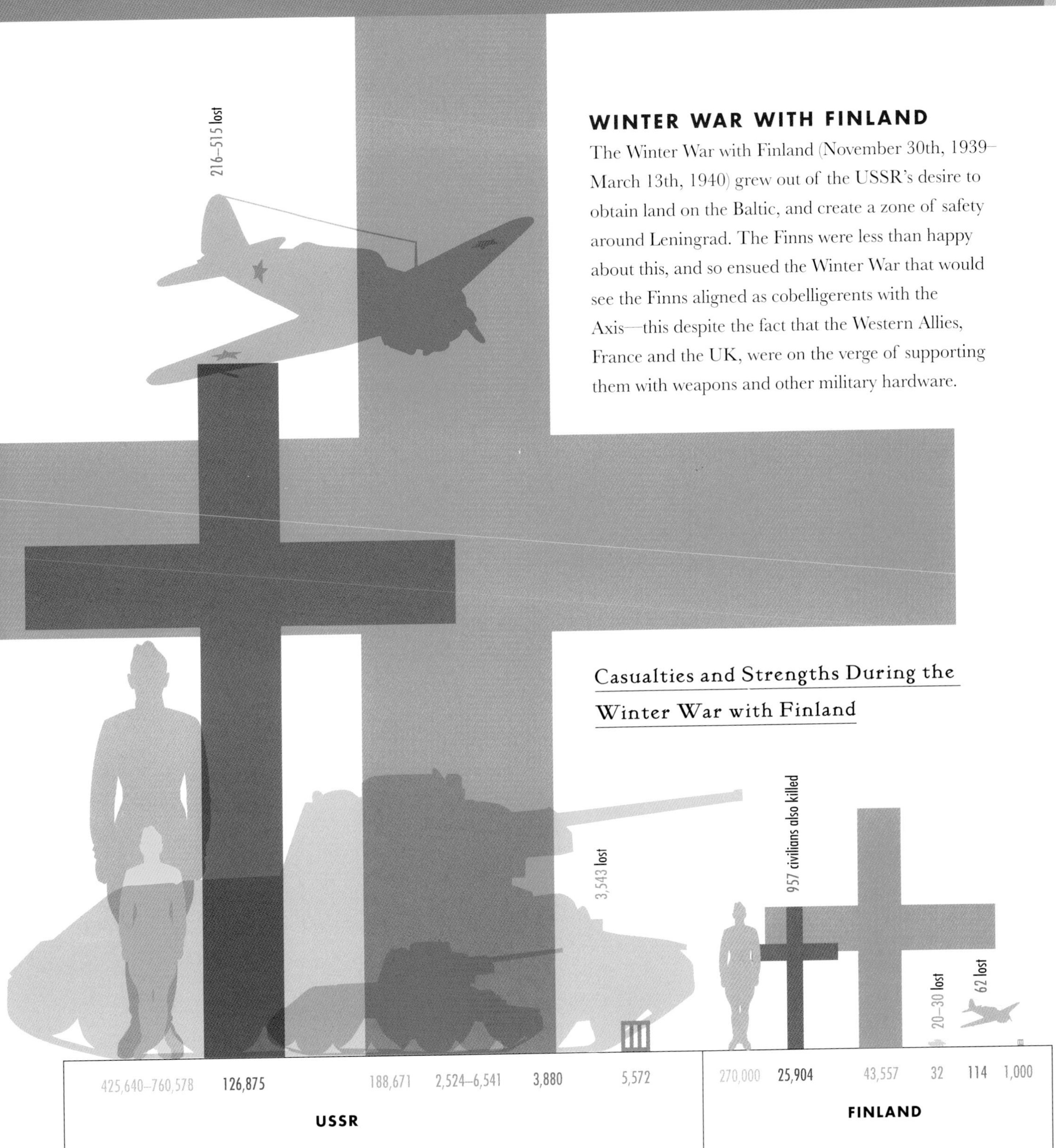

Japan and the Second Sino–Japanese War
1937–1945

The Second Sino–Japanese War was a prelude to Japanese expansionism. The First Sino–Japanese War (1894–1995) resulted in China losing Korea and Taiwan to Japan. China was in a state of unrest, with local warlords exerting power over their regions; even with the declaration of a republic in 1912, there was little opportunity for a unified approach. During 1926–1928, the nationalist Kuomintang government led by Chang Kai-shek (or Jiang Jieshi) attempted to develop a rule of law across the country, with limited success against the communist forces. The vast, unruly territory of China was there for the picking.

FIGHTING OVER CHINA

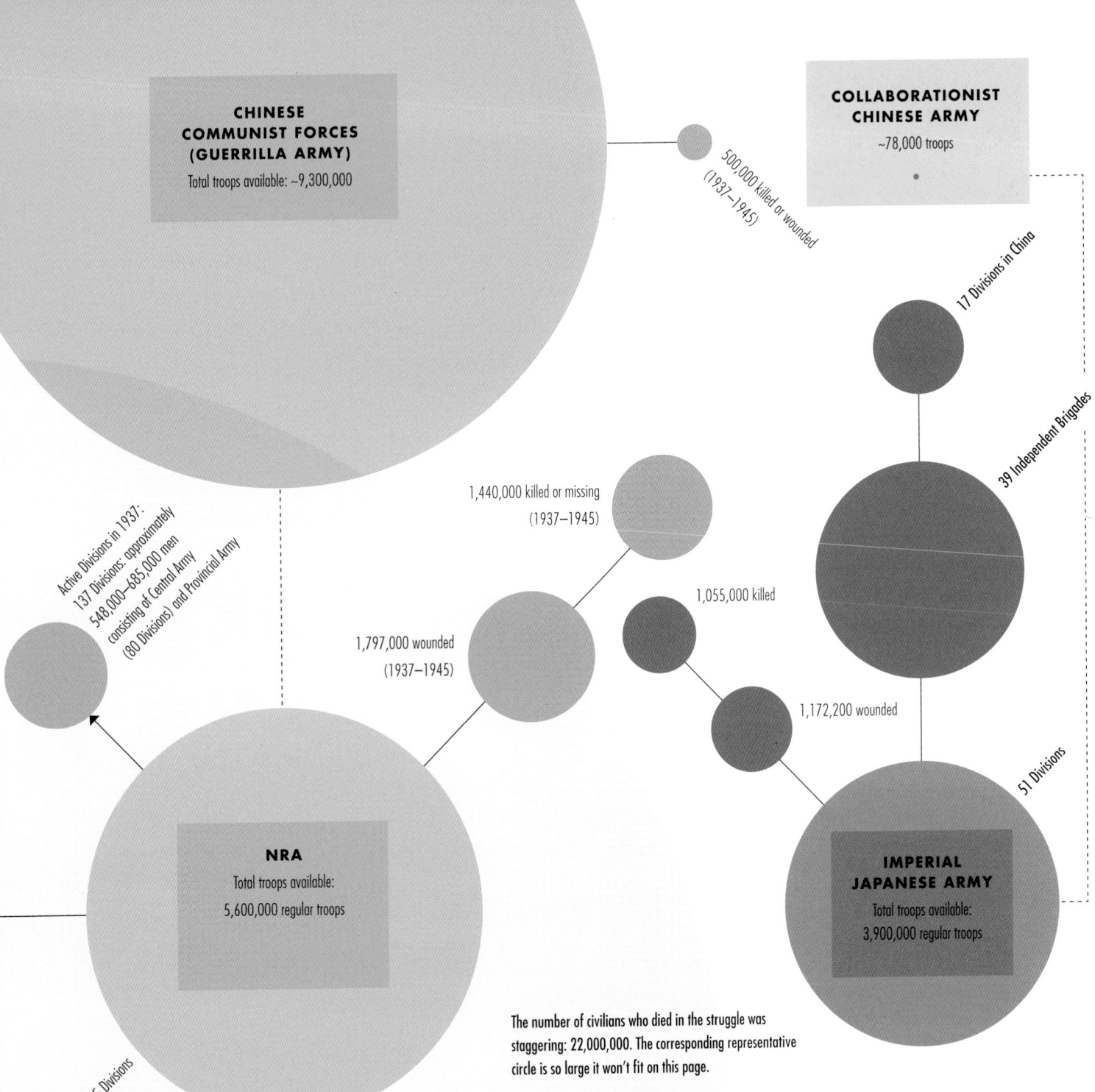

From 1931 to 1933, Japan took over the whole territory of Manchuria, and installed a puppet leader in the form of Pi Yu, the last emperor of China, to lead the newly named territory of Manchukuo. In 1933, Japan (and their allies, the Collaborationist Chinese Army) maintained an uneasy truce with the Chinese nationalists over the territory. For the nationalists, the truce brought with it an opportunity to deal with its internal affairs, and to try to crush the communist rebels once and for all. The Chinese communist forces were pushed back to Shaanxi Province, Mao Zedong leading them in the Long March from disaster, some 7,950 miles (12,800 km). With the rebels subdued, in 1936 there emerged a tentative united front between the National Revolutionary Army (the NRA, or Chinese National Army) and the communist guerrillas, as a means of combining forces to expel the Japanese. The united front was necessary, as the tinderbox was lit once again in July 1937; the result of an outbreak of fighting between Japanese soldiers and the NRA near Beijing. The Japanese responded with the occupation of the region; with tensions escalating, Chang Kai-shek ordered an attack on Japanese forces in Shanghai. The stage was set for the Second Sino–Japanese War, and the expansion of Japanese imperial ambitions across Asia.

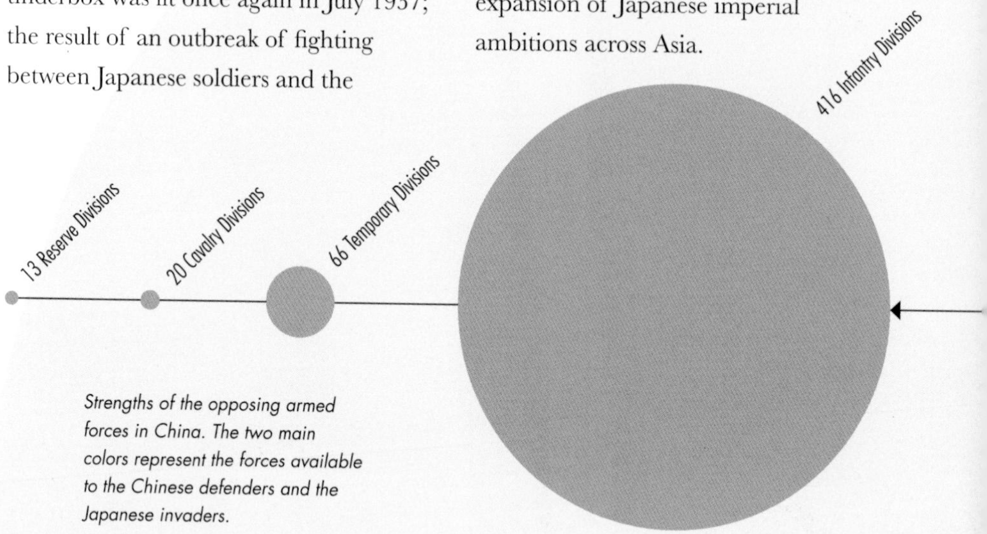

Strengths of the opposing armed forces in China. The two main colors represent the forces available to the Chinese defenders and the Japanese invaders.

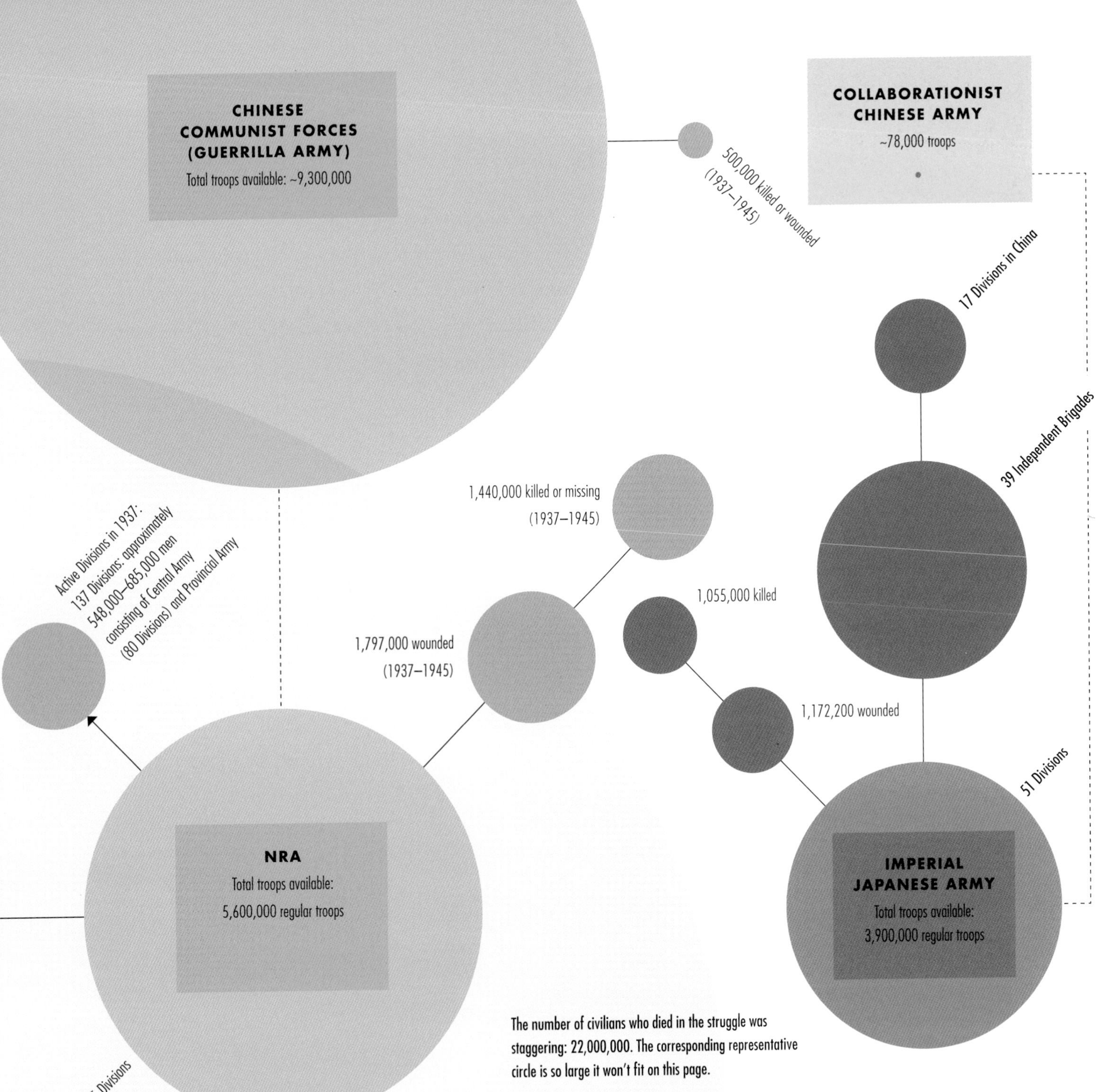

The number of civilians who died in the struggle was staggering: 22,000,000. The corresponding representative circle is so large it won't fit on this page.

Building the US Army
1923–1946

In 1923, the US General Staff produced a plan for the assembly of an army whose numbers could be increased from a standing force of 400,000 (based on the regular army and the National Guard) to a minimum of 1.3 million men—sufficient for the creation of six field armies. Revised in successive years, the concept planned for the provision of manpower, but made few provisions for the increase in matériel. It was the worsening European situation in 1940 that would focus President Roosevelt's attention on the matter.

With the US intent on using up the resources accrued during World War I, there was little impetus to implement a widespread procurement plan, or even a mobilization of industrial resources that would deliver an army capable of fighting a war. Procurement was an issue that was bigger than any one department of state; the US president would need to be directly involved, and industrial procurement became a priority in the 1930s, in the run-up to war. Plans included the creation of four "superagencies" that would handle engagement in war, and for a War Resources Administration that would have sufficient clout to direct resources where they were needed.

Number of US Soldiers Drafted Per Year

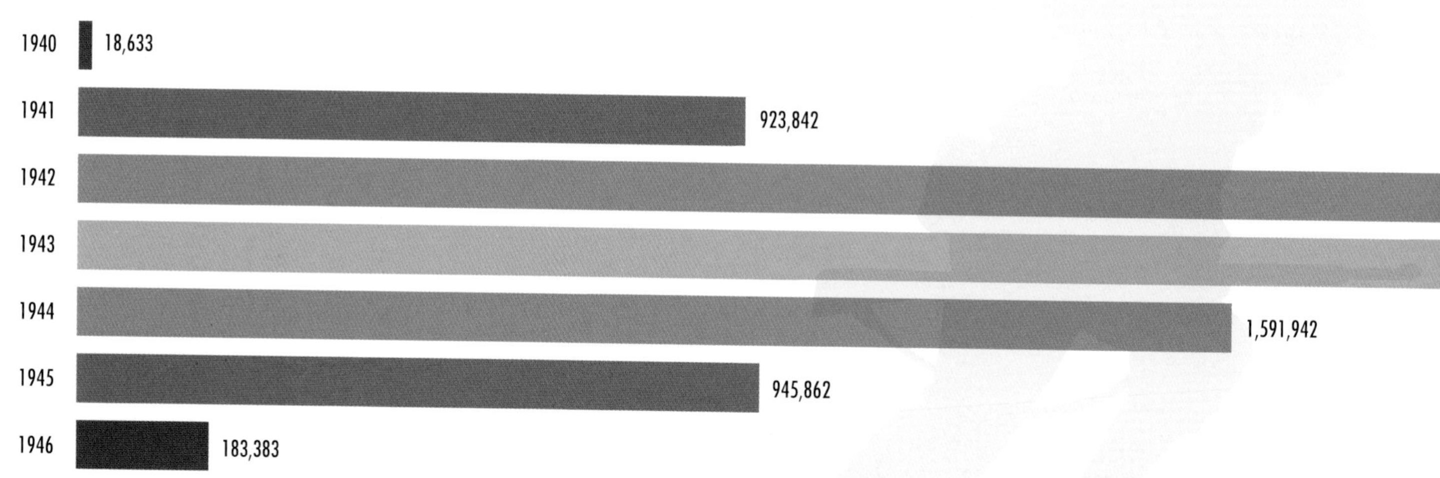

In the 20 years after the end of World War I, the US had largely turned its back on international collaboration—a position that almost guaranteed the failure of the League of Nations and attempts at restricting the proliferation of arms. Despite the obvious expansionist aims of Nazi Germany and Imperial Japan, in train with many of what would become the Allied powers, there was a strong move toward pacifism. It fell to President Roosevelt to tread carefully in preparing for the worsening international situation. In 1939, he launched a policy of "limited preparedness," which was pursued with greater urgency after the invasion of Poland. As part of this, the regular army was increased to 227,000 men and the National Guard to 235,000 men.

It was the *Selective Training and Service Act* of 1940 that brought in the first peacetime conscription draft in US history. It required the registration of all men between 21 and 35 (some 16 million men). The government selected conscripts through a lottery system; these men were then required to serve 12 months in the armed forces. With the international situation worsening, the period of service was extended. On the US joining the war, the draft age was increased from 35 to 45, and the period of service extended beyond a single year. After the US entered the war, that service was set as the duration of the war plus an additional service period of six months. In October 1942, Congress voted for the policy to be continued, albeit only by a single vote.

In the six years from 1940 to 1946 during which the policy remained in place, over 10,000,000 American men were drafted.

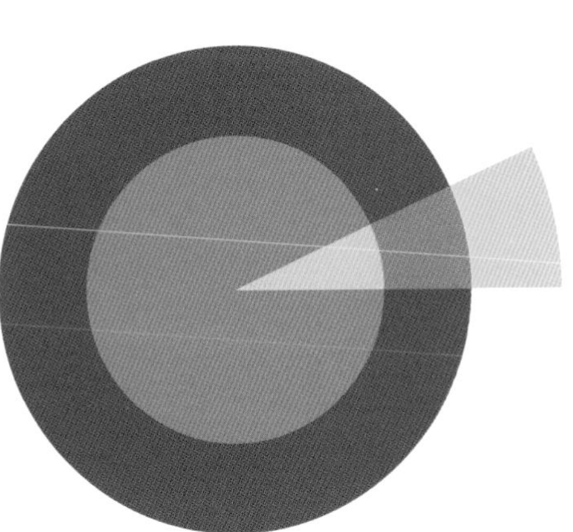

- Total number of WWII servicemen: **16,100,000**
- Total number of draftees: **10,110,114**
- Percentage of US casualties of all types: **6.9%**

US Casualties 1941–1945

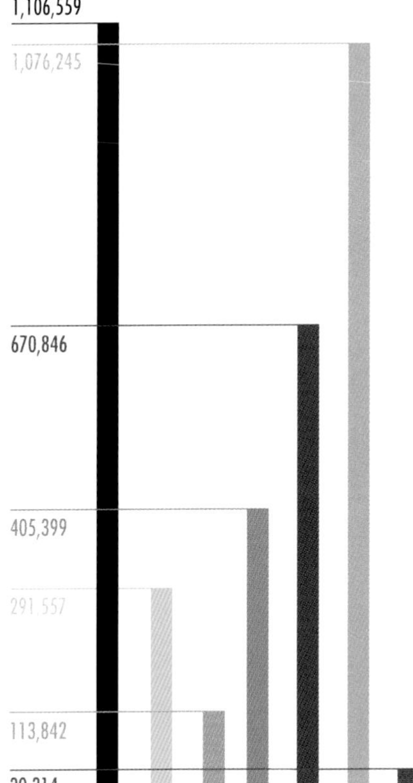

3,033,361

3,323,970

All casualties
Combat losses
Other deaths
Total deaths
Total wounded
Total dead & wounded
Total missing

Lend-Lease
1941–1945

The Lend-Lease program was a means for the US to supply munitions, equipment, and other military supplies to its allies. The idea was part of Roosevelt's policy of "active neutrality" in the years before the attack on Pearl Harbor. With US entry into the war becoming increasingly likely, his primary concern was to strengthen American defences, and reinforcing its allies' war effort was central to this.

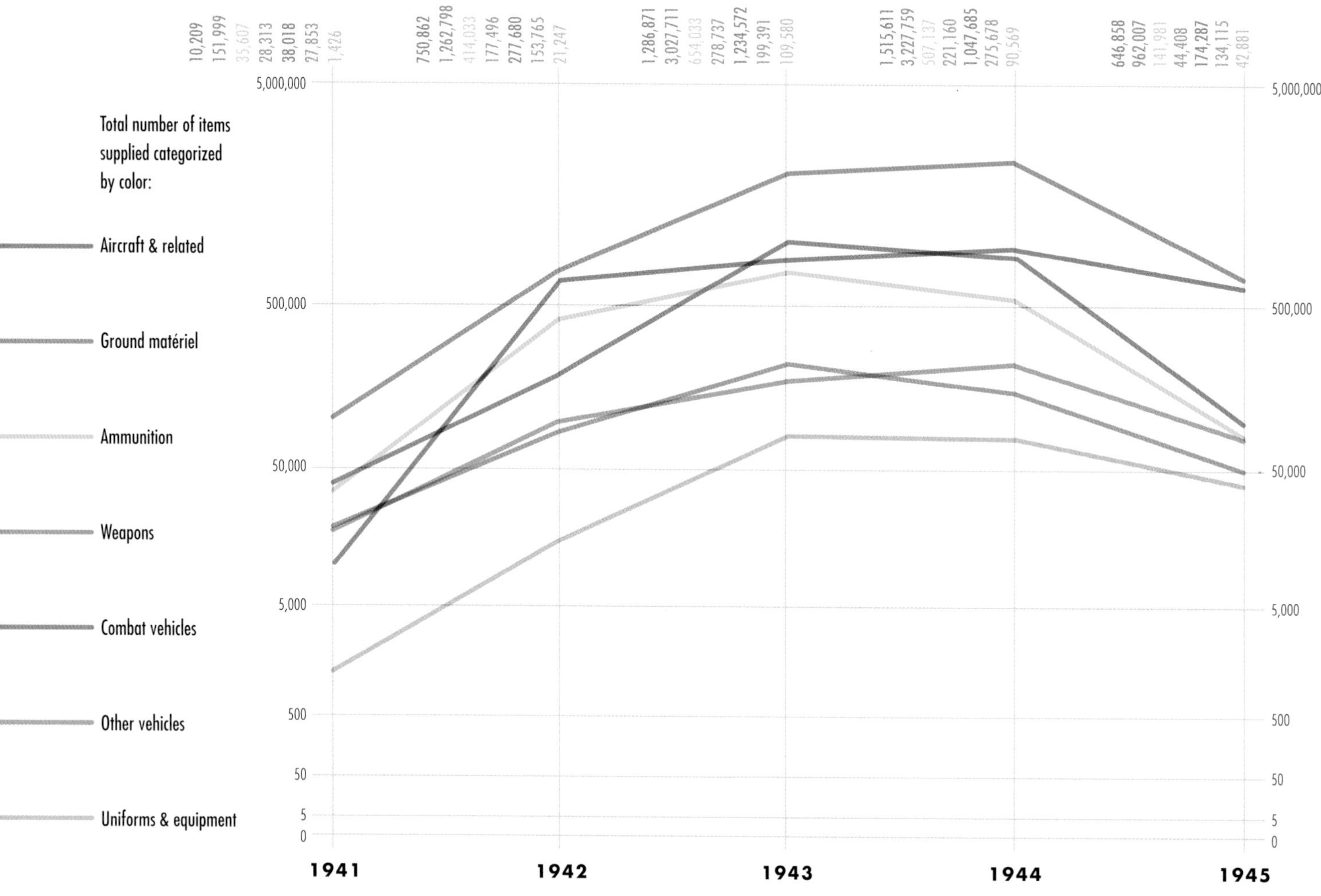

From March 1941 to December 1945, the US government carried out what amounted to $24,000,000 of Lend-Lease transactions under the control of the Secretary of War alone. With the US actively engaged in the war post-Pearl Harbor, the fact that Roosevelt could authorize the Secretary of War, Secretary of the Navy, or the head of any other agency to procure the matériel and then to sell, lend, or lease it to the government of countries that "the president deemed vital to the defence of the United States" made perfect sense. The UK and its empire (excluding Canada) was a beneficiary of just over half of that total and took up 58.5% of the matériel; the USSR received 23%, Free France 8%, China 7%, Brazil and Canada just under 1%, with the rest being distributed among other Allied countries. Without Lend-Lease, Britain would never have been able to rebuild its stocks of war matériel after Dunkirk; it was a vital component of the Anglo–American alliance.

Number of individual pieces of equipment supplied by Lend-Lease; the scale of the chart is logarithmic, increasing in order of magnitude.

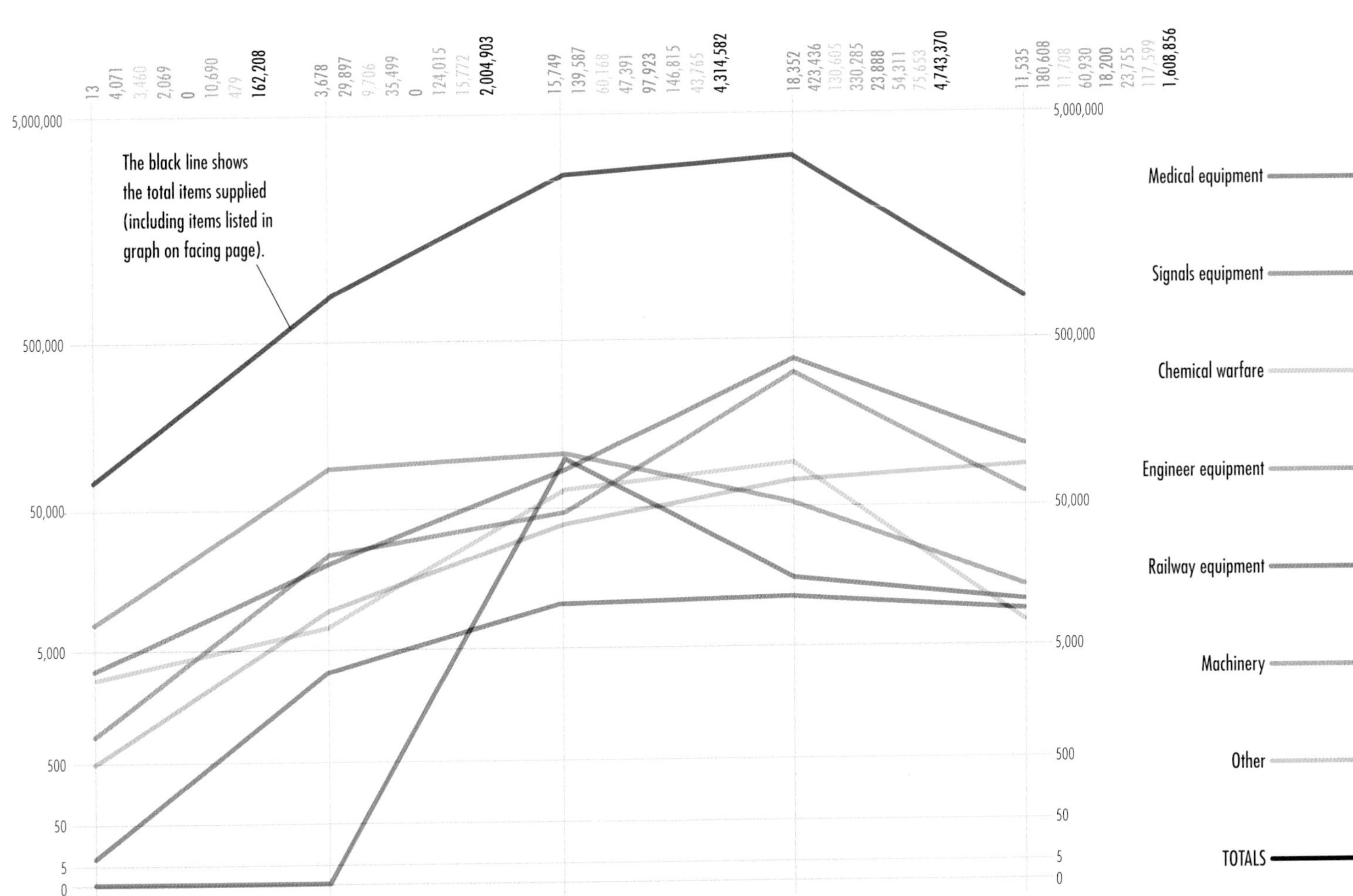

Munitions Production of the Main Powers 1939–1945

The manufacturing capabilities of the main powers were always going to define their ability to wage a global war. Hitler's ambitions were clear: the German economy was geared toward expansion and conflict from him taking the chancellorship in 1935. Japan, too, was focused on war. For the Allied nations, gearing their factories, and people, for war production meant a major change in mindset. The capabilities of the US was one of the major factors in steering the Allies to victory.

THE AXIS

Nazi Germany could draw upon its manufacturing strength and formidable military machine in order to win its early victories. One-sixth of the German economy was devoted to expanding the military in 1938; this would be put to good use during its aggressive campaigns of 1939–1940. The Nazis had not envisaged the mobilization of the whole nation for war, whether in the fighting services or on the home front, until 1943, when the realities of fighting an extended war on two fronts started to bite. Instead, the Nazis made extensive use of captured matériel and manpower, and consumed much of the foodstuffs produced by the occupied nations—who were made to pay for their occupation. Civilian labor and prisoners of war were employed widely in the German war effort.

Despite their aggressive military stance and early military victories, Japan's economy, dependent on imports, was to suffer. Though output grew steadily through the war, the Allied naval and air campaign effectively strangled the Japanese. With other nations taking on a "total war" mindset, Japan also suffered by not mobilizing its people effectively; for example, Japan did not harness the potential of the female population. With capability much reduced, Japan's potential to engage in war faded year on year as the war progressed.

The increasing volume of combat munitions production: amount spent per year by each of the belligerents in billions of US dollars.

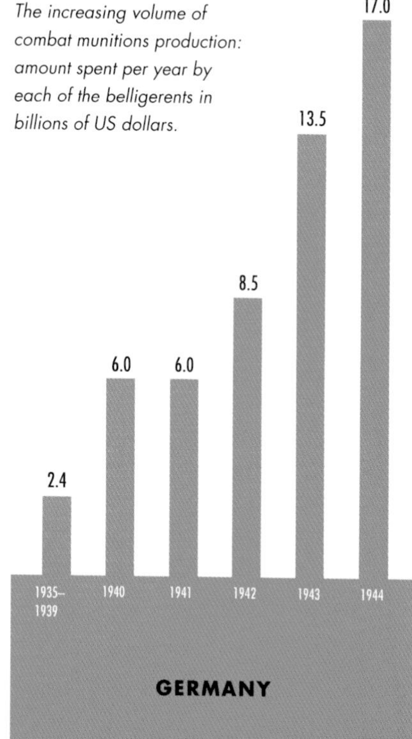

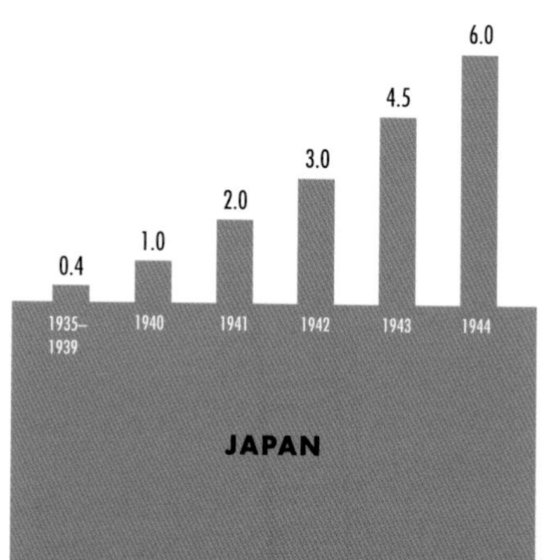

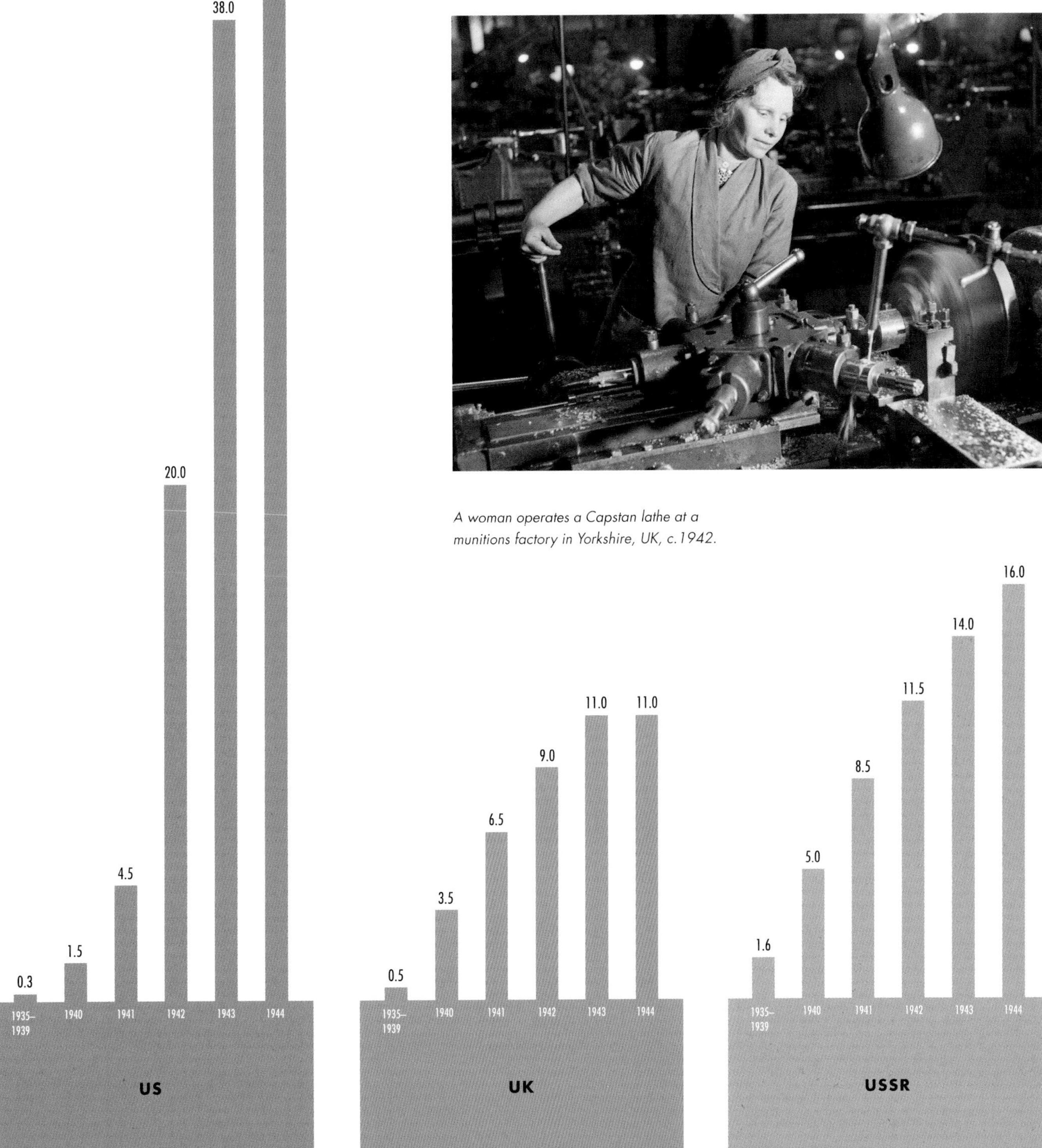

A woman operates a Capstan lathe at a munitions factory in Yorkshire, UK, c.1942.

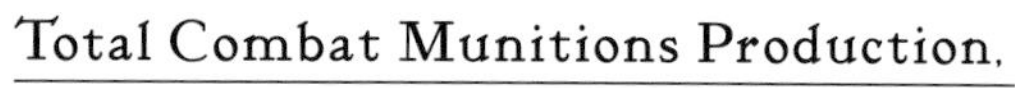

Total Combat Munitions Production, Axis and Allied Powers

The figures on the graphics below are the combined figures of combat munitions production of the Axis and Allied powers for the period 1935–1944, in billions of dollars. Whereas Axis production rose steadily, Allied production increased dramatically for the period.

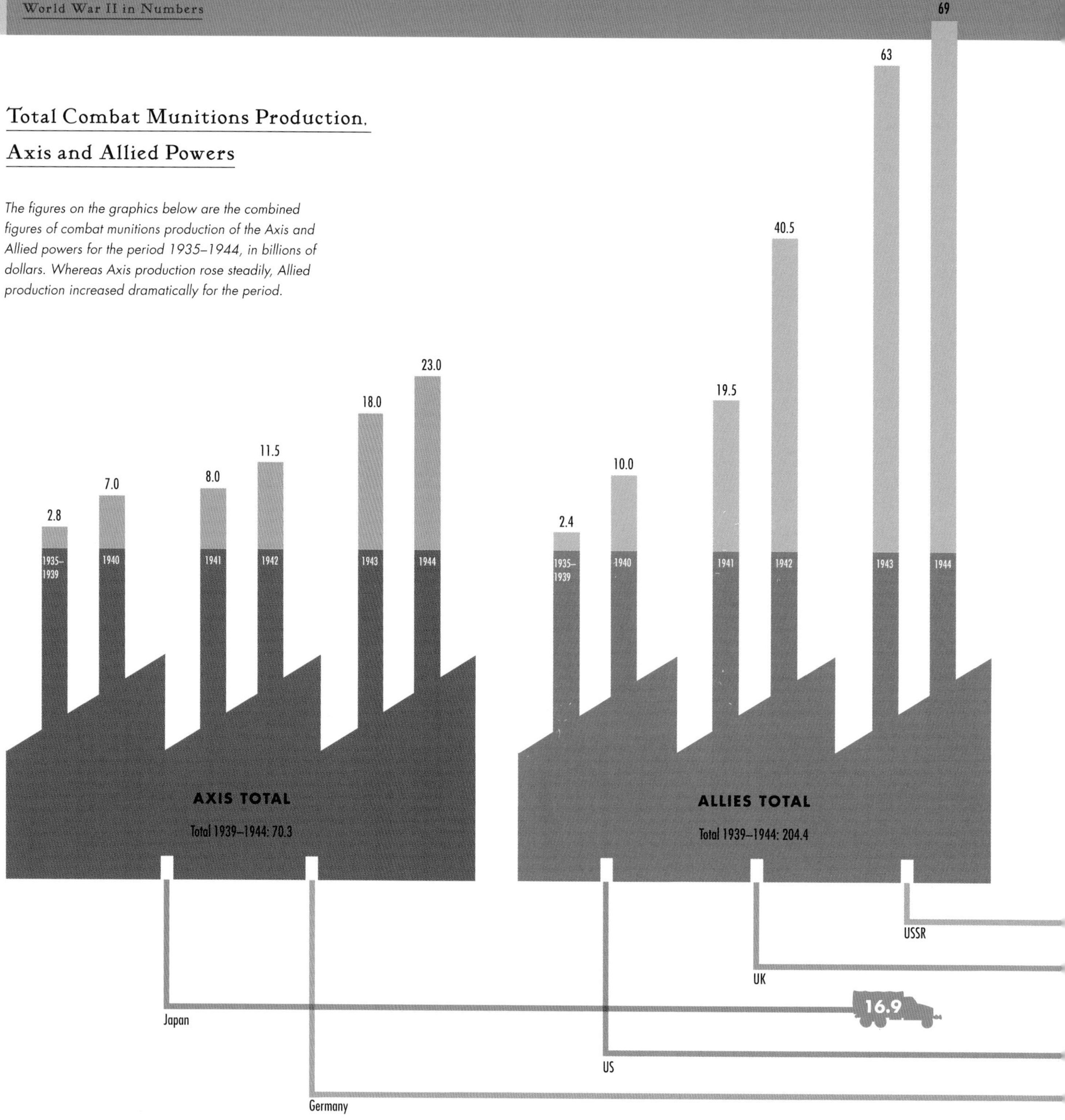

THE ALLIES

The US was a powerhouse; it supplied munitions to its allies through Lend-Lease and bolstered the war effort in many ways. Neutral in 1939–1940, spending on matériel was low, just 2% of national expenditure. But with the attack on Pearl Harbor, and the commitment to the Allied cause, US production rose steeply. During the period there was a vast increase in its Gross Domestic Product (GDP) and the growth of civilian consumerism, even though the population—men and women—was working long hours, and the fact that by 1943 some 47% of the GDP went directly into the nation's war effort. Without the US industrial might, the Allies would have been in a perilous state.

Rearmament in the UK was slow; though Hitler's rise to power had prompted action, much of its effort was pushed into defending the island, with outlay on the navy and air force. Concerned that defence spending might stand in the way of economic progress, the British planned initially for a limited war. They were wrong to do so. With the country on a war footing, the whole of the UK became mobilized for the war effort. The people were subjected to rationing, but they were also highly motivated, with men and women engaged in the production of munitions. Though strongly dependent upon Lend-Lease to make good the deficit, domestic goods factories were transformed into arms manufactories, pushing up production. Some 64% of the UK's national income was to be spent on the war effort.

Unlike the other Allied nations, the Soviet military machine was well geared for war, focused on the probability of invasion or military action. With Germany identified as an aggressor, the Soviets maintained a level of rearmament that was at least on a par with that of Nazi Germany, devoting some 20% of its economy to defence. When the USSR was invaded in 1941, its whole population was mobilized for the war effort. Conditions were harsh; most of the industrial centers were in the west, and many were destroyed or shipped eastward (over 1,500 factories) in order to satisfy the military's needs. Like Britain, over 60% of its economic might was spent on war production.

On average, the major powers devoted 40–65% of their total GDP to munitions production. The Allies produced about three times as much in munitions as the Axis powers; they were to use this to good effect in the delivery of final victory.

Operation Bolero
1943–1944

With planning in progress for the opening of a second front in Europe, it was essential that the US find secure bases within Britain where troops could be trained and acclimatized to the European Theatre of Operations (ETO). The build-up commenced in April 1942, under a plan that was to become known as Operation Bolero.

The plan required the development of a US strategic air force in Britain, as well as the build-up of troops in preparation for the invasion of France. Bolero was coordinated at the highest levels, between Washington and London; with the possibility that Allied troops could set foot on European soil as early as April 1943, it was essential that they act quickly. Thus, plans were developed for the transport and housing of a million US personnel.

The commander of the United States Army Air Forces (USAAF), Major General H. Arnold, was responsible for a plan that would base 525,000 ground troops, 235,000 logistical support troops, and 240,000 air force personnel in the UK. There would also be 21 heavy bomb groups, equipped with B-17 and B-24 bombers (essential if the war was to be brought to the heart of the Reich), 17 medium and light bomb groups, 17 fighter groups (equipped with P-38, P-39, P-40, and P-47 fighters), six observation groups and eight transport groups, amounting to a total of 69 active air force combat groups, and totalling 3,649 aircraft, to be built up from nothing. It was an ambitious plan.

New bases were prepared for the aircraft, with the southeastern counties—the bomber country of England—being the eventual home of many bomber and fighter groups, though Northern Ireland was another attractive proposition for airfield development. The US Army was likewise distributed in the most advantageous regions in the UK—the southern and southwestern counties were most favored.

A staggering number of US Army and USAAF units were distributed across the UK—over 7,000 of them in England alone in the days before the Normandy invasion—ensuring that US soldiers became a familiar sight in Britain.

US Army and USAAF Units

	English county	US Army units	USAAF units	Totals
1	Bedfordshire	10	39	49
2	Berkshire	261	107	368
3	Buckinghamshire	69	46	115
4	Cambridgeshire	28	74	102
5	Cheshire	249	0	249
6	Cornwall	266	6	272
7	Cumberland	0	0	0
8	Derbyshire	77	0	77
9	Devonshire	442	19	461
10	Dorset	253	36	289
11	Durham	0	0	0
12	Essex	27	312	339
13	Gloucestershire	417	21	438
14	Hampshire	327	266	593
15	Herefordshire	88	25	113
16	Hertfordshire	110	25	135
17	Huntingdonshire	15	92	107
18	Kent	17	153	170
19	Lancashire	153	70	223
20	Leicestershire	51	3	54

	English county	US Army units	USAAF units	Totals
21	Lincolnshire	49	71	120
22	London	100	0	100
23	Middlesex	43	8	51
24	Norfolk	33	305	338
25	Northamptonshire	71	97	168
26	Northumberland	6	0	6
27	Nottinghamshire	23	0	23
28	Oxfordshire	145	21	166
29	Rutland	21	0	21
30	Shropshire	102	41	143
31	Somerset	380	1	381
32	Staffordshire	199	2	201
33	Suffolk	69	333	402
34	Surrey	7	0	7
35	Sussex	33	0	33
36	Warwickshire	59	0	59
37	Westmorland	0	0	0
38	Wiltshire	554	13	567
39	Worcestershire	102	3	105
40	Yorkshire	35	1	36
	Totals	**4,891**	**2,190**	**7,081**

Distributed by county in England, May 30th, 1944

TOTALS

51–100
101–150
151–200
201–250
251–300
301–350
351–400
401–450
451–500
501–550
551–600

Waffen SS: Foreign Volunteers and Conscripts 1940–1945

The Waffen SS was the elite military wing of the SS, a component of the Nazi party controlled by Heinrich Himmler. The Waffen SS was never part of the armed forces, or Wehrmacht, but was a separate organization—though its control in the field was a function of the army high command. The use of foreign volunteers in the Waffen SS commenced in 1940, with the creation of the SS Division Wiking, which saw service in Operation Barbarossa. With German success came a flow of volunteers, grouped in 1942–1943 as divisions of the SS. These had up to 60% foreign volunteers.

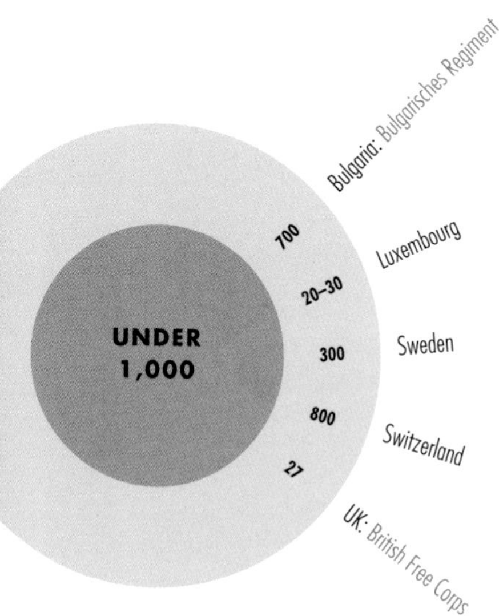

When Waffen volunteers returned home at the end of the war, they all received a very frosty reception, and many were tried for war crimes. There were notable exceptions—the men of the Estonian and Latvian SS units. As conscripts to the Waffen SS, these men were treated as involuntary members, even "freedom fighters" by the authorities.

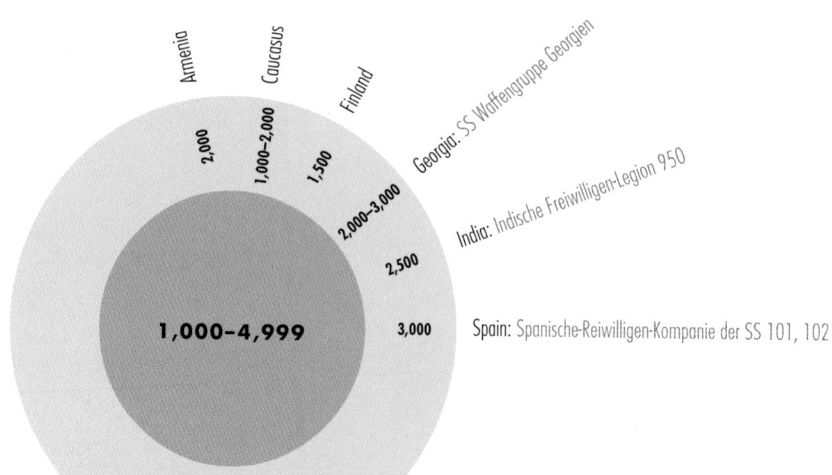

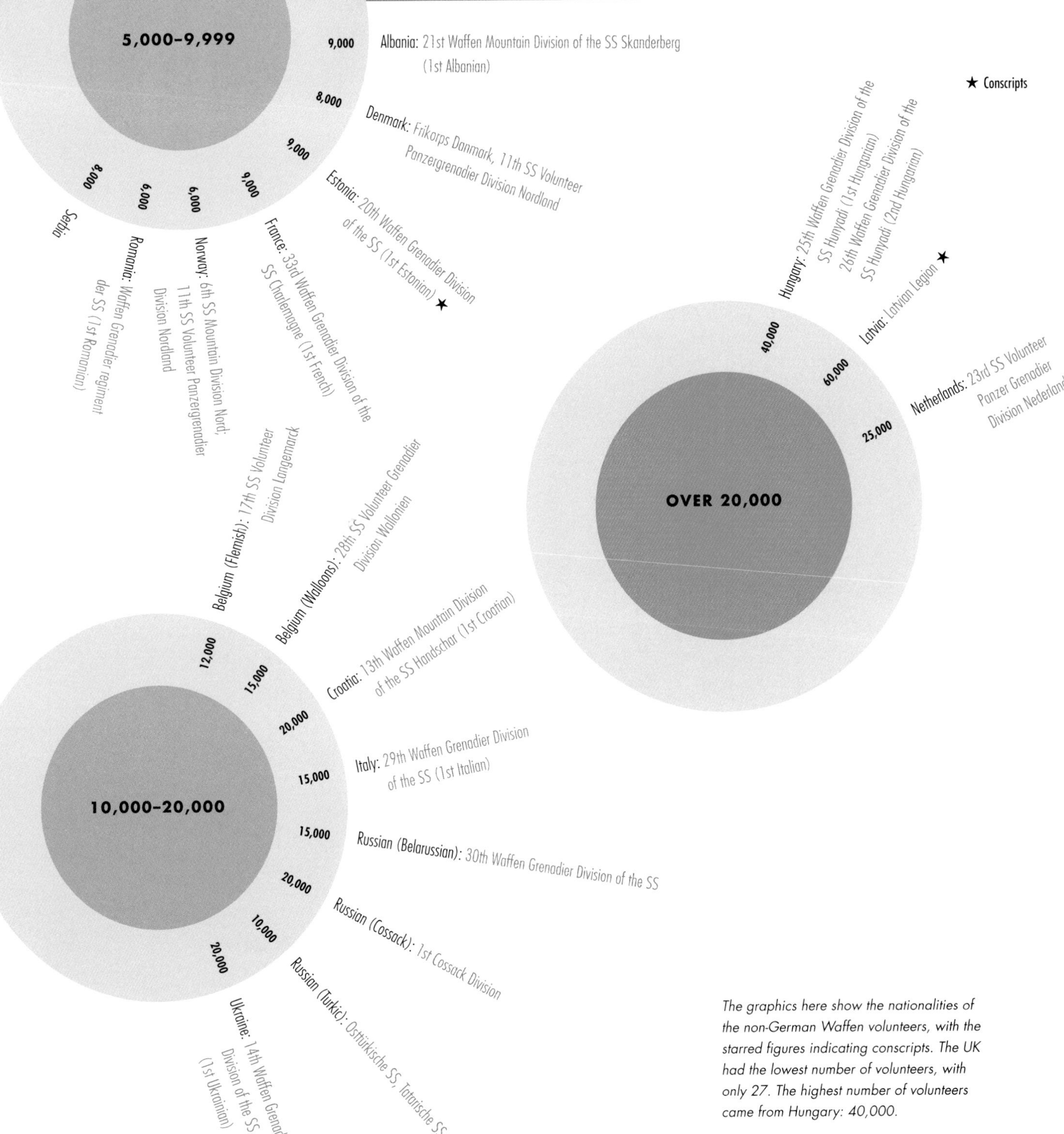

The graphics here show the nationalities of the non-German Waffen volunteers, with the starred figures indicating conscripts. The UK had the lowest number of volunteers, with only 27. The highest number of volunteers came from Hungary: 40,000.

Chapter Two

LAND CAMPAIGNS

Hitler's destruction of Poland in 1939 was the first of many victories, and his armored divisions punched through the French defensive positions in May 1940. In 1941, the Nazi leader turned his attention to the USSR; Operation Barbarossa would prove costly. After El Alamein in 1942, the Allies were in the ascendant, pushing back the fronts after Kursk and D-Day. In the Pacific, the expansionist Japanese were repelled with staggering rates of fatality on the islands of the Pacific, and in the jungles of Burma.

The Invasion of Poland
1939

The German invasion of Poland was the beginning of World War II, shattering the policy of appeasement followed by the Western Allies. With Neville Chamberlain's hopes of "peace in our time" already weakened by the German annexation of Czechoslovakia, in an attempt to control Hitler's territorial ambitions, Chamberlain and the French Prime Minister Édouard Daladier issued a formal guarantee of Poland's borders in March 1939. Unconvinced the Allies would act, Hitler ordered his armed forces to prepare to invade Poland—a country reborn in the wake of the Versailles Treaty, and a territory that stood in the way of the unification of East Prussia and Germany. Hitler's mind was set.

The attack of Poland opened at 06:00 on September 1st with ferocious bombing of the capital, Warsaw. The Luftwaffe attacked all targets, military and civilian, in a bombing campaign that would shock the world. Within a week, the Polish air force defending the capital had taken 70% casualties. Air superiority was quickly achieved across Poland, with many of the Polish aircraft destroyed on the ground. The Luftwaffe attacked transport junctions and troop concentrations, dive-bombed by Ju 87 Stuka aircraft.

Meanwhile, the Wehrmacht smashed into Poland with two army groups fighting in the north from Prussia, and from the south through

FALL WEISS

In the wake of the German–Soviet Non-Aggression Pact, the Fall Weiss, the invasion of Poland was slated for September 1st, 1939. Its pretence was a bizarre staged attack by Germans dressed in Polish uniforms against a radio tower in Silesia, on August 31st, 1939. Any hope of survival was without foundation; the Western Allies were to stand on the defensive in the shadow of the Maginot Line, and the Poles were left to face the might of German blitzkrieg.

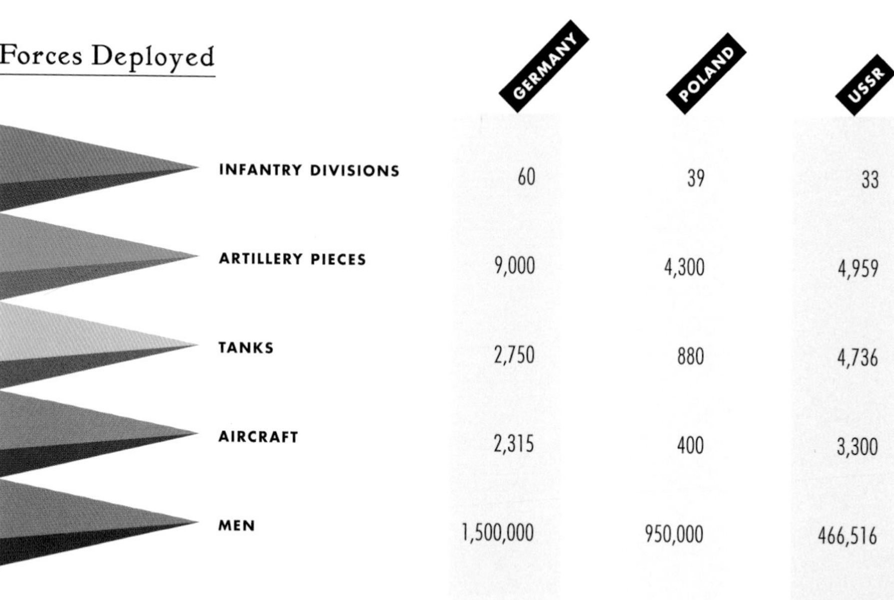

Forces Deployed

	GERMANY	POLAND	USSR
INFANTRY DIVISIONS	60	39	33
ARTILLERY PIECES	9,000	4,300	4,959
TANKS	2,750	880	4,736
AIRCRAFT	2,315	400	3,300
MEN	1,500,000	950,000	466,516

Slovakia—which had been in German hands since Hitler had annexed the country. Armored divisions quickly opened up the front for the infantry, which advanced deeply into Poland, while the very countries that had guaranteed its borders, Britain and France, hesitated. It was not until September 3rd that they declared war on Germany, but by then it was too late. Grimly holding on, the Polish Army—which included 12 divisions of cavalry, the famous lancers that had inspired the world—was broken up into pockets of resistance as the two German army groups met at Lodz. Just eight days after crossing the border, the German panzers were at the gates of the capital, and Polish forces were ordered to make a last stand in the west to soak up the pressure.

With the Nazis approaching USSR borders, Stalin seized the opportunity to build a corridor of security, invading the vulnerable eastern side of the state on September 17th. Though the Poles fought long and hard, there was no hope, and with no help arriving, the battle was over on October 6th, the country split between unlikely bedfellows Hitler and Stalin, and its name removed from the map. The Poles would suffer as perhaps no other nation under occupation.

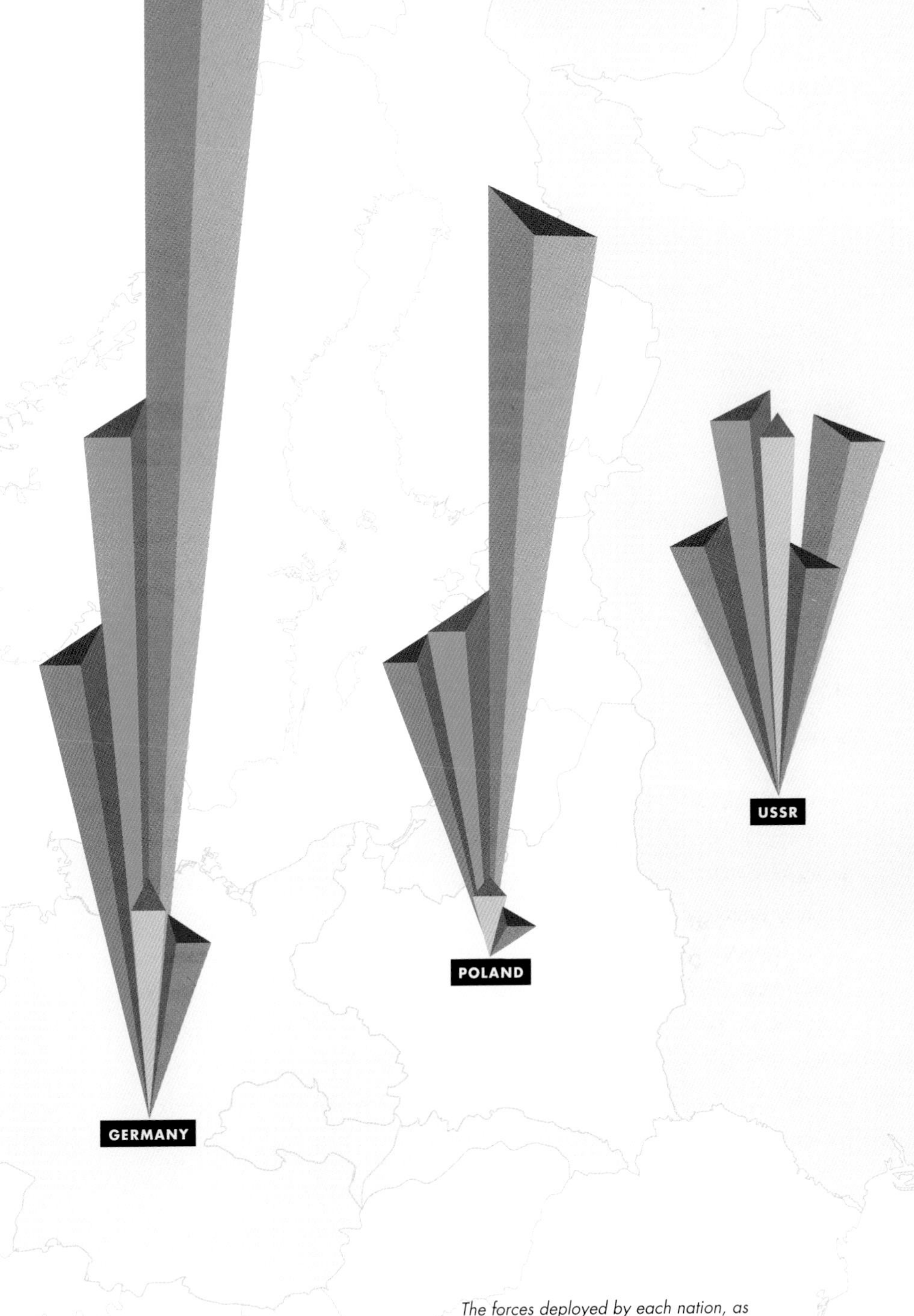

The forces deployed by each nation, as given in the table of figures on the facing page, are represented here visually.

Casualties of the Invasion of Poland

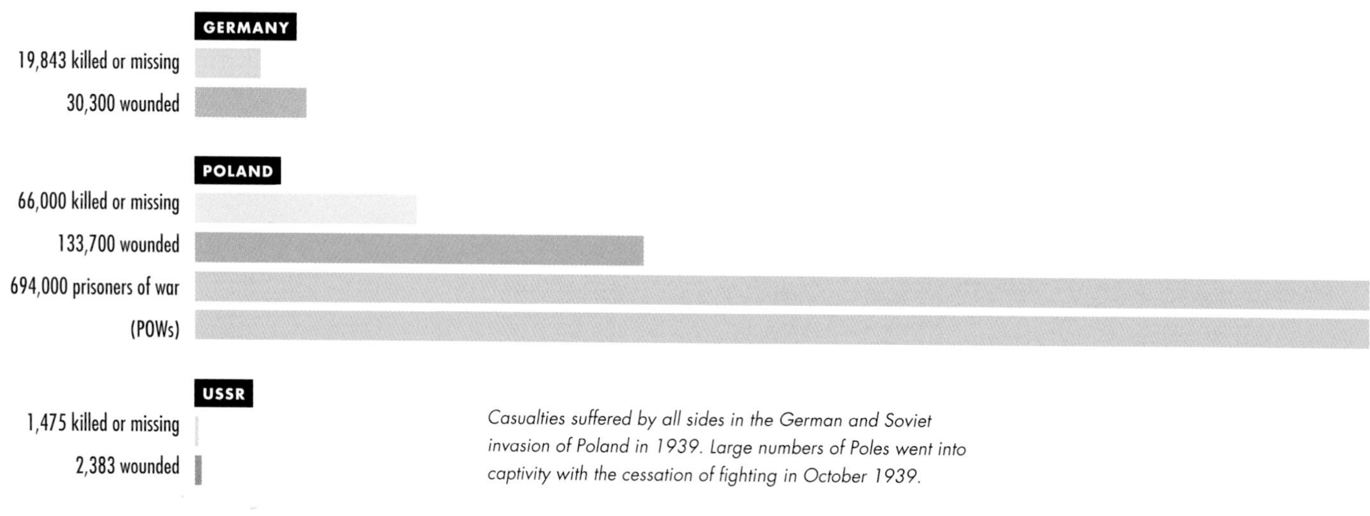

Casualties suffered by all sides in the German and Soviet invasion of Poland in 1939. Large numbers of Poles went into captivity with the cessation of fighting in October 1939.

THE POLISH CAVALRY

The cavalry was the elite of the Polish army. At 70,000 men, organized in 11 cavalry brigades, it represented 10% of the army's strength, with a long tradition that had inspired the world and had led to the growth of lancer elites in most armies of the 19th century, all of whom carried as pennants the red and white flag of Poland. Lances were carried into battle early in World War I by lancers of all the main protagonists; but with Poland partitioned since the early part of the 19th century, Poles would serve in the cavalry arms of many nations. With the re-emergence of Poland after the Treaty of Versailles came the revival of Polish regiments and the readoption of their long histories.

In the interwar years, cavalry figured highly during the Russo–Polish war of 1920, but by the 1930s, tactics had changed. Cavalry was maintained by most nations, but there was recognition of the advances of the mechanized battlefield, even affecting the Poles. The symbolism of the Polish Lancer was altered irrevocably in 1934, its most sacred weapon—the lance—being replaced by the saber, the cavalryman transformed into a mounted infantryman. Now, the purpose of these mounted soldiers was not to take part in massed charges, but rather to act as a light, mobile force that could be

> *"The Polish Pomorska Cavalry Brigade, in ignorance of the nature of our tanks, had charged them with swords and lances and suffered tremendous losses."*
>
> General Heinz Guderian, Panzer Leader, 1952

delivered anywhere within range of their horses, dismounting to fight on foot. The Polish army was aware that this mobility might bring its cavalry forces into direct contact with armored units on a future battlefield. In such cases, cavalrymen were directed to attack tanks from cover, using light anti-tank weapons—but not to charge them directly with sabers.

Yet, on the opening day of the invasion of Poland, Colonel Kazimierz Mastalerz, commander of the 18th Regiment of the Pomorska Cavalry Brigade, was to lead his men in a charge on a German infantry battalion in the village of Krojanty; initially flushed with success, Mastalerz's men were attacked by armored vehicles that appeared from nowhere and that killed 20 of the cavalry troopers before they could retreat. It was from this action that the idea of Polish cavalry charging tanks was born, finding its way into the memoirs of the German panzer leader, Guderian. Despite the mythology of lances against tank turrets, the cavalry demonstrated its position as the elite of the Polish Army by adapting to the new doctrine of lightning warfare so ruthlessly demonstrated by the Wehrmacht. Operating as a mobile force, as intended, the Polish cavalry was able to inflict severe casualties on the German Army and, in at least one instance, to force the 20th Motorized Division to withdraw—much to the consternation of the German commander.

Polish cavalry rides into action during the German invasion of the country, September 1939.

The cavalry were the elite of the Polish Army; a force of 70,000 men in 11 brigades, it was heavily committed during the German invasion.

The Battle of France
1940

The Battle of France was fought between May 10th and June 25th, 1940, and saw the defeat of one of the strongest of the world's military nations—France. The battle also saw the Germans deploy their tactics of blitzkrieg, punching a hole in the French frontier, and avoiding the strength of the fortified Maginot Line. Pushing through the hilly and wooded terrain of the Ardennes, the Germans enacted their plan *Fall Gelb* (Case Yellow).

The German tactics involved the sheer weight of manpower, armor, and aerial supremacy that have become known as blitzkrieg, a limited "lightning war" that ensured their enemies were stunned by the weight of the attack. Though a large part of the German forces were not motorized (relying on horse power, as it had in World War I), it was their superior weight of armor and troops that would be decisive—as would be the means of communicating between tanks by radio, with the result that tanks could operate effectively in relation to changing local conditions. Some 2,439 German tanks and 7,398 artillery pieces would face the French and British armies in 1940.

Yet France possessed the stronger tank force, with machines such as the Somua S35 and Renault D2 more heavily armored than their German counterparts. German tanks were, however, faster, whereas British tanks were either lightly armored or lumbering. It was the effectiveness of German combined arms tactics (coupled with the Allied defensiveness) that saw the defeat of the Allies; and with effective artillery support, the French tanks—deployed in small, ineffective numbers—were to suffer their highest casualties to the German gunners. Those French tanks that survived would be redeployed by the Germans, even if it was only to provide turrets for Hitler's Atlantic Wall.

PzI

Panzerkampfwagen 1.
This light tank formed the bulk of the German armored strength in 1939. It was fast, but lightly armored (see table overleaf).

MATILDA II

The Matilda II was a British tank designed to work with infantry.
It was slow, but heavily armored.

RENAULT FT17

This French light tank was used in World War I and was obsolete, though available in large numbers.

35

Destroyed by aircraft

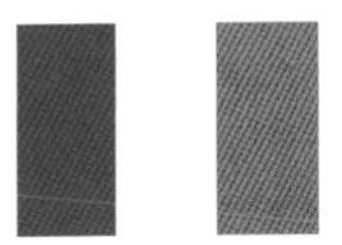

Tank Casualties by Cause

Destroyed by artillery

1,669

1,749

Total French tanks destroyed

Destroyed by mines

45

The number of French tank casualties during the Battle of France, and the means by which they were destroyed. The vast majority were hit by artillery and tank artillery in battle; far fewer were hit by aircraft or destroyed by mines.

Main Tanks Deployed in the Battle of France

	TYPE	NAME	NO.	ARMOR (inches / mm)	Actual armor width
FRANCE	Light tanks:	Hotchkiss H35/H39	802	1 3/8 in (34 mm)	
		Renault R35/39	945	1 5/8 in (43 mm)	
		FCM 36	90	1 9/16 in (40 mm)	
		Renault FT17 (obsolete)	462	1 3/16 in (30 mm)	
	Medium tanks:	Somua S35	264	1 13/16 in (47 mm)	
		Renault D2	45	1 9/16 in (40 mm)	
	Heavy tanks:	Renault B1bis	206	2 3/8 in (60 mm)	
		FCM-2C (obsolete)	8	1 3/4 in (45 mm)	
UK	Light tank:	Vickers MkVIb	208	1/2 in (14 mm)	
	Infantry tanks:	Matilda I	77	2 3/8 in (60 mm)	
		Matilda II	23	3 1/16 in (78 mm)	
GERMANY	Light tanks:	PzI	643	1/2 in (13 mm)	
		PzII	880	1/2 in (14 mm)	
	Medium tanks:	PzIII	349	2 3/4 in (70 mm)	
		Pz35(t)	128	1 in (25 mm)	
		Pz38(t)	207	1 3/16 in (30 mm)	
		PzIV	281	3 1/8 in (80 mm)	

MAIN ARMAMENT	SPEED (mph / km/h)	Visual representation of speed to scale
37 mm	17 mph (28 km/h)	
37 mm	12 mph (20 km/h)	
37 mm	15 mph (24 km/h)	
37 mm	4 mph (7 km/h)	
47 mm	30 mph (41 km/h)	
47 mm	23 mph (23 km/h)	
75 mm	17 mph (28 km/h)	
75 mm	9 mph (15 km/h)	
.303 machine gun	34 mph (56 km/h)	
.303 machine gun	8 mph (13 km/h)	
40 mm (2 pdr)	9 mph (14 km/h)	
7.92 mm machine gun (x 2)	31 mph (50 km/h)	
20 mm (x 2)	25 mph (40 km/h)	
37 mm	25 mph (40 km/h)	
37 mm	21 mph (34 km/h)	
37 mm	26 mph (42 km/h)	
75 mm	26 mph (42 km/h)	

Dunkirk: Operation Dynamo
1940

Operation Dynamo was the code name for the evacuation of the soldiers of the British Expeditionary Force (BEF), and of their French Allies, from Dunkirk in May/June 1940. With the BEF under constant pressure since the German invasion of France on May 10th, 1940, troops were ordered to withdraw to the coast in a continuously contracting perimeter. With British and French troops acting to protect the rear, the retreating force reached Dunkirk, and the evacuations commenced on May 27th.

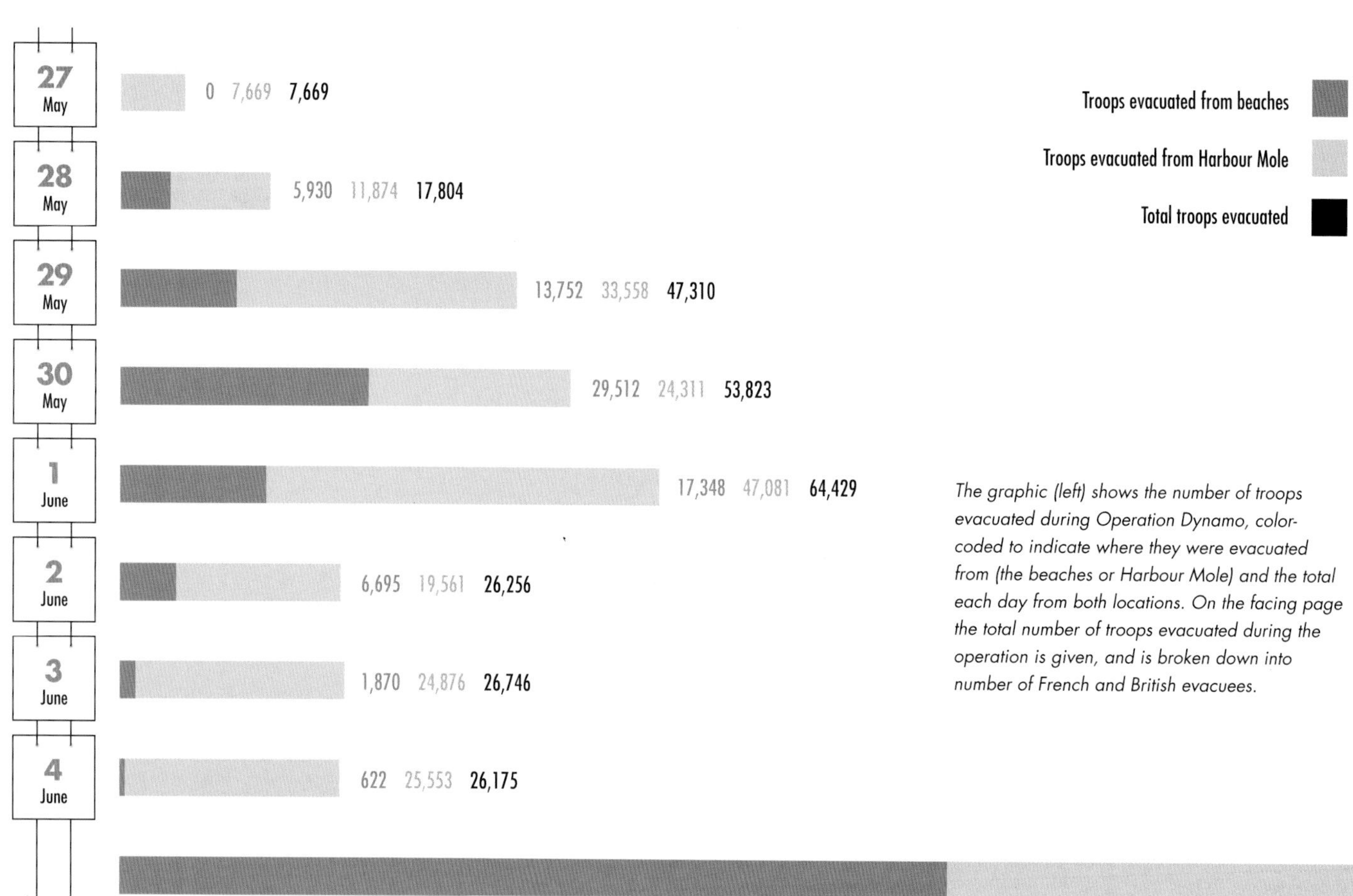

The graphic (left) shows the number of troops evacuated during Operation Dynamo, color-coded to indicate where they were evacuated from (the beaches or Harbour Mole) and the total each day from both locations. On the facing page the total number of troops evacuated during the operation is given, and is broken down into number of French and British evacuees.

Operation Dynamo required that the perimeter be held while much of the BEF was removed from the beaches, and here the remnants of the French First Army assisted in holding back the Germans, while the perimeter was otherwise held by British battalions, some of whom would never escape, and who would be either killed or captured.

The harbor at Dunkirk had a large structure, the mole, which allowed troops direct access to smaller warships, destroyers, that were able to come inshore and load men directly. These suffered at the hands of the Luftwaffe, which sent divebombers and other aircraft to try to prevent the evacuation. Despite criticism, the Royal Air Force (RAF) was active in reducing their impact.

But things were a little more tricky on the shallow shelving beaches to the east of Dunkirk. Here men had to wade into the sea to be picked up by an armada of what became known as "little ships," small craft handled by yachtsmen or a diversity of civilian boats that were able to come inshore to assist with the evacuation. The exact number of little ships will never be known.

Over 330,000 men would be picked up from the beaches or Harbour Mole at Dunkirk, and they would form the basis of a rebuilt British Army and of the Free French forces. More damaging was the loss of equipment; whereas men could be rescued, most of their equipment was abandoned, either to the sands of Dunkirk or to the approaching German forces.

Losses:

British Expeditionary Force:

68,111 men: KIA or POW

French (at Dunkirk):

40,000 men POW

Equipment lost by the BEF:

2,472 guns

63,879 vehicles

20,548 motorcycles

85,228 tons (77,318 tonnes) of ammunition

466,972 tons (423,630 tonnes) of stores

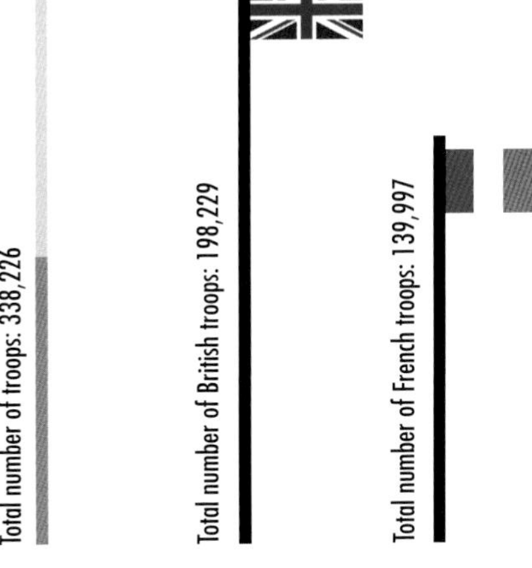

Total troops evacuated

75,729 194,483 270,212

Naval Vessels Involved in the Dunkirk Rescues:

Total number of naval ships (British, French, Dutch, Norwegian) involved in the evacuation: 933

Number of ships unharmed: 636

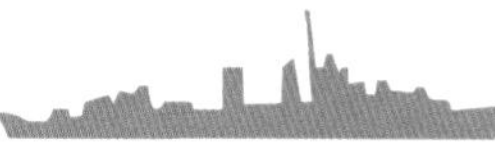

Number of ships damaged: 61

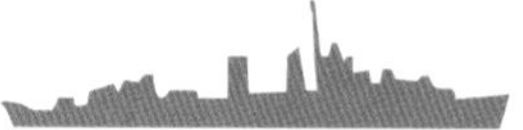

Number of ships sunk or destroyed: 236

Number of little ships: unknown, c. 700–850

British and French prisoners leave the beaches of Dunkirk in June 1940. They would face five long years of captivity in German POW camps.

The Battle of Crete

1941

The Battle of Crete was significant—for the first time in history, an island would be taken by airborne troops rather than direct amphibious assault. Crete was a military target for its strategic position and the location of its airfields, which allowed the Allies aerial access to the Romanian oilfields that were so vital to the Axis war effort, particularly for the coming invasion of the Soviet Union. The battle commenced on May 10th, 1941, and saw ten days of fierce fighting for the German *Fallschirmjäger*.

German paratroopers (Fallschirmjäger) jumping over Crete in 1941. With the Allied troops on the alert, casualties among the Germans were high.

German Forces in Crete

11 Luftflotte

14,000 *Fallschirmjäger*

15,000 *Gebirgsjäger*

500 transports
80 gliders
280 fighters
150 divebombers
180 fighters

The German paratroopers were highly trained and professional. They had been involved in the daring capture of Fort Eben-Emael in 1940, and confidence in their skills was high. It has been estimated that during a jump, 13 paratroopers could exit their delivery aircraft—the functional and tough Junkers 52—in eight seconds. Jumping at 330 ft (100 m) with an air speed of 46 mph (75 km/h), the soldiers would be tightly clustered, with just 75 ft (23 m) between them—but they would be widely scattered if the aircraft were to fly higher or faster. At Crete, many *Fallschirmjäger* jumped at just 250 ft (75 m), 30 ft (9 m) of which was taken up by the static line of the parachute, attached to its canvas bag.

The largest operational unit of the German Luftwaffe was a Luftflotte, or "air fleet," divided into specialist wings (Geswader).

Gebirgsjäger, or mountain infantrymen, were elite troops of the Wehrmacht, drawing on a long tradition of Alpine warfare.

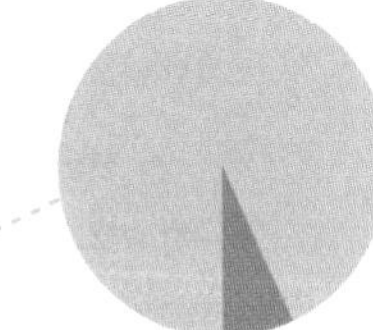

Percentage of Gebirgsjäger strength that were casualties. **6.92%**

Fallschirmjäger were elite German parachute troops serving with the Luftwaffe, first raised in 1935.

At a height of 250 ft (75 m), the paratroopers were easy targets. Their effectiveness as fighting soldiers on their descent was also compromised by the nature of their parachute harness, which meant that each man jumping had to adopt a spread-eagle horizontal stance, facing head-down out of the aircraft. The paratrooper would freefall until the static line deployed his chute, which opened to its full extent at 100 ft (30 m) down. The German jump stance meant that landing would be on all fours—risking both ankle and wrist injury. It also meant that the target was larger, and the descending soldiers more vulnerable to ground fire. Allied paratroopers, who jumped vertically, were less vulnerable.

German paratrooper as seen from below.

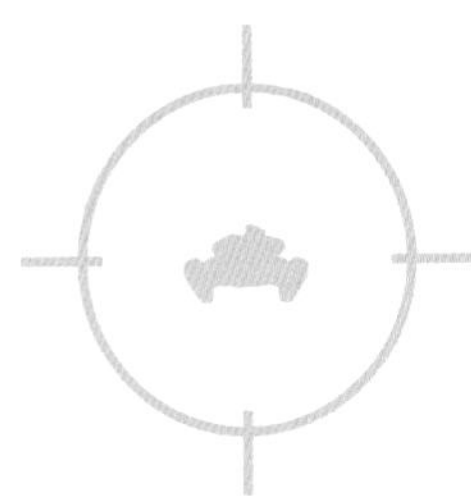

Allied paratrooper as seen from below—the shootable target surface area is much smaller.

Landed

42%

Some 8,100 Fallschirmjäger were dropped over Crete, 58% of the the total 14,000 available, the remainder held in reserve.

63.5%

Casualties were high, amounting to some 63.5% of those dropped over Crete.

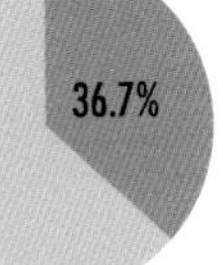

With 36.7% of the total Fallschirmjäger force casualties, Hitler was cautious about committing them elsewhere.

Crete was the largest German airborne operation, and also its last. Picked out on their descent, the German paratroopers were slaughtered. The *Fallschirmjäger* were ferried to the island in two waves, aboard 500 Junkers 52 aircraft of the XI Fliegerkorps. Air-assault troops were delivered in 70 gliders. In total, 8,100 paratroopers were dropped on Crete; of these, almost two-thirds became casualties, half of them killed or missing. The battle was only lost to the Allies when some Junkers 52 aircraft landed and mountain troops (*Gebirgsjäger*) gained a foothold at Hill 107, overlooking Maleme airfield. From here, the Germans were able to pour in more troops and to push back the Commonwealth and Greek forces, and the island was evacuated. Never again would the *Fallschirmjäger* carry out such an audacious assault; they fought the rest of the war as elite ground troops.

Fallschirmjäger *graves on Crete.*

German Casualties

Fallschirmjäger *casualties were high at Crete; ground troops (*Gebirgsjäger*) took fewer casualties, as they did not have to jump out of an aircraft into the face of the Allied guns.*

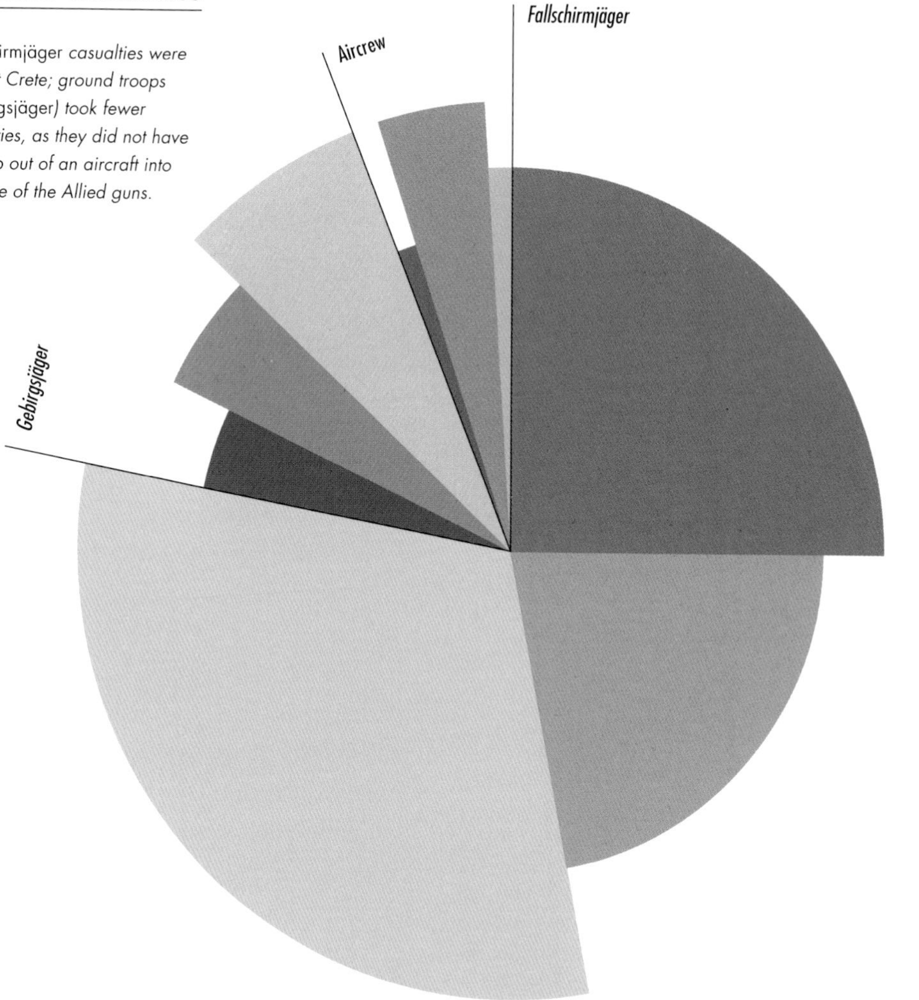

Fallschirmjäger

Aircrew

Gebirgsjäger

	Fallschirmjäger	Gebirgsjäger	Aircrew	
KILLED	1,653	262	76	1,991
MISSING	1,441	318	236	1,995
WOUNDED	2,046	458	90	2,594
Total casualties	5,140	1,038	402	6,580

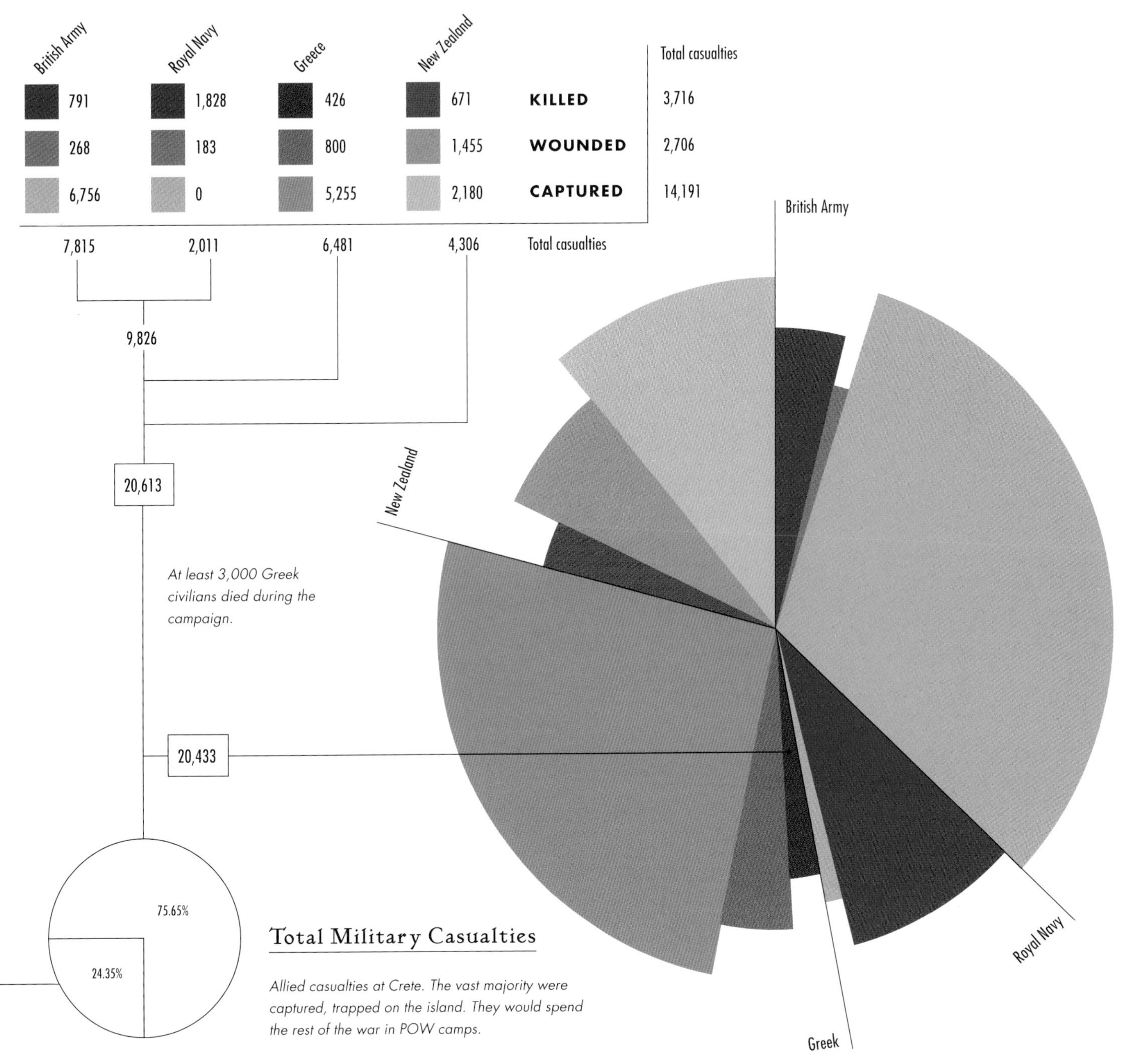

At least 3,000 Greek civilians died during the campaign.

Total Military Casualties

Allied casualties at Crete. The vast majority were captured, trapped on the island. They would spend the rest of the war in POW camps.

The Conquest of Malaya
1941

Japanese expansionist plans included the invasion and capture of the Malay Peninsula, rich in natural resources. For the Japanese, it was a vital target—Malaya supplied over 50% of the world's rubber. The peninsula was actually a federation of states. At its tip lay Singapore, a jewel in the crown of the British Empire; a significant military and naval base supporting Britain's imperial commitments. Singapore was reputed to be an "island fortress," yet its defences were concentrated on the naval base at Changi and were designed to protect that base and harbor from attacks from the sea. This left the northern shore, facing Malaya, vulnerable. On December 8th, 1941, the Japanese landed on the northern Malay Peninsula, their plan to move rapidly southward toward the now vulnerable fortress.

The advance along the peninsula was rapid, the Japanese making use of the roads cut for the rubber workers, deploying men on bicycles and making use of light tanks. Singapore was defended by mostly Indian troops with a leavening of Australian, British, and Malay units (17 Australian, 13 British, and two Malay battalions) that composed the force of 88,000 men. The newly arrived British 18th Infantry Division lacked experience and appropriate training; most of the other units were under-strength. The fortress of Singapore was equipped with 15-inch large-caliber coastal guns; as coastal guns focused on firing on ships to the south, these were said to have been useless against a land force attacking from the north. In fact, they were used against the Japanese, but were ineffective due to their lack of high explosive shells.

Led by Lieutenant-General Sir Arthur Percival, the Allied force was relatively poorly equipped and certainly poorly trained—little match for, and out-generalled by, Lieutenant-General Yamashita and his Japanese 25th Army, 30,000 veterans battle-hardened by the war in China. The attack on Singapore itself commenced on February 7th, 1942. The colony would fall just eight days later, the Japanese penetrating the Allied lines through gaps formed by creeks and swamps, ultimately causing the Allied forces to contract inward. Winston Churchill, believing the Japanese to be outnumbered, demanded no surrender from Percival on February 10th. Three days later, with the Allies still losing ground, senior officers advised Percival to surrender in an attempt to minimize civilian casualties. At first, he refused, but faced with fierce attacks and decreasing supplies, he ruled out the possibility of a counterattack. Unconditional surrender followed on February 15th. The worst defeat in the history of British arms, the Battle of Singapore and the preceding Malayan Campaign saw Percival's command suffer around 7,500 killed, 10,000 wounded, and 120,000 captured, with Indian, Australian, and British troops condemned to the hell of Japanese prison camps. Japanese losses in the fighting for Singapore numbered around 1,713 killed and 2,772 wounded.

Conquest of Malaya: Movement of the Japanese Forces Southward

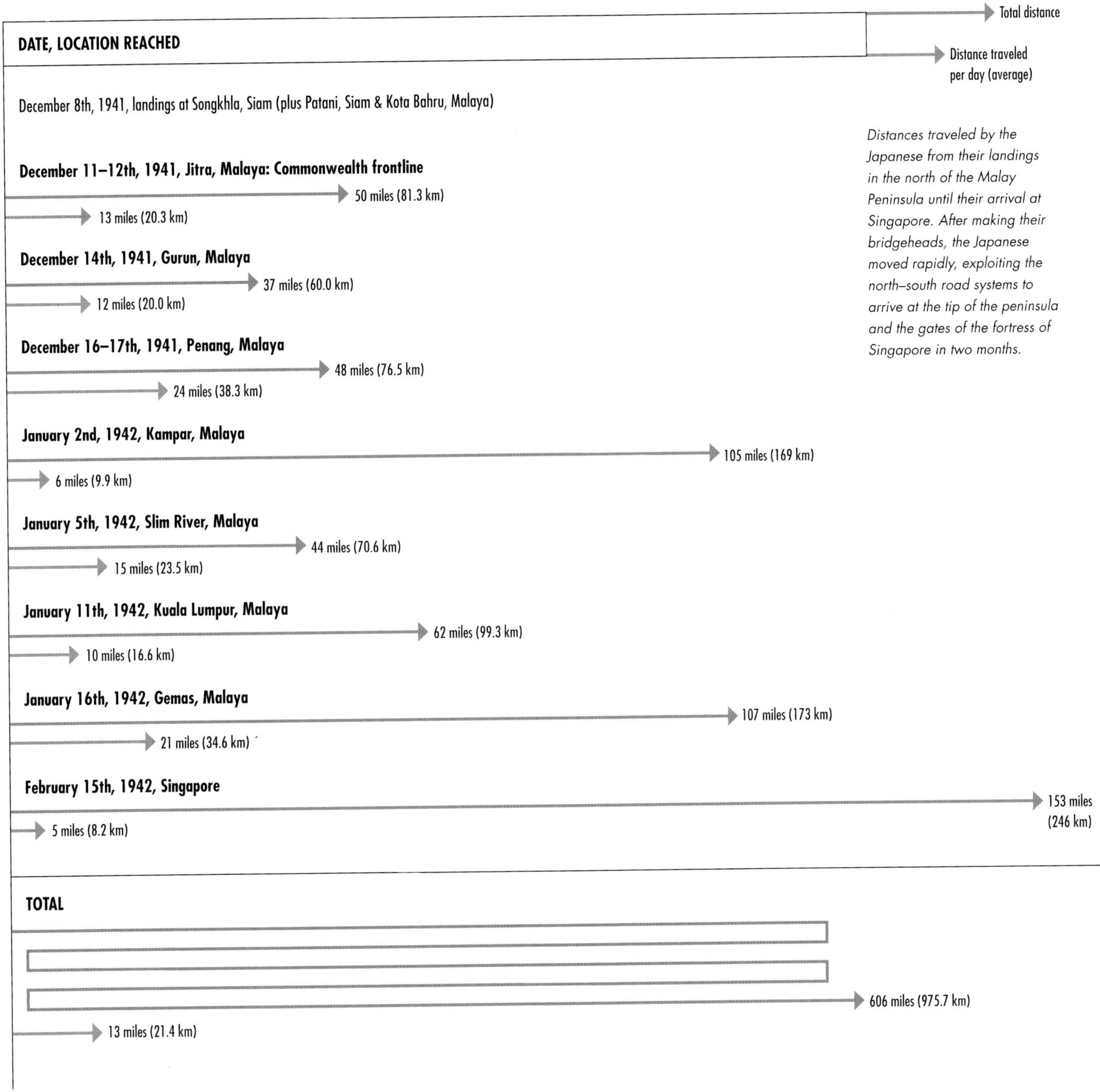

Total distance

Distance traveled per day (average)

DATE, LOCATION REACHED

December 8th, 1941, landings at Songkhla, Siam (plus Patani, Siam & Kota Bahru, Malaya)

Distances traveled by the Japanese from their landings in the north of the Malay Peninsula until their arrival at Singapore. After making their bridgeheads, the Japanese moved rapidly, exploiting the north–south road systems to arrive at the tip of the peninsula and the gates of the fortress of Singapore in two months.

December 11–12th, 1941, Jitra, Malaya: Commonwealth frontline

50 miles (81.3 km)

13 miles (20.3 km)

December 14th, 1941, Gurun, Malaya

37 miles (60.0 km)

12 miles (20.0 km)

December 16–17th, 1941, Penang, Malaya

48 miles (76.5 km)

24 miles (38.3 km)

January 2nd, 1942, Kampar, Malaya

105 miles (169 km)

6 miles (9.9 km)

January 5th, 1942, Slim River, Malaya

44 miles (70.6 km)

15 miles (23.5 km)

January 11th, 1942, Kuala Lumpur, Malaya

62 miles (99.3 km)

10 miles (16.6 km)

January 16th, 1942, Gemas, Malaya

107 miles (173 km)

21 miles (34.6 km)

February 15th, 1942, Singapore

153 miles (246 km)

5 miles (8.2 km)

TOTAL

606 miles (975.7 km)

13 miles (21.4 km)

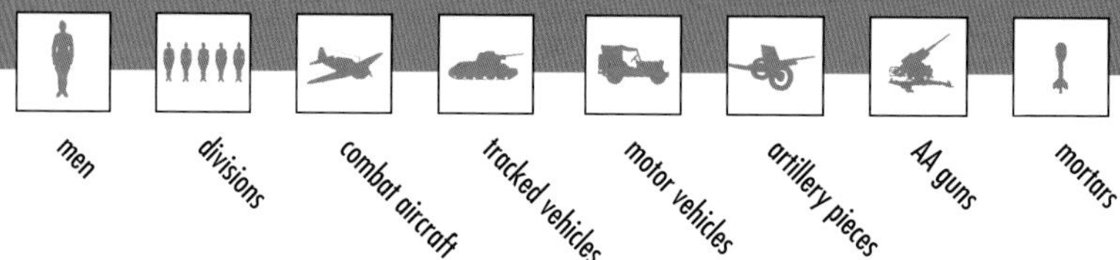

Operation Barbarossa 1941

Operation Barbarossa was the largest invasion in history. Launched on June 22nd, 1941, it was the culmination of Hitler's obsession with the east, and the idea that he might defeat the USSR, a country that, on paper at least, had the greatest army and air force in the world.

The Wehrmacht invasion force was the largest ever assembled, consisting of 138 divisions in three Army Groups. Army Group North (29 Divisions) was focused on Leningrad and the Baltic states (Lithuania, Latvia, and Estonia); Army Group Center (52 Divisions) was focused on the invasion of Byelorussia and the capture of Minsk, Smolensk, and ultimately Moscow; and Army Group South (41 Divisions) was to take on the Ukraine, on to Kiev, and then cross the Dneper into the Crimea. The invasion force was backed up with 4,442 armored vehicles and almost 4,000 aircraft, and would be reinforced by divisions from other Axis countries: 16 Finnish (in the north) and 2 Slovakian, 3 Italian, and 15 Romanian divisions in the south. Altogether, 3,316,000 men were poised to strike on the broad front that was the Soviet Union's western frontier.

Facing them were 304 Soviet Divisions, with a strong tank force; 228 of these (including 75 tank and mechanized divisions) would be distributed in the five western Military Districts (Leningrad, Baltic, Western, Kiev, and Odessa) facing the Wehrmacht. This would amount to 3,310,000 men, 5,465 tanks, and just over 2,000 aircraft. On paper, evenly matched to the German forces. But the Soviet forces were below par, and the Russian command had been purged by Stalin in his attempts to remove opposition. There were few men able to act quickly and decisively enough to hold the invaders back.

Evenly matched, with around 60% of the total forces of both states, Nazi Germany had one advantage essential in a lightning war; over 80% of its tank force was committed to the invasion.

SOVIET FORCES

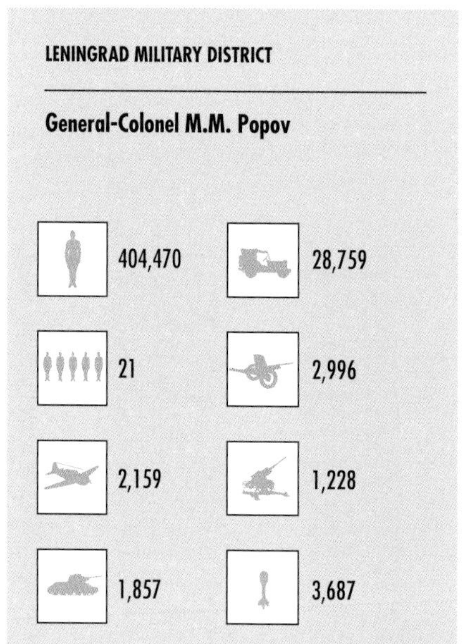

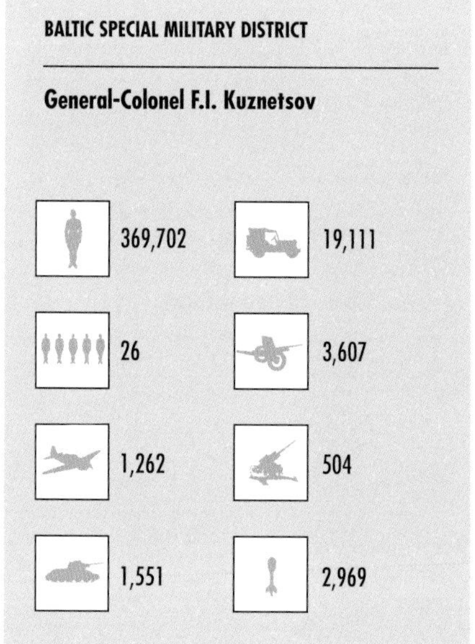

WEHRMACHT FORCES

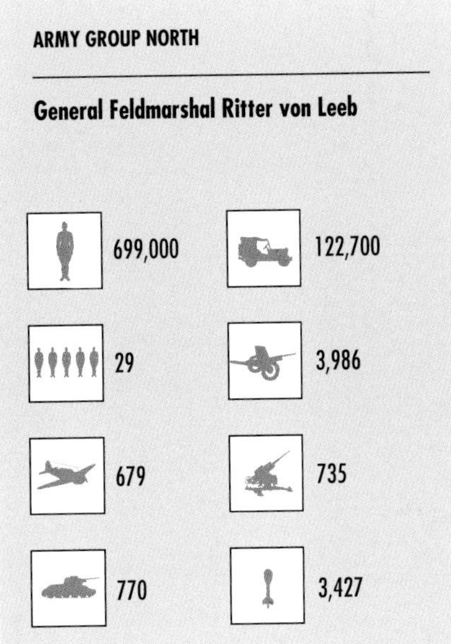
ARMY GROUP NORTH
General Feldmarshal Ritter von Leeb
699,000
122,700
29
3,986
679
735
770
3,427

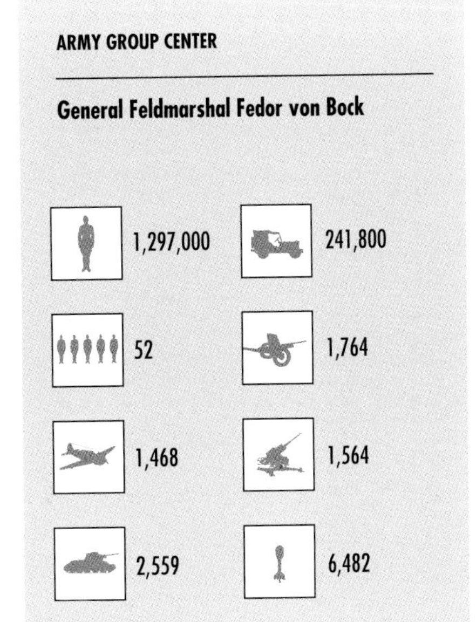
ARMY GROUP CENTER
General Feldmarshal Fedor von Bock
1,297,000
241,800
52
1,764
1,468
1,564
2,559
6,482

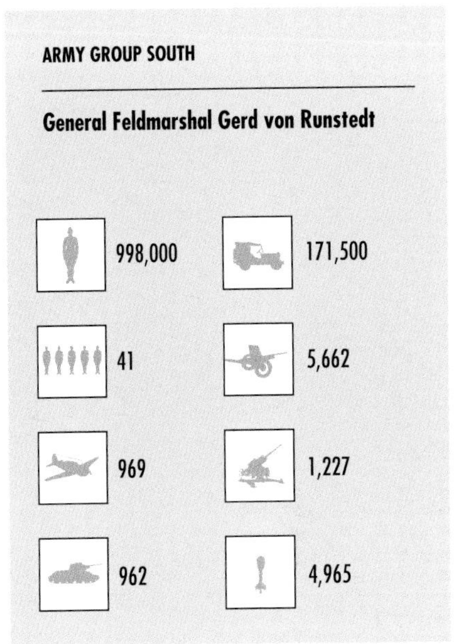
ARMY GROUP SOUTH
General Feldmarshal Gerd von Runstedt
998,000
171,500
41
5,662
969
1,227
962
4,965

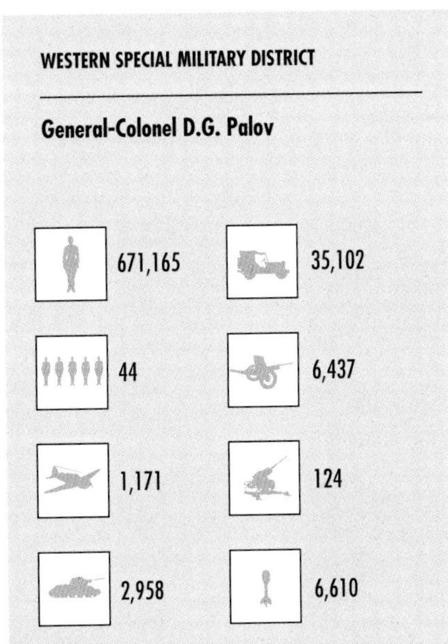
WESTERN SPECIAL MILITARY DISTRICT
General-Colonel D.G. Palov
671,165
35,102
44
6,437
1,171
124
2,958
6,610

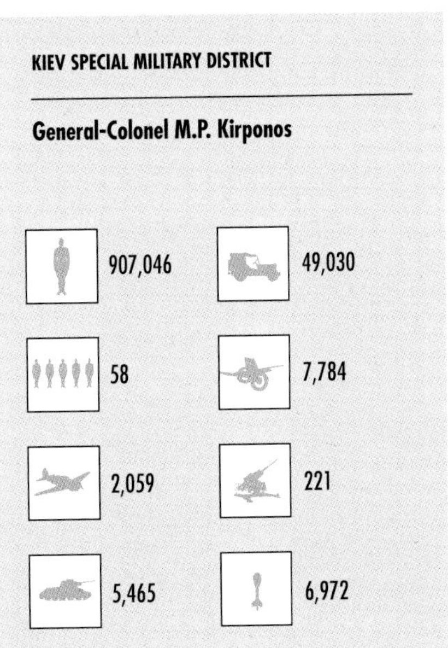
KIEV SPECIAL MILITARY DISTRICT
General-Colonel M.P. Kirponos
907,046
49,030
58
7,784
2,059
221
5,465
6,972

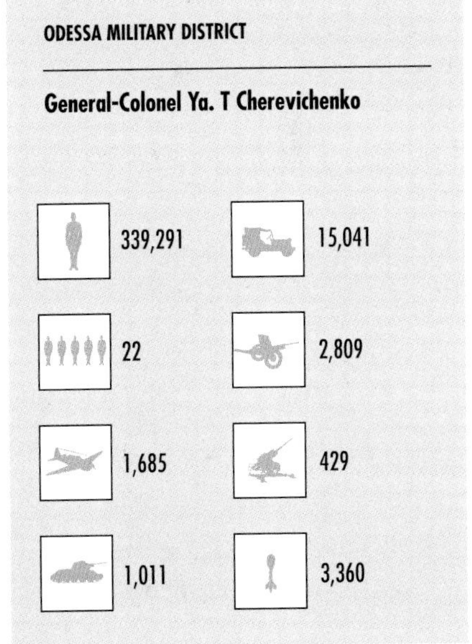
ODESSA MILITARY DISTRICT
General-Colonel Ya. T Cherevichenko
339,291
15,041
22
2,809
1,685
429
1,011
3,360

WEHRMACHT FORCES

The opposing forces during Operation Barbarossa. The total number of men, combat aircraft, tracked vehicles, motor vehicles, artillery pieces, AA guns, and mortars compared.

1 dot = 10,000 soldiers
1 row of dots = 100,000 soldiers
Total Wehrmacht forces committed to Barbarossa, June 22nd, 1941
3,316,000
3,277
4,445
577,000
19,676
3,769
17,113
Total Wehrmacht forces on all fronts, June 22nd, 1941
5,160,000
4,878
5,432
831,400
25,150
16,322
22,650

Percentage Wehrmacht forces committed to Barbarossa
64.3%
67.2%
81.8%
69.4%
78.2%
23.1%
75.6%

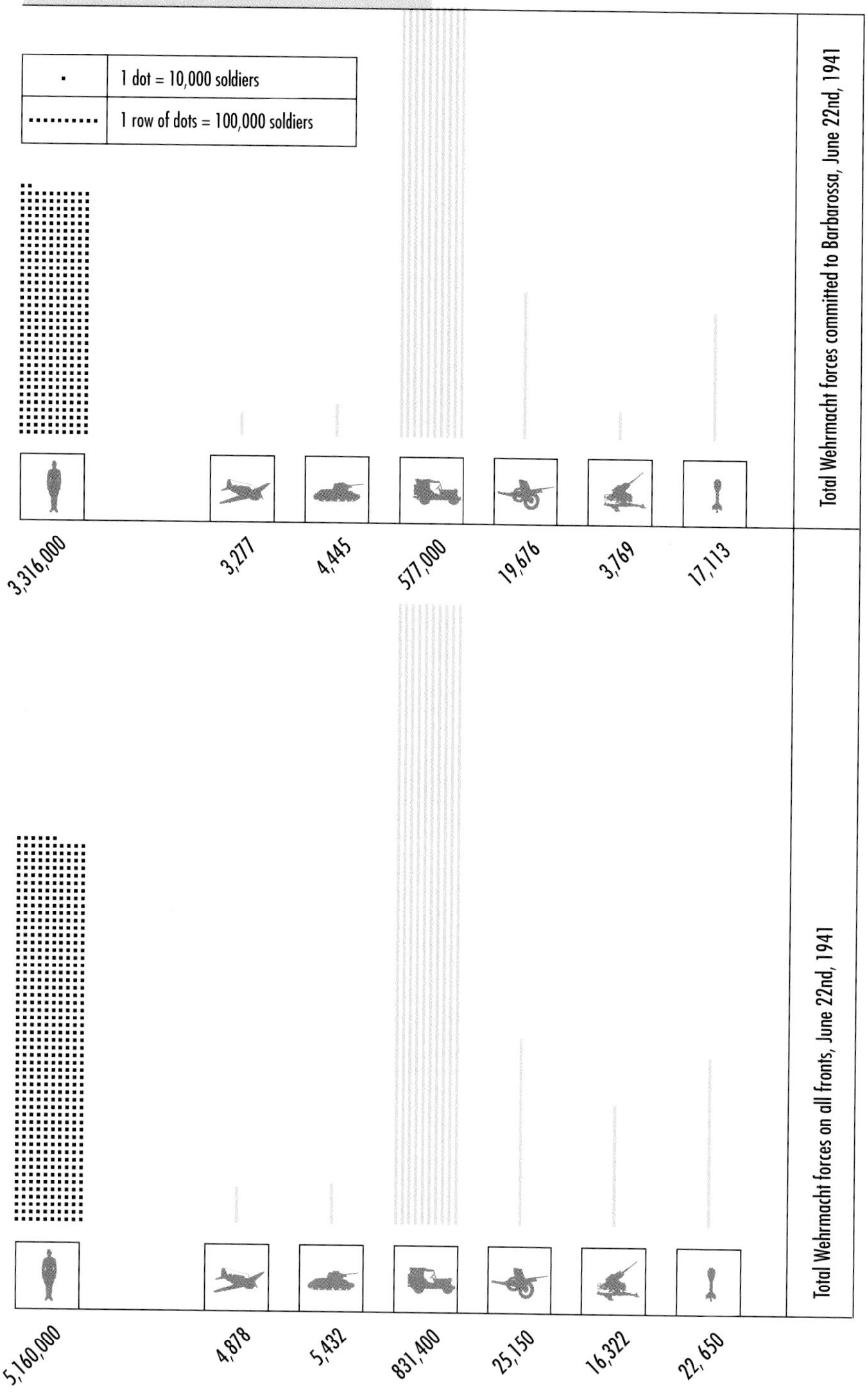

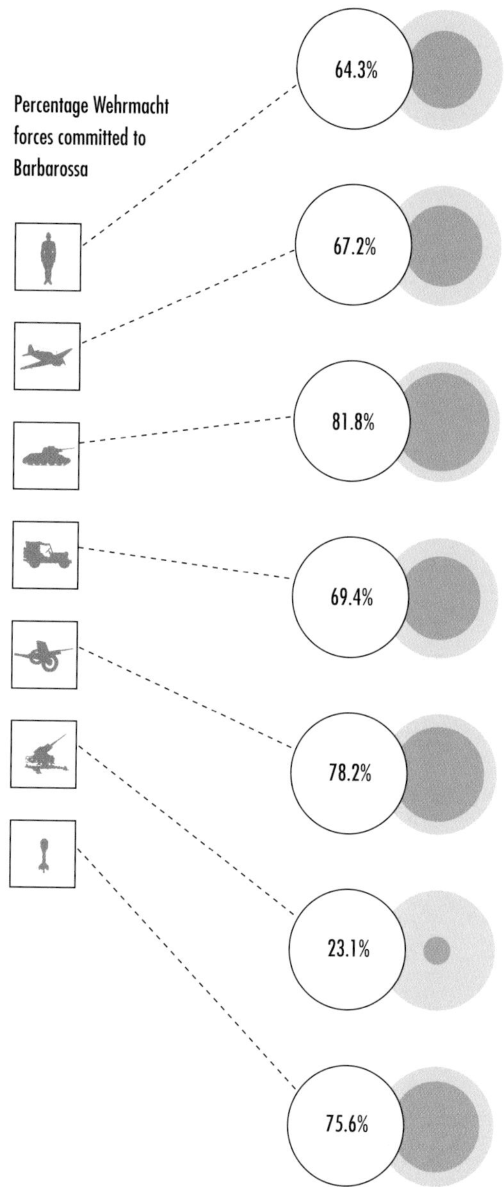

SOVIET FORCES

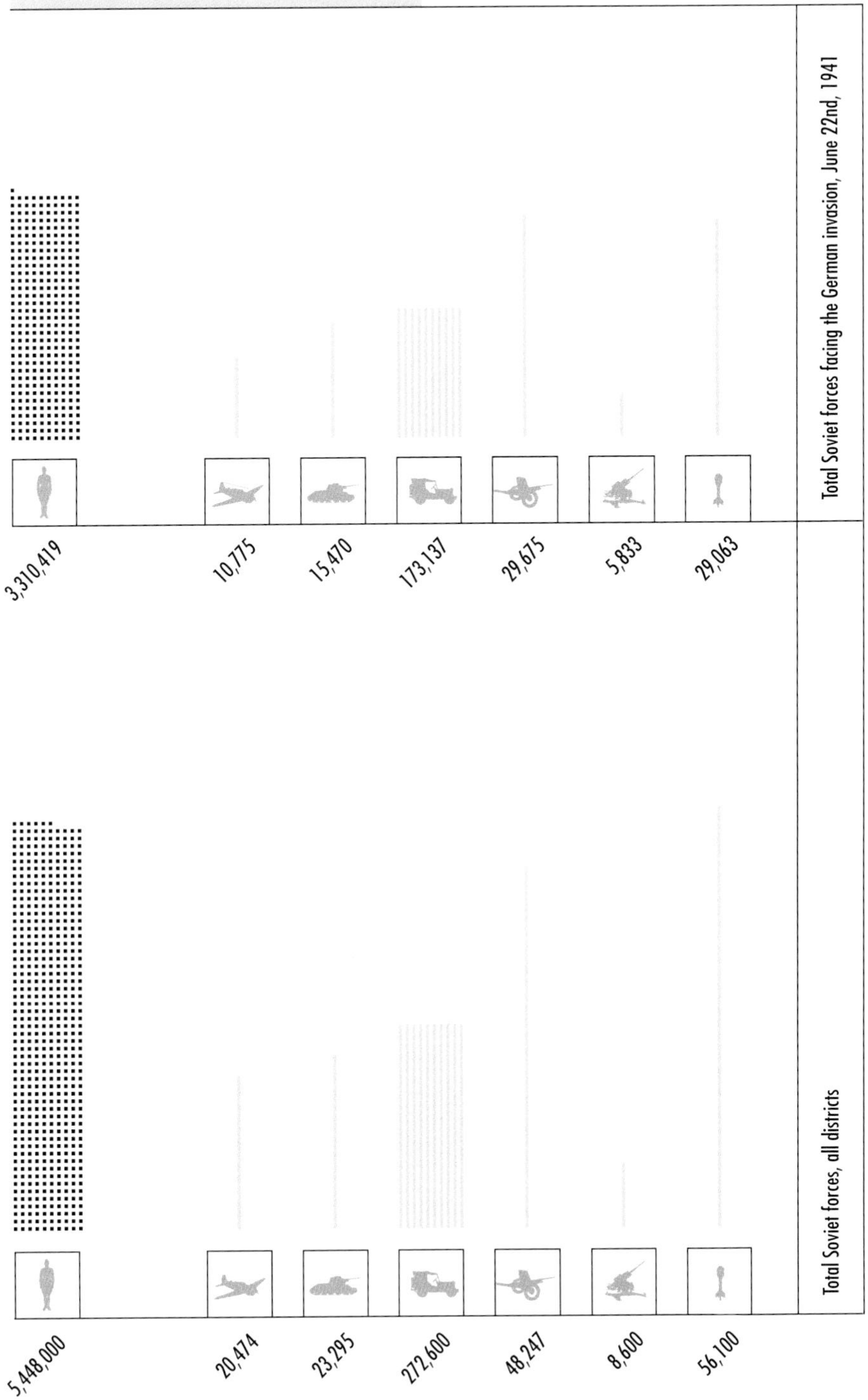
Total Soviet forces facing the German invasion, June 22nd, 1941
3,310,419
10,775
15,470
173,137
29,675
5,833
29,063
Total Soviet forces, all districts
5,448,000
20,474
23,295
272,600
48,247
8,600
56,100

Percentage of total Soviet forces to meet invasion, June 22nd, 1941

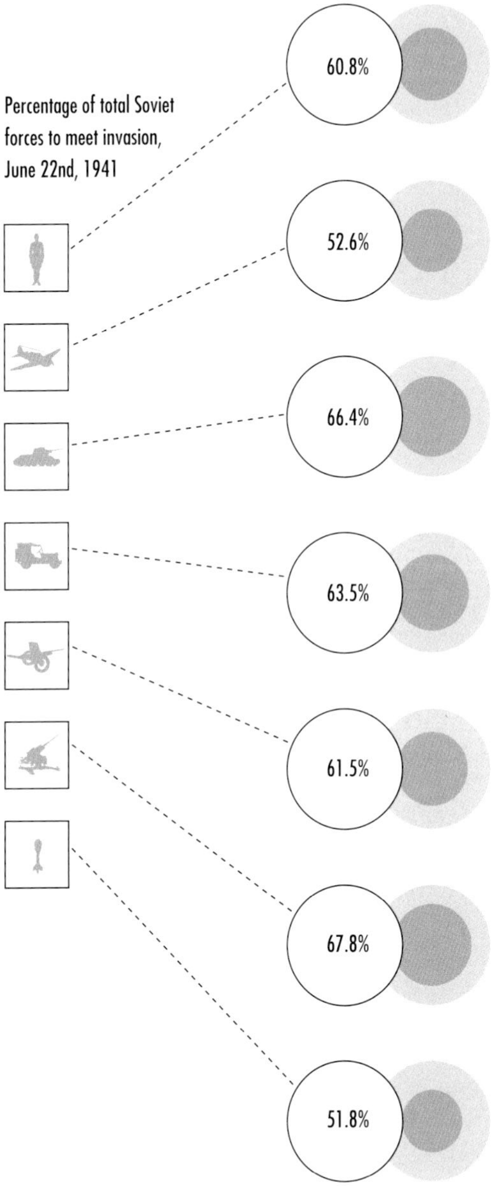
60.8%
52.6%
66.4%
63.5%
61.5%
67.8%
51.8%

Hitler's Allies on the Eastern Front

Operation Barbarossa, the German invasion of the USSR in June 1941, saw the deployment of a great mass of men and matériel in the largest invasion force ever assembled. Although most of the 138 divisions deployed were of German origin, there were also several nationalities that were Axis allies, or were co-belligerents or sympathizers.

	AXIS DIVISIONS/DIVISION EQUIVALENTS						
DATE	GERMANY	ROMANIA	HUNGARY	ITALY	SLOVAK REPUBLIC	FINLAND	SPAIN
June 1941	121	15.5			0.5	16	
September 1941	137	15.5	1.5	3	2	16	1
January 1942	149	7	3	3	2	16	1
June 1942	171	13	9	3.5	1	16	1
November 1942	173	27	12	11.5	1	16	1
April 1943	177	10	5		1	16	1
December 1943	173	9	9		1	16	1
September 1944	134		21				
November 1944	139		16.5				
March 1945	179		11				

Romania supplied the equivalent of 15.5 divisions to the effort on the Eastern Front, more than any other of the Axis allies—and would subsequently suffer heavily during the Soviet counteroffensives. Originally neutral, a fascist coup in 1940 saw the country join the Axis in November of that year. A further uprising in August 1944—led by King Michael—was to realign the country with the Allies, and Romania ended the war fighting against the other Axis powers. Some 370,000 soldiers died in the war.

Hungary had joined the Axis powers in November 1940. Initially involved in the invasion of Yugoslavia in March 1941, Hungarian divisions were not called upon to take part in Barbarossa from the outset, but on July 1st, the Carpathian Group attacked the Soviets in southern Russia. At least 300,000 Hungarian soldiers died in the conflict. With Italy fully committed to the war in June 1940, Mussolini was keen to show solidarity by sending troops to participate in the invasion of the USSR; given the performance of Italian forces in the Western Desert, Hitler was less enthusiastic. Nevertheless, Italians were in the thick of the fighting, and suffered badly at Stalingrad—30,000 died in the fighting, many more as prisoners in the hands of the Soviets. The Slovak Republic was created in the wake of the German invasion of Czechoslovakia in 1939; joining the Tripartite Pact in November 1940, Slovak troops were engaged on the Eastern Front until 1943.

More complex was the relationship between Finland and Germany, particularly following the early-war conflict between the USSR and the Finns: the Winter War, fought between November 1939 and March 1940. With Russia identified as an enemy, the Finns cooperated with the Nazis and fought the Soviets on their border in Karelia in the summer of 1941, in the Continuation War, placing Finland as a Nazi co-belligerent, though this war was over in autumn 1944, when the Finns turned on the Nazis in Lapland.

Spain was officially neutral during the war, but its fascist leader General Franco nevertheless permitted Spanish volunteers to serve on the Eastern Front in the "Blue Division"—though it was withdrawn in 1944 due to increasing diplomatic pressure from the Allies. Some 10% of the 45,000 volunteers are known to have died.

TOTAL	TOTAL NON-GERMAN	PERCENT NON-GERMAN
153	32	21%
176	39	22%
181	32	18%
214.5	43.5	20%
241.5	68.5	28%
210	33	16%
209	36	17%
155	21	14%
155.5	16.5	11%
190	11	6%

The changing commitment of foreign divisions on the Eastern Front. Germany's allies supplied a number of divisions to help put its war aims against the USSR into action. In this diagram, the deeper the color, the stronger the commitment.

Tank Strengths: Western Desert

With Italy entering the war on June 10th, 1940, came the development of a whole new theater of operations for the British: the Western Desert. With France lost, the desert was the perfect place for British and Commonwealth troops to re-engage with the enemy. The main battlefront was in the maritime region of the deserts of Libya and Egypt, as well as in the French colonies of Algeria and Tunisia. Here, the vast expanse of flat terrain allowed for the development of mobile warfare, and the deployment of large numbers of tanks and armored vehicles. Tank supremacy was a significant factor in the outcome of the war in this region.

A comparison of Allied and Axis tank strengths in the Western Desert is shown below. Strengths fluctuated during the war, with the Allies achieving their greatest strength at the Second Battle of El Alamein in 1942.

Axis: German

Axis: Italian

Total Axis reserves

British

Total Allied reserves

The war against the Italians commenced almost immediately; on June 14th, British armored forces invaded Italian-controlled Libya, leading to some early successes against their ill-equipped enemy. The Battle of Sidi Barrani, fought in Egypt on September 16th, 1940, saw the British 8th Army rout the Italians during their failed counteroffensive; 38,000 prisoners were taken into captivity. Following hard on the Allied defeats in Europe, Sidi Barrani was some much-needed good news. Here the British and Commonwealth troops could deploy superior armor and armored tactics against a numerically superior Italian force. By December, the British had captured the

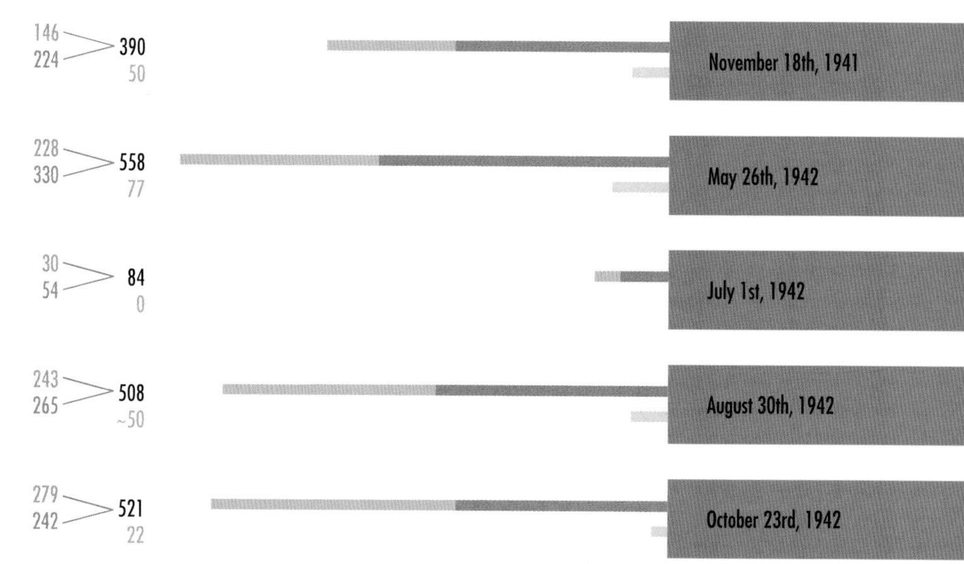

city of Tobruk, and had destroyed the Italian 10th Army, with 130,000 prisoners in total following the Battle of Beda Fomm.

But with the defeat came the need for the Germans to bolster the fortunes of their weaker allies. With the arrival of the Deutches Afrika Korps (DAK) came the development of back-and-forth warfare that would center on maneuver, on the availability of armor, and on extended desert supply lines. With pressures from other theaters, the Allied lines were depleted of experienced troops, and in February, General Erwin Rommel's DAK advanced and the Commonwealth troops were withdrawn to the Egyptian frontier. Tobruk was left under siege, supplied by sea, before being relieved by the Allies during Operation Crusader, in November 1941. A fortified defensive position, the Gazala Line, was developed to resist Axis advances, but was unable to hold off Rommel's offensive. By June the Battle of Gazala saw the 8th Army defeated, with Tobruk falling with the loss of 35,000 Commonwealth troops. With this defeat, the Commonwealth withdrew to the Alamein line, on the flanks of the Qattara Depression—largely impassable to tanks—which helped repel the Axis attacks at the First Battle of El Alamein, on June 30th, 1942. Attacking again in late August, Rommel was stopped at the Battle of Alam el Halfa. The British were now in receipt of American-made tanks, reinforcing the 8th Army—while the Axis were sorely in need of new armor. The seesaw series of battles for control of Libya and parts of Egypt reached a climax in the Second Battle of El Alamein when British Commonwealth forces under the command of Lieutenant-General Bernard Montgomery delivered a decisive defeat to the Axis forces and pushed them back to Tunisia. In all cases, the supply and maintenance of armor was of the greatest significance.

Allied Armor in the Western Desert

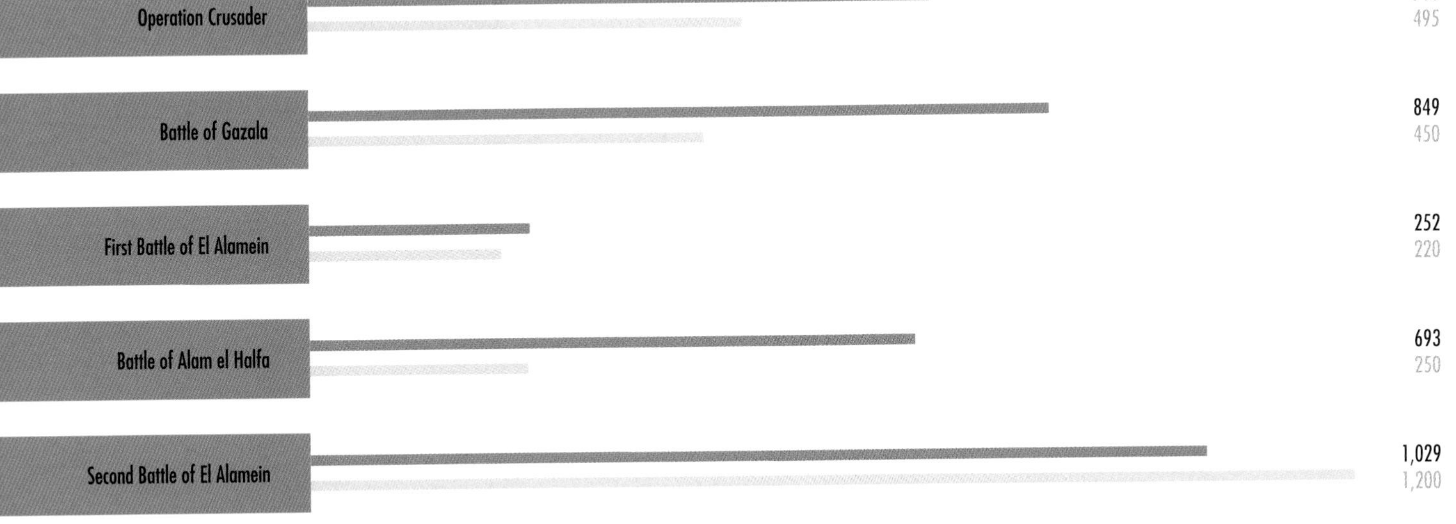

The Second Battle of El Alamein 1942

The Desert War had seen many successes and reverses for the British Commonwealth and other Allied forces. A war of extended supply lines, and a perfect place for tank warfare, there had been many drives across the desert terrain—and many changes in leadership. The final change was the appointment of General Bernard Law Montgomery to command the British 8th Army, and it was his leadership that would ultimately lead to the defeat of the DAK and their Italian Allies, commanded by General Erwin Rommel.

With the Italo-German army no less than 70 miles (113 km) from the key Egyptian city of Alexandria, the situation was dangerous for the Allies in the summer of 1942, and when Rommel attacked at Alam el Halfa in August, he was held by General Montgomery's defensive lines. A skilled organizer and an inspirational leader, Montgomery was set to turn the fortunes of the Allies in the desert, and to close down the cat-and-mouse chases that had ensued since 1940. He stockpiled a large quantity of weapons, artillery, and tanks. His tank force was equipped with new imports from the US, Grant and Sherman tanks replacing the slower and more vulnerable British infantry tanks. By October, Montgomery had an army of 195,000 men, 1,351 tanks, and 1,900 artillery pieces.

Operation Lightfoot was launched on October 23rd, with a 900-gun bombardment of the German lines; 139 tons (127 tonnes) of shells rained down on the Germans. With Rommel sick in Austria, his replacement died of a heart attack, and the general was recalled to face Montgomery. The Germans stuck to their defences, and the operation slowed. Montgomery's response was Operation Supercharge, which attacked the German lines in force, on November 1st. Under great pressure, Hitler demanded the Afrika Korps stand and fight. On November 4th, the 8th Army drove through the Germans, capturing large numbers of men and matériel, Rommel escaping with just 20 tanks left; he had lost over 450 tanks, 1,000 guns, and half of his men—100,000 of them killed, wounded, or taken prisoner. The British and Commonwealth forces suffered 13,500 casualties and 500 of their tanks were damaged. However, of these, 350 were repaired and were able to take part in future battles.

The opposing commanders: British General Bernard Law Montgomery (top, green), and German General Erwin Rommel (bottom, gray). Montgomery kept a picture of Rommel with him to help focus his mind.

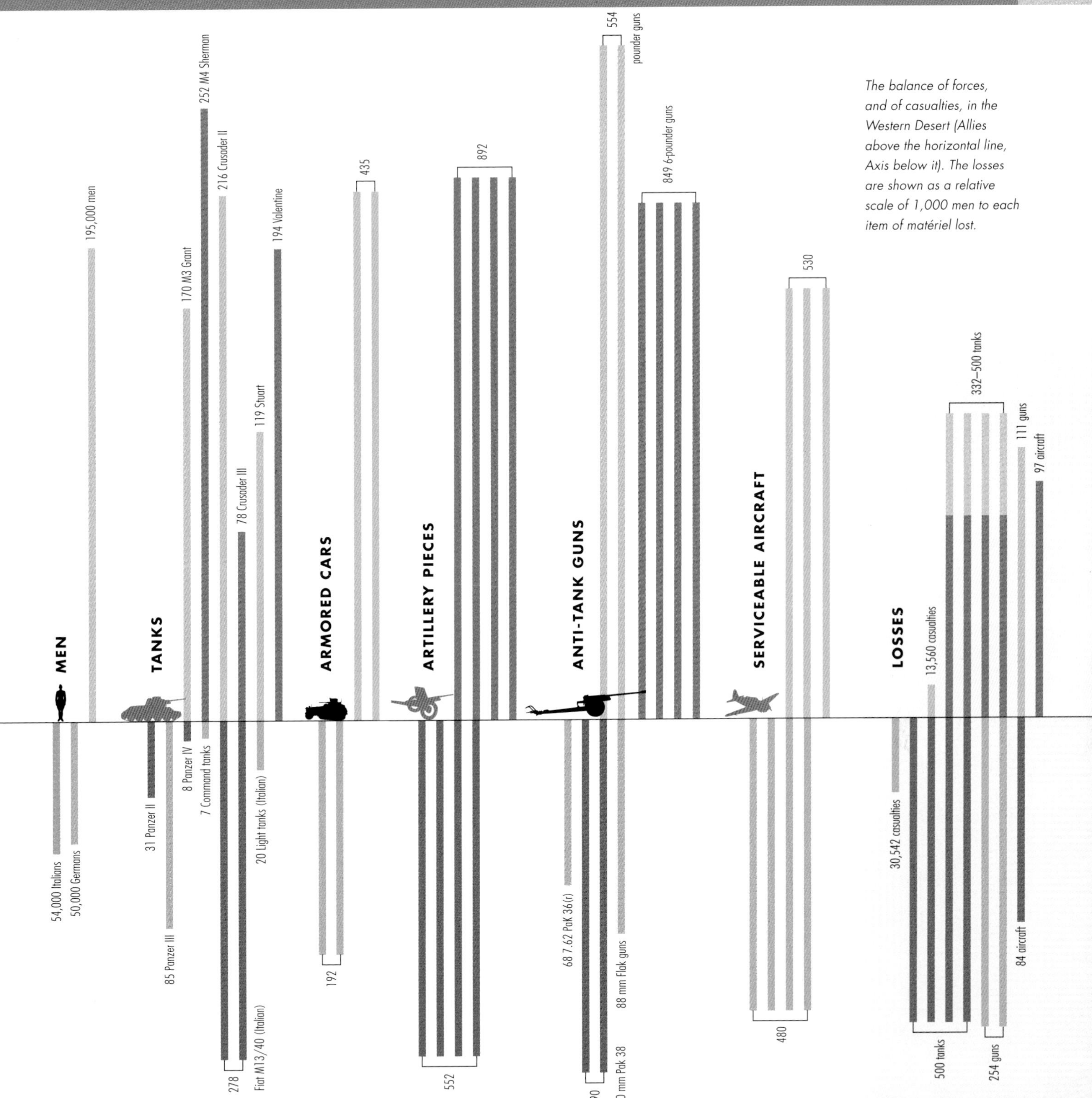

The balance of forces, and of casualties, in the Western Desert (Allies above the horizontal line, Axis below it). The losses are shown as a relative scale of 1,000 men to each item of matériel lost.

Stalingrad: the Doomed 6th Army

1942

Stalingrad was a battle of epic proportions; to many, it defined the most important turning point in a war marked by numerous pivotal battles. Yet this was different. With Hitler's sights set on the invasion of the Caucasus—in order to supply his strategic needs for fuel—in August 1942 the assault on Stalingrad was intended as little more than a holding operation. Fatally splitting his forces, Hitler's ambitions wavered in front of the city that bore his opponent's name—renamed in Stalin's honor in 1925 after he helped to save it during the bitter civil war that followed the revolution.

What started as a modest fight for Stalingrad became a mincing machine that would lead to over 1.25 million casualties on both sides (with at least half a million fatalities for the Red Army alone) and leave at least 40,000 civilians dead. The battle commenced on August 23rd, 1942 with an artillery bombardment of this grim city situated on the banks of the River Volga. The Germans and their Romanian, Hungarian, and Italian allies fought them street by street to wrest control of the city from Soviet hands; by November, the Germans held most of the city. But the assault was taking its toll. And on November 19th, 1942, General Zhukov, Stalin's most able general, launched an assault, Operation Uranus, that would see General Paulus' 6th German Army—and the 3rd and 4th Romanian armies—completely encircled.

As winter set in, this daring assault left the Germans encircled, besieged in an egg-shaped perimeter that could only be supplied by air. Göring

Air Supply at Stalingrad August–October 1942

With the German 6th Army assaulting Stalingrad, air support was essential. In the period August–October 1942, Luftflotte 4 "Richthofen" made prodigious efforts to keep the German forward airfields and troops supplied.

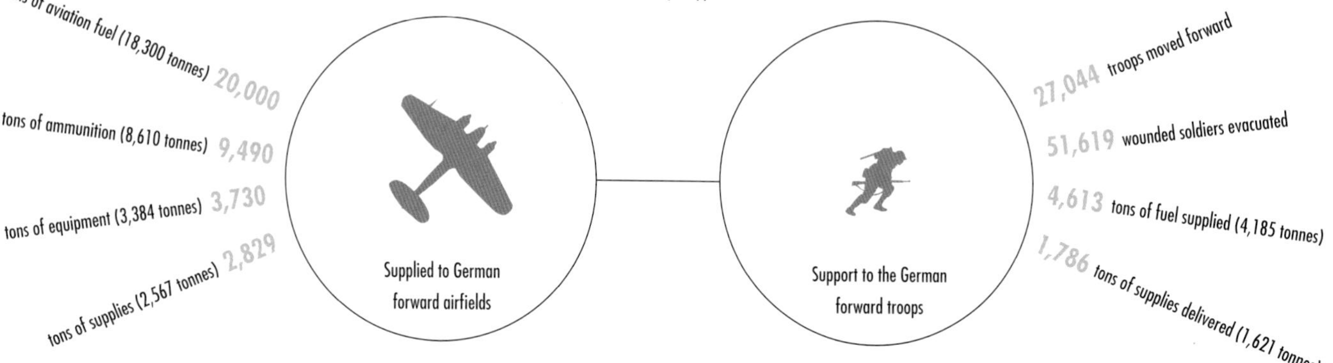

guaranteed that supplies could get through by air; however, the Soviet air force was no longer on the defensive, the tide had turned in favor of its flyers. The encircled 6th Army required 499 tons (453 tonnes) of supplies of all types—food, ammunition, war clothing—if it was to hold out. This was just too much; 299 tons (272 tonnes) were the most that could be supplied, and even then this was at best; in most cases what was delivered was just over 99 tons (90 tonnes). Paulus' army was doomed.

Hitler ordered his men to stand their ground in a titanic battle of ideology; he expected that there would be no surrender, and that each would fight to the end. For this reason, Paulus was made Field Marshal—no German of this rank had ever surrendered. But his gamble did not pay off. Paulus did not do what was expected of him; instead of taking his own life he consigned 90,000 men to captivity, most to certain death in Soviet POW camps. At Stalingrad, the Nazi ambition in the east ground to a halt.

Air Supply at Stalingrad November 1942–February 1943

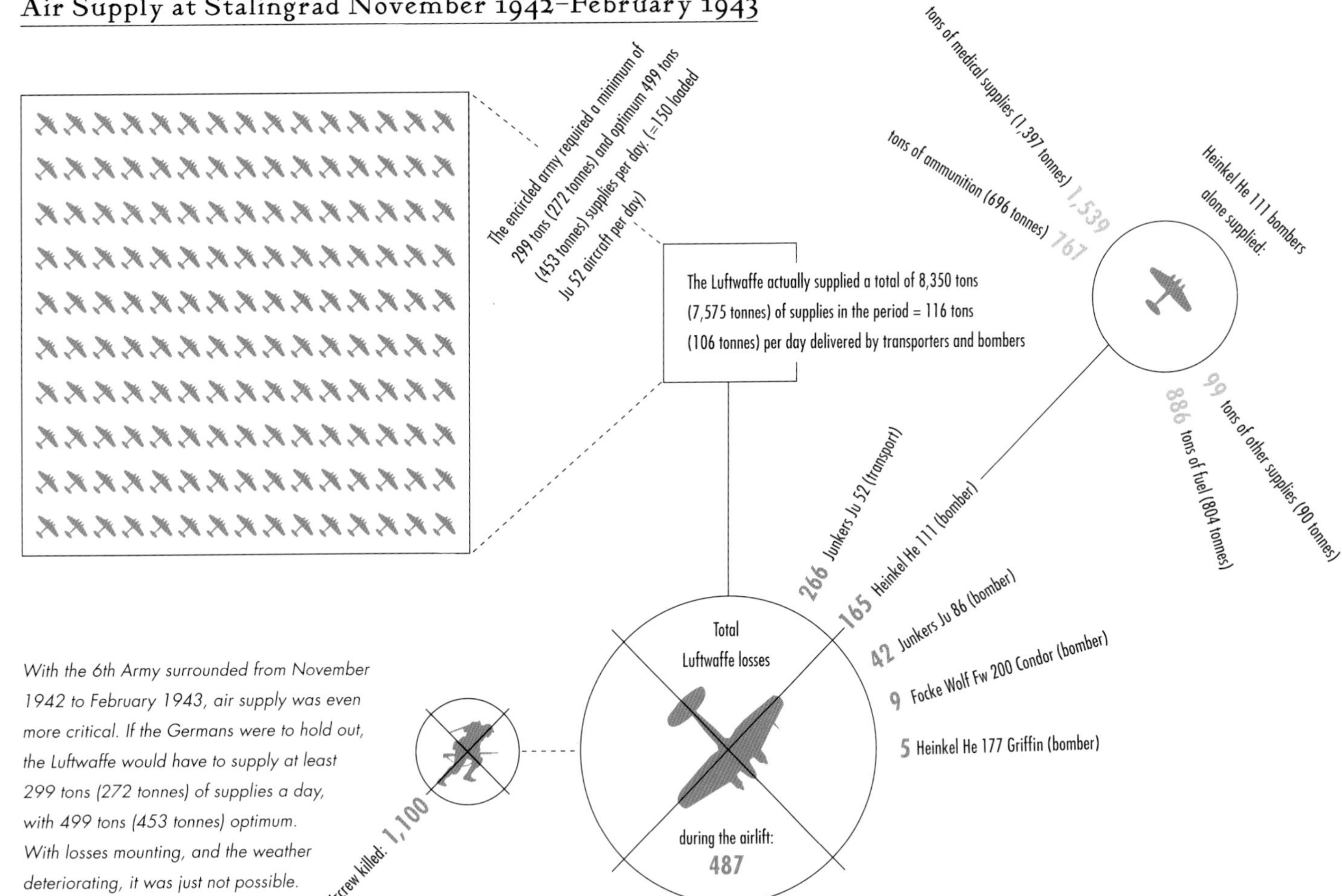

With the 6th Army surrounded from November 1942 to February 1943, air supply was even more critical. If the Germans were to hold out, the Luftwaffe would have to supply at least 299 tons (272 tonnes) of supplies a day, with 499 tons (453 tonnes) optimum. With losses mounting, and the weather deteriorating, it was just not possible.

The Invasion of Italy
1943

Operation Husky, the invasion of Sicily, opened the Italian campaign on July 9–10th, 1943. The British, Canadian, and American landings, using amphibious and airborne troops, were a success, although the Axis forces escaped to the mainland on August 17th, 1943, abandoning the island to its fate. Assaulting the mainland of Italy, with its easily defended central rocky spine, was to be another matter.

The campaign in Italy was one of the most costly fought by the Allies, and was to be a point of disagreement between the British and Americans. Impatient to get the war against the Germans underway, the Americans favored an invasion of Europe as soon as possible after the defeat of the Axis in Africa, with no diversions of effort or resources on "sideshows." Churchill felt otherwise; the "soft-underbelly of Europe" was tantalizing. Italy was to prove to be no picnic, and Roosevelt was also convinced that knocking Italy out of the war would more than repay the effort of invasion.

The battle-hardened British 8th Army was to land on the toe of Italy on September 3rd, 1943. This was too much for the Italians, and an armistice with the invaders followed shortly afterward, on September 8th. The Germans, however, were in no mood to hand over Italy to their enemies so easily, and what ensued was one of the most costly European campaigns of World War II. Further Allied landings took place by the American-led 5th Army on September 9th, the British at Taranto, and the Americans, heavily opposed, at Salerno. The Allies would battle their way up the peninsula, the British in the east, the Americans in the west, the port of Naples being the target. As the Allies battled northward,

MAINLAND ITALY

September 3rd
British 8th Army lands at toe of Italy

September 3rd
Italians sign armistice

September 4th
Germans occupy Italy as far as Naples

September 9th
Taranto landing

September 9th
American 5th Army lands at Salerno

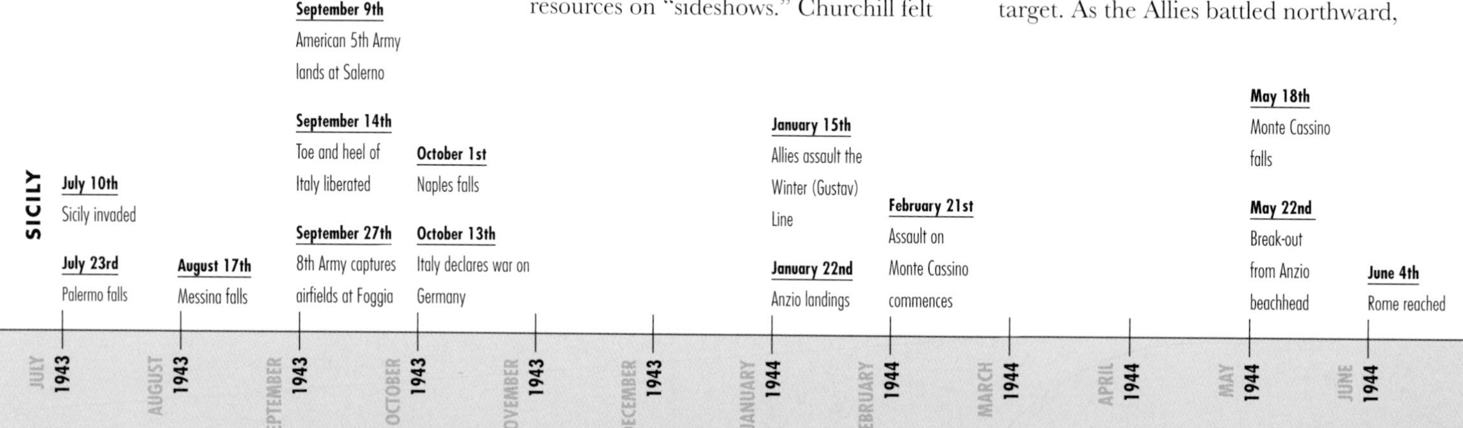

the difficulty of the terrain became a major issue. The Germans had largely abandoned southern Italy as a dead loss; they were later to exploit and aggressively defend the terrain advantages given to them by the 3,000 ft (900 m) high Appennine Mountains farther north.

By October 1943, the Germans had laid out defensive lines that would serve to contain the Allies as far south—and therefore as far away from Germany—as possible. The most famous of these was the Gustav Line, which, together with other minor positions, proved to be a major obstacle at the end of 1943, halting the Allies in mountain snowstorms. The Gustav Line was to prove almost impregnable, and it took repeated offensives by the multinational 8th and 5th Armies (with British, American, Canadian, French, and Polish troops) to break it, between January and May 1944. One particular position, that of the mountain-top monastery of Monte Cassino, was to become infamous, a byword for the strength of the positions, and the tenacity of its defenders. This was to prove one of the toughest nuts to crack, an essential objective in the invasion route of the Allied forces up the spine of the Italian peninsula. Four battles would be fought between January 24th and May 18th, 1944, for the control of Monte Cassino. Assaulted by Allied troops of many nations, the monastery was finally taken on May 18th, 1944.

Rome fell to the US forces previously bottled up at Anzio on June 4th, 1944. The way ahead into northern Italy was blocked by another defensive position, the Gothic Line, along the Apennine Mountain chain between Florence and Bologna. An offensive by the 8th and 5th armies on August 25th, Operation Olive, saw no decisive breakthrough, and the war ground to a halt, with little hope of resuming the attack in early 1945 due to the severity of the winter weather conditions. The Allies were forced to sit and wait for spring. The final phase commenced on April 9th, 1945, and by the end of that month, the Axis forces were beaten; the Germans formally surrendering on April 29th, with the end of the war in Italy on May 2nd. Some 60,000 Allied soldiers had died, with total casualties reaching 320,000; for the Axis, this figure was over 658,000.

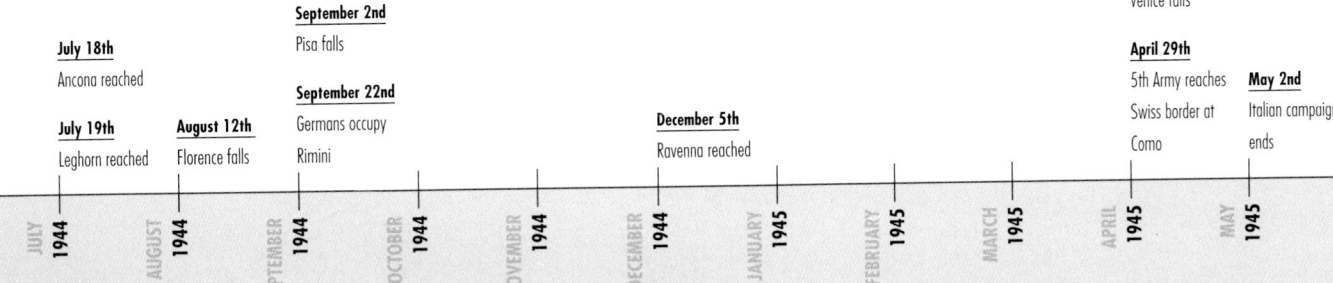

July 18th Ancona reached

July 19th Leghorn reached

August 12th Florence falls

September 2nd Pisa falls

September 22nd Germans occupy Rimini

December 5th Ravenna reached

April 6th Final offensive commences

April 21st Bologna reached

April 23rd 5th Army crosses Po River

April 23rd Ferrara falls

April 23rd La Spezia falls

April 29th Milan falls

April 29th Venice falls

April 29th 5th Army reaches Swiss border at Como

May 2nd Italian campaign ends

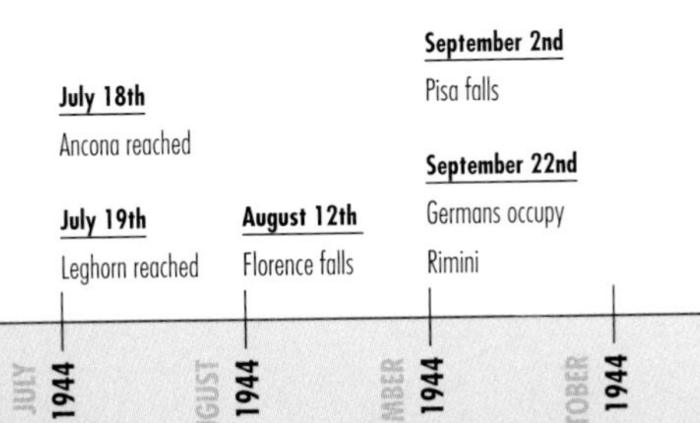

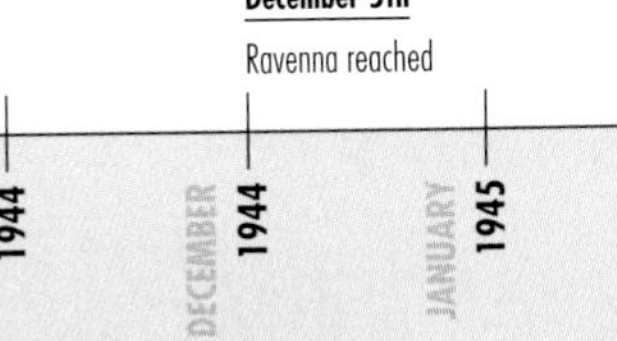

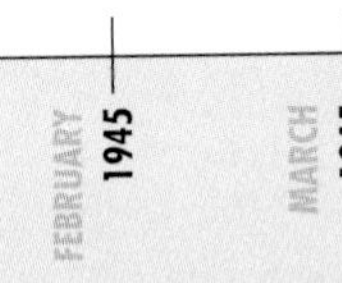

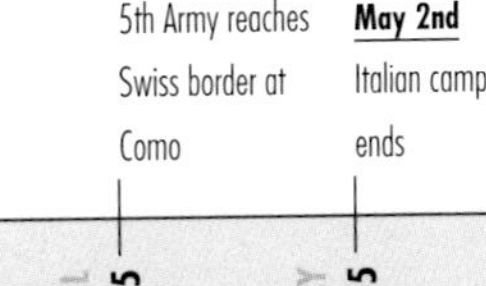

JULY 1944 · AUGUST 1944 · SEPTEMBER 1944 · OCTOBER 1944 · NOVEMBER 1944 · DECEMBER 1944 · JANUARY 1945 · FEBRUARY 1945 · MARCH 1945 · APRIL 1945 · MAY 1945

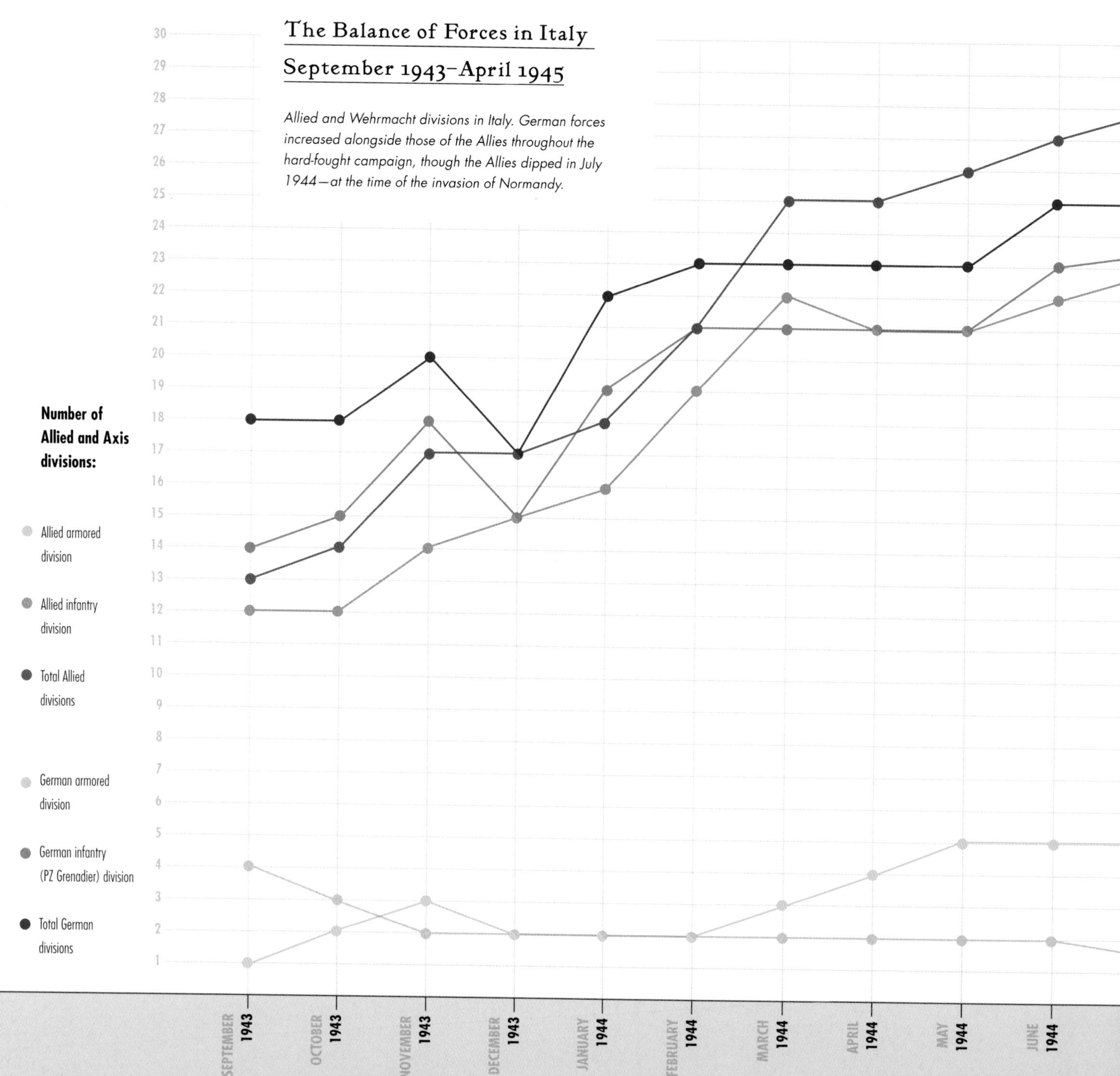
The Balance of Forces in Italy
September 1943–April 1945
Allied and Wehrmacht divisions in Italy. German forces increased alongside those of the Allies throughout the hard-fought campaign, though the Allies dipped in July 1944—at the time of the invasion of Normandy.
Number of Allied and Axis divisions:
Allied armored division
Allied infantry division
Total Allied divisions
German armored division
German infantry (PZ Grenadier) division
Total German divisions
30
29
28
27
26
25
24
23
22
21
20
19
18
17
16
15
14
13
12
11
10
9
8
7
6
5
4
3
2
1
SEPTEMBER 1943
OCTOBER 1943
NOVEMBER 1943
DECEMBER 1943
JANUARY 1944
FEBRUARY 1944
MARCH 1944
APRIL 1944
MAY 1944
JUNE 1944

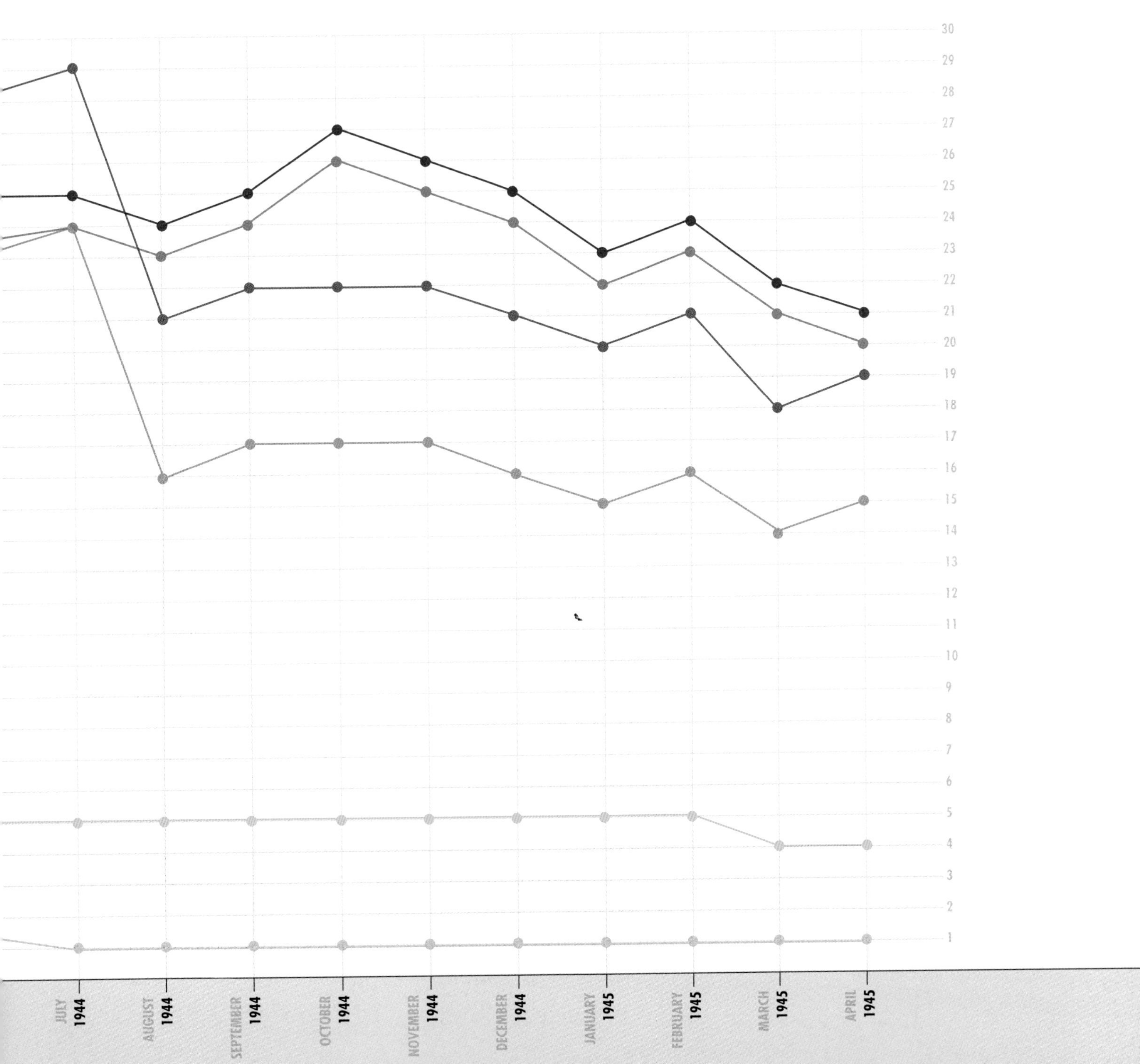
30
29
28
27
26
25
24
23
22
21
20
19
18
17
16
15
14
13
12
11
10
9
8
7
6
5
4
3
2
1
JULY 1944
AUGUST 1944
SEPTEMBER 1944
OCTOBER 1944
NOVEMBER 1944
DECEMBER 1944
JANUARY 1945
FEBRUARY 1945
MARCH 1945
APRIL 1945

Monte Cassino: Polish War Crosses

1944

The abbey at Monte Cassino after it was reduced to rubble by the Allied attack.

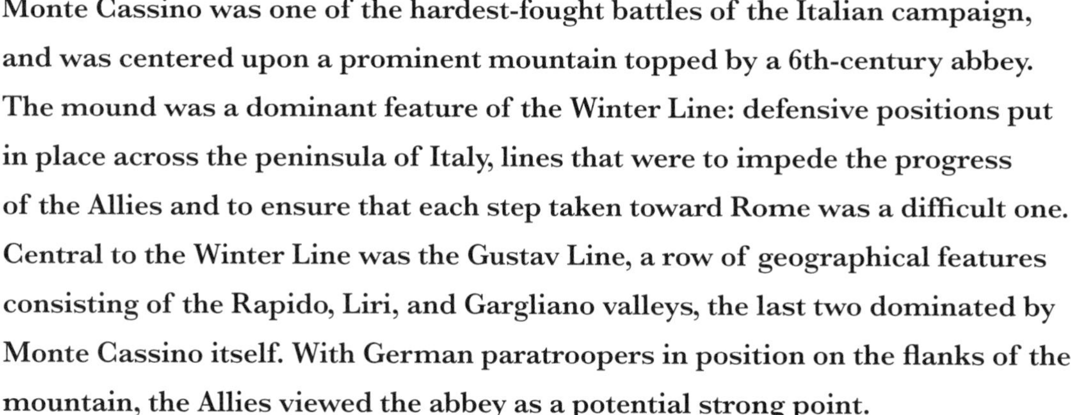

Monte Cassino was one of the hardest-fought battles of the Italian campaign, and was centered upon a prominent mountain topped by a 6th-century abbey. The mound was a dominant feature of the Winter Line: defensive positions put in place across the peninsula of Italy, lines that were to impede the progress of the Allies and to ensure that each step taken toward Rome was a difficult one. Central to the Winter Line was the Gustav Line, a row of geographical features consisting of the Rapido, Liri, and Gargliano valleys, the last two dominated by Monte Cassino itself. With German paratroopers in position on the flanks of the mountain, the Allies viewed the abbey as a potential strong point.

To pass northward up the peninsula, the Allies assaulted the Gothic Line at Cassino no less than four times, with increasing force between January 17th and May 18th, 1944, leaving the abbey a pile of smoking ruins, and running up a casualty list that was fearsome: the Allies suffered 55,000 casualties, the Germans, 20,000.

The Polish war cemetery at Monte Cassino.

The Allied army at Monte Cassino was truly international, with US, British, Canadian, New Zealand, South African, French, French colonial, and Polish troops committed to the battle. The fourth assault, from May 11–25th, 1944, saw the II Polish Corps attack, forming the right flank. The II Corps was created in 1943 and was made up of Poles from a variety of sources. The 3rd Carpathian Division was formed in the Middle East, mostly from Poles who had been evacuated from the USSR. The Corps became an independent unit of the British 8th Army, and in 1944 it numbered 50,000 men. At Cassino, the Corps was heavily engaged, not only with the fighting troops committed to the line; support troops were also to serve in the front. For three days Polish attacks and German counterattacks brought heavy losses to both sides. The Polish Corps lost 281 officers and 3,503 other ranks in the assault. At the conclusion of the battle, the Polish government in exile was quick to establish a war cross for all Poles who had been engaged at Monte Cassino; only those who took part in the battle were entitled to receive one. Like the huge Polish war cemetery at Monte Cassino, the war crosses are a testimony to Polish endurance in battle.

Polish Monte Cassino Crosses

UNIT	NUMBER AWARDED
Commanders	13
Headquarters Group	731
3rd Carpathian Rifle Division	13,922
5th Kresowa Division	13,941
2nd Armored Brigade	3,519
Carpathian Lancers	677
2nd Artillery Group	2,645
2nd Corps Artillery	3,123

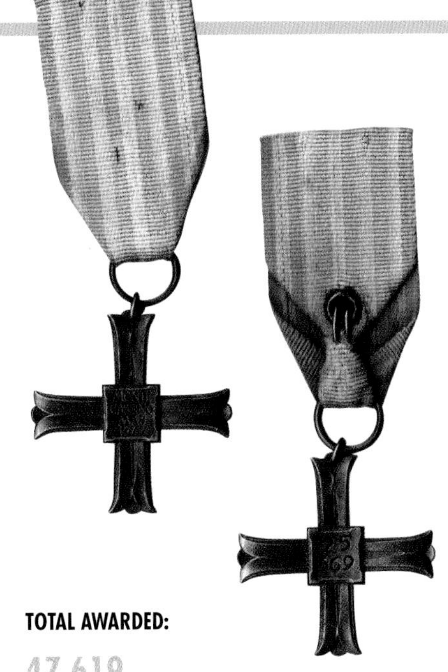

TOTAL AWARDED:

47,619

UNIT	NUMBER AWARDED
2nd Corps Regiment	1,660
Signal Corps	1,038
Medical Corps	1,221
Medical hospital	841
Supply & transport	2,956
Military Police	201
Commando Company	91
Miscellaneous	1,040

The Battle of Kursk: Operation Citadel 1943

The Battle of Kursk represented a major turning point in the war. Hitler was "sick to his stomach" and wanted to once more demonstrate German superiority by taking a salient in the defensive line that had settled since the defeat at Stalingrad. The salient lay in front of the Soviet city of Kursk, some 280 miles (450 km) south of Moscow in the southern sector of the Eastern Front; the Germans hoped to eliminate it with a massive blow, breaking through its northern and southern flanks and encircling the Soviet armies within. With the doctrine of combined warfare known as blitzkrieg, the Germans planned to rely upon the armored strength of their new heavy tanks, their previously unchallenged air superiority, and the weight of arms. They would then once more take on the offensive, driving the Soviets back, shortening their lines, and creating new opportunities to defeat Stalin.

Events in 1943

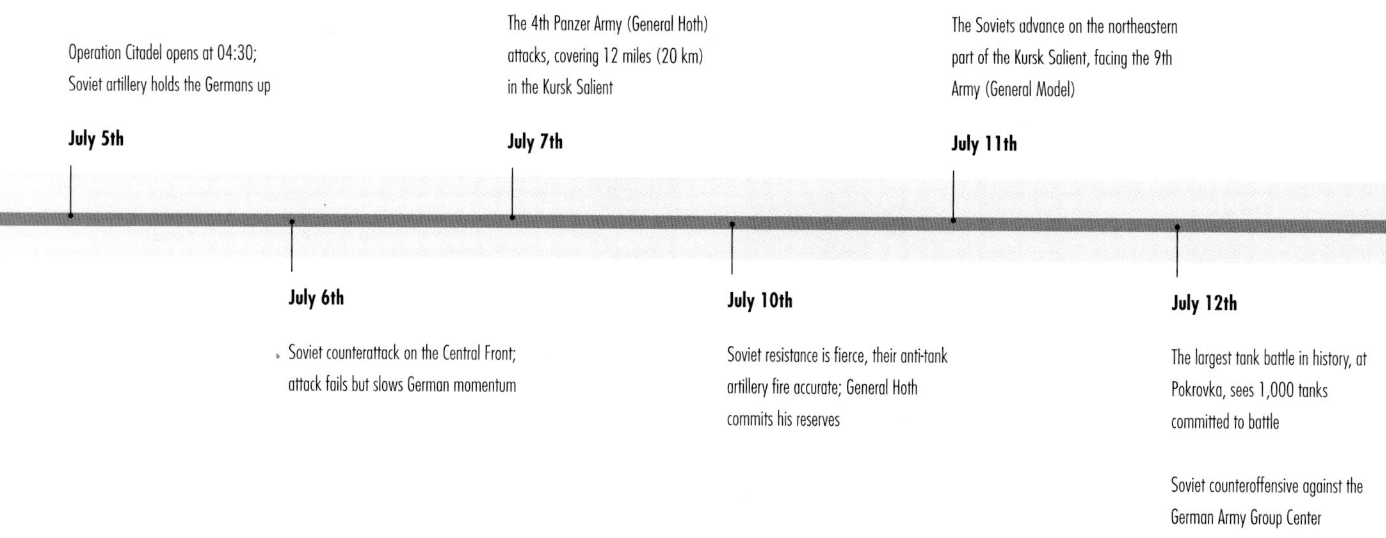

July 5th

Operation Citadel opens at 04:30; Soviet artillery holds the Germans up

July 6th

Soviet counterattack on the Central Front; attack fails but slows German momentum

July 7th

The 4th Panzer Army (General Hoth) attacks, covering 12 miles (20 km) in the Kursk Salient

July 10th

Soviet resistance is fierce, their anti-tank artillery fire accurate; General Hoth commits his reserves

July 11th

The Soviets advance on the northeastern part of the Kursk Salient, facing the 9th Army (General Model)

July 12th

The largest tank battle in history, at Pokrovka, sees 1,000 tanks committed to battle

Soviet counteroffensive against the German Army Group Center

Soviet troops and T-34s advance at Orel, August 1943.

Yet it was Hitler's uncharacteristic nervousness that would doom this battle to failure; the campaign was delayed twice as he waited for the new super tanks, the Tiger and the Panther, to become available, and with ample warning of the operation gained through a spy ring in Switzerland, Marshall Zhukov secretly created a fortified hell of trenches, defensive strong points, and other concealed features that were among the heaviest yet prepared in the history of the war. This would challenge the German armored offensive head-on, and create the opportunity for what would become known as the largest tank battle of the whole war. It was the strength of this defensive position, and the fact that the Soviets could rely upon their anti-tank guns, that created an effective killing zone that was to put a stop to the German intentions. There would never again be a Nazi offensive of this scale in the east; the tide of the advance was now flowing back westward. Though the losses to the Soviet military machine would be titanic, there were immediate Soviet counteroffensives at Orel and Kharkov that would commence a "push" that would ultimately end at the gates of Berlin, the ambition of Hitler's Third Reich nothing but burned embers.

With accounting difficult, the exact numbers of men and machines is open to some interpretation, and many authors have tried to perfect the details. What is sure is that, for once, the Germans were at least matched and in most cases outnumbered by the Soviet effort.

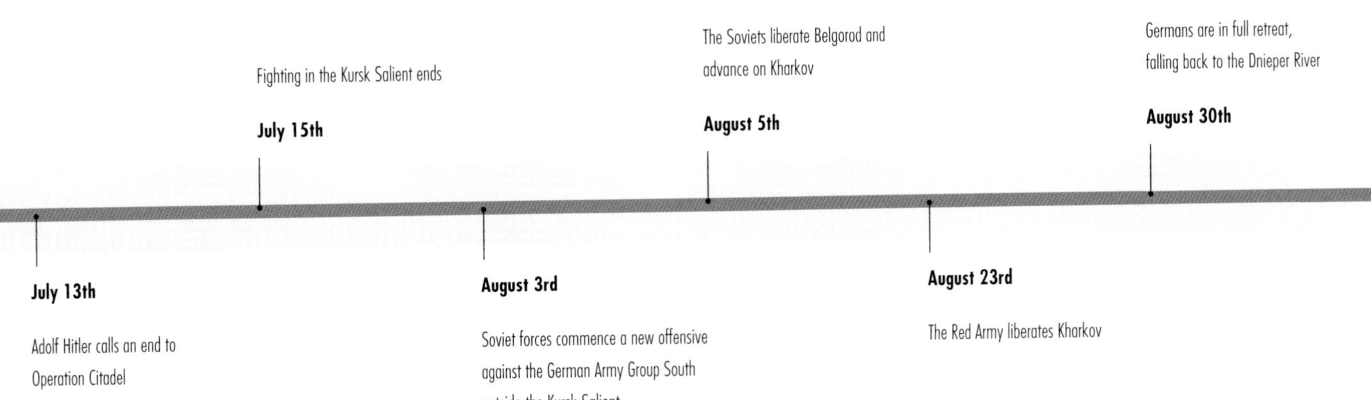

July 13th

Adolf Hitler calls an end to Operation Citadel

July 15th

Fighting in the Kursk Salient ends

August 3rd

Soviet forces commence a new offensive against the German Army Group South outside the Kursk Salient

August 5th

The Soviets liberate Belgorod and advance on Kharkov

August 23rd

The Red Army liberates Kharkov

August 30th

Germans are in full retreat, falling back to the Dnieper River

Battle of Kursk: Strengths

The graphic shows the military strengths of the German (left) and Soviet (right) forces during the Battle of Kursk and the distribution of forces across the various fronts in the battle (bottom). The grand totals are given far right.

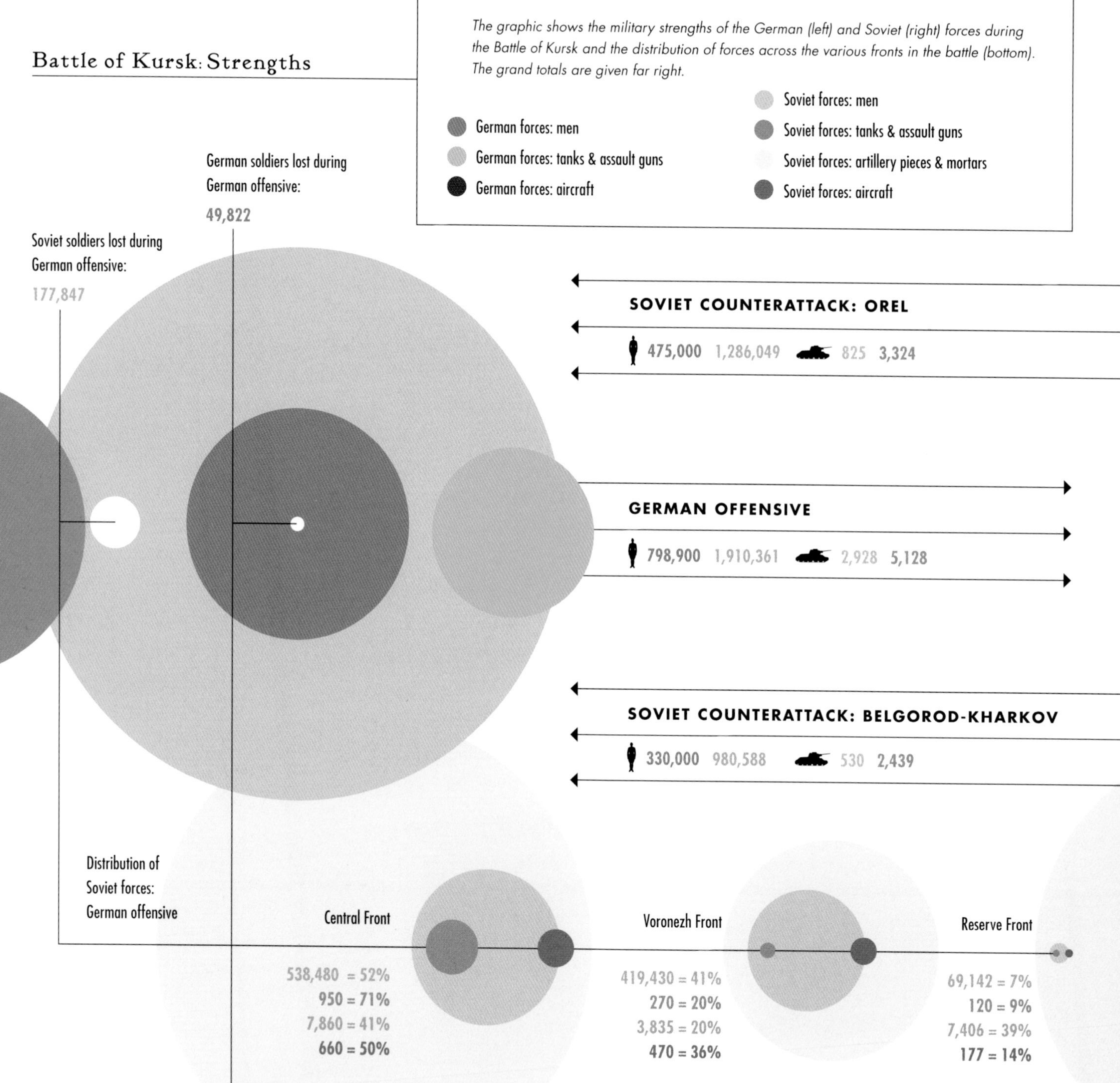

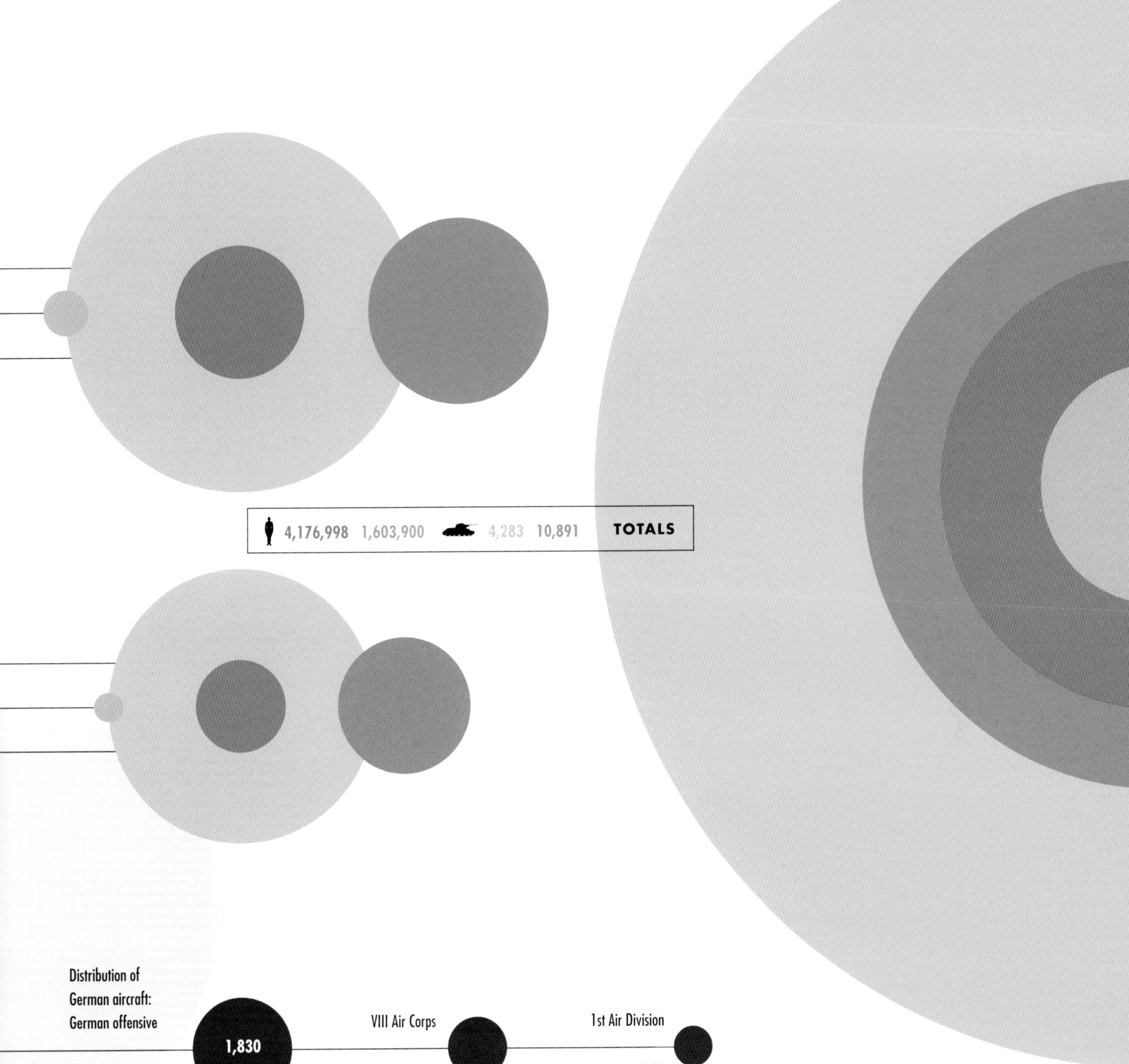
4,176,998 1,603,900 4,283 10,891 TOTALS
Distribution of German aircraft: German offensive
1,830
VIII Air Corps
1,100 = 60%
1st Air Division
730 = 40%

The Raid on Dieppe
1942

Wounded Allied soldiers on the beach at Dieppe. A Churchill tank is pictured in the background.

The Raid on Dieppe was the first time the Allies had set foot, in force, on the northern coast of France since they were bundled out at Dunkirk in 1940. The fact that the coast was vulnerable to raids had already been established through the daring raids of Winston Churchill's Commandos, who had put the static defence units of Hitler's Atlantic Wall on the defensive. But with the German invasion of the USSR came calls for an invasion to draw away some of the pressure from the newly joined ally. Dieppe was conceived as a heavily armed raid on the coast of France, with the limited aim of taking and holding a beachhead, and more particularly a port, under the noses of the heavily entrenched Germans.

Dieppe, a port in Normandy, was selected as the target for Operation Rutter, a location that, it was felt, could be taken and held as a demonstration of the capability of the Allies—building on the successes of the much more limited Commando Raids. It was to take place on August 19th, 1942, with troops assembling in five English south-coast ports. The total military manpower was to be 6,100. Some 5,100 of these would be Canadians of the 2nd Canadian Division, bolstered by 1,000 British troops, mostly Commandos, all to be landed from around 237 ships and landing craft.

The raid commenced at 04:50 with Commandos assaulting the coastal batteries at the margins of the beaches. This action was beset with difficulties, with Canadians of the Royal Regiment of Canada and the South Saskatchewan Regiment taking heavy casualties. The main assault followed 30 minutes later; its armored heart was ripped out when the tanks quickly became bogged down on the beach and lost their tracks, or were held up by beach defences.

The Canadian troops were trapped on the beaches and mowed down by a murderous crossfire. The raid had failed. At 11:00, the troops were withdrawn from their exposed beach positions. The Canadians lost 3,367 men, killed, wounded or taken prisoner (around 1,950 POWs); only 2,210 were to return to England, many of them wounded. The Commandos suffered too, though proportionately less, with 275 casualties; those taken prisoner would have a tough time in Nazi Germany. The Royal Navy lost a destroyer and 33 landing craft (75 men killed, 269 missing or captured). The RAF lost 106 aircraft—most of them fighters, the highest single-day loss in World War II. There were 74 RAF men killed or missing, just 17 POW. German casualties numbered 591, with 48 aircraft destroyed, and 24 damaged at a loss of 13 pilots killed or missing.

Dieppe was an unmitigated disaster; but its lessons, learned hard, were put to good use, again in Normandy, just under two years later on D-Day, June 6th, 1944.

Allied Fatalities at Dieppe

By far the greatest number were from the 2nd Canadian Division, and specifically the 4th Canadian Infantry Brigade. Deaths per regiment are listed (right).

CANADIAN FATALITIES:

2nd Canadian Infantry Division (Major General J. Hamilton) Headquarters and miscellaneous detachments	5
14th Army Tank Regiment (The Calgary Regiment (Tank))	13
3rd Light Anti-Aircraft Regiment, Royal Canadian Artillery (Detachment) & 4th Field Regiment, Royal Canadian Artillery (Detachment)	13
Corps of Royal Canadian Engineers	27
Royal Canadian Corps of Signals	9
4th Canadian Infantry Brigade (Brigadier S. Lett) The Essex Scottish Regiment The Royal Hamilton Light infantry (Wentworth Regiment) The Royal Regiment of Canada	 121 197 227
6th Canadian Infantry Brigade (Brigadier W.W. Southam) Les Fusiliers Mont Royal The Queen's Own Cameron Highlanders of Canada The South Saskatchewan Regiment	 119 76 84
5th Canadian Infantry Brigade The Black Watch (Royal Highland Regiment) of Canada (three platoons) The Calgary Highlanders (anti-aircraft gunners on LCT)	 4 0
The Toronto Scottish Regiment (Machine Gun)	1
Royal Canadian Army Service Corps	1
Royal Canadian Ordnance Corps	2
Canadian Provost Corps	1
Canadian Intelligence Corps	3

BRITISH & US FATALITIES:

No. 3 Commando, No. 4 Commando, A Commando, Royal Marines	52
No. 10 Commando	0
1st US Ranger Battalion	1

Total Canadian fatalities (including those who died in captivity or of their wounds)	**903** 909
Total British and US military fatalities	**53**
Total Allied military fatalities	**956**
Total Allied naval and air force fatalities	**149**
Total Allied fatalities	**1,105**

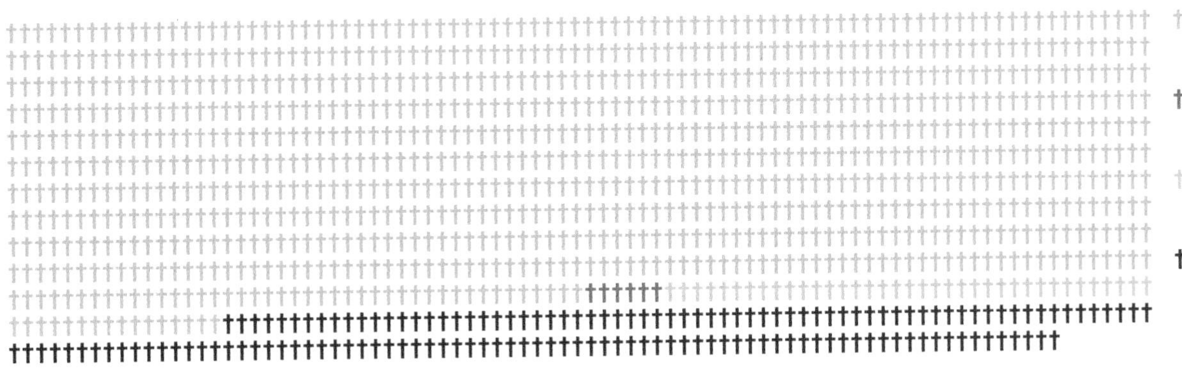

Canadian battle fatalities

Canadian soldiers captured at Dieppe who died as POWs

British and US fatalities

Naval and air force fatalities

Normandy: Balance of Forces
1944

The graphics show the number of British, US, and German troops deployed during the Allied invasion of Normandy.

BRITISH US GERMAN

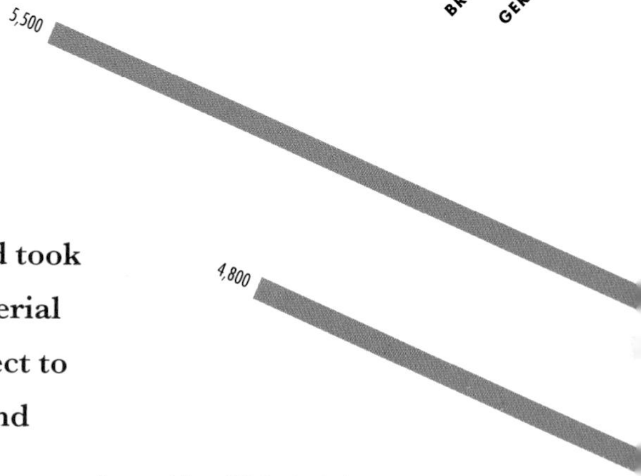

5,500

4,800

The Allied invasion of Normandy in 1944 represents the largest amphibious landings ever undertaken, and was the result of scrupulous planning. The landings, Operation Neptune, were an integral part of the Normandy invasion, Operation Overlord, and took place at 06:30 on June 6th, 1944. The attacking force would have aerial supremacy over the beaches; the coastal fortifications were subject to intense preliminary aerial bombardment prior to the invasion, and were backed up by naval bombardment during the campaign.

The landings, involving 61,715 British, 21,400 Canadian, and 73,000 US troops, committed an armada of some 5,000 ships. The landings would be backed up by airborne assaults to hold the perimeter, and Commando landings to ensure the flanks of the individual landing beaches would be secure.

The Allied force was well-equipped with many innovations; a variety of specially adapted tanks ("Hobart's Funnies"), a floating harbor ("Mulberry"), and a submarine fuel line ("Pluto"). This huge assault force would also make use of a wide variety of landing craft intended to put ashore the troops and their armor, capable of attacking Hitler's Atlantic Wall, along a stretch of 50 miles (80 km) of the Normandy coast. The wall comprised a complex interlocking set of blockhouses, artillery emplacements, tank turrets, and mined beach obstacles, behind which a still formidable enemy force of four divisions lurked. Though most were "second line," at least two were composed of non-German nationals from the eastern part of the Reich, and another was formed

GROUND TROOPS

700,000

REPLACEMENTS

120,000

20,000

OTHER MEN

780,000

of men of lower categories of fitness, destined to take on a garrison role for the Atlantic Wall fortifications. Inland, however, there were Panzer divisions to act as a reserve; though their deployment caused some controversy among the commanders, there would be at least four panzer divisions available to take on the Allies in Normandy.

In all ways, however, the Allies outnumbered the Germans; though the ground troops were evenly matched in numbers, there was no way that the Germans could match them in reserves and replacements; the Allies would have at least a 6:1 advantage here. In tanks, and in aircraft, the Germans would be some way behind the Allies, and have a massive disadvantage in stemming the tide of the Allied invasion force.

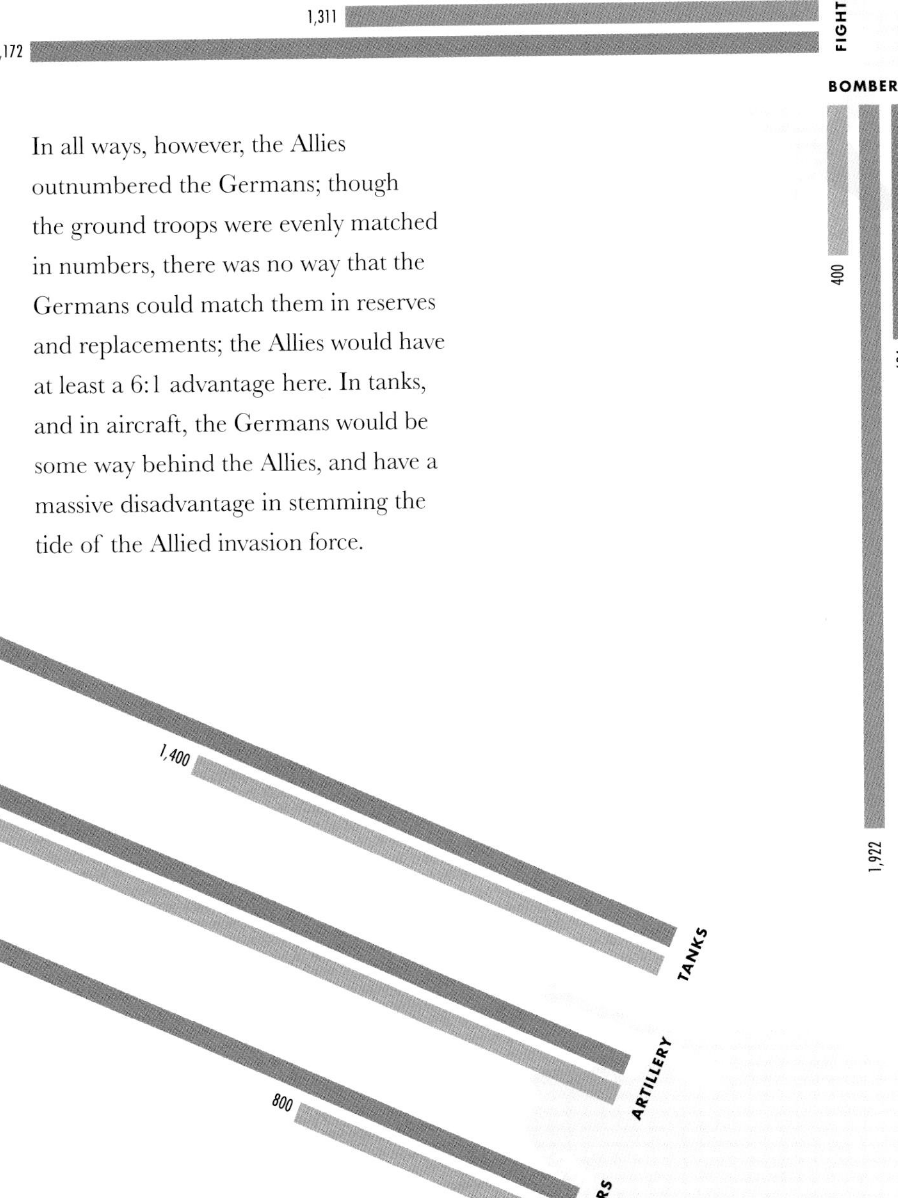

D-Day: Casualties and Strong Points
1944

General Eisenhower was the popular choice for Commander-in-Chief of the Invasion Force that was to land in Normandy in June 1944. He was an able diplomat and leader, well liked and respected by all. Unafraid of taking decisions, Eisenhower also knew how to handle his men, and particularly the big personalities of the generals immediately under his command, such as Bernard Montgomery. Monty, triumphant leader of the 8th Army in the Western Desert and in Italy, was called to take charge of the Army Group that was actually to invade Europe in 1944. The 21st Army Group was to consist of two armies: the 2nd British (General Dempsey) and the 1st US (General Bradley). British drive and ingenuity would be severely tested in the assault on fortress Europe.

American troops ready to embark for Britain and the invasion of Europe, 1944.

The invasion beaches first selected in 1943 were in Normandy; these provided sufficient tactical space for maneuver, and the Atlantic Wall defences—Hitler's very own Maginot Line designed to keep the Western Allies at bay while he took on the might of the USSR—were much weaker than those across the Straits of Dover in the Pas de Calais, just 22 miles (35 km) away. They were much farther away from the coast of Britain, but the Allies were not going to land in ignorance. Intelligence gathering had been part of the Commandos' brief, with small-scale operations ascertaining, for example, whether the beach sands would support armor, and the scale of the defences recently bolstered by Montgomery's old adversary, General Erwin Rommel.

The Allies had comprehensive dossiers on all aspects of the chosen beaches, spreading from the River Douvres in the west, to the Orne and the Caen Canal in the east. The ground would vary considerably: the British and Canadian landing beaches (code-named Gold, Juno and Sword), and one of the American (Utah) were character-ized by open beaches backed by dune fields or sea walls; the remaining American beach, Omaha, was backed by cliffs. All beaches would be tough nuts to crack, as Rommel had ensured that their defences were in good order, intended to stop an invader in a maze of tetrads and "Belgian hedgehogs," and to rip the bottom out of thin-skinned invasion craft.

To counter these, and instrumental in the success on the British and Canadian beaches, was the 79th Armored Division, led by Major General Hobart. Hobart was the originator of the "funnies," a series of specialist armored vehicles based on Sherman and Churchill tanks that were designed to take on the might of Hitler's Atlantic Wall fortifications. Examples included the crab or flail tank, intended to take out the mine-fields, and the Armored Vehicle Royal Engineers (AVRE), which were equipped with a petard-firing weapon that could dispatch most concrete fortifications it met.

The British and Canadian landings took place at around 07:30, after the Americans had come ashore at Utah and Omaha. Embarking from a range of specialist landing craft, they were everywhere opposed by their defenders. Resistance was nevertheless patchy on all beaches; toughest at the easiest beach to defend, Omaha, but tough elsewhere, too. The availability of specialist tanks from the 79th Armored Division, reducing the defences and assaulting the defenders, was of the greatest significance. The "funnies" had done their job well. By nightfall, the Allies had established their beachhead and had captured the city of Bayeux, symbolic as the seat of the Duke of Normandy, William the Conqueror. Caen, however, was an altogether tougher challenge.

Royal Marine Commandos practicing beach landings in advance of D-Day.

Assembling a Grant tank in Detroit, one of many intended for Normandy.

Allied Strengths: Normandy

ALLIED TROOPS LANDED IN NORMANDY	
Airborne troops	23,400
American (Omaha & Utah beaches + airborne)	73,000
British (Gold & Sword beaches + airborne)	61,715
Canadian (Juno Beach)	21,400
Totals:	**179,515**

AIRCRAFT IN OPERATION	
Aircraft supporting the landings	11,590
Sorties flown by allied aircraft	14,674
Aircraft lost	127
	26,391

German Defences: D-Day Beaches

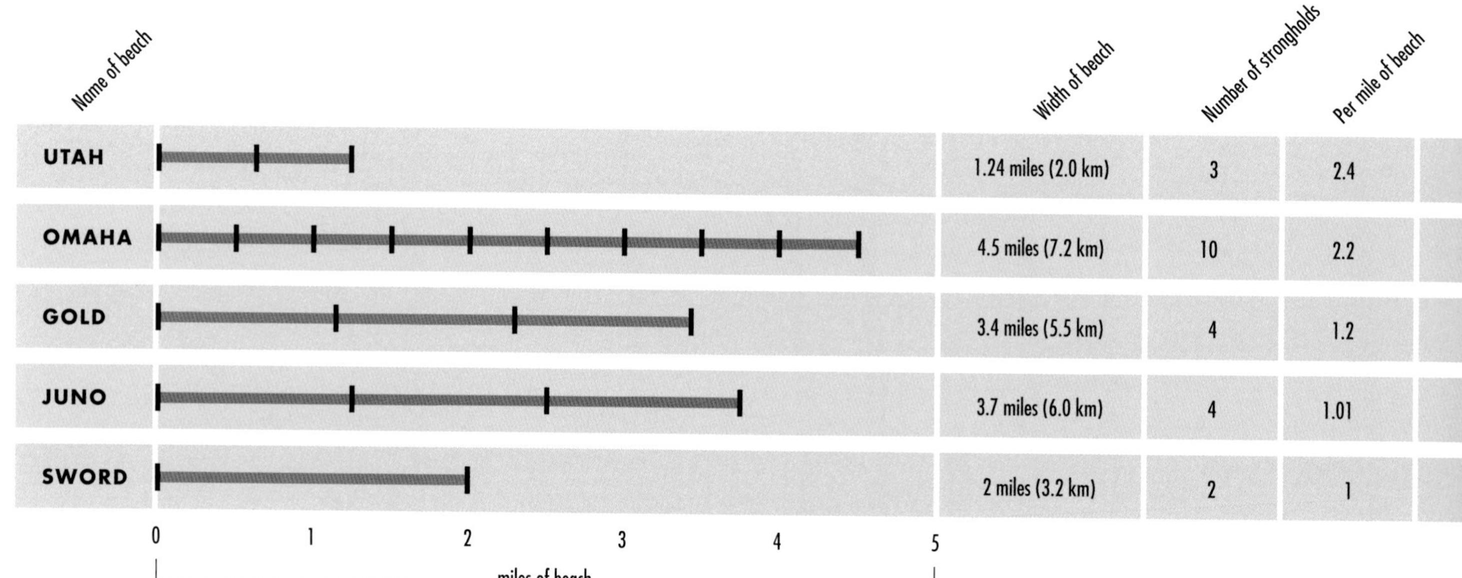

Name of beach	Width of beach	Number of strongholds	Per mile of beach
UTAH	1.24 miles (2.0 km)	3	2.4
OMAHA	4.5 miles (7.2 km)	10	2.2
GOLD	3.4 miles (5.5 km)	4	1.2
JUNO	3.7 miles (6.0 km)	4	1.01
SWORD	2 miles (3.2 km)	2	1

NAVAL VESSELS IN OPERATION NEPTUNE

Naval combat ships	1,213
Landing ships and landing craft	4,126
Ancillary craft	736
Merchant vessels	864
6,939	

PERSONNEL IN OPERATION NEPTUNE

American	52,889
British	112,824
Canadian (and other allied)	4,988
170,701	

German infantry companies	Machine guns	Mortars	Field guns	Anti-tank guns	Allied casualties (6.6.44)	Allied casualties per mile of beach	Allied casualties per strong point	Allied casualties per machine gun
1	17	3	7	6	197	159	66	12
8	85	28	20	15	2,374	527	237	28
4	18	1	5	9	413	121	103	23
4	33	5	4	9	805	217	201	24
2	14	7	8	7	630	315	315	45

The Polish Home Army

The resistance of the Polish Army to invasion in 1939 came as a surprise to the Wehrmacht, and its troops fought valiantly in the face of the German armored assault, only to be stabbed in the back by the invasion of the Soviet Union, who, seizing an opportunity, expanded its borders deep onto Polish soil in order to create a buffer zone that would hopefully cushion Hitler's ambitions eastward. Despite being invaded, the Poles did not capitulate, and with the movement of the Polish government in exile to London, many Poles sought to fight on within the Allied armies abroad.

Though there were many Polish combatants serving in diverse theaters of war, also created was a resistance force, at first known as the "Polish Victory Service," and then the "Union of Armed Combat," or ZWZ, that was born out of adversity in September 1939, through to the AK or Armia Krajowa, the Home Army, in 1942. These organizations were responsible for armed acts of sabotage, or the development of more passive resistance on the shop floor, or in the transport industries—all designed to slow down the capabilities of the German invad-

Polish Home Army and Union of Armed Combat Sabotage (January 1941–June 1944)

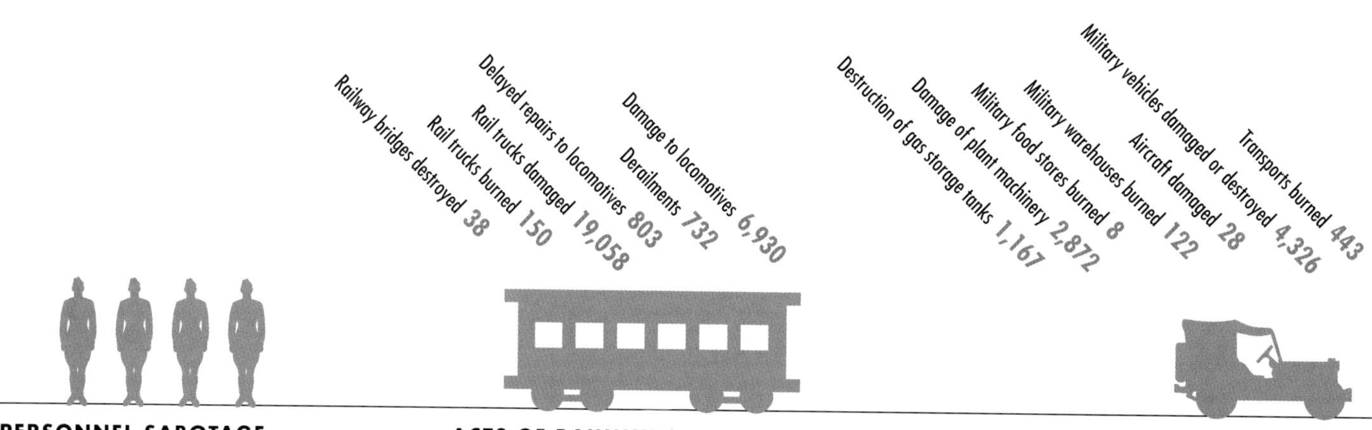

Individual attacks on German personnel
5,733

Number of individual attacks on railways
27,711

Number of individual acts
8,966

ers. The Home Army was involved in sabotage, and retaliatory attacks on the occupying Germans, as well as providing a source of intelligence to the Allies, feeding back information on troop movements, and the development of the German revenge weapons. Successfully unifying a number of armed insurrectionist units, the army rose from a disparate band of saboteurs to a well-armed and determined force of some 350,500 soldiers. Its actions were directed from abroad by the Polish commander-in-chief, based with the government in exile in London. With the whole of Poland under the Nazi jackboot, its population subject to some of the worst atrocities of the whole war, the Armia Krajowa had been created with one thing in mind; the preparation and execution of an armed uprising in Poland, intended to take the war back on the offensive from within the borders of the occupied state. And so it was that a force of some 40,000 soldiers (10% of them women) would rise up against the Germans in the Polish capital, Warsaw, in August 1944.

Successfully using the city's network of sewers on August 1st, the soldiers of the Home Army, with improvized equipment (and helmets painted in the red and white of the national flag) attacked the German forces with skill and tenacity, hoping that they could clear their city and be supported by the advancing Allies, particularly the Soviets in the east. Early successes were followed by tragedy as the Soviets halted and the Western Allies refused to press Stalin to push on. In a battle that lasted for just over two months, the biggest losses would be sustained by the civilians, with 150,000 killed and the remaining 650,000 transported from the city, which was systematically razed to the ground. The Home Army itself suffered 20,000 casualties, half the number sustained by the Germans.

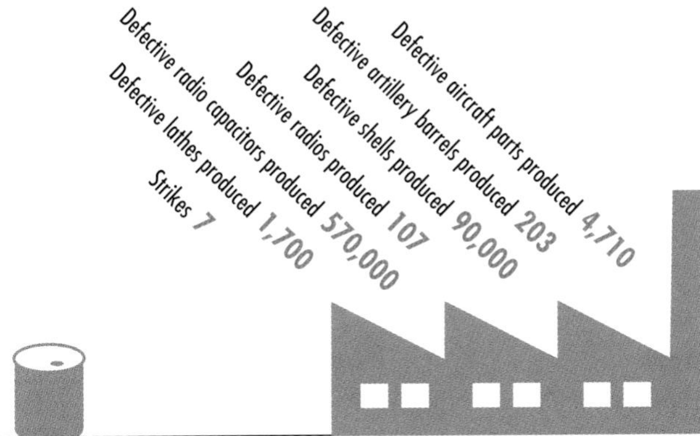

The graphic shows a breakdown of the acts of sabotage perpetrated by the Polish Army against the Germans between January 1941 and June 1944.

GAS	SABOTAGE DURING MANUFACTURING		TOTAL
49,244 tons (44,674 tonnes) of gas destroyed	Number of individual acts 666,727	Other acts of sabotage 25,154	Total number of sabotage activities 733,691

Operation Market Garden
1944

Operation Market Garden of September 1944 was one of the most audacious gambles of the war. The airborne assault was designed to take and hold the succession of bridges across waterways standing in the way of the Allies slogging toward the Rhine and into Germany. In true airborne fashion, these troops would be vulnerable behind the lines, fighting as self-contained units surrounded by the enemy. The relief would be by a mobile armored column, supplied by the men of XXX Corps along a single, narrow road in just 48 hours.

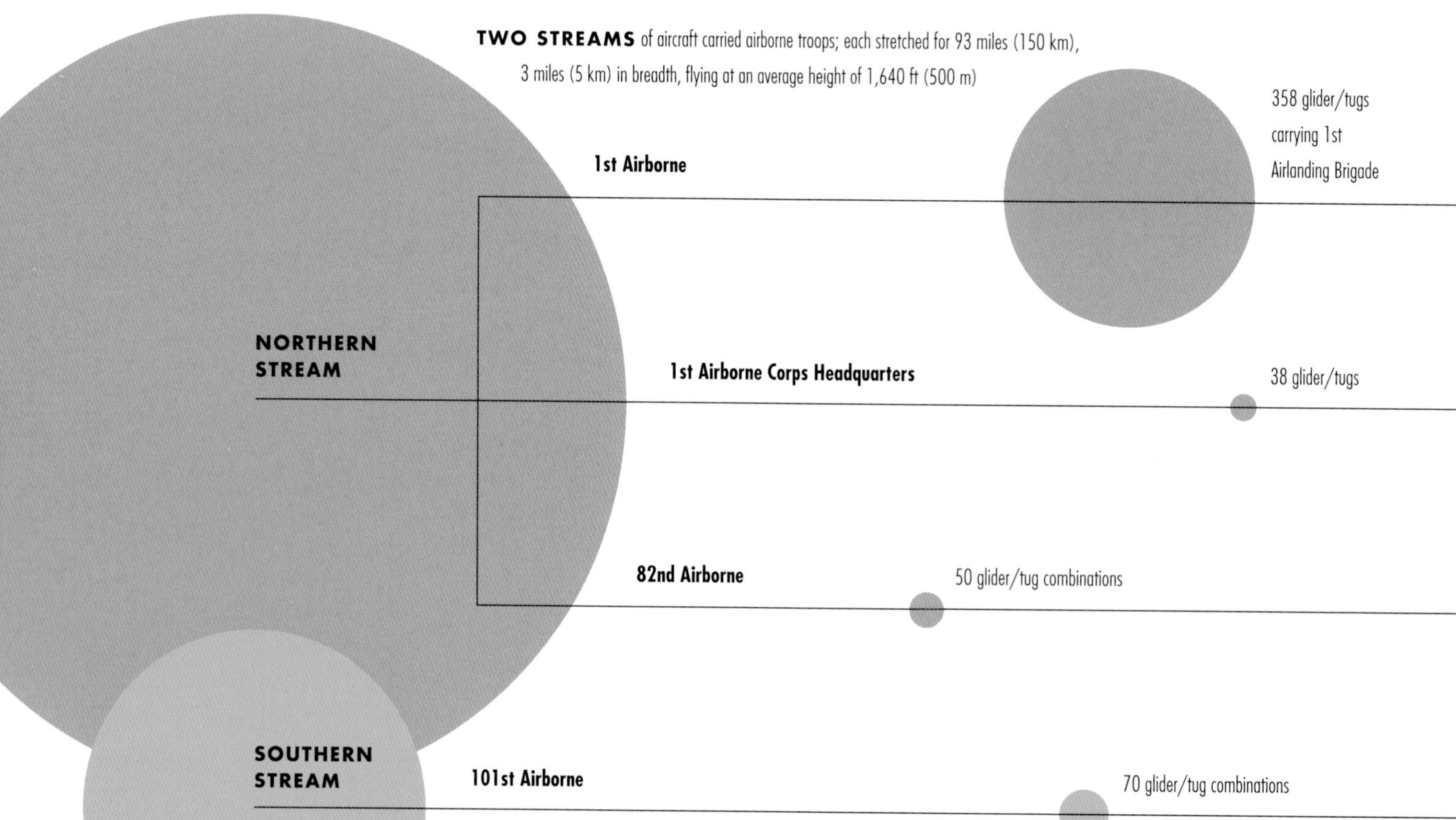

The First Allied Airborne Army were to drop three airborne divisions along a corridor from Eindhoven to Arnhem, each division to take and hold the bridges across the main waterways, and await the arrival of the armor and infantry of the British 2nd Army, spearheaded by XXX Corps. Commencing at "Joe's Bridge" across the Meuse-Escaut Canal, it was the role of XXX Corps to link up each of the airborne divisions in turn: first the US 101st Airborne Division from Eindhoven to Veghel; second the US 82nd Division from Grave to Nijmegen; and finally, the British 1st Airborne Division at Arnhem, the farthest advance into enemy-held territory.

The operation was doomed to failure by poor operational planning and logistical issues; the failure of XXX Corps to reach Arnhem in time meant that the operation had failed; the controversial decision to halt XXX Corps north of Nijmegen doomed the British paratroops' operation in the advanced position. The battle was effectively over on September 21st. In all, 20,011 paratroopers and 14,589 glider troops were deployed; at Arnhem, the surrounded paratroopers were to see some 6,000 taken into captivity. The operation, though audacious, failed in its intent; for XXX Corps, driving along a difficult, narrow front into strongly enemy-held territory, it was certainly a "bridge too far."

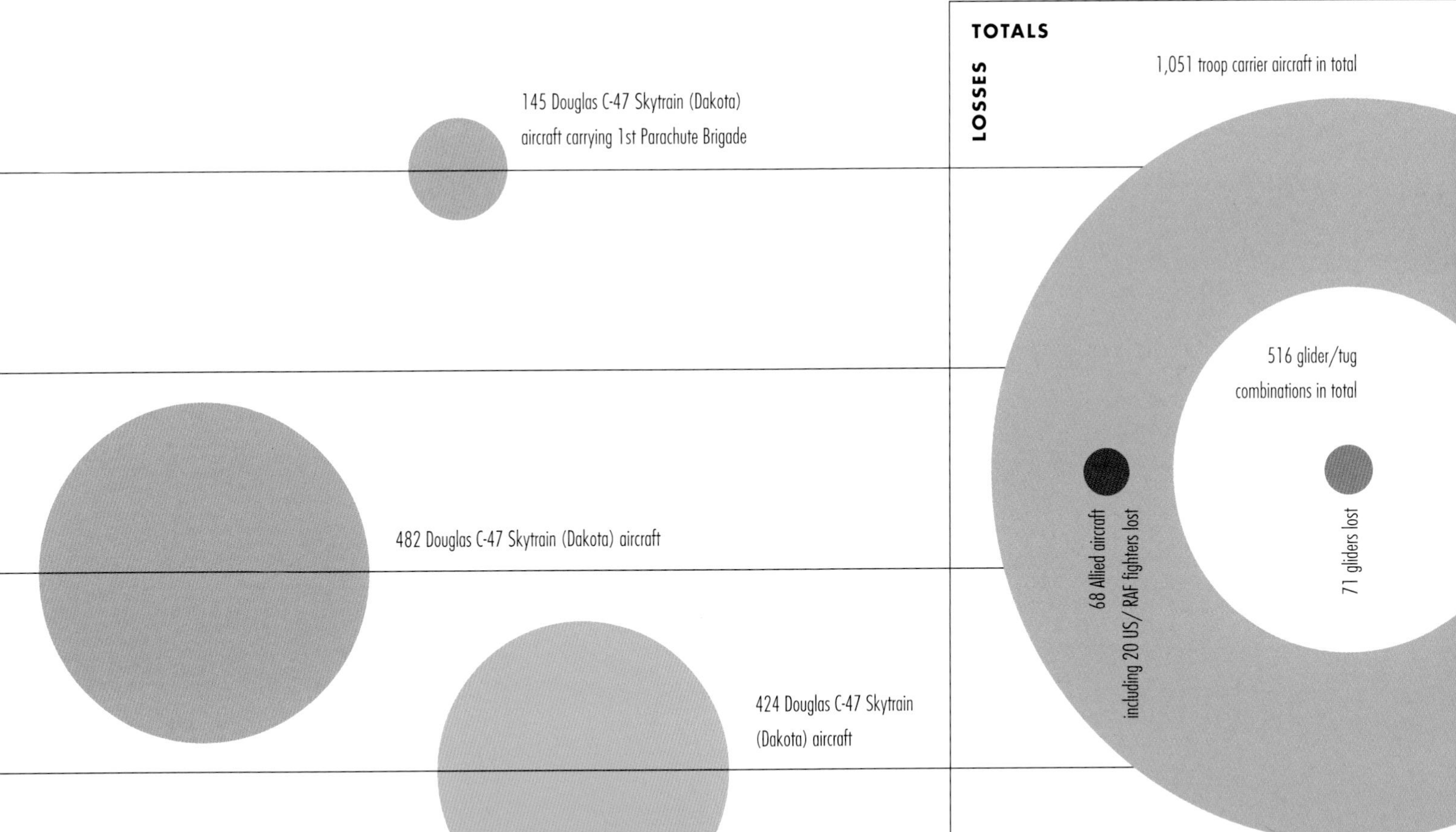

Operation Market Garden timeline

Operation Market Garden was composed of two components: "Market," which was the airborne assault, intended to take and hold the successive bridges along the route, and "Garden," the ground component, intended to drive a corridor through enemy-held territory and relieve the airborne troops holding the bridges. XXX Corps was unable to punch its way through to Arnhem in time—"a bridge too far."

SUNDAY, SEPTEMBER 17TH, 1944

AIRBORNE INVASION — OPERATION GARDEN

- **09:30** Slow glider tugs took off
- **10:25** Faster Pathfinders took off
- **11:35** Last aircraft left ground
- **12:40** Pathfinders dropped at Arnhem (21st Independent Parachute Company), Eindhoven (101st Airborne), and Grave (82nd Airborne)
- **13:00** Gliders of 1st Airlanding Brigade land at Arnhem; 6,769 men of 101st Airborne land north of Eindhoven; 6,527 men of 82nd Division jumped south of Nijmegen
- **13:30** 1st Airborne Headquarters' gliders landed at Groesbeek
- **13:53** 1st Parachute Brigade jumped west of Arnhem
- **14:08** By this time ~20,000 troops, 511 vehicles, 330 artillery pieces, 590 tons (535 tonnes) of equipment had been landed
- **15:00** 1st Airlanding Brigade secured defensive perimeter around landing zones west of Arnhem
- **15:40** 1st Parachute Brigade moved toward Arnhem
- **16:00** By this time 101st Airborne reached objectives (north of Eindhoven), road and rail bridges at Heeswijk, Veghel and St Oedenrode captured; Son Bridge destroyed; 82nd Airborne captured Grave and Heumen bridges, two bridges over Maas-Waal canal destroyed
- **18:30** Arnhem rail-bridge blown up; road bridge intact
- **19:30** 2nd Parachute Battalion in position at southern end of Arnhem road bridge

XXX CORPS — OPERATION MARKET

- **14:00** Opening bombardment at "Joe's Bridge," 408 artillery pieces
- **14:35** Guards Armored Division and infantry of 50th (Northumbrian) Division attacked along the narrow front
- **19:30** Guards Armored Division halted, 9 miles (14 km) traveled

MONDAY, SEPTEMBER 18TH, 1944

AIRBORNE INVASION — OPERATION GARDEN

- **06:00** Second airlift delayed due to poor weather; airborne troops continue their attacks
- **10:00** 904 glider/tug combinations took off flying northern route (91 lost in transit)
- **13:00** 428 gliders delivered 2,656 men, 146 jeeps, 2 bulldozers to 101st Airborne area; 385 gliders delivered 1,782 men, 12 (75 mm) guns, 12 (105 mm) guns, and 8 (57 mm anti-tank) guns to 82nd Airborne Area
- **15:00** 124 C-47 aircraft (I lost) and 296 gliders delivered 2,119 men to 1st Airborne area at Arnhem

XXX CORPS — OPERATION MARKET

- **06:00** Guards Armored Division advanced from Valkenswaard to reach 101st Division
- **c.18:00** Arrived at destroyed Son Bridge, 11 miles (18 km) traveled

Operations of IX Troop Carrier Command: Operation Market Garden

	SEPT 17TH	SEPT 18TH	SEPT 19TH	SEPT 20TH	SEPT 21ST	SEPT 23RD	SEPT 25TH	TOTAL
Aircraft dispatched	1,053	126	60	387	177	41	34	1,878
Aircraft aborted	–	–	24	1	49	–	–	74
Aircraft destroyed	27	6	2	–	5	–	–	40
Aircraft damaged	236	24	16	11	33	–	–	320
Aircrew killed	51	22	5	–	11	–	–	89
Troops carried	16,292	2,119	–	125	1,511	560	–	20,607
Troops dropped	16,220	2,110	–	125	998	558		20,011
Drop casualties	233	?	–	2	?	?	–	235+
Artillery pieces carried	12	–	–	6	–	–	–	18
Cargo carried in tons (tonnes)	7,470 (6,777)	50.7 (46)	70.5 (64)	488.3 (443)	97 (88)	27.5 (25)	48.5 (44)	8,255 (7,489)

OPERATION GARDEN AIRBORNE INVASION

OPERATION MARKET XXX CORPS

TUESDAY, SEPTEMBER 19TH, 1944

03:30 1st Parachute Brigade attack at Arnhem

10:00 1st Parachute Brigade attack at Arnhem failed

13:00 Third wave took off after being fogbound: 385 gliders with artillery for 101st Airborne (189 lost/returned); other reinforcements mostly grounded by poor weather

06:00 Bailey Bridge complete at Son, Guards Armored Division resumed advance

08:20 Guards Armored reached Grave Bridge (82nd Airborne), 28 miles (45 km) traveled; division presses on to Nijmegen but fails to take the bridge; a river assault on the Waal is proposed, 9 miles (15 km) traveled

WEDNESDAY, SEPTEMBER 20TH, 1944

c.08:00 Reinforcements grounded due to bad weather; 1st Airborne Division seriously depleted

14:40 82nd Airborne troops made the river assault over the Waal to take the bridge at Nijmegen

18:00 Sustained German attacks at Arnhem Bridge

19:10 Guards Armored Division crossed the bridge across the Waal at Nijmegen

20:00 Guards Armored Division halted, controversially, north of the river, just 2.5 miles (4 km) more. There was 10 miles (16 km) to go to reach the beleaguered 1st Airborne at Arnhem.

Battle of the Bulge
1944–1945

The Ardennes Offensive, known as the "Battle of the Bulge" from the "bulge" made in the Allied front, was Hitler's last offensive in the west. Intended to split the Allies, it was to lead to 89,987 US casualties, 19,276 dead, 47,493 wounded, and 23,218 men captured. The battle commenced on December 16th, 1944 and was fought in the winter months in the Ardennes, over roughly similar ground to where the Germans had broken through during the Battle of France in 1940.

Hitler hoped to deploy three armies (the 6th and 5th Panzer armies and the 7th Army), equipped with the latest and most powerful tanks, to punch through the Allied lines at the junction between the British and Canadian forces, and those of the Americans. The main attack by the 6th Panzer Army led by Sepp Dietrich would press on to capture the strategically important port of Antwerp—which was actively supplying the Allies—while the 5th Panzer Army would face the Americans, and force their way through to Brussels. The battle would become the largest fought by the Americans in World War II.

Increasing Size of German Tanks 1941–1944

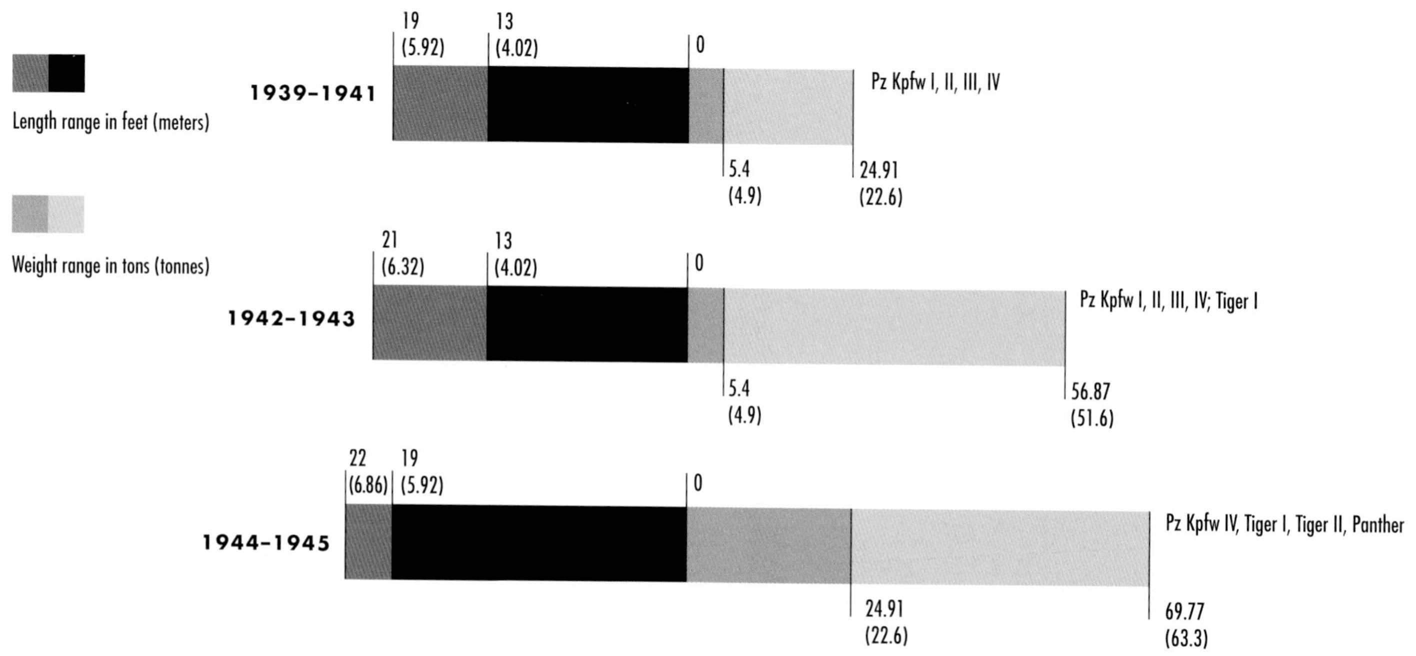

The attacks were unsuspected and the surprise was total. In just two days, December 16–17th, 1944, the Germans were able to punch a hole in the Allied line and advance some 60 miles (96 km) into Allied territory. With the weather poor, the Allied "tank-busting" aircraft such as the RAF Typhoons were not able to function, and the German heavy tanks operated with impunity.

But the Ardennes was less forgiving to the larger and heavier tanks of 1944–1945 than it was to the tanks of 1940. The Ardennes terrain is wooded, hilly, and dissected by rivers. With little opportunity to cross country, the German tanks had to maintain their positions on roadways. With the increase in length and weight, this meant that the German tanks became stuck or bogged down if they attempted to move off road.

And, as the German tanks were fuel-thirsty in 1944, the Germans were reliant on the capture of Allied supplies. As the momentum broke down, the Panzer troops were forced to abandon their vehicles. With the Americans holding out until reinforced, and the German initiative slipping away, the battle was lost, Hitler's gamble wasted.

Increasing Fuel Consumption

The tanks used by the Wehrmacht in the closing campaigns of the war may have been heavily armored and impressively gunned, but they were exceedingly thirsty of fuel. With fuel difficult to source in the Reich, this represented a serious problem during the last-ditch Ardennes Offensive.

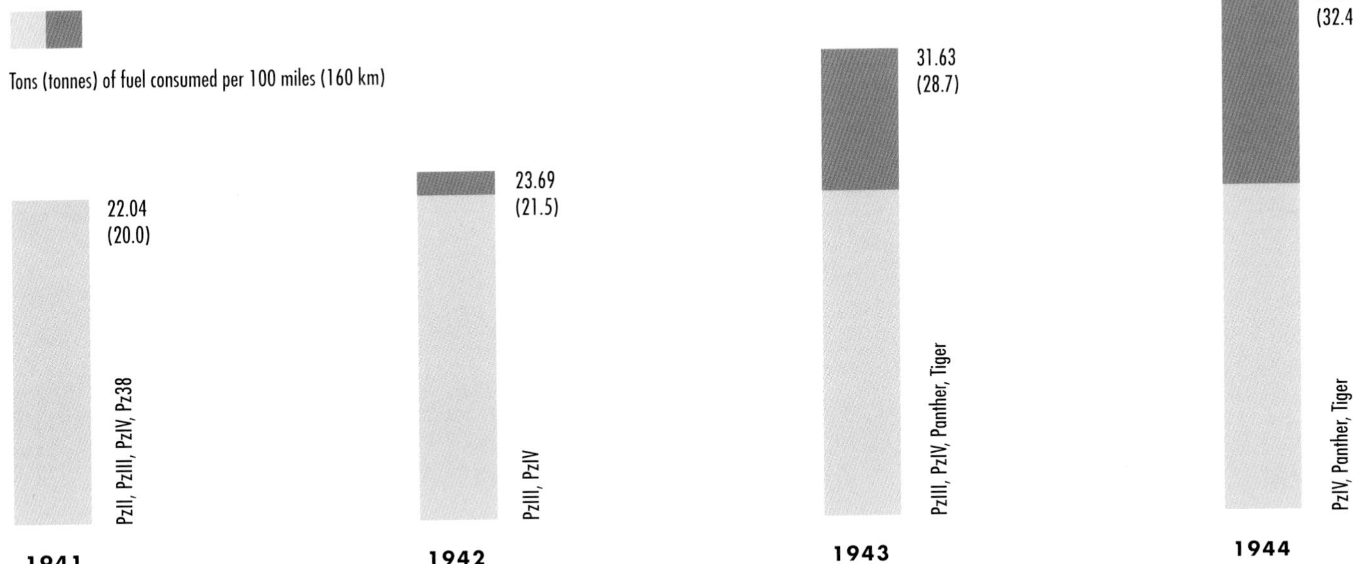

Battle of Kohima
1944

Kohima was one of the most important battles to be fought in the Pacific theater, and was to influence directly the outcome of the war in Burma; it would be one of the largest defeats suffered by the Japanese in land combat.

In March 1944, the Japanese Army launched Operation U-Go, an attack on India intended to seize British supplies in Assam, inspire an uprising by the Indian people against British rule and relieve pressure on other fronts in the Western Pacific. The Japanese were aware of the growing aerial threat from the British, flying out of Assam, and with Allied aerial superiority the Japanese needed to create a larger buffer zone between them and the Allied air bases in north-east India. This part of India was also the start point for Allied ground operations; a plain across which any invading army would have to pass in order to get into India, or over to Burma. Strategically significant, this was the focal point of Japanese intentions to neutralize Allied efforts against them.

As with their 1942 campaign, the Japanese relied on mobility, infiltration, and captured supplies to maintain the momentum of the attack. As the Japanese attacked northward in Arakan, British and Indian forces employed defensive boxes, supplied by air, to hold out against determined assaults until the Japanese were forced to withdraw, short of supplies. These tactics were again employed on a larger scale when Imphal and Kohima were surrounded. In all cases, air operations were significant; the supply of the beleaguered Allies by air meant that they were able to hold on while the Japanese were ground down. And the only way that this was achieved was through the total domination of the airspace over the ground.

The Japanese 15th Army consisted of three infantry divisions and a unit of the "Indian National Army." The Japanese commander planned to cut off and destroy the forward Allied forces, before capturing strategically important Imphal, on the main route to India, isolating the town by the capture of Kohima. Kohima lay on the road to Imphal, and was a small village located on a spur of a wooded ridge, a difficult piece of terrain. The Japanese 31st Division, with more than 12,000 men, attacked on April 5th, and continued to press the defenders of the 161st Indian Brigade back to the cluster of buildings

Air Supply, Kohima, April–May 1944

- USAAF Troop Carrier Command (TCC) (Integrated USAAF & RAF), Brig. Gen W.D. Old
- 1st, 2nd, 27th & 315th Troop Carrier Squadrons, USAAF 177th Transport Wing (31st, 62nd, 117th, 194th Transport Squadrons) RAF

Supplies delivered in tons (tonnes)			Casualties evacuated			Nonessential personnel evacuated		
RAF	USAAF	Total	RAF	USAAF	Total	RAF	USAAF	Total
18,097 (16,418)	14,216 (12,897)	32,314 (29,315)	4,717	10,210	14,927	29,101	29,658	58,759

that represented the residence of the British deputy commissioner. The Japanese pressed the defenders with numerous attacks, but by April 14th, the attacks had abated, and the Allied troops took heart.

The Japanese aims to defeat the Indian and British troops and remove the threats to their supply lines were not achieved; the defenders of Kohima were besieged for almost two weeks on April 5–18th, 1944 before being relieved by the British 2nd Division, which began its own counteroffensive on May 15th. The Allied air forces contributed greatly to the battle as aircraft delivered most of the supplies the British and Indian forces needed; the RAF alone flew 18,999 short (17,236 tonnes) of supplies and 12,000 men into the Kohima-Imphal region and flew out 13,000 casualties and 43,000 noncombatants. The fighting continued until the Japanese withdrew with heavy casualties, the Imphal operation finally abandoned in July. The Japanese retreated to the Chindwin River, the largest defeat they had suffered up to that point, with 55,000 casualties, including 13,500 dead—and with them, the reputation of the Japanese soldier as invincible.

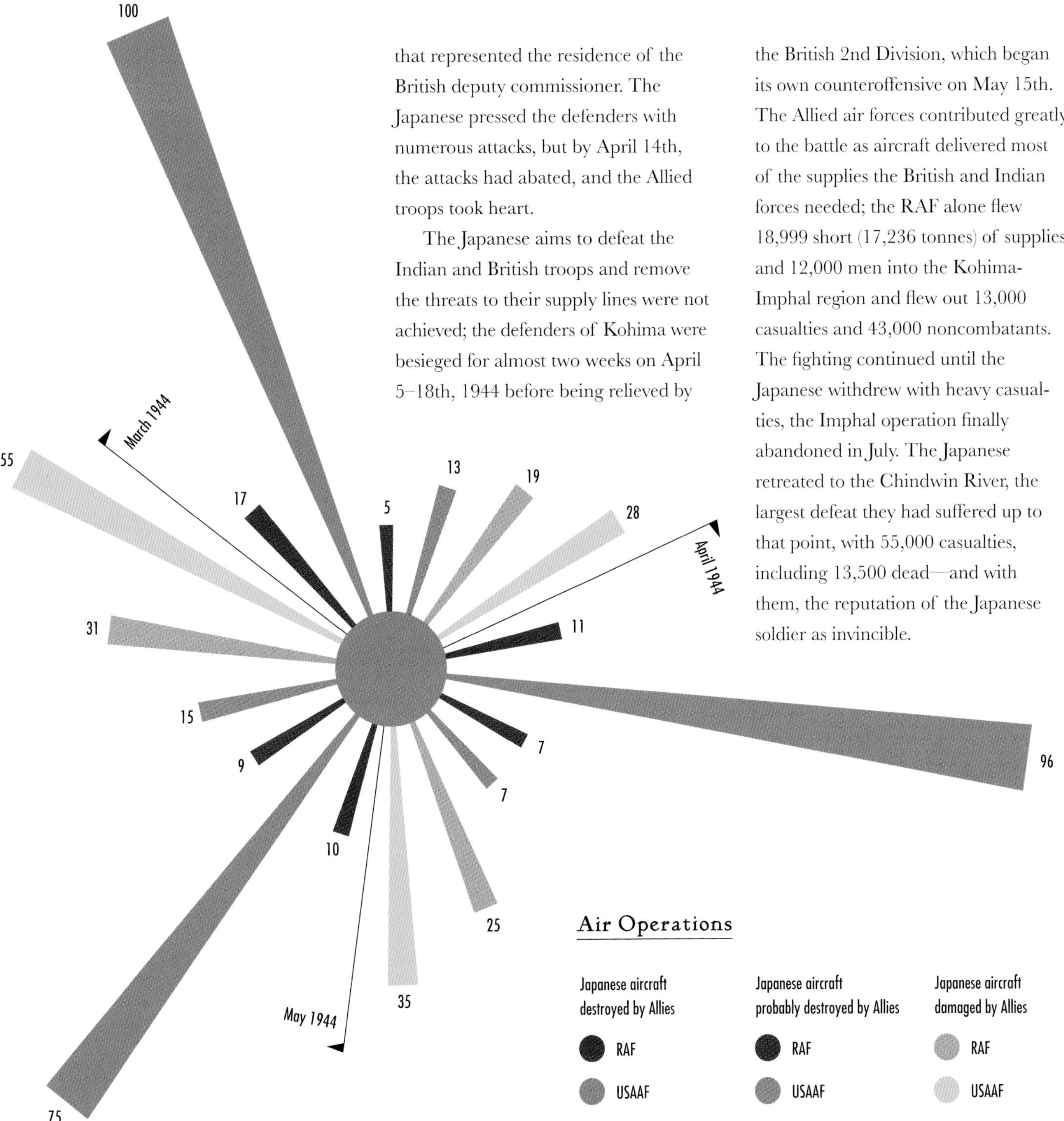

Island-Hopping in the Pacific

1943

In 1943, the Allied strategy was to push the Japanese off the Pacific islands gained during their expansionist phase in 1941–1942. The idea was to strangle the Japanese hold on a range of islands, bypassing some of the strongest held and allowing them to "wither on the vine," in the words of General Douglas MacArthur. The United States Marine Corps (USMC) and United States Navy (USN) took the brunt of the fighting in what became a very bloody conflict. First was Tarawa, in the Gilbert Islands—essential for a base if the Allies, principally the USMC, were to embark on their strategic campaign. The marines were held up offshore, and their advance was painfully slow—particularly in the face of the stiff Japanese resistance that became emblematic of the whole engagement.

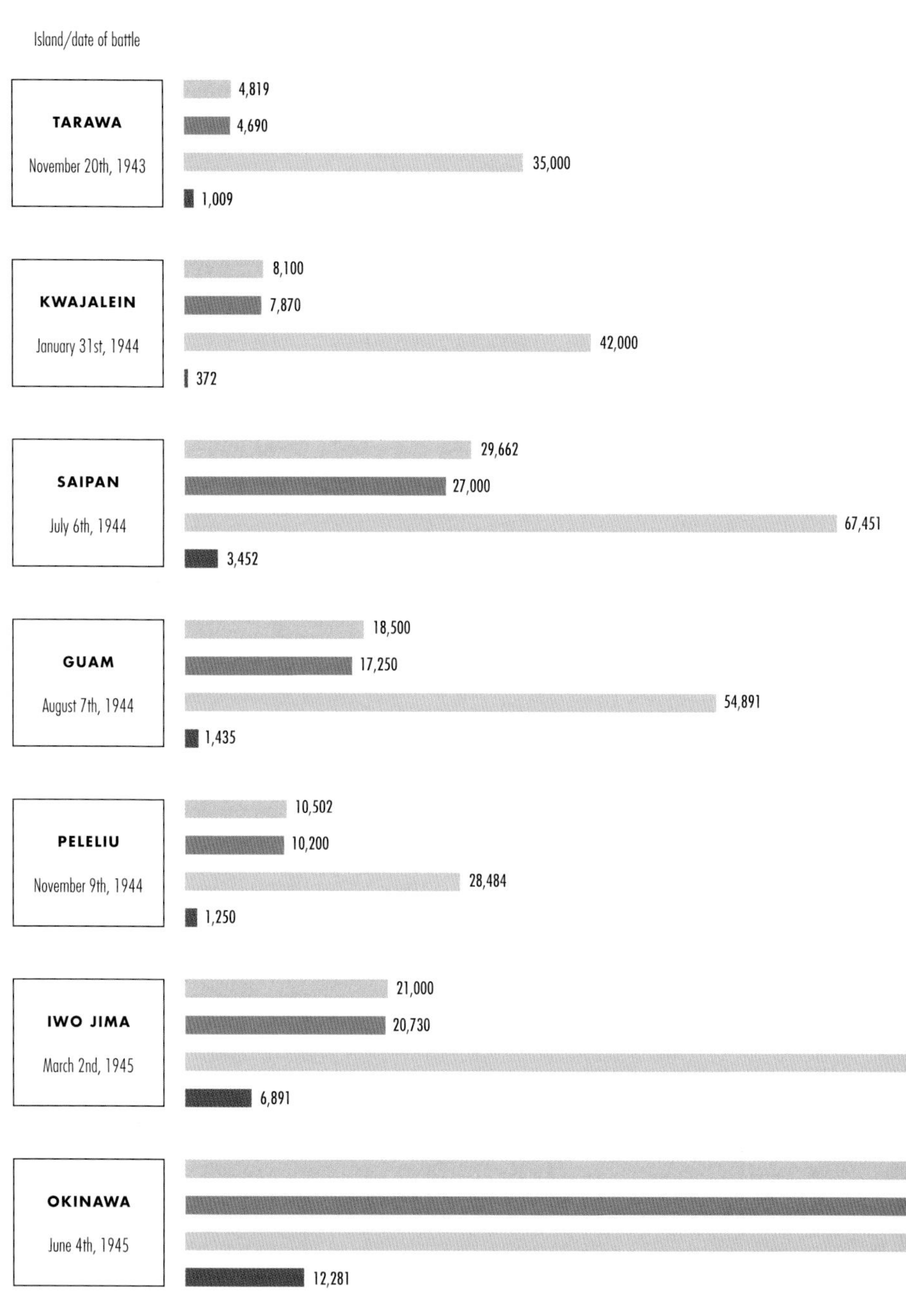

Percentage of Forces Dead

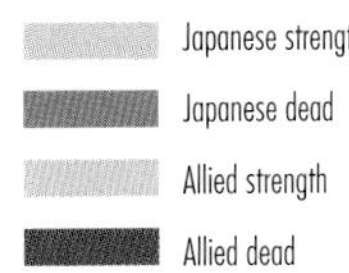

The fanaticism shown by Japanese troops in the Pacific is well demonstrated by the proportion of fatalities in a given battle. For the Japanese, 90% fatalities were common; for the Allies, 4% was average.

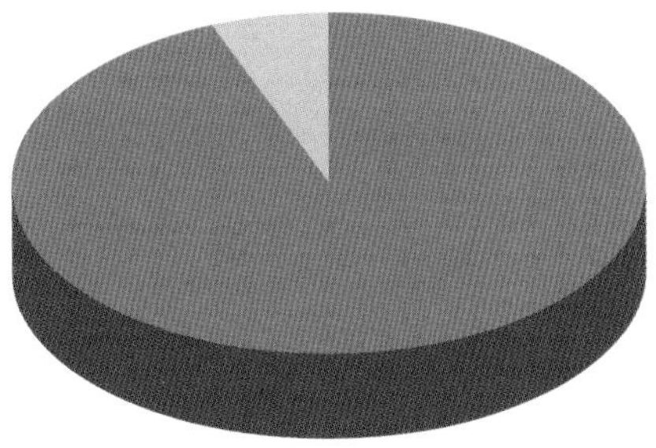

Japanese forces = 94%

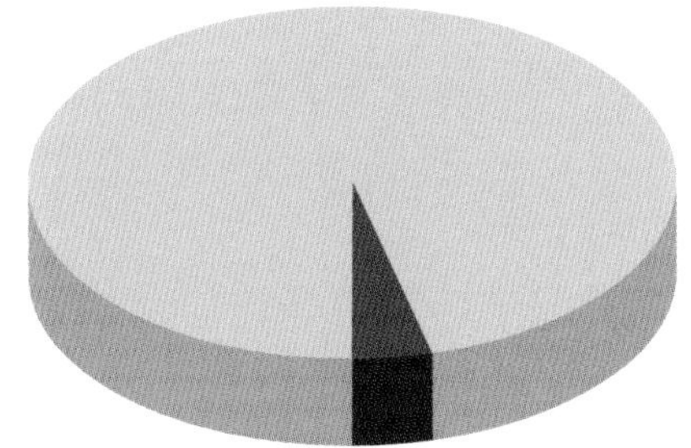

Allied forces = 4%

Suffering extreme losses, the Japanese fought with a blind determination that saw more than 90% of their garrisoned troops dead. And this would not be an isolated occurrence; the Japanese would fight almost to the last man on all the Pacific islands. After Tarawa came Kwajalein in the Marshall Islands. Kwajalein was part of the inner ring of the Japanese defences, and the battle there was particularly tough. Next, the US Marines would have to face attacking the Marianas, with Saipan and Guam significant. With General Douglas MacArthur wishing to liberate the Philippines after his immortal "I will return" statement, Peleliu in the Palau islands was next, opening the way for the liberation of the islands. From there it was pressing to the heart of Japanese territory, with Iwo Jima and Okinawa next in line before the planned invasion of the Japanese homeland. With Japan directly threated, the resolve of the defenders was not distinguished; and the American losses were hard fought.

220,000

118,000

110,071

208,750

Top Ten Costliest Battles in the Two World Wars

The battles of the two world wars have one thing in common: their terrible loss of life. Although casualty figures are often difficult to determine accurately (comprising the dead, wounded, missing, and captured), their scale is hard to comprehend.

The costliest battles from both wars bear comparison—and not only in the level of casualties. While World War I is usually seen from the perspective of trench warfare, this can be considered as an extended siege. With Stalingrad or Monte Cassino, significant siege battles of World War II, both can be considered in the light of Verdun, the Somme or the Third Battle of Ypres. Open warfare, particularly in the first hours and days of a campaign, is similarly costly. The fight for France, in 1914 and again in 1940, and over much the same ground, both figure highly in the list. Other comparisons can be made: amphibious landings such as Luzon and Gallipoli, or all-out, all-arms assaults such as the Hundred Days and the Ardennes. And, throughout history, battles on the open steppes of Russia have been among the bloodiest ever fought.

World War II

Date: September 1st, 1939–September 2nd, 1945

Location: Europe, Pacific, Atlantic, South-East Asia, China, Middle East, Mediterranean, and Africa, briefly North America

Result:
- Allied victory
- Dissolution of the Third Reich
- Creation of the United Nations
- Emergence of the United States and the Soviet Union as superpowers
- Beginning of the Cold War

Axis (WWII)

Allies (WWII)

The different sized circles illustrate the total deaths for each of these costliest battles comparatively.

Central powers (WWI)

Allies (WWI)

World War I

Date: July 28th, 1914–November 11th, 1918

Location: Europe, Africa, the Middle East, the Pacific Islands, China, and off the coast of South and North America

Result:
- Allied victory
- End of the German, Russian, Ottoman, and Austro-Hungarian empires
- Formation of new countries in Europe and the Middle East
- Transfer of German colonies and regions of the former Ottoman Empire to other powers
- Establishment of the League of Nations

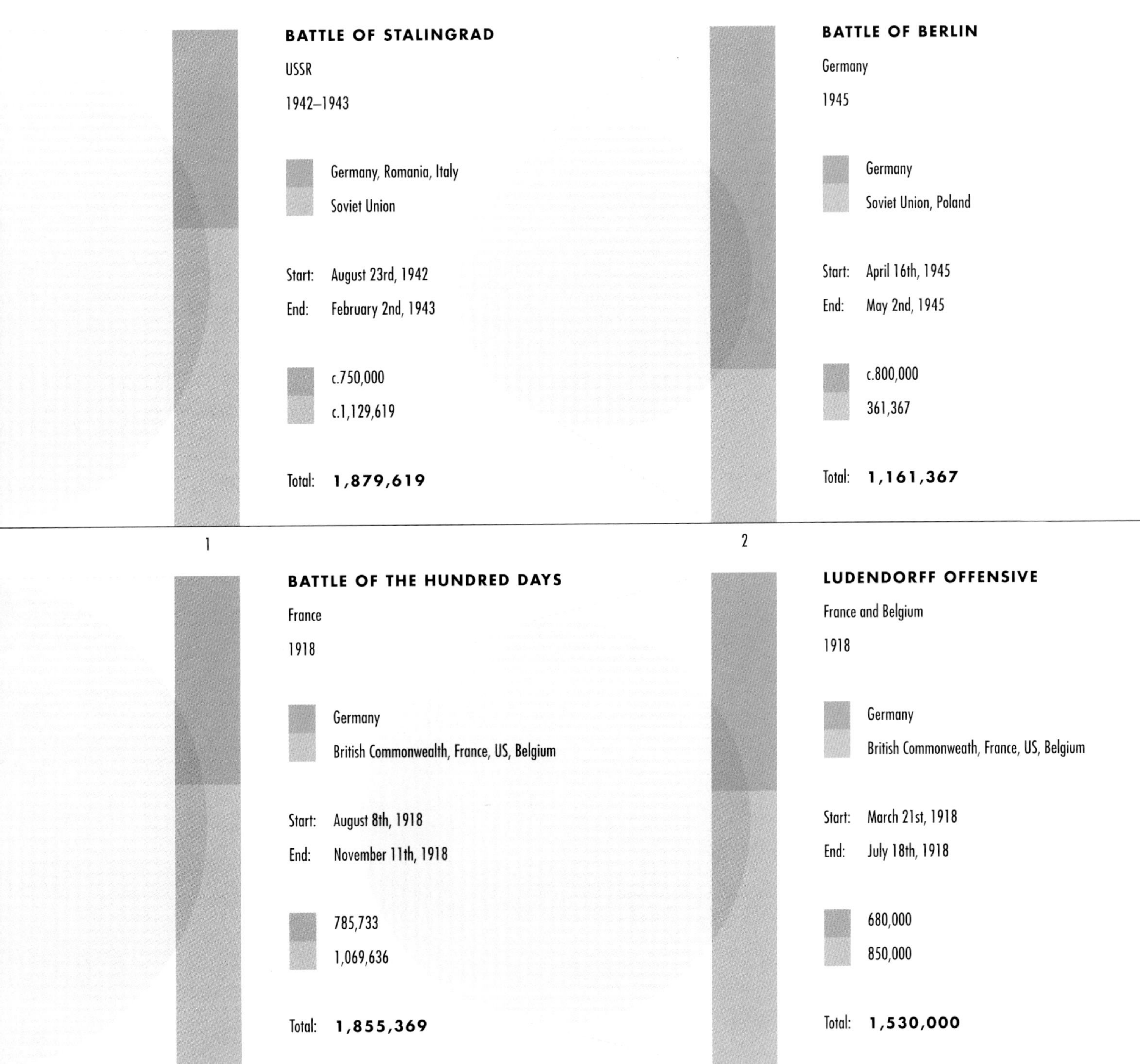

BATTLE OF STALINGRAD

USSR

1942–1943

Germany, Romania, Italy

Soviet Union

Start: August 23rd, 1942

End: February 2nd, 1943

c.750,000

c.1,129,619

Total: **1,879,619**

1

BATTLE OF BERLIN

Germany

1945

Germany

Soviet Union, Poland

Start: April 16th, 1945

End: May 2nd, 1945

c.800,000

361,367

Total: **1,161,367**

2

BATTLE OF THE HUNDRED DAYS

France

1918

Germany

British Commonwealth, France, US, Belgium

Start: August 8th, 1918

End: November 11th, 1918

785,733

1,069,636

Total: **1,855,369**

1

LUDENDORFF OFFENSIVE

France and Belgium

1918

Germany

British Commonweath, France, US, Belgium

Start: March 21st, 1918

End: July 18th, 1918

680,000

850,000

Total: **1,530,000**

2

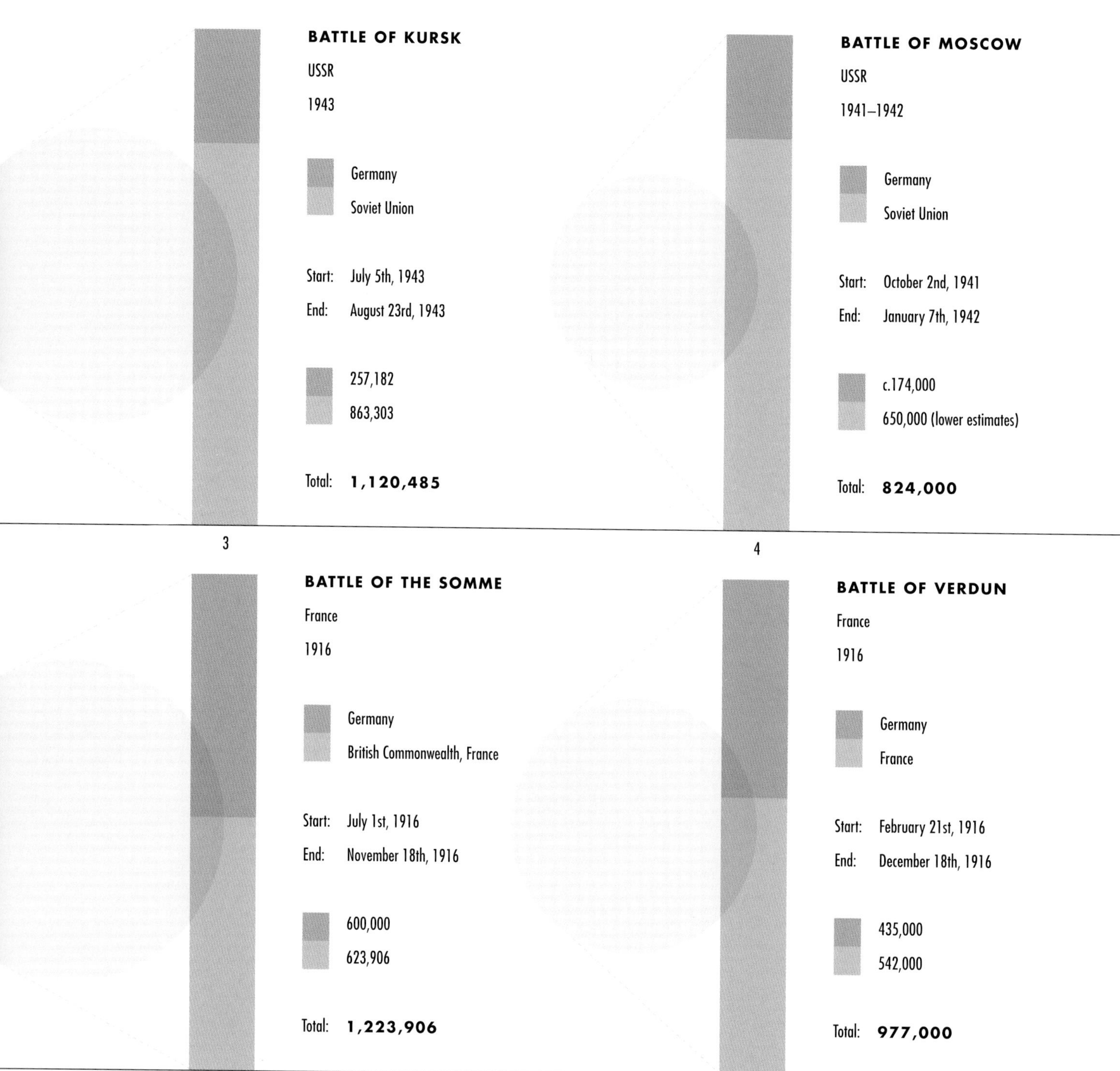

BATTLE OF KURSK

USSR

1943

Germany

Soviet Union

Start: July 5th, 1943

End: August 23rd, 1943

257,182

863,303

Total: **1,120,485**

3

BATTLE OF MOSCOW

USSR

1941–1942

Germany

Soviet Union

Start: October 2nd, 1941

End: January 7th, 1942

c.174,000

650,000 (lower estimates)

Total: **824,000**

4

BATTLE OF THE SOMME

France

1916

Germany

British Commonwealth, France

Start: July 1st, 1916

End: November 18th, 1916

600,000

623,906

Total: **1,223,906**

3

BATTLE OF VERDUN

France

1916

Germany

France

Start: February 21st, 1916

End: December 18th, 1916

435,000

542,000

Total: **977,000**

4

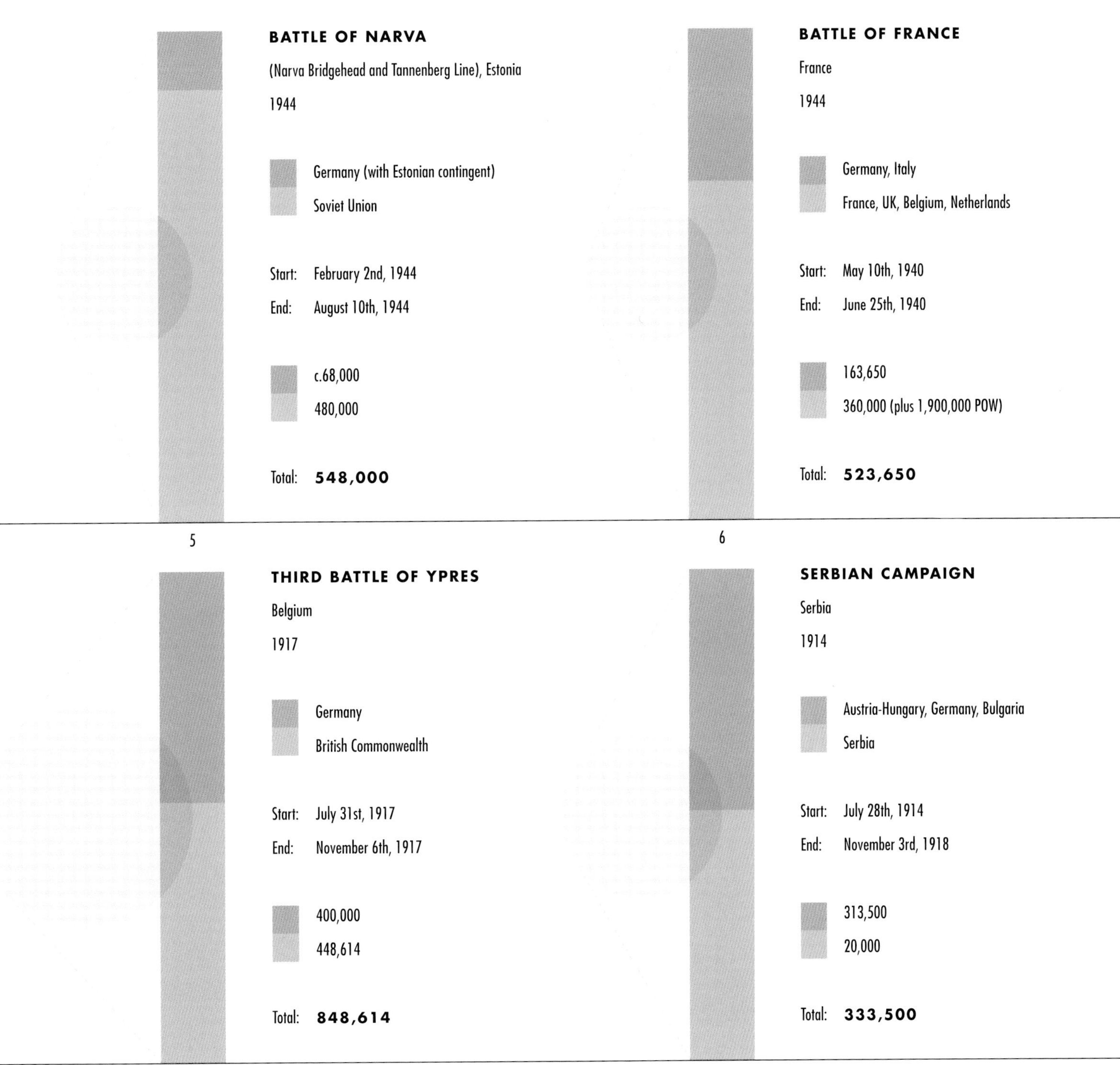

BATTLE OF NARVA

(Narva Bridgehead and Tannenberg Line), Estonia

1944

Germany (with Estonian contingent)

Soviet Union

Start: February 2nd, 1944

End: August 10th, 1944

c.68,000

480,000

Total: **548,000**

5

BATTLE OF FRANCE

France

1944

Germany, Italy

France, UK, Belgium, Netherlands

Start: May 10th, 1940

End: June 25th, 1940

163,650

360,000 (plus 1,900,000 POW)

Total: **523,650**

6

THIRD BATTLE OF YPRES

Belgium

1917

Germany

British Commonwealth

Start: July 31st, 1917

End: November 6th, 1917

400,000

448,614

Total: **848,614**

5

SERBIAN CAMPAIGN

Serbia

1914

Austria-Hungary, Germany, Bulgaria

Serbia

Start: July 28th, 1914

End: November 3rd, 1918

313,500

20,000

Total: **333,500**

6

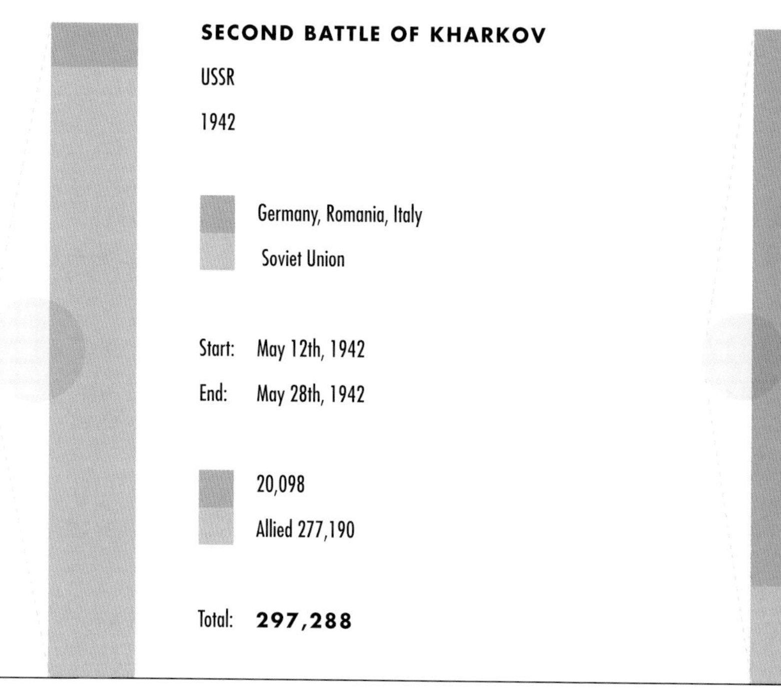

SECOND BATTLE OF KHARKOV

USSR

1942

Germany, Romania, Italy

Soviet Union

Start: May 12th, 1942

End: May 28th, 1942

20,098

Allied 277,190

Total: **297,288**

7

BATTLE OF LUZON

Philippines

1945

Japan

US, Philippines, Australia, Mexico

Start: January 9th, 1945

End: August 15th, 1945

214,585

37,690

Total: **252,275**

8

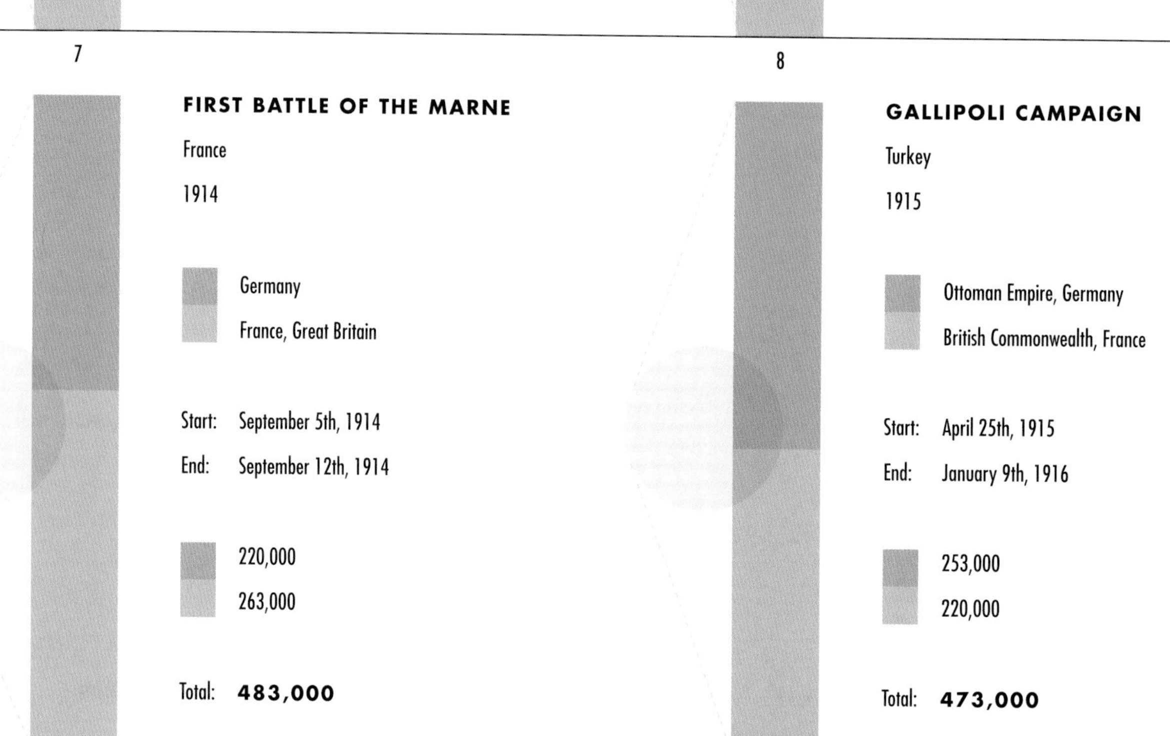

FIRST BATTLE OF THE MARNE

France

1914

Germany

France, Great Britain

Start: September 5th, 1914

End: September 12th, 1914

220,000

263,000

Total: **483,000**

7

GALLIPOLI CAMPAIGN

Turkey

1915

Ottoman Empire, Germany

British Commonwealth, France

Start: April 25th, 1915

End: January 9th, 1916

253,000

220,000

Total: **473,000**

8

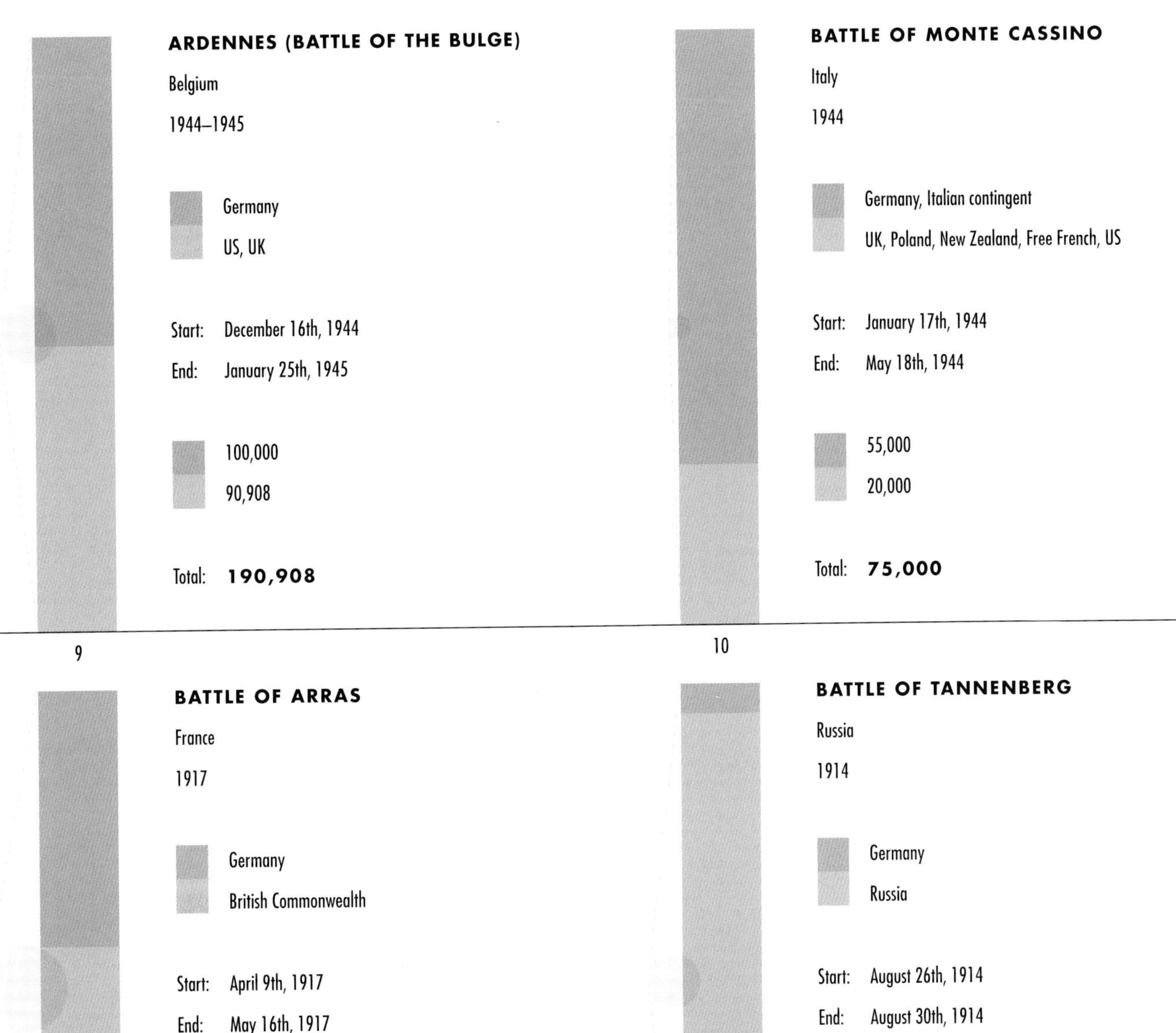

ARDENNES (BATTLE OF THE BULGE)

Belgium

1944–1945

Germany

US, UK

Start: December 16th, 1944

End: January 25th, 1945

100,000

90,908

Total: **190,908**

9

BATTLE OF MONTE CASSINO

Italy

1944

Germany, Italian contingent

UK, Poland, New Zealand, Free French, US

Start: January 17th, 1944

End: May 18th, 1944

55,000

20,000

Total: **75,000**

10

BATTLE OF ARRAS

France

1917

Germany

British Commonwealth

Start: April 9th, 1917

End: May 16th, 1917

120,000

158,000

Total: **278,000**

9

BATTLE OF TANNENBERG

Russia

1914

Germany

Russia

Start: August 26th, 1914

End: August 30th, 1914

12,000

170,000

Total: **182,000**

10

7B
DB

Chapter Three

WEAPONS AND INNOVATIONS

It is well known that with war comes innovation. In World War II military aviation made great strides; from ballistic missiles came the first rockets into space; from the Nazi jet aircraft came the birth of the jet age. Similar advances were made at sea, and on land—in the handheld weapons of the infantryman, capable of taking on even the most formidable tank. The greatest innovation would be the most terrifying. The atomic bomb was developed, designed, built and dropped, unleashing its awful destructive power.

Aircraft in the Battle of Britain
1940

The Battle of Britain in August–September 1940 was primarily a battle between the fighters of Royal Air Force (RAF) Fighter Command and the bombers of the Luftwaffe. The Luftwaffe's primary targets were the airfields, military installations, and transport links; it was the RAF's task to destroy the bombers before they could carry out their tasks. Pitted against them was the Luftwaffe's Messerschmitt 109 fighter, which was operating at extreme range and only had minutes over southern England. Its twin-engined sister, the Messerschmitt 110, was no match for the British fighters.

Aircraft Production During the Battle of Britain

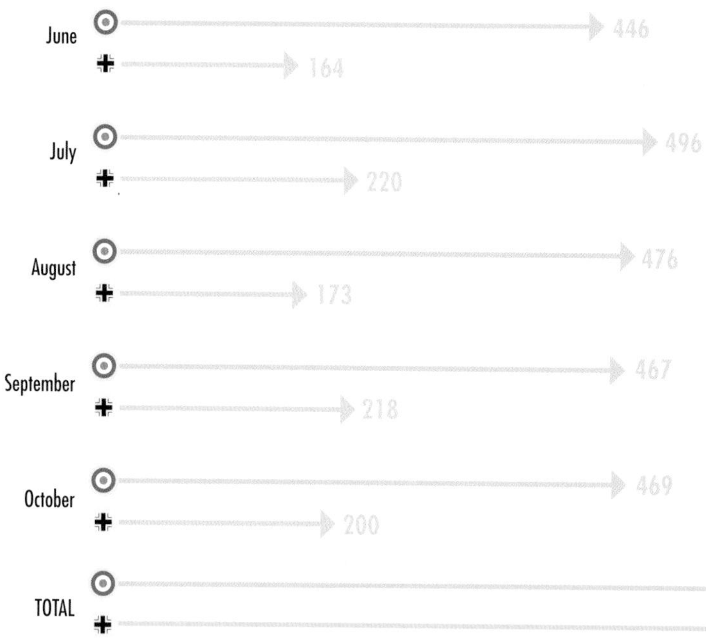

Hawker Hurricanes of RAF Fighter Command flying in formation during the Battle of Britain.

6 Dornier Do 215

66 Others

74 Junkers Ju 87

76 Others

53 Blenheim

171 Dornier Do 17

229 Messerschmitt Bf 110

246 Heinkel He 111

281 Junkers Ju 88

357 Spitfire

533 Messerschmitt Bf 109

601 Hurricane

1,087 TOTAL

1,606 TOTAL

2,354

Losses by Type

The ability of the RAF fighters to destroy the German bombers (and their fighter escorts) at a rate that would damage the capability of the Luftwaffe to fight the battle was critical—as were the losses of trained aircrew.

Luftwaffe aircraft

RAF fighters

A Heinkel He 111 bomber over the East London docks, September 7th, 1940.

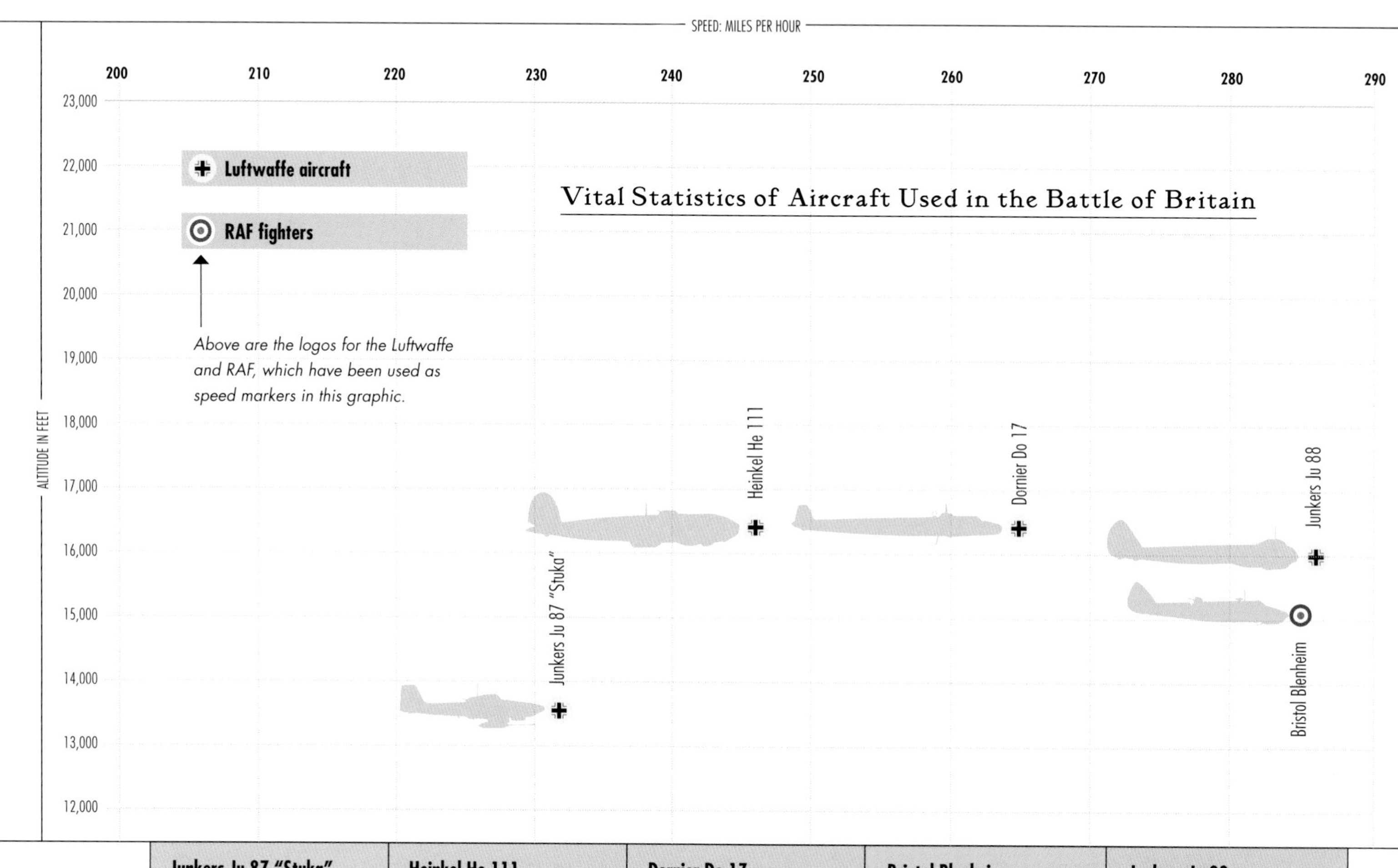

	Junkers Ju 87 "Stuka" Divebomber	**Heinkel He 111** Bomber	**Dornier Do 17** Bomber	**Bristol Blenheim** Night fighter	**Junkers Ju 88** Bomber
Engines	1,100 hp Junkers Jumo	Two 1,100 hp Dailmler Benz DB601	Two 1,000 hp bramo	Two 840 hp Bristol Mercury engines	Two 1,200 hp Junkers Jumo
Wingspan	45 ft (13.80 m)	74 ft (22.6 m)	59 ft (18.0 m)	46 ft (14.14 m)	60 ft (18.25 m)
Length	36 ft (11.0 m)	54 ft (16.39 m)	52 ft (15.85 m)	40 ft (12.11 m)	47 ft (14.35 m)
Max speed	232 mph (373 km/h) at 13,500 ft (4,100 m)	247 mph (398 km/h) at 16,400 ft (5,000 m)	265 mph (426 km/h) at 16,400 ft (5,000 m)	285 mph (459 km/h) at 15,000 ft (4,600 m)	286 mph (460 km/h) at 16,000 ft (4,900 m)
Armament	Two 7.9 mm machine guns in wings, one in cockpit	Three 7.9 mm machine guns	Four to eight 7.9 mm machine guns	Four .303 Browning machine guns in ventral fairing; one in a dorsal turret	Three 7.9 mm machine guns
Bomb load	One 2,425 lb (1,100 kg) bomb plus four 242 lb (110 kg) wing bombs	4,413 lb (2,002 kg)	2,204 lb (1,000 kg)		3,970 lb (1,801 kg)

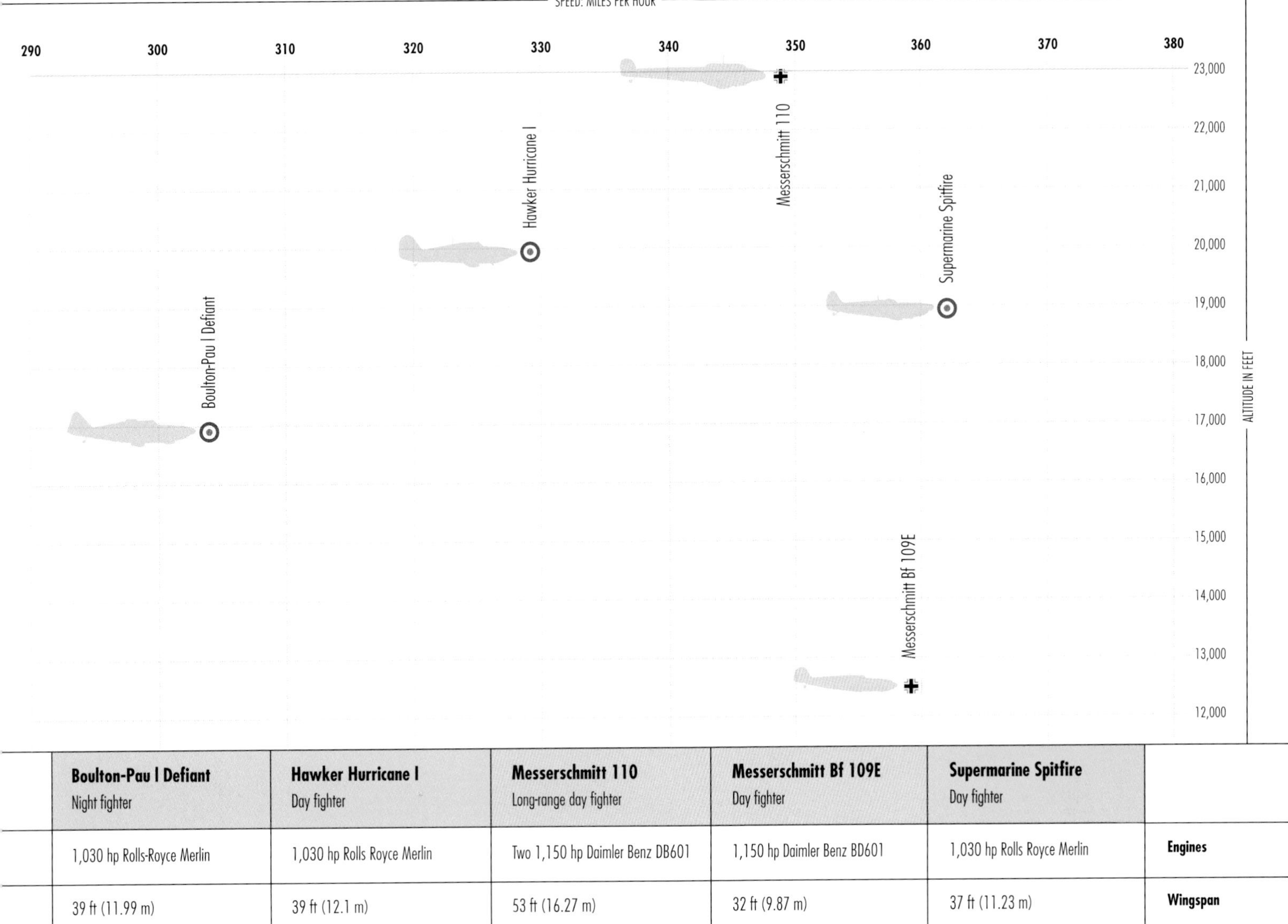

Boulton-Pau l Defiant Night fighter	Hawker Hurricane I Day fighter	Messerschmitt 110 Long-range day fighter	Messerschmitt Bf 109E Day fighter	Supermarine Spitfire Day fighter	
1,030 hp Rolls-Royce Merlin	1,030 hp Rolls Royce Merlin	Two 1,150 hp Daimler Benz DB601	1,150 hp Daimler Benz BD601	1,030 hp Rolls Royce Merlin	**Engines**
39 ft (11.99 m)	39 ft (12.1 m)	53 ft (16.27 m)	32 ft (9.87 m)	37 ft (11.23 m)	**Wingspan**
35 ft (10.77 m)	32 ft (9.8 m)	40 ft (12.11 m)	29 ft (8.74 m)	30 ft (9.12 m)	**Length**
304 mph (489 km/h) at 17,000 ft (5,200 m)	329 mph (529 km/h) at 20,000 ft (6,100 m)	349 mph (562 km/h) at 22,960 ft (7,000 m)	357 mph (575 km/h) at 12,300 ft (3,700 m)	362 mph (583 km/h) at 19,000 ft (5,800 m)	**Max speed**
Four .303 Browning machine guns in dorsal turret	Eight .303 wing-mounted Browning machine guns	Four 7.9 machine guns and two 20 mm cannon in nose, one rear-firing 7.9 mm machine gun	Two 7.9 mm machine guns on engine crankcase firing through the nose; two 20 mm cannon in wings	Eight .303 wing-mounted Browning machine guns	**Armament**

Allied and Axis Rifles

Even with the advent of armored warfare, the infantryman was still as relevant as ever in this new age. Though World War I had quickly descended into a positional warfare of trenches and dugouts, in preparation for a future conflict, Britain at least believed that its soldiers would not have to carry a personal entrenching tool into action again. But the lot of the soldier to carry out war fighting with his personal weapons—rifle and bayonet—would not change.

The graphics here and on the following two pages are a visual representation of the comparitive weights, lengths, and so on, of the rifles used by the Axis and Allied soldiers during World War II.

Weight

Length

Muzzle velocity

Effective range

Cartridge

Action

Weight

Length

Muzzle velocity

Effective range

Cartridge

Action

Weight

Length

Muzzle velocity

Effective range

Cartridge

Action

American soldiers comparing their rifles, a bolt-action Springfield M 1903 model and the M1 Garand.

GERMANY

Mauser Karabinier 98K

3–9 lb (3.7–4.1 kg)

3.6 ft (1.11 m)

2,493 fps (760 mps)

1,640 ft (500 m)

7.92 x 57 mm Mauser

Bolt action

Gewehr 41

10.8 lb (4.9 kg)

4.6 ft (1.4 m)

2,542 fps (775 mps)

1,312 ft (400 m)

7.92 x 57 mm Mauser

Gas operated, semi-automatic

Gewehr 43

9.7 lb (4.4 kg)

3.7 ft (1.13 m)

2,542 fps (775 mps)

1,640 ft (500 m)

7.92 x 57 mm Mauser

Gas operated, semi-automatic

JAPAN

Arisaka Type 38

8.7 lb (3.95 kg)

4 ft (1.28 m)

2,509 fps (765 mps)

1,968 ft (600 m)

6.5 x 50 mm Arisaka

Bolt operated

Arisaka Type 44 Carbine

7.3 lb (3.3 kg)

3 ft (0.97 m)

2,247 fps (685 mps)

1,640 ft (500 m)

6.5 x 50 mm Arisaka

Bolt operated

Arisaka Type 99

8.1 lb (3.7 kg)

3.6 ft (1.12 m)

2,395 fps (730 mps)

1,640 ft (500 m)

7.7 x 58 mm Arisaka

Bolt operated

Most nations went to war with bolt-action rifles, a traditional format in which the bolt is operated manually, thereby opening the breech and ejecting the spent cartridge case. This action then cocks the firing pin and reloads the rifle—but this is very much dependent on the skill of the rifleman. Reliable, tough, and capable of releasing at least 15 rounds a minute, the bolt-action rifle was nevertheless replaced during World War II by the semi-automatic gas-operated rifle, most notably by the United States and Germany. As the war progressed, semi-automatics became more prevalent; as did cut-down or carbine versions of standard rifles—essential for motorized infantry short on space.

In semi-automatics the gases released by the cartridge during firing are reused to eject the cartridge case, cock the weapon, and load. This provided a much greater rate of fire; for the M1 Garand, the iconic service rifle of the US infantryman, this would equate to 30 rounds a minute, twice that of the traditional bolt-action rifles carried by his British counterpart. This, in turn, required a larger number of rounds to be carried by the infantryman. However, most sniper rifles remained bolt action; here, the emphasis was on accuracy and range of the shot, rather than number of rounds released in the heat of battle.

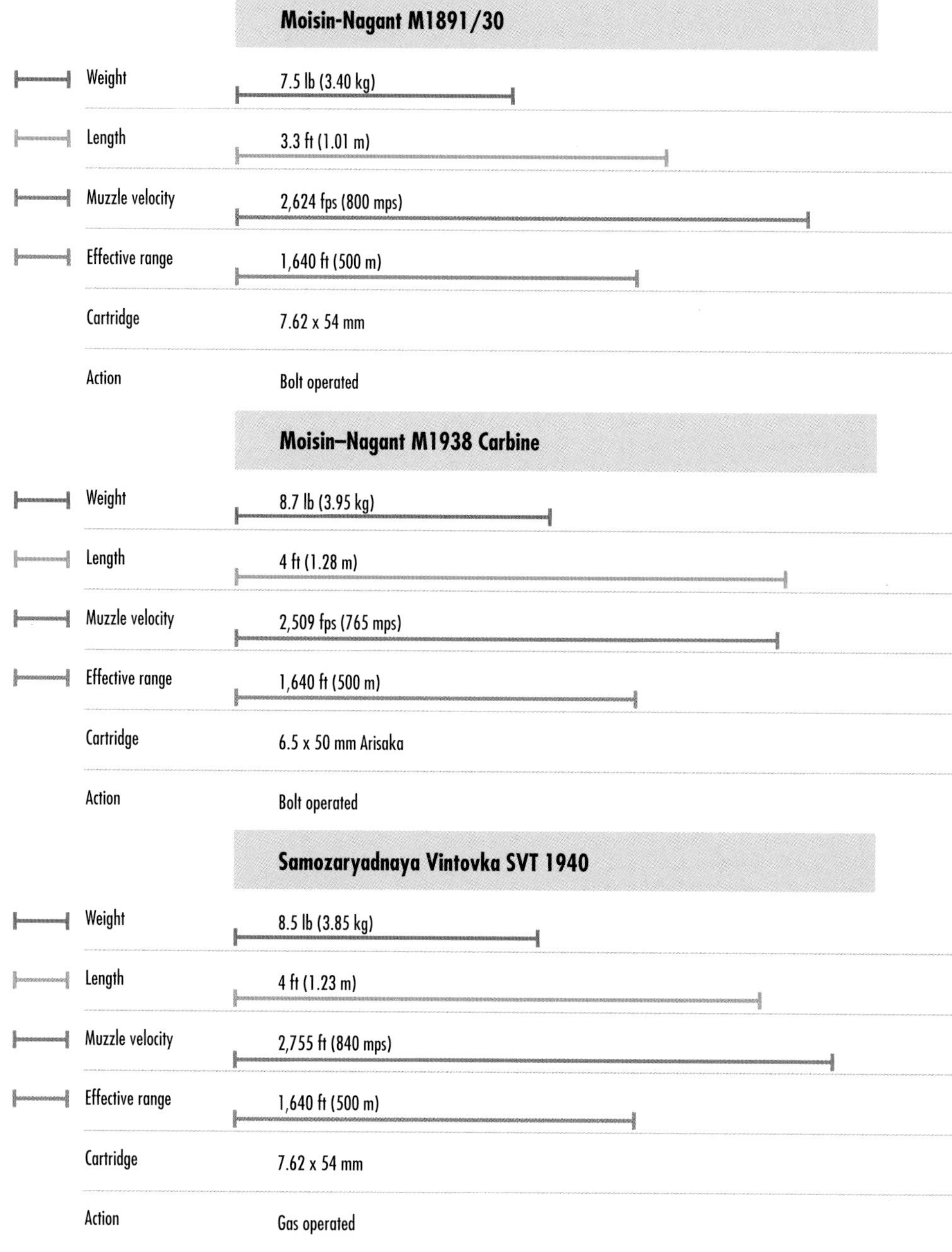

SOVIET UNION

Moisin-Nagant M1891/30	
Weight	7.5 lb (3.40 kg)
Length	3.3 ft (1.01 m)
Muzzle velocity	2,624 fps (800 mps)
Effective range	1,640 ft (500 m)
Cartridge	7.62 x 54 mm
Action	Bolt operated

Moisin–Nagant M1938 Carbine	
Weight	8.7 lb (3.95 kg)
Length	4 ft (1.28 m)
Muzzle velocity	2,509 fps (765 mps)
Effective range	1,640 ft (500 m)
Cartridge	6.5 x 50 mm Arisaka
Action	Bolt operated

Samozaryadnaya Vintovka SVT 1940	
Weight	8.5 lb (3.85 kg)
Length	4 ft (1.23 m)
Muzzle velocity	2,755 ft (840 mps)
Effective range	1,640 ft (500 m)
Cartridge	7.62 x 54 mm
Action	Gas operated

UK/COMMONWEALTH

No. III Short Magazine Lee Enfield

8.8 lb (4 kg)

3.6 ft (1.118 m)

2,440 fps (744 mps)

1,650 ft (503 m)

.303 Mk VII

Bolt operated

No. 4 Mk 1 Lee Enfield

9 lb (4.1 kg)

3.7 ft (1.129 m)

7,440 fps (744 mps)

1,650 ft (503 m)

.303 Mk VII

Bolt operated

No. 5 Mk 1 Rifle

15.6 lb (7.1 kg)

3.28 ft (1.00 m)

2,539 fps (774 mps)

1,791 ft (546 m)

.303 Mk VII

Bolt operated

US

M1903 Springfield

8.6 lb (3.9 kg)

3.6 ft (1.115 m)

2,798 fps (853 mps)

1,968 ft (600 m)

.30-06 Springfield

Bolt operated

M1 Garand

9.5–11.7 lb (4.31–5.3 kg)

3.6 ft (1.1 m)

2,798 fps (853 mps)

1,443 ft (440 m)

.30-06 Springfield

Gas operated, semiautomatic

M1 Carbine

5.3 lb (2.4 kg)

2.9 ft (0.9 m)

1,991 fps (607 mps)

1,318 ft (402 m)

.30-06 Springfield

Gas operated, semiautomatic

Hitler's Battleships

Hitler's fleet of battleships—seven *panzerschiffes* (armored ships) were originally limited to a displacement of 11,199 tons (10,160 tonnes) by the Treaty of Versailles, but soon developed into a number of formidable ships—with Winston Churchill considering them a greater threat to the merchant fleets than the U-boats.

The ships were originally conceived as the heart of the new German Navy following the scuttling of the Grand Fleet at Scapa Flow in 1919. The first to be launched, the *Deutschland*, was created at the shipyards in Kiel and was sent on its way by Paul von Hindenburg. The ship was launched as a means of protecting the "peaceful coexistence" of Germany with the rest of the world. This peaceful aim was soon turned on its head when a new chancellor, Adolf Hitler, came to power in 1933. With the *Deutschland* commissioned into the Kriegsmarine (as the German Navy was known, 1935–1945), its sister ships, the *Admiral Scheer* and the *Admiral Graf Spee* would follow, launched in 1933 and 1934 respectively. These three were restricted in size by the constraints of the Versailles treaty, but any restrictions would soon be thrown off by Hitler, who had his sights set on repudiating the treaty obligations in 1935. With Britain and France, the main naval powers, willing to renegotiate the terms of the treaty, Hitler seized upon the opportunity. From the first three "pocket battleships"—cruisers in size but armed with guns equivalent to any battleship—came the development of the ships that would become famous as commerce raiders, and that, as icons of Nazi Germany, would expend the Allied nations' efforts in tracking them down and destroying them: the monstrous

The Admiral Graf Spee was the first of Hitler's battleships to be sunk: it was scuttled on December 17th, 1939 following British attacks during the Battle of the River Plate.

Bismarck and *Tirpitz*. Though Germany had great plans for its capital ships, the Kriegsmarine entered the war with only four battleships in a fit state to take on the Allies. These were the *Deutschland*, *Admiral Graf Spee*, *Scharnhorst*, and *Gneisenau*. The *Admiral Scheer* was undergoing a refit, and the *Bismarck* and *Tirpitz* were still being fitted out as warships. The first to be lost was the *Graf Spee*, when it was trapped at the mouth of the River Plate by the British. Unable to emerge from neutral waters, it would be scuttled in December 1939. Two other pocket battleships would receive similar fates, in 1945. But it would be the might of the *Bismarck* and the mighty *Tirpitz* that would expend the efforts of most of the Royal Navy. The *Bismarck* was hunted down in 1941 after the destruction of HMS *Hood*, while the *Tirpitz* survived until 1944, when it sank after being targeted by RAF Lancaster bombers.

The Deutschland *was the first of Hitler's capital ships to be commissioned, and the last to be sunk, scuttled on May 4th, 1945.*

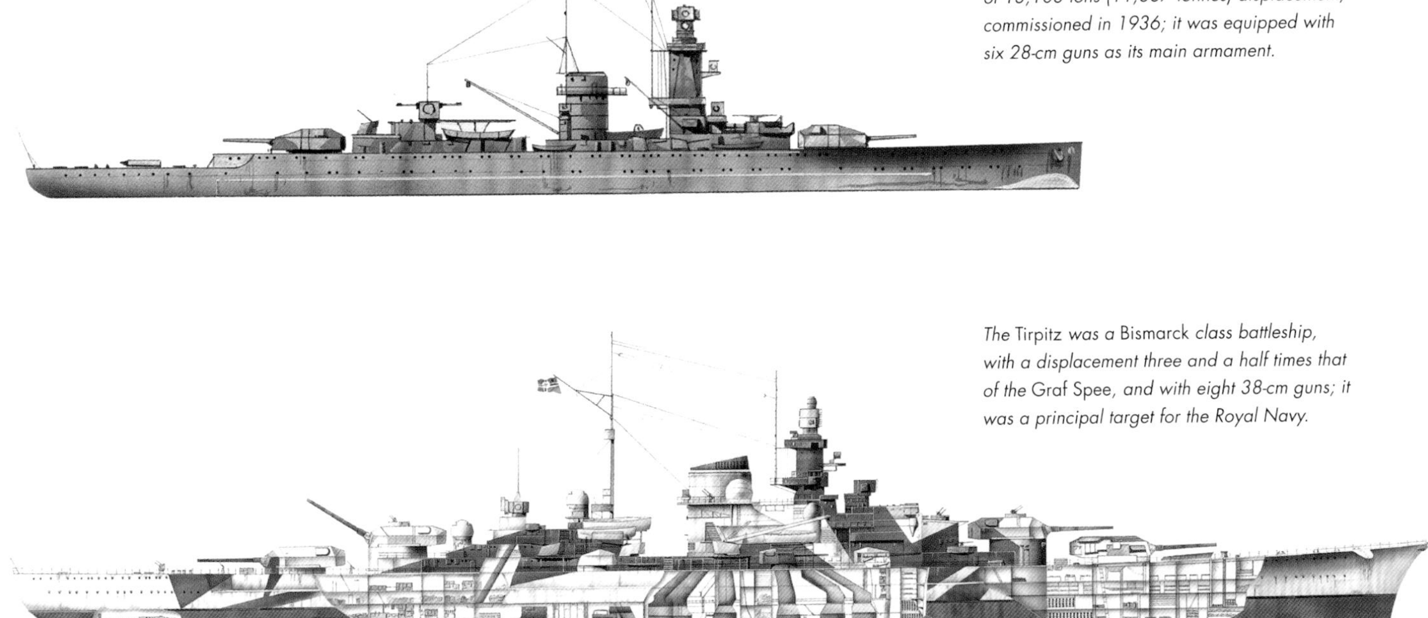

The Graf Spee *was a* Deutschland *class ship of 13,103 tons (11,887 tonnes) displacement, commissioned in 1936; it was equipped with six 28-cm guns as its main armament.*

The Tirpitz *was a* Bismarck *class battleship, with a displacement three and a half times that of the* Graf Spee*, and with eight 38-cm guns; it was a principal target for the Royal Navy.*

Specifications of Hitler's Battleships

	DEUTSCHLAND	ADMIRAL SCHEER	ADMIRAL GRAF SPEE
Commissioned	May 19th, 1933	November 12th, 1934	January 6th, 1936
Standard displacement	13,103 tons (11,887 tonnes)	13,103 tons (11,887 tonnes)	13,551 tons (12,294 tonnes)
Length	617 ft (188 m)	617 ft (188 m)	617 ft (188 m)
Beam (breadth)	68 ft (20.8 m)	68 ft (20.8 m)	71 ft (21.7 m)
Draught (standard load)	19 ft (5.8 m)	19 ft (5.8 m)	19 ft (5.8 m)
Main armament	6 x 28 cm guns	6 x 28 cm guns	6 x 28 cm guns
Secondary armament	8 x 15 cm guns	8 x 15 cm guns	8 x 15 cm guns
A-A armament	6 x 10.5 cm guns	6 x 10.5 cm guns	6 x 10.5 cm guns
Other guns	8 x 37 mm, 10 x 20 mm	6 x 88 mm	6 x 88 mm
Torpedo tubes	8	8	8
Belt armor	82.6 mm	101.6 mm	101.6 mm
Deck armor	38.1 mm	38.1 mm	38.1 mm
Conning tower	139.7 mm	139.7 mm	139.7 mm
Turret armor (face)	139.7 mm	139.7 mm	139.7 mm
Turret armor (side)	101.6 mm	76.2 mm	76.2 mm
Aircraft capacity	2	2	2
Complement	1,150	1,124	1,124
Engines (shaft horsepower)	48,390 SHP	52,050 SHP	54,000 SHP
Top speed (knots)	28	28.3	28.5
Fate	Scuttled (after bomb damage) May 4th, 1945	Capsized (after bombing) April 9th, 1945	Scuttled (Battle of River Plate) December 17th, 1939

GNEISENAU	SCHARNHORST	BISMARCK	TIRPITZ
May 21st, 1938	January 7th, 1939	August 29th, 1940	January 25th, 1941
35,615 tons (32,310 tonnes)	35,615 tons (32,310 tonnes)	46,703 tons (42,369 tonnes)	48,047 tons (43,588 tonnes)
771 ft (235 m)	771 ft (235 m)	823 ft (251 m)	823 ft (251 m)
100 ft (30.5 m)	100 ft (30.5 m)	118 ft (36.0 m)	118 ft (36.0 m)
27 ft (8.2 m)	27 ft (8.2 m)	28 ft (8.7 m)	9 ft (9.0 m)
9 x 28 cm guns	9 x 28 cm guns	8 x 38 cm guns	8 x 38 cm guns
12 x 15 cm guns	12 x 15 cm guns	12 x 15 cm guns	12 x 15 cm guns
14 x 10.5 cm guns	14 x 10.5 cm guns	16 x 10.5 cm guns	16 x 10.5 cm guns
16 x 37 mm, 14 x 20 mm	18 x 20 mm	36 x 20 mm	70 x 20 mm
6	6	0	8
304.8 mm	304.8 mm	323.9 mm	323.9 mm
108 mm	108 mm	108 mm	108 mm
355.6 mm	355.6 mm	355.6 mm	355.6 mm
362 mm	362 mm	355.6 mm	355.6 mm
247.7 mm	247.7 mm	317.5 mm	317.5 mm
4	4	6	6
1,754	1,754	2,065	2,430
160,000 SHP	160,000 SHP	138,000 SHP	138,000 SHP
32	32	30.8	29
Scuttled (as block-ship, Gotenhafen) March 12th, 1945	Sunk in action December 26th, 1943	Sunk in action May 27th, 1941	Sunk (after bombing) November 12th, 1944

Panzers

With the doctrine of combined arms warfare, the tank, Panzerkampfwagen Pz kpwf or simply Panzer, was an integral part of German military success early in the war. Though facing a significant force of excellent tanks during the Battle of France in 1940, the tactics employed by the Germans—blitzkrieg—was to cement belief in the centrality of the armored vehicle in warfare. There were significant numbers of the lighter Panzer I and Panzer II tanks in the early campaigns. However, production of what became some of the most significant tank designs, out-performing those of the Allies in both armor and weaponry, ramped up in 1941, in preparation for Barbarossa, the invasion of the Soviet Union. It was here, though, that the German Panzer III met the Soviet T-34, and was outclassed.

German innovation in tank design meant that new machines like the Tiger and Panther were produced mid-war, and were capable of taking on and beating Allied armor in the field. Tank production hit new heights in 1943–1944, producing these formidable machines equipped with 75 or 88 mm guns, and with vastly increased armor. Though not invulnerable, these tanks were immune to many of the Allied anti-tank weapons, and could pack a significant punch. The Panzer IV was joined by the super tanks, the Tiger I, Tiger II, and Panther; though equipped with stronger armor, and impressive weaponry, they were thirsty—and this at a time when the Allies were attacking the Nazi fuel supplies. The value of these giants was severely limited.

German Tank Production

German tank production, 1938–1945: number of tanks produced in a given year. Production of heavier armored and armed tanks took off in 1943.

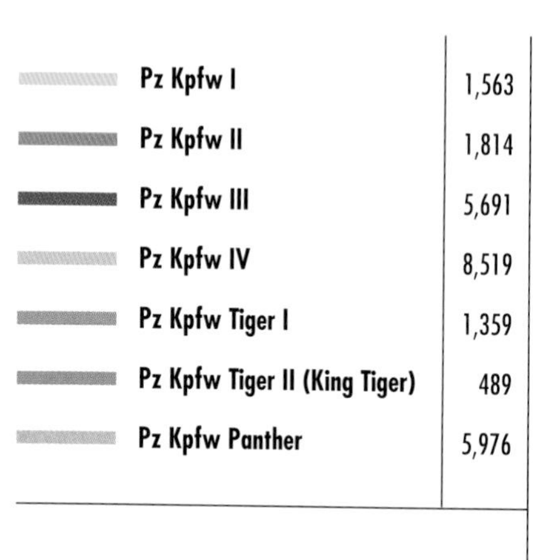

	Total
Pz Kpfw I	1,563
Pz Kpfw II	1,814
Pz Kpfw III	5,691
Pz Kpfw IV	8,519
Pz Kpfw Tiger I	1,359
Pz Kpfw Tiger II (King Tiger)	489
Pz Kpfw Panther	5,976
Total	25,411

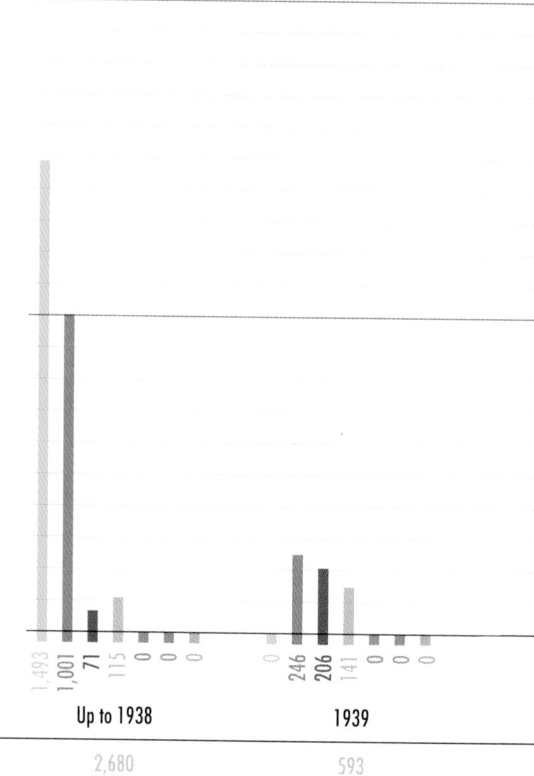

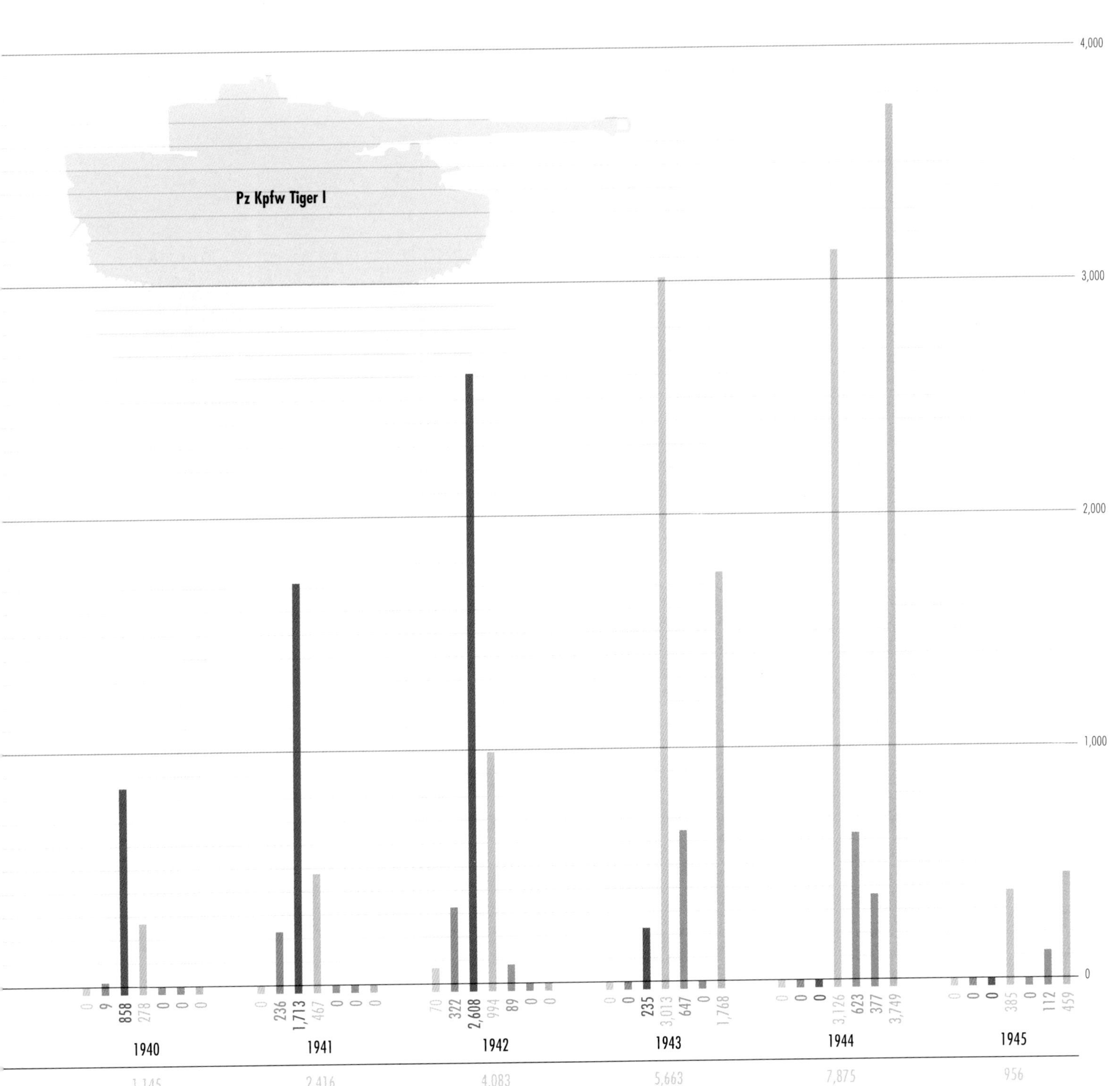

4,000
3,000
2,000
1,000
0
Pz Kpfw Tiger I
0 9 858 278 0 0 0
1940
1,145
0 236 1,713 467 0 0 0
1941
2,416
70 322 2,608 994 89 0 0
1942
4,083
0 0 235 3,013 647 0 1,768
1943
5,663
0 0 0 3,126 623 377 3,749
1944
7,875
0 0 0 385 0 112 459
1945
956

Specifications of the Main German Battle Tanks in World War II

	LENGTH	WEIGHT	ARMAMENT
Pz Kpfw I	13 ft (4.02 m)	5.95 tons (5.4 tonnes)	2 x 7.92 MG13 machine guns
Pz Kpfw II	16 ft (4.81 m)	9.8 tons (8.9 tonnes)	20 mm KwK 30, or 20 mm
Pz Kpfw III	21 ft (6.41 m)	25.35 tons (23.0 tonnes)	37 mm KwK 36, 50 mm KwK
Pz Kpfw IV	23 ft (7.02 m) to gun muzzle 19 ft (5.92 m)	27.5 tons (25 tonnes)	75 mm KwK 40
Pz Kpfw Tiger I	20 ft (6.32 m)	62.7 tons (56.9 tonnes)	88 mm KwK 36
Pz Kpfw Tiger II (King Tiger)	34 ft (10.29 m) to gun muzzle 21 ft (6.4 m)	75.5–76.9 tons (68.5–69.8 tonnes)	2 x 7.92 mm MG34
Pz Kpfw Panther	28 ft (8.66 m) to gun muzzle 22 ft (6.86 m)	49.4 tons (44.8 tonnes)	88 mm KwK 43

SECONDARY ARMAMENT	TOP SPEED	ARMOR (actual thickness)
none	31 mph (50 km/h)	1/4–1/2 in (7–13 mm)
1 x 7.92 mm MG34	25 mph (40 km/h)	3/8 in–1 3/8 in (10–35 mm)
2 x 7.92 MG34	25 mph (40 km/h)	1/4–2 3/4 in (5–70 mm)
2 x 7.92 MG 34	26 mph (42 km/h)	1/2–3 1/8 in (14.5–80 mm)
2 x 7.92 mm MG34 machine guns	24 mph (38 km/h)	1–4 3/4 in (25–120 mm)
2 x 7.92 mm MG34 machine guns	26 mph (41.5 km/h)	1–7 in (25–180 mm)
2 x 7.92 mm MG34 machine guns	34 mph (55 km/h)	5/8–4 3/4 in (15–120 mm)

Artillery

Adequate artillery is essential in modern warfare; World War II was no different.

The Wehrmacht used two main howitzers and three flat trajectory field guns, in addition to the super-heavy railway gun Schwerer Gustav, and the self-propelled howitzer Karl-Gerät.

The 15-cm sIG 33 has a claim to the heaviest infantry support gun, intended for the demolition of defensive positions, and clearing barbed wire and minefields. It balanced the much lighter leichtes Infanteriegeschütz infantry support weapon. There was also the larger 15-cm Kanone.

The US Army deployed a wider range of howitzers. The 75 mm Pack Howitzer was destined for difficult terrain, and could be broken down for use with pack animals, or in airborne deployments. The M-114 155 mm howitzer was a towed artillery piece that saw wide deployment—as did its lighter version, the M101A1, the standard light howitzer used by US forces in all theaters. The heaviest was the 240 mm M1 (Black Dragon), used in the reduction of field fortifications.

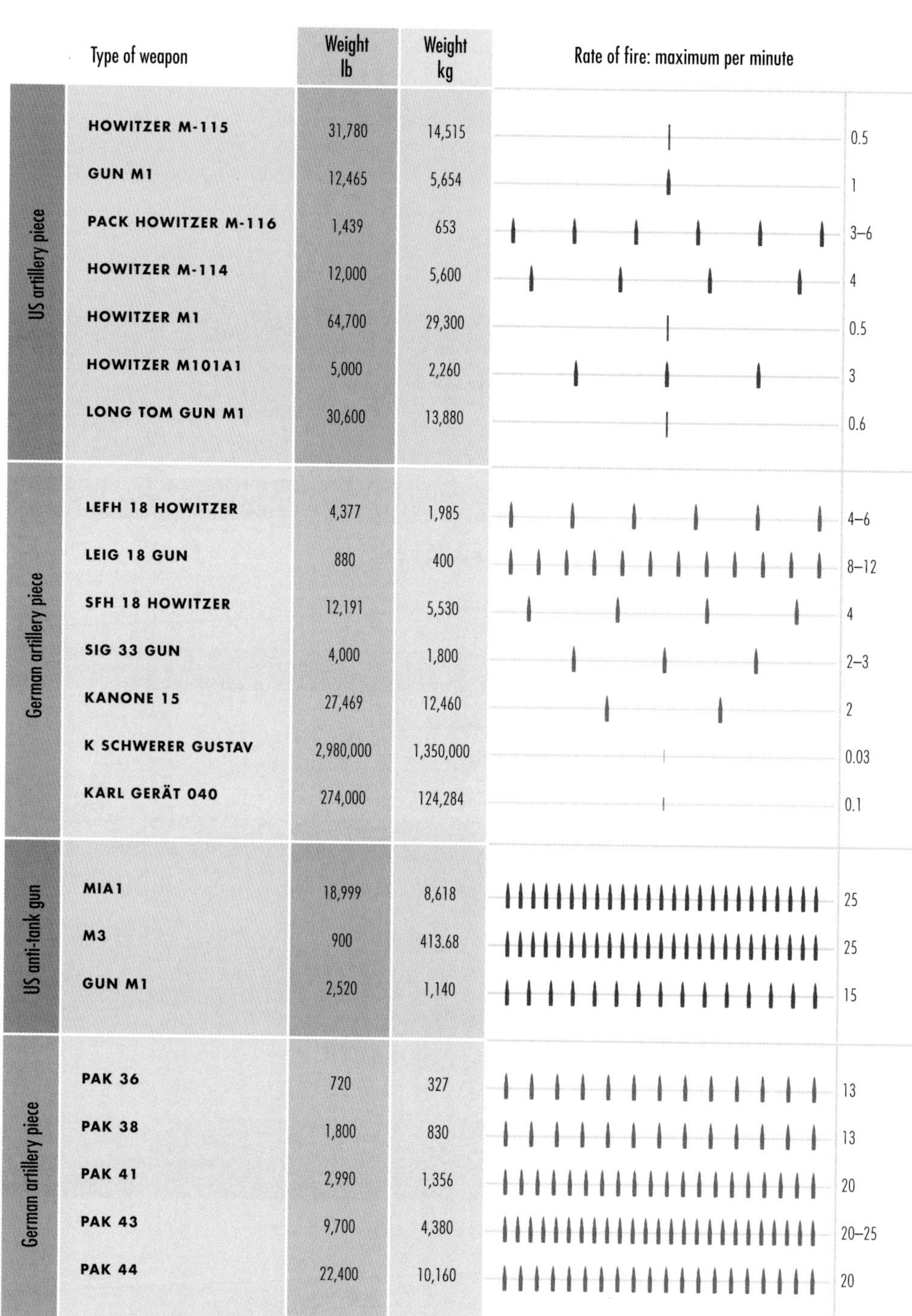

Category	Type of weapon	Weight lb	Weight kg	Rate of fire: maximum per minute
US artillery piece	HOWITZER M-115	31,780	14,515	0.5
US artillery piece	GUN M1	12,465	5,654	1
US artillery piece	PACK HOWITZER M-116	1,439	653	3–6
US artillery piece	HOWITZER M-114	12,000	5,600	4
US artillery piece	HOWITZER M1	64,700	29,300	0.5
US artillery piece	HOWITZER M101A1	5,000	2,260	3
US artillery piece	LONG TOM GUN M1	30,600	13,880	0.6
German artillery piece	LEFH 18 HOWITZER	4,377	1,985	4–6
German artillery piece	LEIG 18 GUN	880	400	8–12
German artillery piece	SFH 18 HOWITZER	12,191	5,530	4
German artillery piece	SIG 33 GUN	4,000	1,800	2–3
German artillery piece	KANONE 15	27,469	12,460	2
German artillery piece	K SCHWERER GUSTAV	2,980,000	1,350,000	0.03
German artillery piece	KARL GERÄT 040	274,000	124,284	0.1
US anti-tank gun	MIA1	18,999	8,618	25
US anti-tank gun	M3	900	413.68	25
US anti-tank gun	GUN M1	2,520	1,140	15
German artillery piece	PAK 36	720	327	13
German artillery piece	PAK 38	1,800	830	13
German artillery piece	PAK 41	2,990	1,356	20
German artillery piece	PAK 43	9,700	4,380	20–25
German artillery piece	PAK 44	22,400	10,160	20

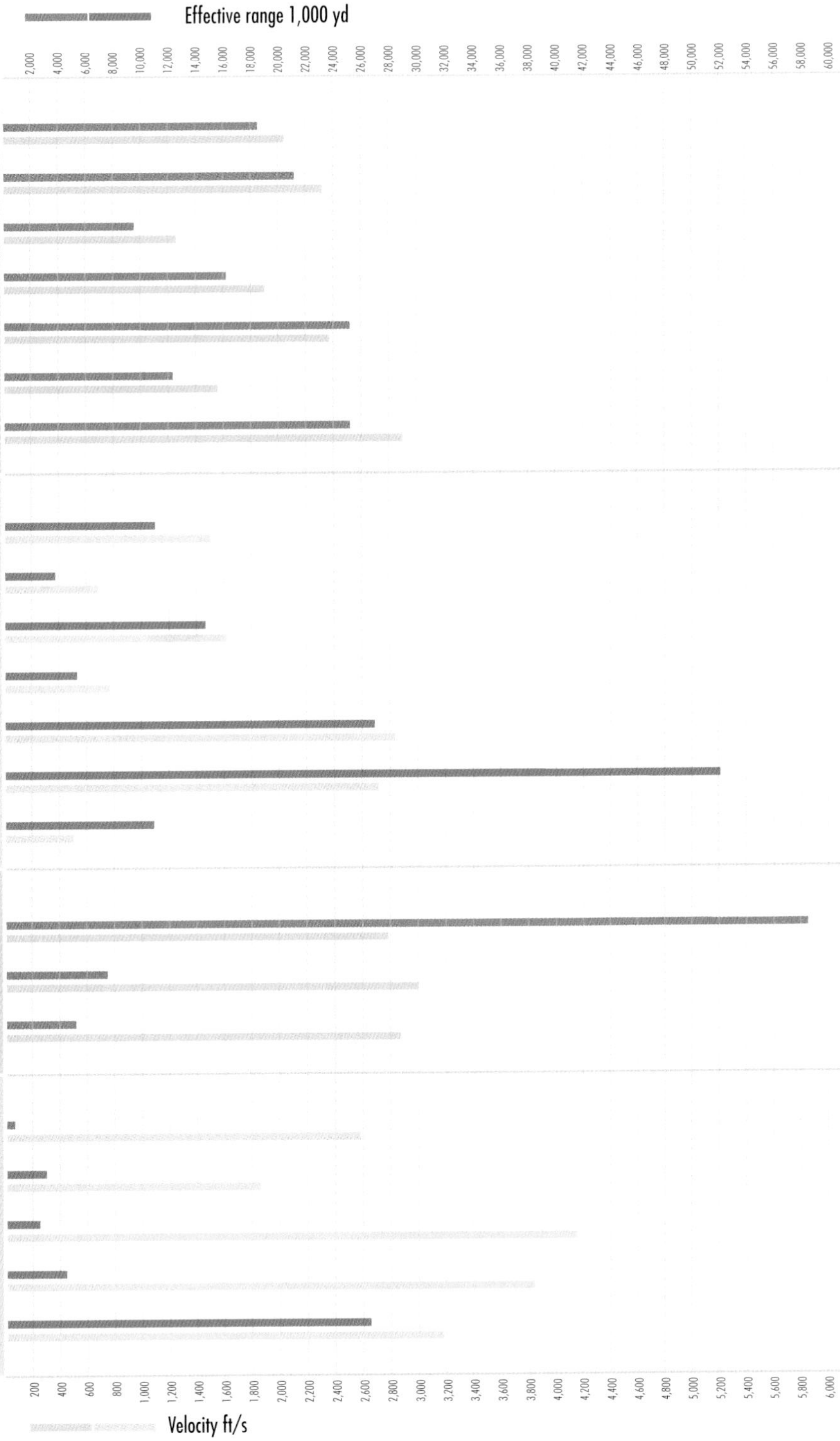

Effective range 1,000 yd

Velocity ft/s

Caliber inch	Caliber mm	Range ft/s	Range m/s	Velocity ft/s	Velocity m/s
8.0	203	18,373	16,800	1,926	587
4.5	114	21,125	19,317	2,274	693
2.95	75	9,610	8790	1,250	381
6.1	155	16,000	14,600	1,847	563
9.4	240	25,168	23,100	2,300	701
4.1	105	12,320	12,700	1,550	472
6.1	155	25,344	23,200	2,800	853
4.13	105	11,675	10,675	1,542	470
2.95	75	3,880	3,550	690	210
5.87	149.1	14,490	13,250	1,620	495
5.87	149.1	5,100	4,700	790	240
5.87	149.1	26,793	24,500	2,838	865
31	800	52,000	48,000	2,700	820
24	600	10,912	9,978	710	220
3.5	90	58,474	17,823	2,700	823
1.45	37	7,550	6,900	2,900	884
2.2	57	5,000	4,600	2,799	853
1.45	37	328	300	2,500	762
1.97	50	3,000	2,743	1,804	550
2.95	75	2,185	2,000	4,035	1,230
3.5	88	4,400	4,000	3,70	1,130
5.0	128	26,70	24,410	3,070	935

Special Operations Executive

The Special Operations Executive (SOE) was set up in 1940 as Winston Churchill's private army, intended to "set Europe ablaze" through a series of clandestine operations in occupied countries. The SOE was a secret, autonomous organization, using skilled and courageous operatives. It had a strength of around 13,000—some 3,200 of whom were women—and most of whom could merge into the background of their chosen country. Those operatives with the benefit of dual nationality, or people who had escaped from an occupied country, were highly prized as operatives.

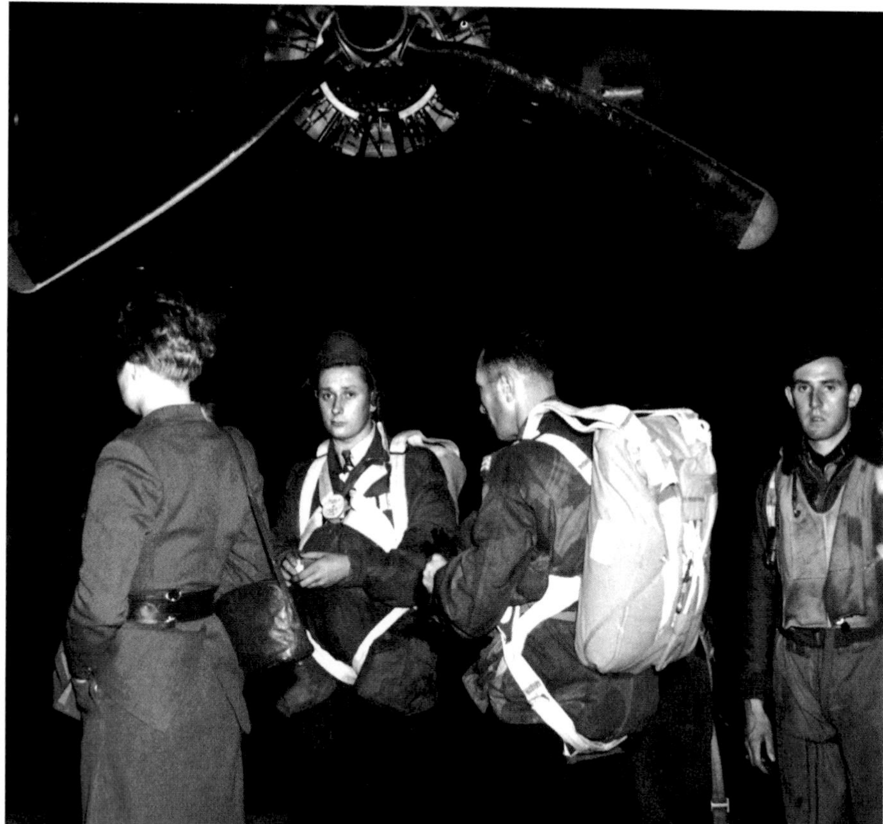

Officially, the SOE was prepared to turn a blind eye on any former criminal activity carried out by its operatives, in order to pursue its private war against the Nazis. SOE agents were trained in a variety of locations within Britain, and were to deploy a range of tools and weapons that had been especially designed for them; suppressed pistols, sten guns, plastic explosives, and a host of other innovative designs created in what became known as "Churchill's toyshop."

SOE operatives getting ready for a drop into enemy territory in 1944.

BELGIUM

57 (1942–1944)
35 (1941–1945)
54 (1941–1945)

ITALY

19 (1944–1945)
20 (1944–1945)
8 (1944–1945)

ALBANIA

18 (date uncertain)

Known SOE Operations (281 Missions)

Known SOE operations across Europe, by type. Many operations required contact with local resistance teams (communications), while sabotage and working with local resistance or partisans was significant. It is likely that many more operations actually took place across occupied Europe.

40	**Partisan support**
102	**Communications**
71	**Sabotage**
68	**Resistance support**

AUSTRIA

5 (1943–1945)
7 (1945)
5 (1943–1945)

FRANCE

4 (1943–1944)
8 (1941–1944)
3 (1943–1945)

NETHERLANDS

6 (1944–1945)
1 (1942)
4 (1944)

GERMANY

2 (1944–1945)
7 (1943–1945)
1 (1944)

SPAIN

7 (1941–1945)
2 (1941–1943)

BALKANS

3 (1942–1943)
1 (1942)

PORTUGAL

1 (1941)

NORTH AFRICA

1 (1941)

WEST AFRICA

1 (1942)

GREECE

1 (1942)

Operations were complex and clandestine: they included active engagement in sabotage or the provision of training to resistance agents in sabotage acts; the provision of expertise and/or weaponry to deliver sabotage; the support and organization of partisan activities, or the encouragement of resistant groups. It could also involve the creation of communication pathways and links, providing intelligence information sources and creating opportunities for the movement of personnel, escaped prisoners of war and so on.

The activities were extremely dangerous and operatives were prone to betrayal. Operatives were often killed, taken captive and despatched, or tortured or left to die in concentration camps.

SOE operatives training in England, 1944: climbing walls.

Hobart's Funnies

After the Dieppe Raid in 1942, when armored vehicles were held up and destroyed by mines, concrete bunkers, and beach walls, a new breed of modified tanks that could tackle these obstacles was developed under the guidance of Major General Percival Hobart. Operated by the 79th Armored Division, they were mostly based on the British Churchill and the American Sherman. The deployment of these "Hobart's funnies" by British and Canadian forces on D-Day greatly enhanced their success. US General Omar Bradley chose not to use them (other than the DD Sherman) on Omaha Beach; if he had, things might have turned out differently.

CHURCHILL TANKS:

BASIC SPECIFICATION, STANDARD CONFIGURATION

Crew:

5

Battle weight:

87,360 lb (39,625 kg) (Marks III–VI);

89,600 lb (40,641 kg) (Marks VII–VIII)

Length:

24 ft 5 in (7.4 m)

Width:

9 ft (2.74 m)

Height:

10 ft 8 in (3.25 m) (Marks I–VI);

11 ft 4 in (3.45 m) (Marks VII–VIII)

Armor:

Maximum: 102 mm (Marks I–VI),

152 mm (Marks VII–VIII)

Minimum: 16 mm (Marks I–VI),

25 mm (Marks VII–VIII)

Maximum speed:

15.5 mph (25 km/h) (Marks I–VI);

12.5 mph (20 km/h) (Marks VII–VIII);

cross-country, 8 mph (13 km/h) (all marks)

Trench crossing capability:

10 ft (3 m)

Vertical obstacle crossing capability:

2 ft 6 in (0.76 m)

Crocodile: Flamethrower tank based on Mark VII tank with armored trailer containing 400 gallons (1,800 liters) of fuel, with a flamethrower range of 357 ft (109 m). Purpose: bunker and trench clearance. Number produced: 800.

AVRE (Assault Vehicle, Royal Engineers): Based on Churchill Marks III or IV. Main armament, 29-cm caliber petard mortar capable of firing a 40 lb (18 kg) HE projectile some 450 ft (137 m). This "flying dustbin" was effective against concrete fortifications. Number produced: 180 for D-Day, 574 for European campaign. AVRE's were fitted with additional engineering features:

Bobbin: a reel of 3 ft (1 m) wide steel-reinforced canvas deployed on soft ground.

Fascine: a bundle of brushwood that could be used to fill trenches.

SBG (Small Box Girder): assault bridge that could be deployed to cross 30 ft (9 m) gaps, and that could be deployed in 30 seconds.

CIRD (Canadian Indestructible Roller Device): a roller for destroying mines.

Bullshorn plough: a front-fitted plough to remove mines.

Double onion: demolition charges that could be placed over walls for safe detonation.

The Crocodile was a flamethrower tank based on the British Churchill. The Churchill made a good platform for many "funnies."

ARV (Armored Recovery Vehicle): Based on Churchill Mark III or IV. Turret removed and fitted with jibs, an earth spade at rear and two-speed winch capable of pulling 27.5 tons (25 tonnes). Large numbers produced.

ARK (Armored Ramp Carrier): Based on the Churchill Mark II or IV, with turret removed and timber tracks laid across the top, linked to ramps. Used for laying ramps across fortifications or sea walls. At least 50 produced.

Bridgelayer: Based on Churchill III or IV, this version was turret-less, and could pivot a 30 ft (9 m), 5.3-ton (4.8-tonne) bridge into position that could support vehicles of up to 67 tons (61 tonnes). Developed in small numbers.

SHERMAN TANKS:

BASIC SPECIFICATION, STANDARD CONFIGURATION

Crew:

5

Battle weight:

66,500 lb (30,163 kg) (M4A1);

69,000 lb (31,297 kg) (M4A2);

68,500 lb (31,071 kg) (M4A3)

Length:

19 ft 4 in (5.8 m)

Width:

8 ft 7 in (2.6 m)

Height:

9 ft (2.7 m)

Armor:

Maximum: 75 mm

Minimum: 12 mm

Maximum speed: 24–29 mph (39–47 km/h); cross-country, 15–24 mph (24–39 km/h)

Trench crossing capability:

7 ft 5 in (2.26 m)

Vertical obstacle crossing capability:

2 ft (0.6 m)

DD (Duplex Drive): Waterproofed and fitted with a collapsible canvas screen (lifted by rubber tubing and compressed air), the Sherman was transformed into an amphibious vehicle, driven at a speed of 4 knots by two small propellers. Produced in large numbers. The first British tanks to land on D-Day.

BARV (Beach Armored Recovery Vehicle): M4A2 Sherman with turret removed, fitted with winch, jibs, and other lifting equipment, together with bilge pump and air-intake trunking for wading. Number produced: 52.

Crab: Sherman fitted with rotating drum with 43 weighted flailing chains intended to explode and clear mines, and with arms fitted with wire cutters to clear barbed wire.

The Crab was a "funny" that cleared mines using flail chains attached to a rotating drum. It was essential to the operations in Normandy.

Panzerfaust

The Panzerfaust (originally called the Faustpatrone) was one of the most effective weapons of World War II. It was easy to produce and use, and was disposable. It was to be one of the most important weapons in Hitler's declining military forces at the end of the war, capable of being used with minimal training. Handled with nerve, these weapons proved devastating against Allied tanks in the latter stages of the war, and were to be influential in the development of hand-held anti-tank devices in the post-war world.

The weapon had a simple smooth-bore launcher, open at both ends, with the result that there is a significant back-blast from the tube—up to 33 ft (10 m), but without a recoil. The propellant was black powder. The warhead, containing TNT and tri-hexogen explosives, was stabilized in the air by folding fins. There were only rudimentary sights, and the launcher was discarded—single shot, one use. With armor penetration set at between 150 and 200 mm, no Allied tank was safe from it. It is estimated that 70% of late-war Soviet tank losses were to Panzerfaust weapons.

The Panzerfaust was designed by Dr Heinrich Langweiler, and the first of its type, the small 30 mm version, entered service on the Eastern Front in November 1943. Given a larger warhead it had more dramatic results, and successive improvements increased both the range and the explosive power of the warheads, with the Panzerfaust 100 being the most significant, entering service almost exactly a year later, in 1944. These weapons would see service in the declining fortunes of Nazi Germany. There were plans to increase the size of the weapon still further, but the end of the war hastened the end of production. Millions were produced. Nevertheless, the weapon would be copied by the Russians after the war.

Panzerfaust Details

The Panzerfaust was an effective weapon, easy to use, relatively light and just over 3 ft (1 m) long. Successive versions were capable of penetrating increasingly heavy tank armor.

	Weight	Max effective range	Caliber Warhead/barrel
Panzerfaust 30 m Klein	7 lb (3.25 kg)	98 ft (30 m)	101 mm / 33 mm
Panzerfaust 30 m	12 lb (5.35 kg)	98 ft (30 m)	149 mm / 33 mm
Panzerfaust 60 m	14 lb (6.25 kg)	196 ft (60 m)	149 mm / 50 mm
Panzerfaust 100 m	17 lb (8 kg)	328 ft (100 m)	149 mm/50 mm

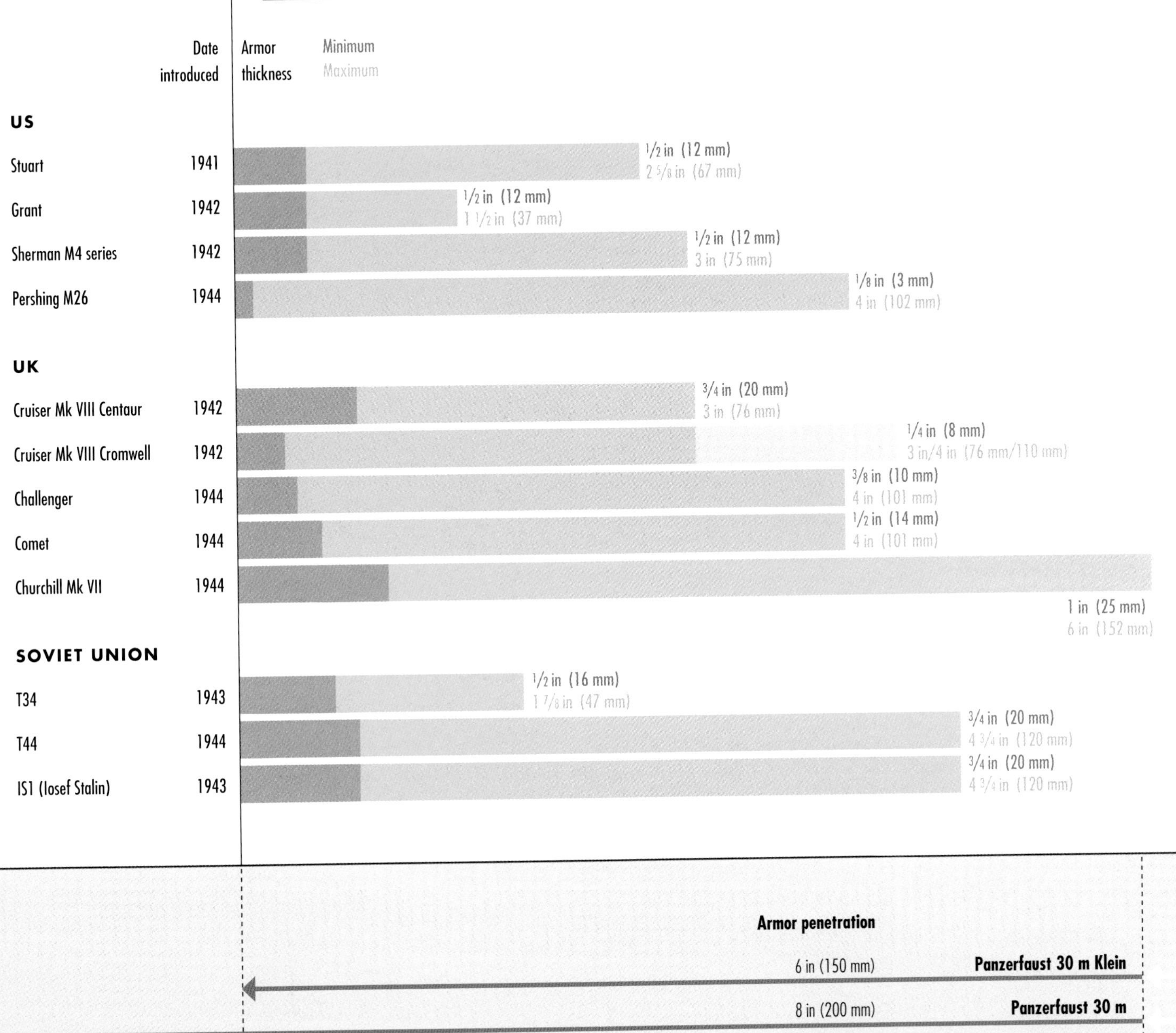
Allied Tank Armor (Actual Thicknesses)
Date introduced
Armor thickness
Minimum
Maximum
US
Stuart 1941 1/2 in (12 mm) 2 5/8 in (67 mm)
Grant 1942 1/2 in (12 mm) 1 1/2 in (37 mm)
Sherman M4 series 1942 1/2 in (12 mm) 3 in (75 mm)
Pershing M26 1944 1/8 in (3 mm) 4 in (102 mm)
UK
Cruiser Mk VIII Centaur 1942 3/4 in (20 mm) 3 in (76 mm)
Cruiser Mk VIII Cromwell 1942 1/4 in (8 mm) 3 in/4 in (76 mm/110 mm)
Challenger 1944 3/8 in (10 mm) 4 in (101 mm)
Comet 1944 1/2 in (14 mm) 4 in (101 mm)
Churchill Mk VII 1944 1 in (25 mm) 6 in (152 mm)
SOVIET UNION
T34 1943 1/2 in (16 mm) 1 7/8 in (47 mm)
T44 1944 3/4 in (20 mm) 4 3/4 in (120 mm)
IS1 (Iosef Stalin) 1943 3/4 in (20 mm) 4 3/4 in (120 mm)
Armor penetration
6 in (150 mm) Panzerfaust 30 m Klein
8 in (200 mm) Panzerfaust 30 m
8 in (200 mm) Panzerfaust 60 m
8 3/4 in (220 mm) Panzerfaust 100 m

Anti-tank Guns

With the creation of the doctrine of rapid armored advances into enemy territory, the Germans ensured that they were able to sweep the field of their ill-equipped enemies. Though there is considerable debate over the use of the term blitzkrieg, or lightning war, the doctrine was clear; the use of all arms on the battlefield, with tanks at the spearhead, followed by motorized infantry, artillery, and aerial attack. It was through this approach that the Allies suffered their first, decisive defeats on the battlefield.

If tanks were to be the spearhead of blitzkrieg, then the only defence against them were aerial superiority and anti-tank weaponry. For their part, tanks had to be sufficiently capable of taking on their enemies with stronger armor and more powerful guns. In 1939–1940, the German tanks were relatively lightly armored and under-gunned; but though many French tanks were heavily armored, the Germans were able to take the front by force of arms and drive. Allied anti-tank guns at this stage were poor and incapable; the use of anti-tank rifles, like the 14 mm Boys, was widespread, even though its 14 mm round was only capable of penetrating 23 mm of armor at short range (Panzer II and III tanks had a maximum of 14 mm, rising to 30 mm). More powerful guns were needed, and anti-tank artillery became a more significant component of the battlefield.

This defence was tested to its fullest extent on the rolling steppes of the Eastern Front. Here, massed armor on both sides was used to great effect, and it was here that the greatest tank battle in history, at Kursk in 1943, was played out. Significant anti-tank weaponry was required to take on the might of the Soviet T-34 tank, perhaps the greatest produced during the war, as well as the Tigers and Panthers of the Wehrmacht. For their part, the Germans deployed the 88 mm Flak gun—a powerful anti-aircraft weapon—in an anti-tank role, and this was to be a devastating weapon in the east, and particularly in the west when used against the more lightly armored British and American tanks. The 88 was rightly feared. On the Ostfront, the Soviets were able to mass large numbers of their 57 mm anti-tank gun against the Germans. At Kursk, the depth of the Soviets' defences, and their numerical superiority of effective anti-tank weapons, meant that the Nazi drive to break into the Kursk Salient failed, and Hitler's offensive drive in the east was effectively over.

German troops bringing up a 37 mm anti-tank gun during the invasion of Belgium in 1940.

GERMANY Maximum thickness of armor (mm) penetrated at (m) range

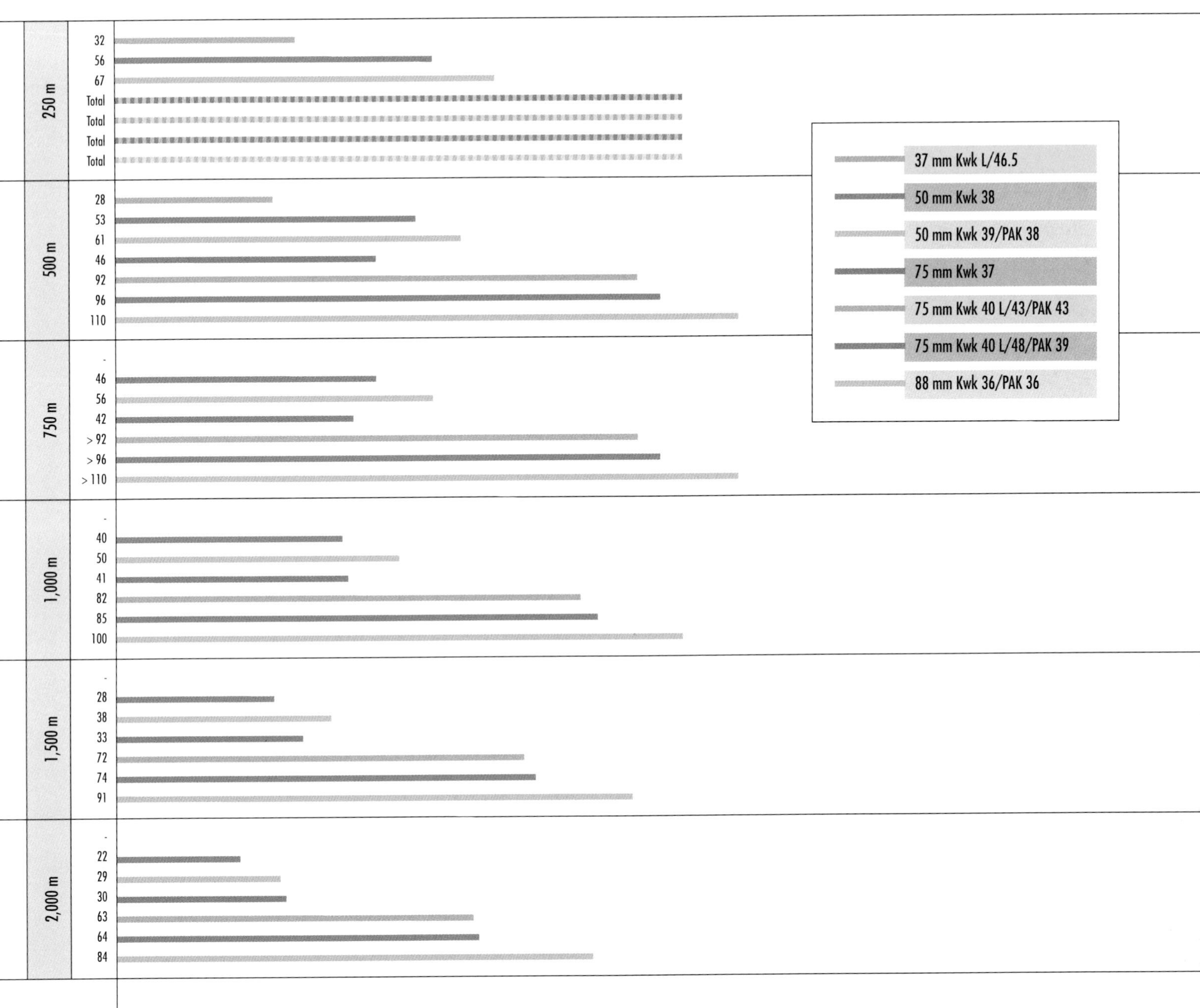

Maximum armor penetration of German anti-tank guns at successive ranges. At the close range (250 m) armor penetration of Allied tanks was total for 75 mm guns and above.

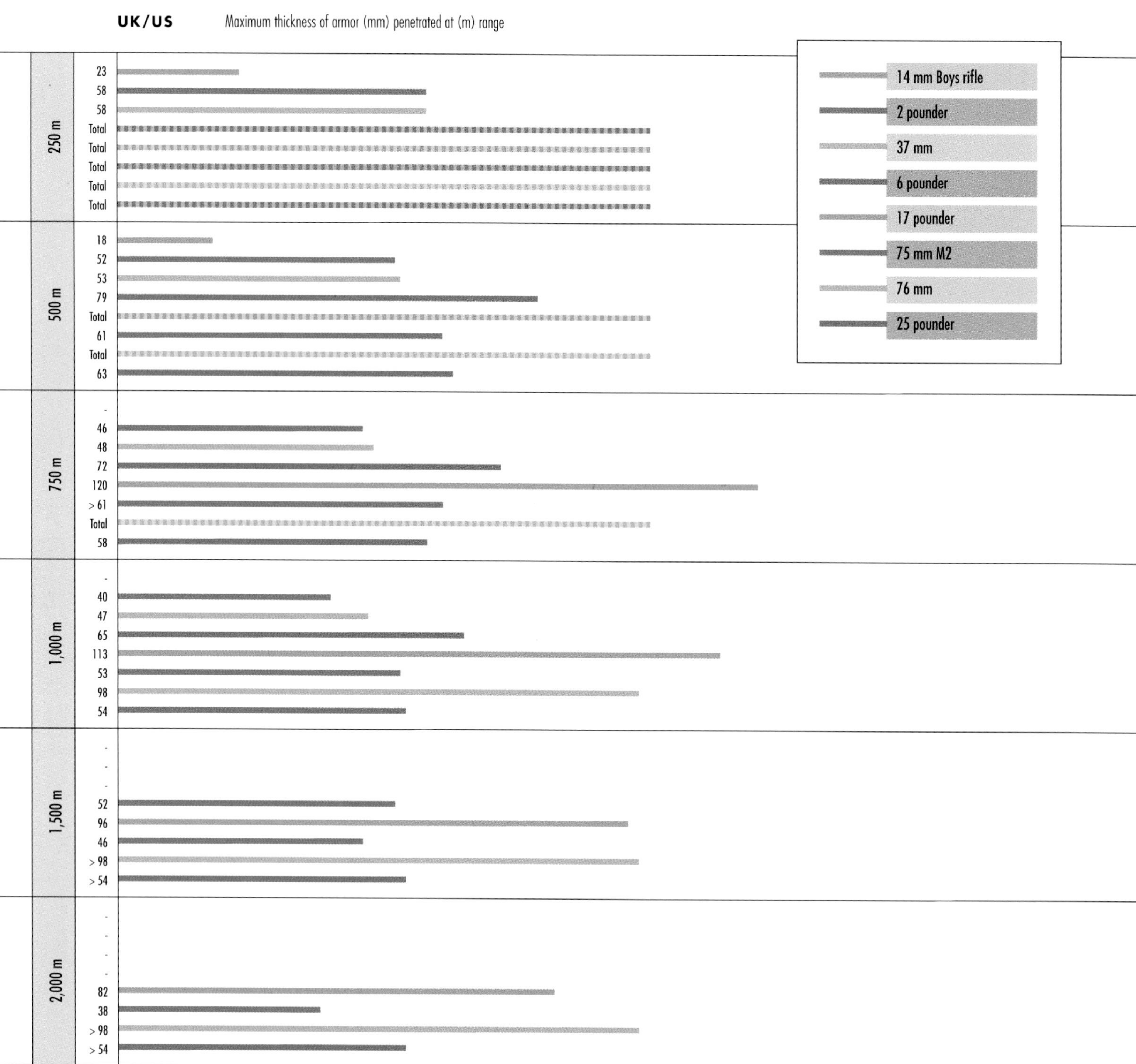
UK/US
Maximum thickness of armor (mm) penetrated at (m) range
14 mm Boys rifle
2 pounder
37 mm
6 pounder
17 pounder
75 mm M2
76 mm
25 pounder
250 m
23
58
58
Total
Total
Total
Total
Total
500 m
18
52
53
79
Total
61
Total
63
750 m
-
46
48
72
120
> 61
Total
58
1,000 m
-
40
47
65
113
53
98
54
1,500 m
-
-
-
52
96
46
> 98
> 54
2,000 m
-
-
-
-
82
38
> 98
> 54

USSR Maximum thickness of armor (mm) penetrated at (m) range

Range	37 mm M-1930	45 mm M-1942	57 mm ZiS-2	100 mm M1944
250 m	?	?	Total	Total
500 m	25	61	90	195
750 m	20	> 61	84	> 195
1,000 m	-	51	74	185
1,500 m	-	> 51	64	?
2,000 m	-	-	56	?

Maximum armor penetration of Allied anti-tank guns at successive ranges is represented with a dashed line. Total penetration was achieved for some guns at closer ranges.

The ZiS-2 57 mm anti-tank gun was a decisive weapon for the Soviet Union, put to good effect during the Battle of Kursk in 1943.

The V-1 Flying Bomb

The final air assault on Britain was the launching of the "V"-weapons offensive following the Allied invasion of Europe in June 1944. The pilotless "flying bomb," the V-1, wrought havoc over London, with over 6,000 people killed and 17,000 wounded.

The first of Hitler's "revenge weapons," the Vergeltungswaffe 1 or V-1, designed to take the fight back to the British in a particularly brutal and random manner, was prepared in the autumn of 1943. Consisting of a simple, winged fuselage of welded steel, and packed with 1,829 lb (830 kg) of amatol explosive, the weapon was designed to bring terror to the shores of the British Isles. The V-1 was distinguished by the throbbing sound of its pulsejet, a sound that would stop as the aircraft's fuel ran out, the engine spluttering before cutting out, and the bomb turning headlong for earth, with an eerie hush before impact. These sounds would lead to the weapon being christened the "buzz-bomb" or "doodle-bug."

Most V-1s were launched from simple "ski-ramp" sites constructed along the French, and later Dutch, coast. By June 1944—just as the Allies were landing in Normandy—they were ready for action. London was to receive the first of these unmanned, pulsejet propelled aircraft on June 13th, 1944, when ten were launched. Only four would reach England, the first landing harmlessly near Swanscombe in Kent. Near Mile End in London's East End,

The Flying Bomb Offensive Against the UK in the Whole Campaign (June 12th, 1944–March 29th, 1945)

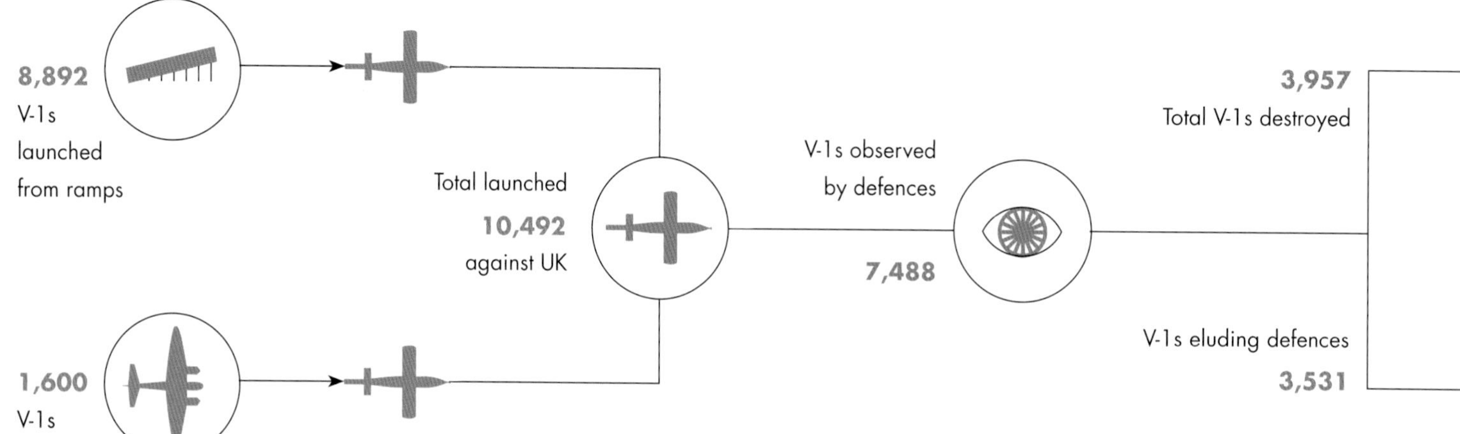

"If the deafening pulse engine cut out on the approach there was a heart stopping 7 to 12 second silence. This terrible silence was followed by a huge bang as it exploded just before it hit the ground or on rooftops." —VICTOR SPINK, LONDON RESIDENT

however, a bridge was destroyed and six people killed and nine injured. A plaque records this today on the rebuilt bridge at Grove Road. The V-1 was very simply aimed, and set roughly on target by gyroscopes; that target was permanently set on Tower Bridge.

The V-1 attacks became sustained—a hundred a day was typical, with 500 launched over the first weekend of deployment (June 16–17th, 1944). The majority of the bombs would fall on the southern and eastern parts of the city. South of London, Croydon was on the flight path and suffered severely, taking 142 hits. A large number were to fall across Kent, and many others would overshoot into Essex; several would hit Winston Churchill's parliamentary constituency in Wanstead and Woodford. The most devastating single bomb attack would fall on June 17th. Here, close by the Cabinet's secret war rooms, the Guards Chapel was hit during a service; 121 people were killed and 60 badly injured. There were many tragedies enacted by this weapon.

View of a V-1 rocket in flight over London, c.1944.

In all, a total of 10,492 V-1s were launched at Britain, the vast majority aimed at London; 2,419 were to reach the city, killing 6,184 civilians and injuring 17,984.

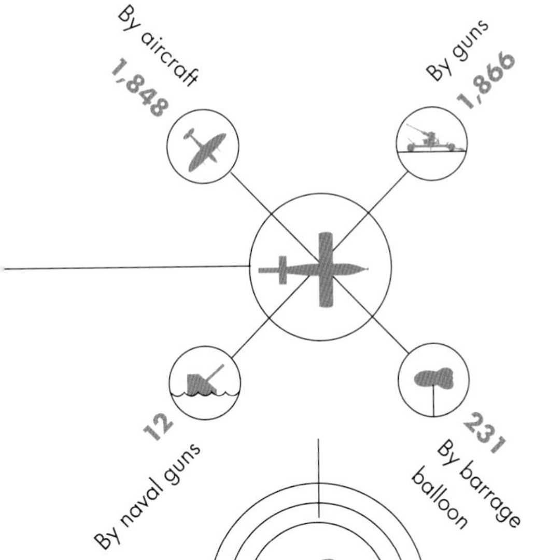

By aircraft **1,848**

By guns **1,866**

12 By naval guns

231 By barrage balloon

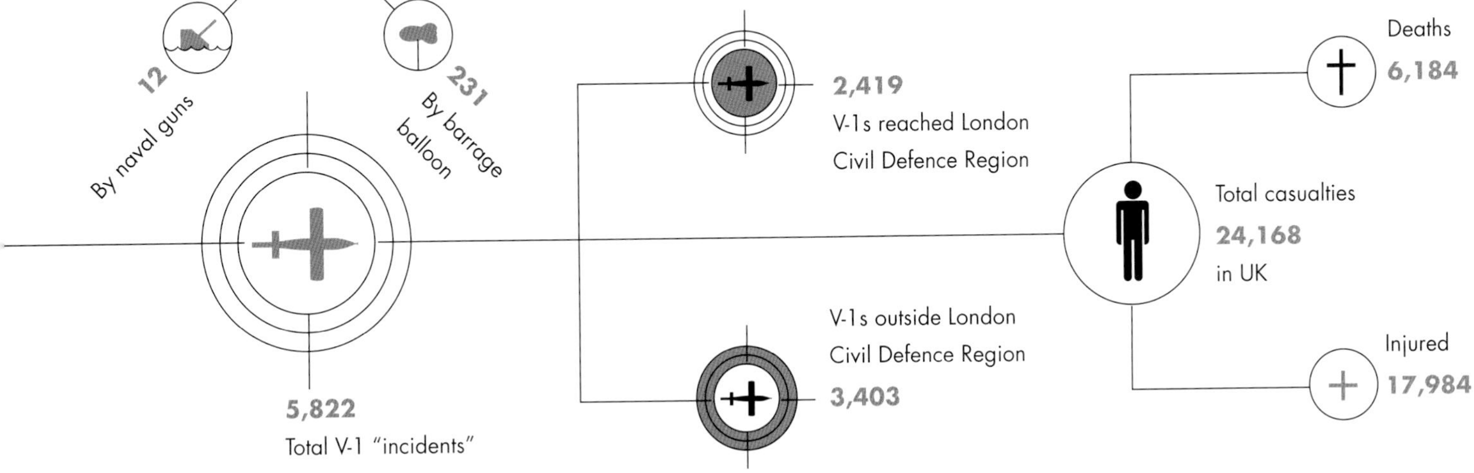

5,822 Total V-1 "incidents"

2,419 V-1s reached London Civil Defence Region

V-1s outside London Civil Defence Region **3,403**

Total casualties **24,168** in UK

Deaths **6,184**

Injured **17,984**

Carrier Fighter Aircraft in the Pacific War

Naval aircraft launched from aircraft carriers fell into three basic types during World War II: fighters, divebombers, and torpedo-bombers. The purpose of the bombers was simple: to attack and destroy ships and onshore installations. The primary purpose of the fighters was also simple: to intercept and destroy enemy aircraft, thereby preventing them from carrying out their own missions. Typically, this would be the destruction of bombers; but it would also mean attacking other fighters in the pursuit of their duties.

JAPANESE FIGHTER AIRCRAFT

Comparative specifications for Japanese and US carrier-borne fighter aircraft used during the Pacific War, 1941–1945. The Zero was an all-round fighter aircraft with excellent manoeuvrability; the Hellcat was faster in a diving attack, but much larger.

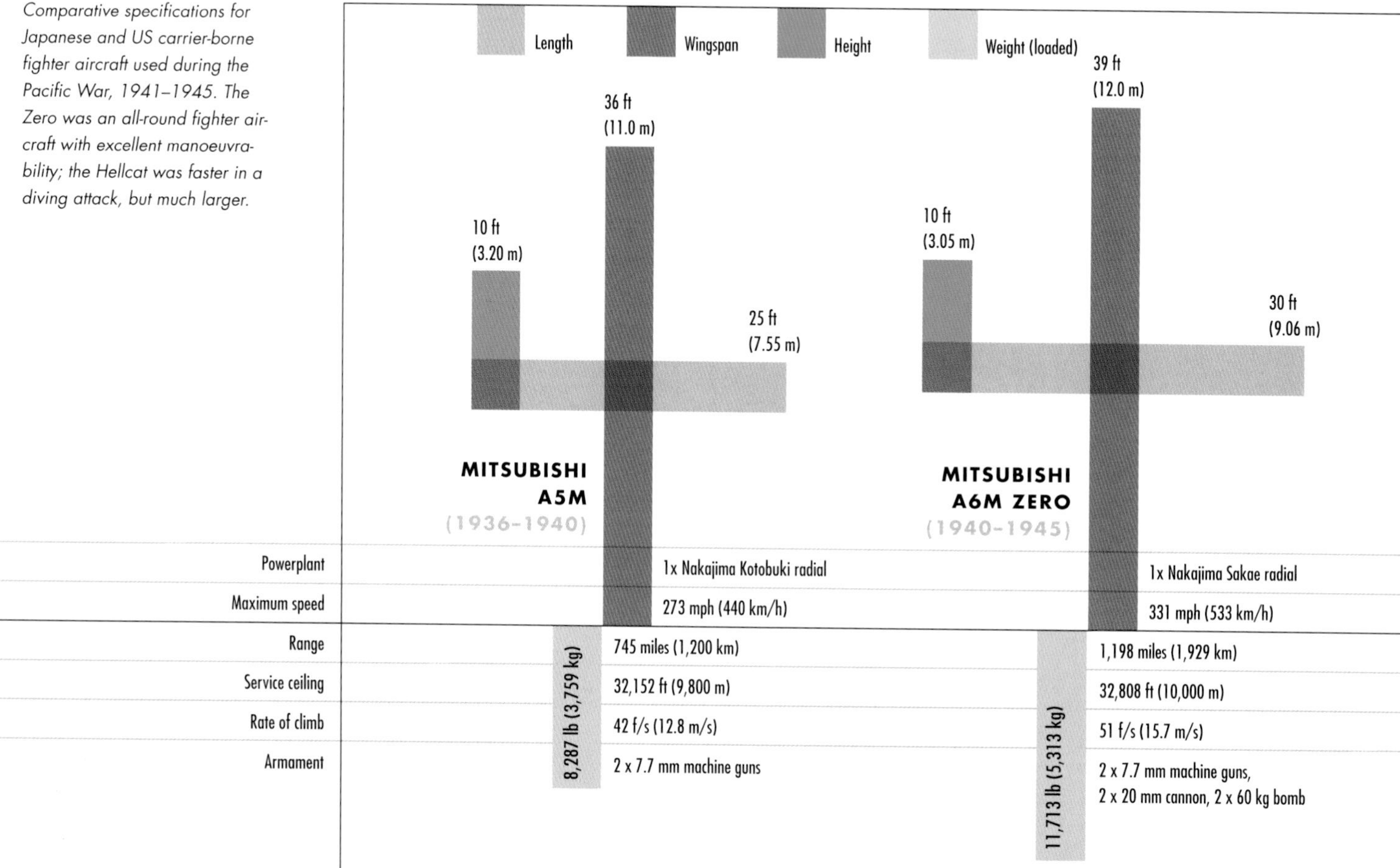

	Mitsubishi A5M (1936–1940)	Mitsubishi A6M Zero (1940–1945)
Powerplant	1x Nakajima Kotobuki radial	1x Nakajima Sakae radial
Maximum speed	273 mph (440 km/h)	331 mph (533 km/h)
Range	745 miles (1,200 km)	1,198 miles (1,929 km)
Service ceiling	32,152 ft (9,800 m)	32,808 ft (10,000 m)
Rate of climb	42 f/s (12.8 m/s)	51 f/s (15.7 m/s)
Armament	2 x 7.7 mm machine guns	2 x 7.7 mm machine guns, 2 x 20 mm cannon, 2 x 60 kg bomb

At the beginning of the Pacific War, the most advanced aircraft was the Mitsubishi A6M Zero. The Zero could not be matched for range rate of climb or speed, though its performance varied at height. Zeros were used almost exclusively as carrier-borne fighter aircraft by the Japanese. Countering the Zero was a difficult proposition, and the US Navy introduced its mainstay, the Grumman Hellcat, in 1943. The Hellcat was designed to challenge the Zero, while being capable of soaking up considerable battle damage. The Hellcat was faster than the Zero, and had a better climb rate, but still the navy advised pilots not to take on the Japanese fighter on level terms. The Hellcat was responsible for over 75% of all naval air victories during the Pacific War.

AMERICAN FIGHTER AIRCRAFT

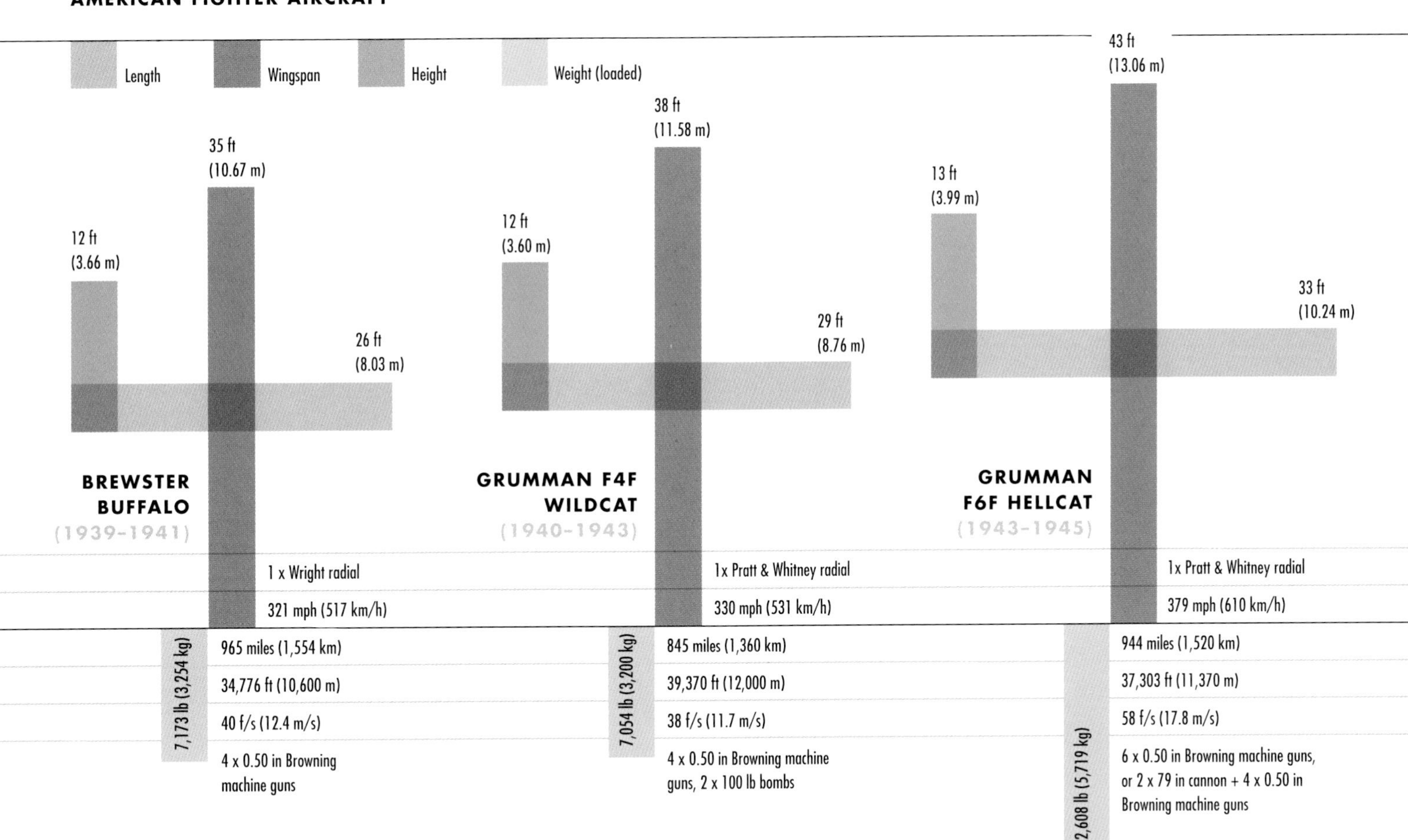

Allied Landing Craft

With the need for the Allies to land on hostile shores in Europe and the Pacific came the need for vessels that could deliver troops, armor, and equipment in sufficient numbers and in relative safety. The disastrous landings at Gallipoli in 1915, when men landed from open boats into a hostile fire fight, were always in the minds of the planners of amphibious operations. For this reason, the Royal Navy and the US Navy both developed a suite of specialist craft that were flat-bottomed, and capable of running up onto a beach in order to divulge their cargo directly.

Allied Landing Craft

Displacement (full load)	Load: Troops	Load: tons (tonnes)	NAME OF CRAFT
435.4 tons (395 tonnes)	210	38.5 (35)	LCI (Landing Craft, Infantry)
38.5–116 tons (35–106 tonnes)	100–200	16.5 –33 (15–30)	LCM (Landing craft, Mechanized; LCM1–8)
10.7 tons (9.7 tonnes)	25–36	0 0	LCPL (Landing Craft Personnel, Large)
280 tons (254 tonnes)	No troops; carried armament for support 0	280–391 (254–355)	LCSL (Landing Craft Support, Large)*
317.5–660 tons (288–599 tonnes)	0	167.5 (152)	LCT (Landing Craft Tank)
1,007.5 tons (914 tonnes)	54	606 (550)	LCM (Landing Ship, Medium)
4,345–6.058 tons (3,942–5,496 tonnes)	300	3.0 (2.8)	LST (Landing Ship Tank)
0	30		LVT (Landing Vehicle Tracked)

*later (Landing Ship Support)

Typically, infantry landing craft, and those designed to carry one or two vehicles, were designed with a forward-facing ramp, which could be lowered to act as a bridge down onto the beach, allowing the assaulting troops to hit the beach running.

Larger craft were also required; ocean-going vessels that were capable of delivering larger numbers of men and/or vehicles to the invasion beaches. These were pivotal in the landings in Italy and North Africa, as well as in the delivery of larger numbers of matériel at Normandy, and in the assaults on the Pacific islands.

A Landing Ship, Tank (LST) loading in preparation for Normandy, 1944.

Length	Speed (knots)	Number built
158 ft (48.3 m)	16	923
45–74 ft (13.6–22.5 m)	7–12	11,350
36 ft (11.1 m)	7–11	4,820
158 ft (48.3 m)	11.5	130
151–193 ft (46.0–59.0 m)	7–8	2,633
203 ft (62.0 m)	13.3	539
325–394 ft (99–120 m)	9	1,040
26 ft (7.95 m)	4	18,620

German Operational Jet Aircraft

In 1943–1944, with the Allies pouring thousands of tons of bombs into the Reich, day and night, Hitler was desperate to find a way of delivering more bombs to his enemies, while Göring was committed to ensuring that the Allied bombers roving the skies over Germany were knocked out. With jet engines available on both sides of the English Channel from the late 1930s, there was a rush to achieve an important milestone—the first operational jet aircraft. For the Germans, fighters and bombers powered by Jumo turbojets seemed to be an option that was too good to turn down, and it was Willy Messerschmitt who produced the first effective aircraft.

GERMAN JET AIRCRAFT

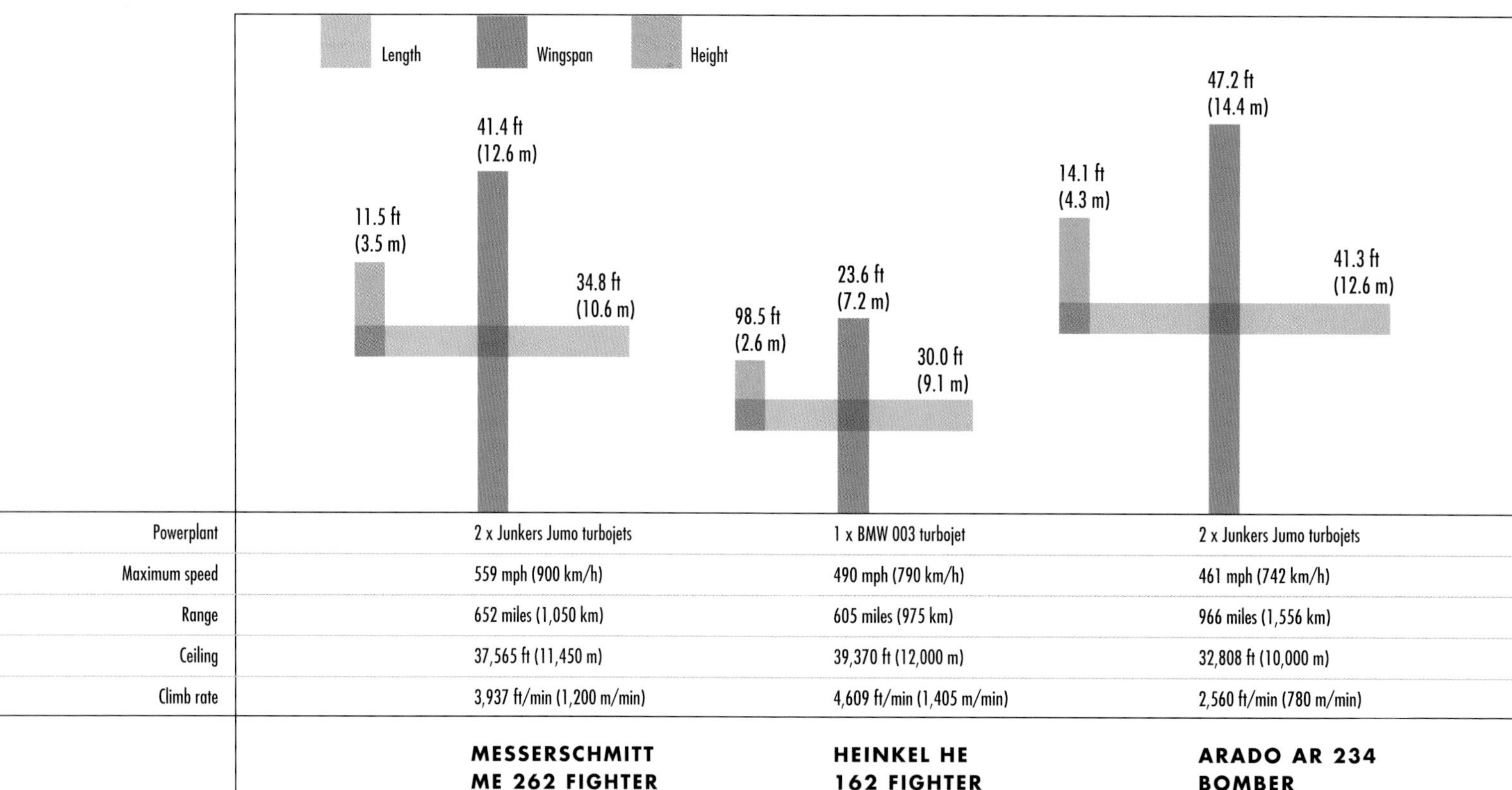

	MESSERSCHMITT ME 262 FIGHTER	HEINKEL HE 162 FIGHTER	ARADO AR 234 BOMBER
Powerplant	2 x Junkers Jumo turbojets	1 x BMW 003 turbojet	2 x Junkers Jumo turbojets
Maximum speed	559 mph (900 km/h)	490 mph (790 km/h)	461 mph (742 km/h)
Range	652 miles (1,050 km)	605 miles (975 km)	966 miles (1,556 km)
Ceiling	37,565 ft (11,450 m)	39,370 ft (12,000 m)	32,808 ft (10,000 m)
Climb rate	3,937 ft/min (1,200 m/min)	4,609 ft/min (1,405 m/min)	2,560 ft/min (780 m/min)

In 1944, the Germans put into production the Me 262, revolutionary for its aerodynamic shape and speed. Hitler at first seized upon the opportunity to use the aircraft to deliver bombs to the heart of Britain. But it slowed the jet aircraft to the point where it was vulnerable to Allied piston-engined fighters. The bombs created much more drag than was warranted, and fighters that could have been knocking out the British and American bombers that were now flying with impunity over the Reich were wasted. Fortunately, an alternative existed, the Arado Ar234, and it was this aircraft that was pressed into service as a fast bomber. It was not successful in this role; it was best deployed in fast reconnaissance. But it allowed the Me 262 to be used in its most impressive role.

The Me 262 was a formidable machine; though equipped with rockets to destroy Allied bombers, these two reduced speed. Once launched, the fighter was largely untouchable, and had a high success rate against the giant Allied bomber force. As the war moved toward its conclusion, the Germans produced the Heinkel He 162, the Volksjager or people's fighter, which flew in combat in early 1945. It was too late to make a difference, and had limited success, though it did make a mark; it was the first jet in history to be equipped with an ejection seat.

ALLIED PISTON-ENGINED FIGHTERS

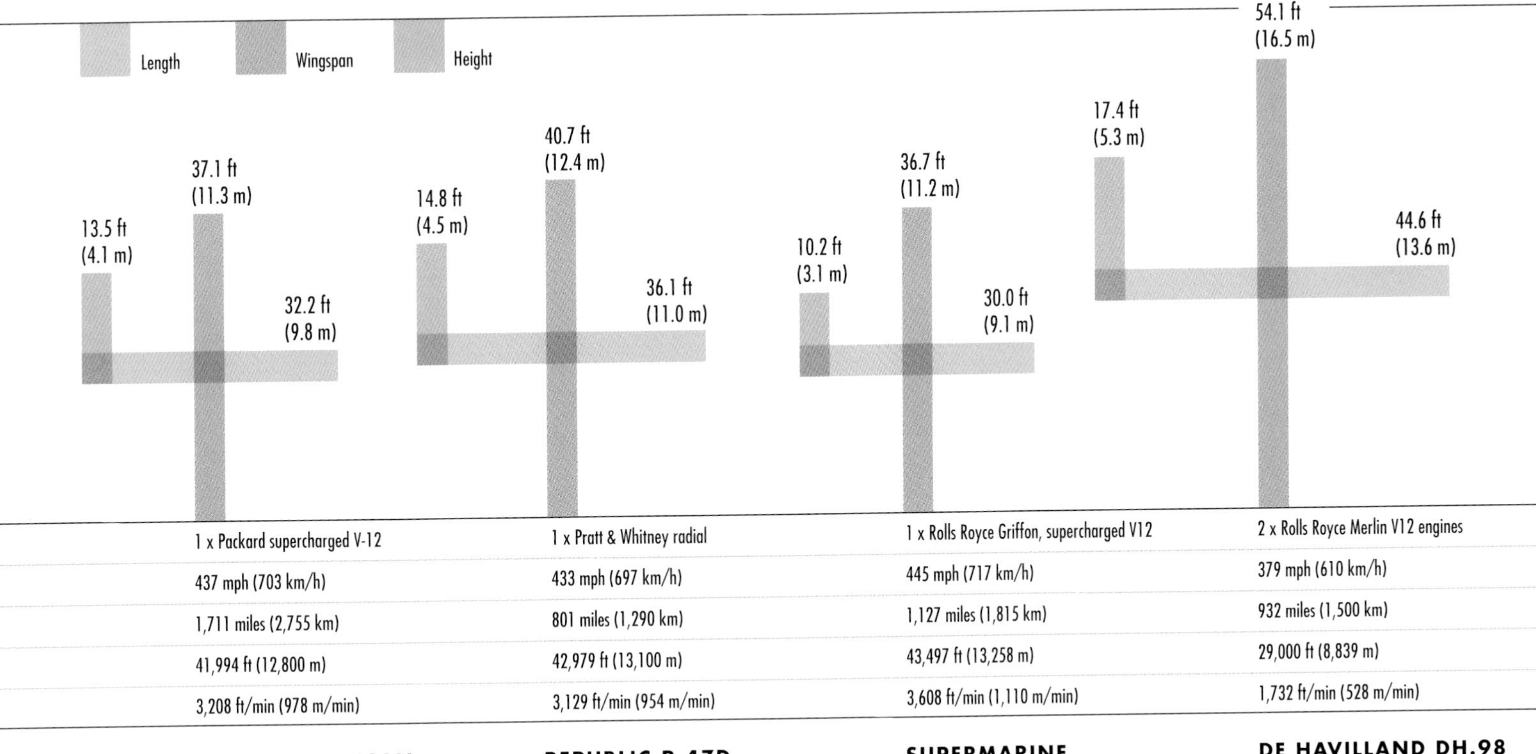

NORTH AMERICAN P-51D MUSTANG	REPUBLIC P-47D THUNDERBOLT	SUPERMARINE SPITFIRE MK XIV	DE HAVILLAND DH.98 MOSQUITO MK II
1 x Packard supercharged V-12	1 x Pratt & Whitney radial	1 x Rolls Royce Griffon, supercharged V12	2 x Rolls Royce Merlin V12 engines
437 mph (703 km/h)	433 mph (697 km/h)	445 mph (717 km/h)	379 mph (610 km/h)
1,711 miles (2,755 km)	801 miles (1,290 km)	1,127 miles (1,815 km)	932 miles (1,500 km)
41,994 ft (12,800 m)	42,979 ft (13,100 m)	43,497 ft (13,258 m)	29,000 ft (8,839 m)
3,208 ft/min (978 m/min)	3,129 ft/min (954 m/min)	3,608 ft/min (1,110 m/min)	1,732 ft/min (528 m/min)

Kamikaze

Japanese aerial suicide attacks—known officially as Special Attacks, but that became known as "kamikaze" (divine wind)—were a means for the Japanese to hold off the inexorable advance of the Allied fleet toward the home islands. The attacks required the piloting of aircraft packed with explosive into naval targets, with the aim of destroying their capability. Aircraft carriers were a major target (and particularly the vulnerable, wooden-decked US carriers), but any large battleship was also under threat from these attacks.

US carrier USS Bunker Hill *is attacked by two Kamikazes in 30 seconds while offshore of the Japanese island Kyushu on May 11th, 1945.*

Japanese Kamikaze Sorties During the Okinawa Campaign

Operation	Date	Navy aircraft	Army aircraft	Total
Kikusui 1	April 6–7th, 1945	230	125	355
Kikusui 2	April 12–13th, 1945	125	60	185
Kikusui 3	April 15–16th, 1945	120	45	165
Kikusui 4	April 27–28th, 1945	65	50	115
Kikusui 5	May 3–4th, 1945	75	50	125
Kikusui 6	May 10–11th, 1945	70	80	150
Kikusui 7	May 24–25th, 1945	65	100	165
Kikusui 8	May 27–28th, 1945	60	50	110
Kikusui 9	June 3–7th, 1945	20	30	50
Kikusui 10	June 21–22nd, 1945	30	15	45
Sorties from Taiwan	April–June 1945	50	200	250
Misc. sorties	April–June 1945	140	45	185
Total	–	**1,050**	**850**	**1,900**

* The numbers of aircraft represent approximate figures

The attacks commenced in October 1944, following the defeats on the Pacific islands, and particularly the fall of Saipan, which allowed the US to bomb the mainland with B-29 bombers. The declining fortunes of the Japanese required some direct action.

The first attacks were recorded in the Battle of Leyte Gulf, with a Japanese aircraft targeting Australian Navy heavy cruiser HMAS *Australia* on October 21st, 1944. The ship did not sink. The main attacks were on US ships, on October 25th, with the primary casualty being the carrier USS *St Lo*, when a Zero fighter was crashed into the flight deck, causing the ship's magazine to explode, thereby sinking the vessel. Between October 25th and 26th, there were 55 attacks, resulting in five sinkings, and 35 ships damaged. The loss of the *St Lo* sponsored an increase in such attacks by the Japanese.

With the Allied landings on the Japanese home island of Okinawa came the peak of the Kamikaze attacks. In April 1945, waves of suicide aircraft made attacks on Allied shipping during Operation Kikusui, and at the cost of 1,465 planes and their pilots, 33 US ships were damaged or sunk.

Kamikaze Damage on Allied Ships During the Okinawa Campaign

The effectiveness of Kamikaze attacks on Allied shipping during the Okinawa Campaign, April–June 1945. Only 30% of attacks actually hit ships, with just 15% actually achieving sinkings. Statistically, Kamikaze attacks were less likely to result in irreparable damage than torpedo attacks.

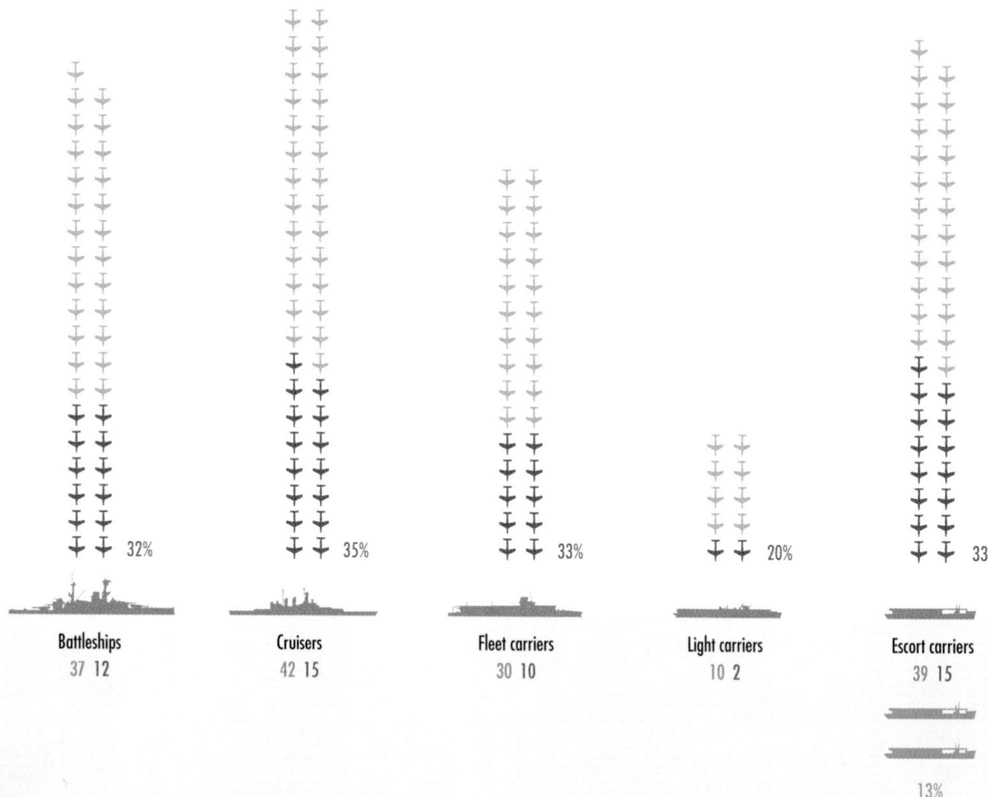

	Number of aircraft in attack	944	
	Hit number	296	31%
	Ships sunk	45	
	Sinkings per hit		15%

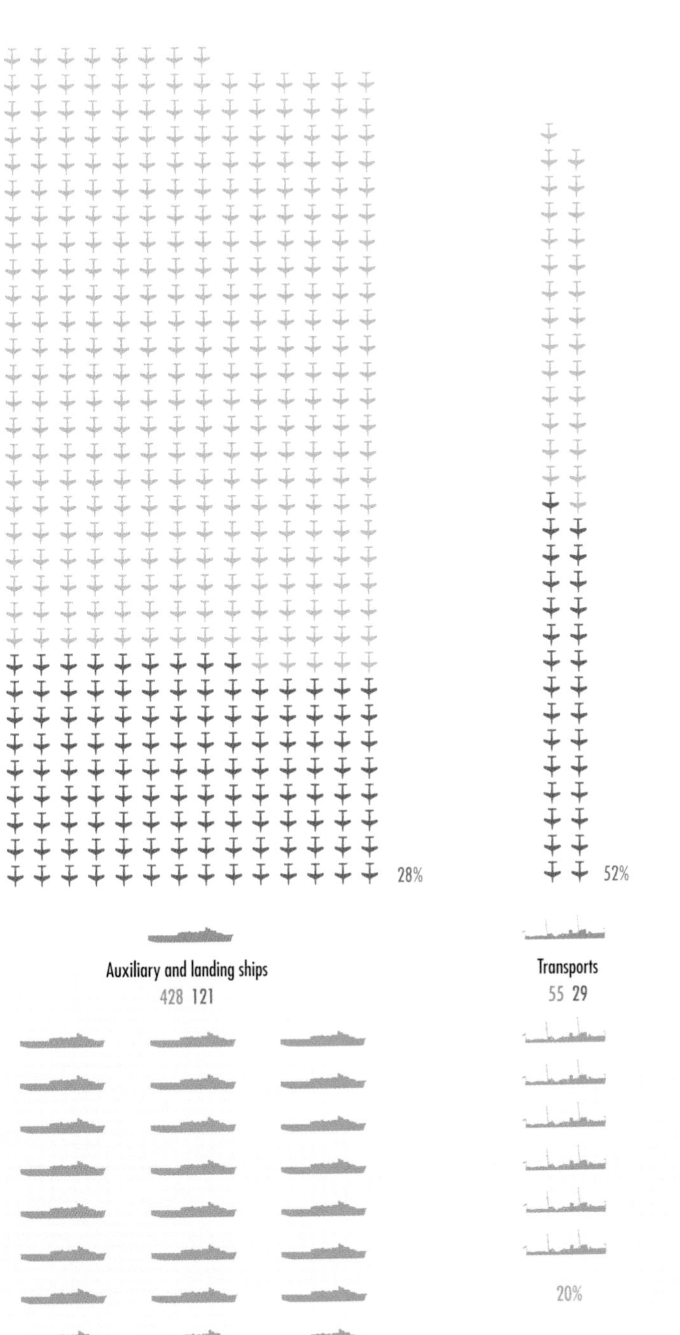

Japanese "Kamikaze" special attack pilots, 1945.

Effectiveness of Japanese Attacks Against Allied Aircraft Carriers

	Divebombing	Submarine torpedo	Aerial torpedo	Kamikaze attack
Average number of weeks in repair	0.3	10	10	1.8
Average number of weeks out of action	0.7	12.4	17.5	4.3
Percentage of damaged carriers requiring repairs	40%	100%	100%	70%

"Fat Man" and "Little Boy": Atomic Bombs 1945

The atomic bombing of Japan in August 1945 effectively ended the war in the east, and on August 15th, 1945, the Japanese announced their surrender. Up until this point, with the Japanese generals against capitulation, Japan looked set to continue the war. What had been needed was a direct word from the emperor, but this was not forthcoming.

Newly discovered ground-level photograph of the mushroom cloud created by the explosion of "Little Boy" over Hiroshima, August 6th, 1945.

The generals' determination to hold out was in spite of US Air Force General Curtis LeMay's conventional and firebombing campaign against Japanese cities, which commenced on March 9th, 1945 and that by July had left most in ruins with a likely death toll of some 800,000 civilians. Japan was beleaguered by sea, too; with supply ships targeted by American submarines, and bombers seeding Japanese seas with mines, the calorific intake of the Japanese fell alarmingly to 1,680—some 1,000 calories less than the average British citizen, even in the depths of war. On land, sea, and in the air, the Japanese were being pressed hard, the Allies in control. On July 26th, 1945, the Western Allies delivered a stark declaration to the Japanese: "We call upon the government of Japan to proclaim… unconditional surrender… The alternative for Japan is prompt and utter destruction." The declaration was ignored, the Japanese set to fight on.

The dropping of "Little Boy" on Hiroshima was the first step in delivering the Allies' promise. The Japanese Government gave little response. It was only after the dropping of the bomb on Nagasaki (and the declaration of war on Japan by the Soviet Union) that surrender was even mooted. It was on August 9th, 1945 that Hirohito declared in favor of surrender; the generals had little choice but to follow his wishes.

The justification for the bombing is that ultimately it saved the lives of the many servicemen who would have had to invade the Japanese mainland—an act, it is argued, that could have resulted in many more Japanese casualties—given the high attrition rate of Japanese defenders. With American losses at Iwo Jima and Okinawa set at 72,000 casualties, American estimates of the invasion of the first of the mainland islands, Kyushu, would be more like 260,000. The Japanese had fought largely "to the last man" on the two islands of Iwo Jima and Okinawa; their losses would surely continue to be astronomical.

The ethical debate continues today; but "Little Boy" and "Fat Man" remain the first—and only—atomic weapons to be used in warfare. The devastating effects they caused were never far from the minds of the military leaders of the Cold War.

"Little Boy" was the first of the atomic bombs dropped on Hiroshima in August 1945. It used a "gun method" to force a subcritical mass of Uranium 235 with a solid target cylinder in order to achieve fission.

LITTLE BOY

"Little Boy" was the first of the two atomic bombs to be dropped on Japan, and that signalled the end of World War II. The result was the second nuclear explosion in history, and the consequent loss of life. The design of "Little Boy" required a subcritical hollow cylinder of Uranium 235 to be explosively driven onto a solid target, thereby initiating the nuclear reaction. The bomb was dropped over the Japanese city of Hiroshima on August 6th, 1945 by Colonel Paul Tibbets of the United States Army Air Forces (USAAF), flying the B29 bomber, Enola Gay. Hiroshima was selected as a target due to the presence of an army depot and point of embarkation.

The devastation wrought by the atomic explosion at Hiroshima.

Characteristics of "Little Boy" and "Fat Man"

The characteristics of "Little Boy" and "Fat Man," code names for the atomic bombs dropped on Hiroshima and Nagasaki in August 1945. The shapes of the two bombs differed substantially due to the method of achieving fission.

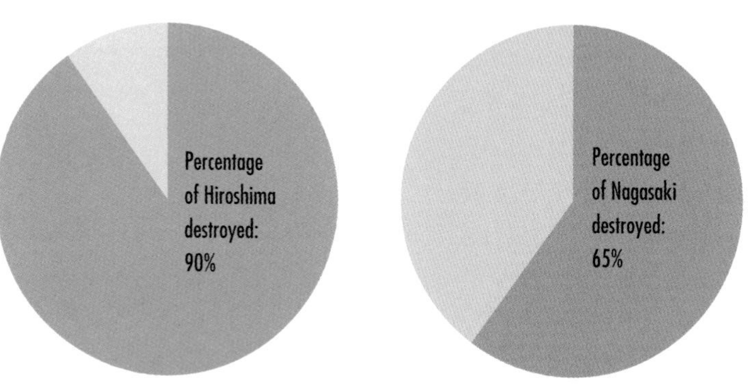

HIROSHIMA BOMB (LITTLE BOY)

NAGASAKI BOMB (FAT MAN)

Percentage of Hiroshima destroyed: 90%
Percentage of Nagasaki destroyed: 65%

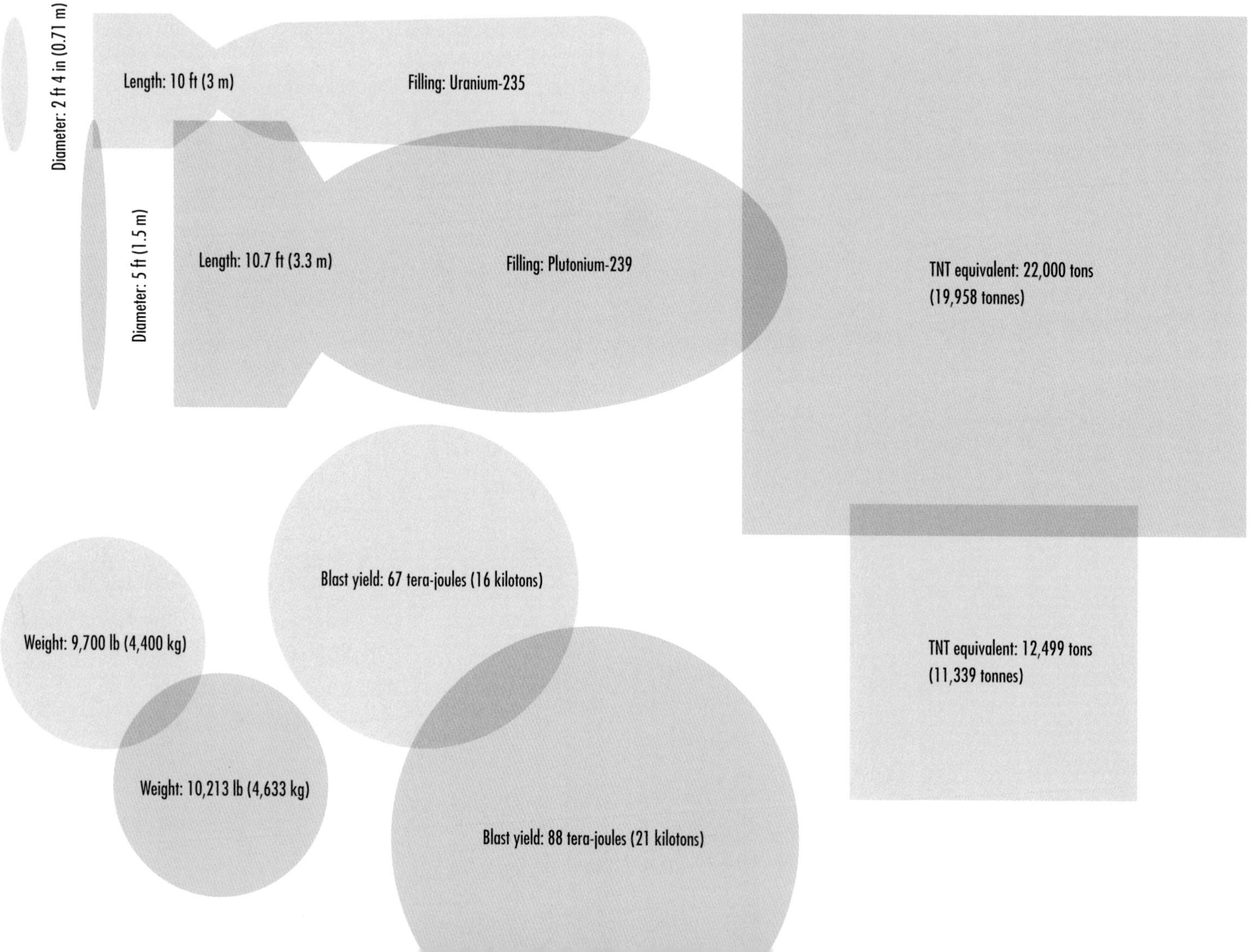

Diameter: 2 ft 4 in (0.71 m)
Length: 10 ft (3 m)
Filling: Uranium-235
Diameter: 5 ft (1.5 m)
Length: 10.7 ft (3.3 m)
Filling: Plutonium-239
TNT equivalent: 22,000 tons (19,958 tonnes)
Blast yield: 67 tera-joules (16 kilotons)
Weight: 9,700 lb (4,400 kg)
TNT equivalent: 12,499 tons (11,339 tonnes)
Weight: 10,213 lb (4,633 kg)
Blast yield: 88 tera-joules (21 kilotons)

FAT MAN

"Fat Man" was the second atomic bomb to be dropped over mainland Japan, when it was used over the Japanese city of Nagasaki. It had been intended for Kokura, a large munitions manufacturing center; but this target was obscured by cloud, so the bomb was delivered to the secondary target by Major Charles Sweeney USAAF piloting the B-29 bomber Bockscar on August 9th,1945. The name of the bomb was derived from its shape, which was designed to house two spheres of explosive; an inner core of subcritical Plutonium 239, and an outer sphere of high explosives, with 32 detonators all designed to create inward pressure on the plutonium, and thereby set off a chain reaction.

"Fat Man," the second of the atomic bombs, dropped on Nagasaki. It used an implosion method to achieve fission, with subcritical Plutonium 239 in a hollow sphere of explosives.

Fatalities From the Atomic Bombing of Japan

At both Hiroshima and Nagasaki, the majority of deaths were from blast effects and burns; up to 20% died from long-term radiation sickness.

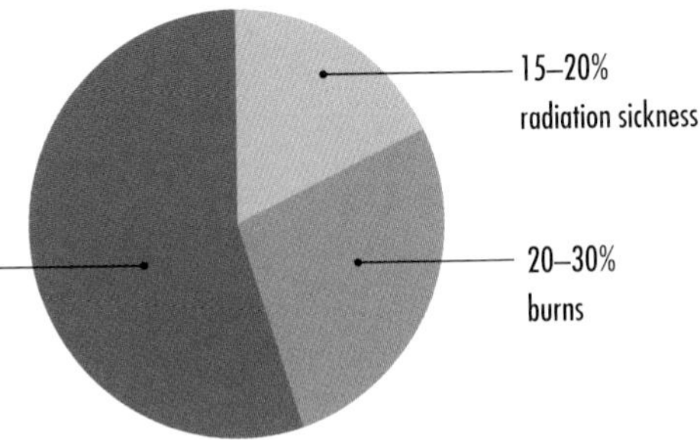

Half of those who were killed died immediately in the two cities; injuries sustained in the attacks and long-term effects of radiation sickness accounted for the remainder.

Casualties:
90,000–166,000 died

Casualties:
60,000–80,000 died

The mushroom cloud created by the detonation of "Fat Man" over Nagasaki, August 9th, 1945, taken from one of the B-29 Superfortress bombers in the attack.

Chapter Four

IN THE AIR

The Battle of Britain in 1940 was one of the most important in history. Reichsmarshall Hermann Göring vowed that he could destroy the Royal Air Force (RAF): he could not. Here, the first air aces of the war were created; many more would be made over the steppes of Russia. Bombing was employed by the Axis and Allies to destroy both –the morale of the people and the industrial means of prosecuting the war and, controversially, incendiaries were used by both sides to burn ancient cities.

The Battle of Britain
1940

The Battle of Britain is one of the most important battles in the history of warfare, and the first to be fought entirely with aircraft. The background to the battle was the hope that Britain could be subdued to pave the way for invasion; after the defeat of the Allies in France there seemed to be little standing in the way of a German invasion.

With this in mind, Hermann Göring, chief of the Luftwaffe, gave Hitler the guarantee that his air force could destroy Britain's air fighting capability while the aircraft were still on the ground. The Kriegsmarine was aware that the only way of successfully mounting any kind of invasion was to have absolute dominance in the air, and Göring promised that his Luftwaffe would be able to dispense with the Royal Air Force in the first four days of the battle. This was quickly

Royal Air Force Casualties by Month (1940)

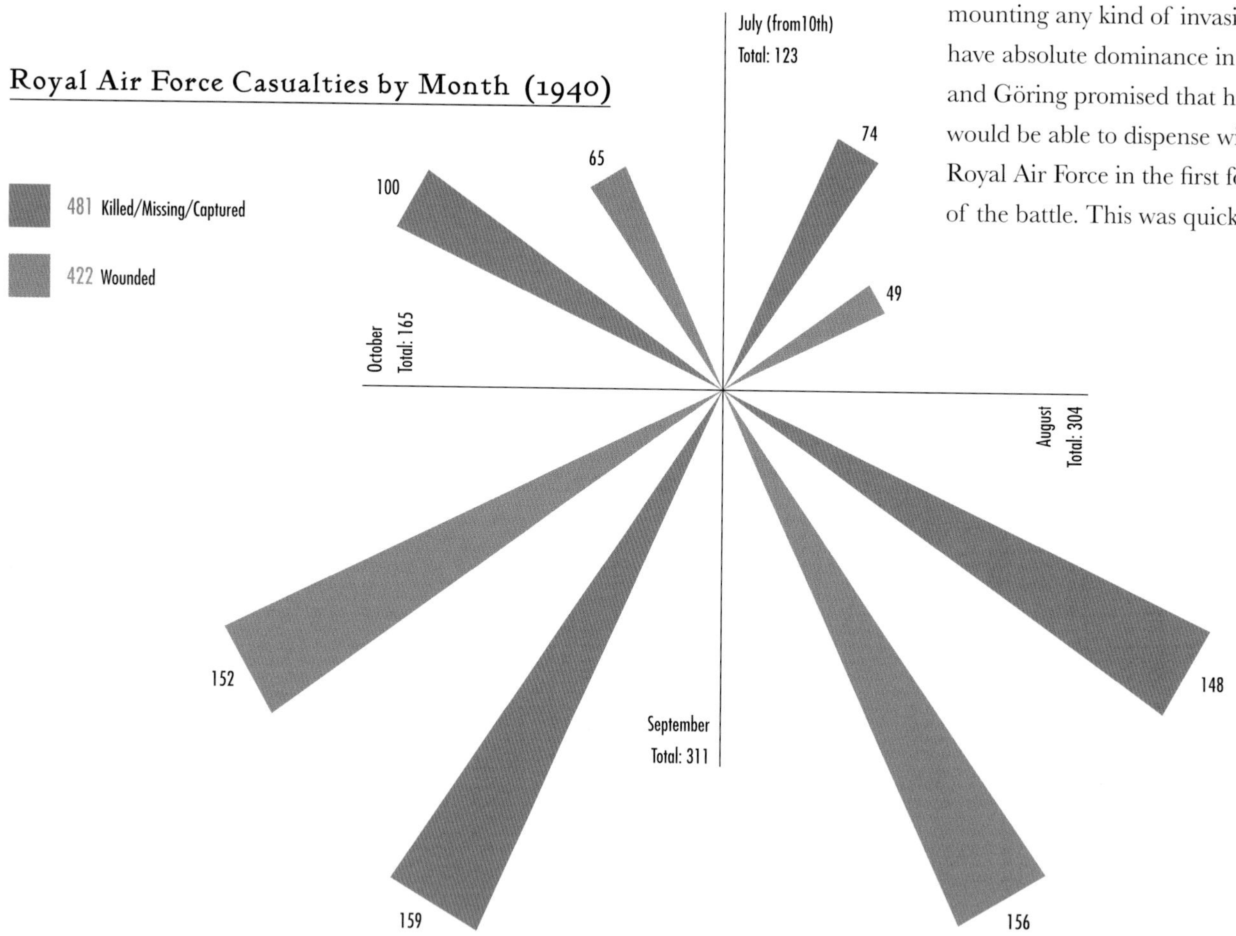

Nationalities of RAF Aircrew

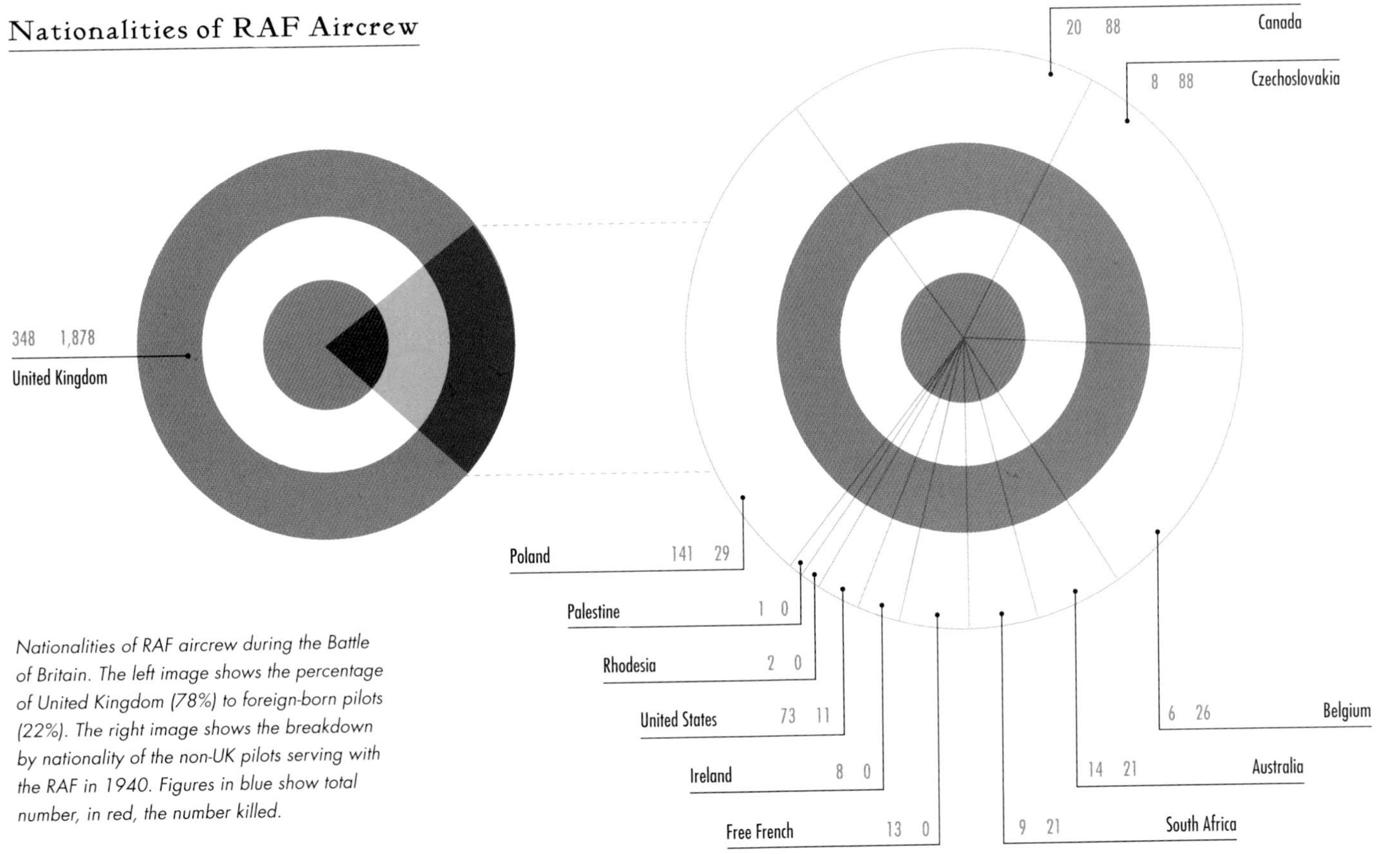

Nationalities of RAF aircrew during the Battle of Britain. The left image shows the percentage of United Kingdom (78%) to foreign-born pilots (22%). The right image shows the breakdown by nationality of the non-UK pilots serving with the RAF in 1940. Figures in blue show total number, in red, the number killed.

reassessed to five weeks. The battle would commence on August 8th, 1940, and continue until just over a month later, on September 15th.

Pivotal was the destruction of the airfields and aircraft of the RAF, and to do so three Luftflotten were assigned to the task of bombing Britain into submission. Targeted were airfields, military installations and transport links, and tasked were bombers and twin-engine fighters. Fighters such as the Messerschmitt 109 could only have limited time over southern Britain due to their fuel capacity; this would mean that the RAF fighters would have the advantage in taking on the bomber fleets. There needed to be a high "kill ratio" if the Luftwaffe was to defeat the RAF.

Supplying the RAF with fighters was one thing, but finding adequately trained pilots to fly them was another. With the numbers of aircrew losses ramping up, it was essential that new pilots be trained quickly. And with a significant number of pilots available from the occupied nations, the RAF was to rely upon a large number of them to prosecute the battle. By September 15th, the Luftwaffe shifted its attention to the bombing of London, and the battle was over.

The Blitz

The "Blitz" was the sustained period of bombing of Britain's cities from September 1940 through to May 1941. The first bombs on the capital fell by chance; in a bungled raid on Purfleet on August 24th, 1940, bombers strayed off target, releasing their loads over the East End and north London. The first bombs on the capital began the escalation of the aerial campaign; the RAF was to bomb Berlin the next evening. There was very little damage—yet at Berlin's Sportsplatz on September 4th, Hitler called for comprehensive retaliatory action against British cities: "If they attack our cities, we shall raze theirs to the ground." With this, on September 7th, the Luftwaffe's bombers were turned away from the ports and airfields targeted as part of the preparations for the invasion of Britain, and were refocused on the capital—the Battle of London had begun.

With London deliberately targeted, the rambling docks concentrated along the Thames as it snaked its way through London's East End were the main focus of the attack. Flying at first in daylight, and then at night, the Luftwaffe was to hit London hard. A concentrated force of 364 bombers made the attack. At 16:56, the sirens were sounded, warning Londoners to take shelter. And from 17:00, the German bombers appeared over the city—large numbers of high-explosive bombs were unloaded on the docks and city areas. The enemy attacked at night too, returning at 20:00 after a break of just two hours. The attack continued into the early-morning hours; its effect was devastating. The port areas were vulnerable; warehouses packed with flammable materials were to be set alight, burning through into the evening, and acting as a beacon for the second wave of bombers that would arrive at night. London's fire services struggled to deal with this concerted attack.

Guided by the flames, the bombers pounded London with high explosives. Surrounding the docks and industrial areas targeted by the Luftwaffe, thousands of homes were destroyed or damaged beyond repair; mainline stations were rendered useless and vessels in the bustling Thames basin were sunk, burned or bombed. Many of the fires were burning out of control as conflagrations—huge areas of spreading flame. In all, 436 Londoners would be killed, and 1,666 injured from this raid. In the days that followed, the bombers returned by night. The damage wrought on September 7th was repeated again on Sunday September 8th; another 412 Londoners would be killed that night, 747 seriously wounded.

In order to enact the loud promises of destruction made by both Göring and Hitler, between 100 and 200 bombers attacked London every night but one between mid-September and mid-November. These bombers destroyed houses and people's lives;

they severed transport links and damaged war production. But all of these were temporary. London carried on. Shop fronts were emblazoned with chalked messages, such as "more open than usual" or "Hitler can't stop us." That 5,730 people were killed and 10,000 were badly injured was an inescapable fact of the bombing campaign; but there can be no doubt that Londoners carried on.

By mid-November, the Germans had dropped more than 14,559 tons (13,208 tonnes) of high-explosive bombs, and more than 1 million incendiary bombs on London. Unopposed other than by the then ineffective "barrage" of anti-aircraft guns, and by largely obsolete aircraft pressed into service as "catseye" night fighters—relying on nerve and common sense but lacking all-important radar at this early part of the war—the Luftwaffe would suffer losses of only 1% by combat casualties. More would be lost in accidents and mechanical failure than would be shot down; new technology would be needed to effectively combat the attackers.

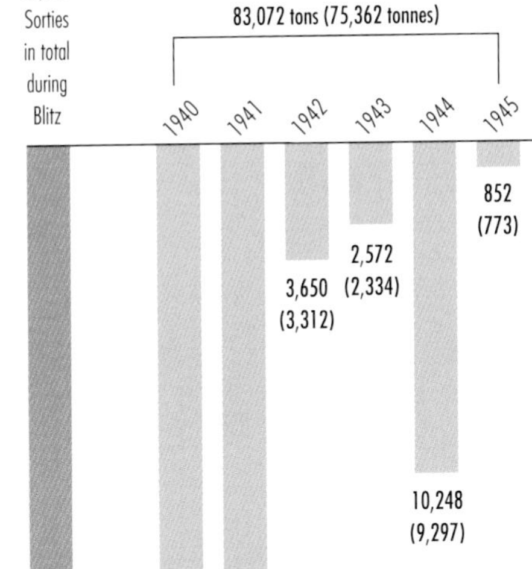

Tonnages and Sorties During the Blitz on London

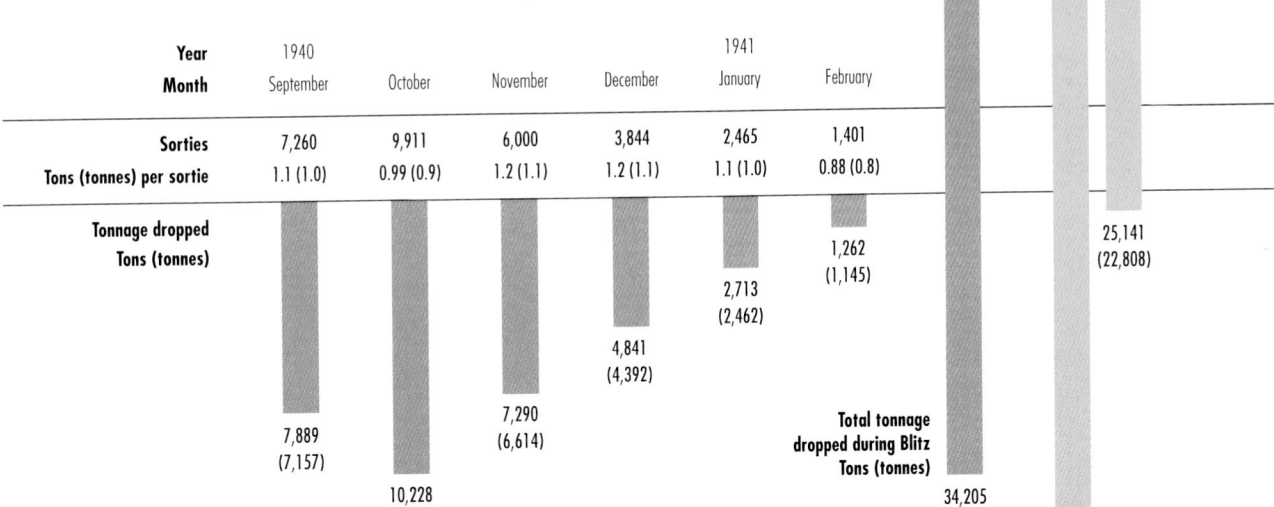

Year	1940				1941	
Month	September	October	November	December	January	February
Sorties	7,260	9,911	6,000	3,844	2,465	1,401
Tons (tonnes) per sortie	1.1 (1.0)	0.99 (0.9)	1.2 (1.1)	1.2 (1.1)	1.1 (1.0)	0.88 (0.8)
Tonnage dropped Tons (tonnes)	7,889 (7,157)	10,228 (9,279)	7,290 (6,614)	4,841 (4,392)	2,713 (2,462)	1,262 (1,145)

30,881 Sorties in total during Blitz

Total tonnage dropped during Blitz Tons (tonnes) 34,205 (31,031)

The average tons per sortie dropped by the Luftwaffe on London during the Blitz, 1940–1941 (left); there were 30,881 sorties flown in this period, with 34,205 tons (31,031 tonnes) of bombs dropped. In all, some 83,072 tons (75,362 tonnes) of bombs were dropped over the UK, the majority in 1940, but with an increase in activity in 1944, "The Baby Blitz."

The Doolittle Raid
1942

The Doolittle Raid was a daring aerial attack on the Japanese mainland. Masterminded by Lieutenant Colonel James Doolittle of the United States Army Air Forces (USAAF), the raid was intended to demonstrate to the Japanese that their home islands were not invulnerable to attack. It was carried out on April 18th, 1942, little over four months after the devastating attack on Pearl Harbor in December 1941. The effects of the raid would have much wider repercussions than the simple act of dropping bombs on the Japanese; it would force the Imperial Japanese Navy into action in the Coral Sea and at Midway that would alter the whole course of the war.

The Doolittle Raid. Strengths and Casualties

16	B-25 Mitchell Bombers
15	Destroyed
1	Interned in USSR

80	Airmen
5	POWs
3	Killed in action
3	Executed
1	Died in captivity

Serial number	40-2344	40-2292	40-2270	40-2282	40-2283	40-2298	40-2261	40-2242
Squadron	(HQ personnel, no squadron)	37th BS	95th BS	95th BS	95th BS	95th BS	95th BS	95th BS
Target	Tokyo	Tokyo	Tokyo	Tokyo	Tokyo	Tokyo	Tokyo	Tokyo
Result	Bombed target	Bombed target	Bombed target	Jettisoned bombs before target	Bombed target	Bombed target	Bombed target	Bombed target
Pilot	Lt. Col. James H. Doolittle	Lt Travis Hoover	Lt Robert Gray	Lt Everett W. Holstrom	Capt. David M. Jones	Lt Dean E. Hallmark	Lt Ted W. Lawson	Capt. Edward J. York
Fate	Crew bailed out; Crashed north Chuchow, China	Crash landed Ningbo, China	Crew bailed out; Crashed south-east Chuchow, China	Crew bailed out; Crashed south-east Shangjao, China	Crew bailed out; Crashed south-west Chuchow, China	Ditched in the sea Wenchu, China	Ditched in the sea Shangchow, China	Landed and interned, Primorsky Krai, Siberia
Fate of crew	Escaped, helped by locals	Escaped; aided by guerrillas	Cpl Faktor died when crew bailed out; others escaped	Escaped	Escaped	Sgt Dieter & Sgt Fitz-maurice drowned, rest captured, Lt Hallmark executed by firing squad; 2 POW	Escaped	Interned in Siberia; escaped May 11th, 1943

The Doolittle Raid was to be carried out by 16 B-25B Mitchell bombers launched from the aircraft carrier USS *Hornet*. Given the distances to Japan from US territory, the *Hornet* was required to get close enough to the Japanese island of Honshu for the B-25s to deliver their 500 lb (226 kg) bombs and then fly on to China; there was no way of landing these large aircraft back on the carrier. The intention was to get within 480 nautical miles of the island; but having been spotted by a Japanese patrol craft, the bombers were launched early, some 650 nautical miles out.

Flying at wave height, only one bomber was damaged, though another ditched its bombs before reaching its target. All the aircraft involved in the bombing were lost and 11 crewmen were either killed or captured—with three of the captured men executed by the Japanese after their capture in China. One B-25 landed at Vladivostok, and was interned by the still neutral Soviets. The raid caused negligible damage, but demonstrated with startling clarity that the Japanese mainland was not invulnerable to attack.

James Doolittle (fifth from the left) and his flight crew in China, after his bombing mission over Japan, April 1942.

Serial	40-2303	40-2250	40-2249	40-2278	40-2247	40-229	40-2267	40-2267
Squadron	34th BS	89th BS	89th BS	37th BS	37th BS	89th BS	89th BS	34th BS
Target	Tokyo	Tokyo	Yokohama	Yokohama	Yokosuka	Nagoya	Kobe	Nagoya
Result	Bombed target	Bombed target	Bombed target	Bombed target	Bombed target	Bombed target	Bombed target	Bombed target
Pilot	Lt Harold F. Watson	Lt Richard O. Joyce	Capt. C. Ross Greening	Lt William M. Bower	Lt Edgar E. McElroy	Major John A. Hilger	Lt Donald G. Smit	Lt William G. Farrow
Fate	Crew bailed out; Crashed south Nanchang, China	Crew bailed out; Crashed north-east Chuchow, China	Crew bailed out; Crashed north-east Chuchow, China	Crew bailed out; Crashed north-east Chuchow, China	Crew bailed out; Crashed north Nanchang, China	Crew bailed out; Crashed south-east Shangjao, China	Ditched in the sea; Shangchow, China	Crew bailed out; Crashed south Ningbo, China
Fate of crew	Escaped	Escaped	Escaped	Escaped	Escaped	Escaped	Escaped	Captured, Lt Farrow & Sgt Spatz (gunner) executed by firing squad; 3 POW

The Bombing of Malta

Malta is situated in a strategically important part of the Mediterranean; controlling Malta meant controlling the sea, particularly important given the heavy Axis involvement in North Africa. Yet Malta was also under British control, as it had been since 1800. The British Empire had fortified the island, a stepping stone for British ships from Gibraltar, off the coast of Spain, to Alexandria in Egypt, and from there on to the Suez Canal and ultimately, India. Yet Malta was only a stone's throw from Italy, and was a considerable thorn in the side of the Axis, and Mussolini's ambitions to control the Mediterranean. The Axis resolved to lay siege to the island, preventing maritime or aerial supply routes, and bombing the nation into submission.

Number of Luftwaffe Air Raids on Malta

Malta	No. of night raids	No. of day raids	Total	No. of aerial sorties
March 1942	90	185	**275**	4,927
April 1942	96	187	**283**	9,599
Totals	**186**	**372**	**558**	**14,526**

Total bomb tonnage **7,495 tons (6,800 tonnes)** Average per raid **13.2 tons (12 tonnes)**

The island has an area of just 100 square miles (260 square kilometers), equal in size to the Isle of Wight, and in 1937 had a population of just 250,000, most of them Maltese; its most dense population was focused around Valetta and the Grand Harbour area, two areas covering just 0.75 square miles (2 square kilometers)—but also home to the Royal Navy. These areas would receive the attentions of the Axis, and would ultimately become the most bombed place on the planet. The Royal Engineers, charged with the disposal of unexploded bombs, would have a major task on their hands to deal with the amount of ordnance thrown their way.

The first attacks came from the Regia Aeronautica in June 1940, but with outdated aircraft, the effects of the Italian campaign were limited, and the RAF—itself flying obsolete Gloster Gladiator biplanes (though joined by Hawker Hurricanes)—claimed 35 aircraft destroyed and 194 damaged. But the real threat to the island came with the deployment of German forces to North Africa. With the supply line of the Deutches Afrika Korps (DAK) under threat, the Oberkommando der Luftwaffe despatched Fliegerkorps X to attack the island, in January 1941. With aerial superiority assured through the support of Messerschmitt 109 fighters, the German bombers continually

Composite image of German Ju 88 bombers attacking the Maltese port of Valetta while a British Spitfire and Italian Macchi MC-202 dogfight, c.1942.

pounded the island, with an estimated 2,799 tons (2,540 tonnes) of high explosive dropped in its first four months of operations. People were forced out of Valetta, though stonemasons and miners toiled to build stone shelters for the people in the wake of the attacks.

Though Fliegerkorps X was withdrawn to assist on other fronts in April 1941, allowing the RAF to resupply, and permitting attacks on Axis shipping, by January 1942 the Luftwaffe were back in business. Though casualties suffered in the airborne assault on Crete in June 1941 quashed any idea of invasion, the bombing attacks were doubled. Tactics changed to targeting the convoys feeding the island's population in mid-1942, but by the autumn, arrival of Spitfires meant that the RAF was to claim aerial superiority, and with the Luftwaffe losing aircraft, and the DAK requiring aerial support, the attacks were called off on October 16th. The situation improved and the ships got through. The last raid on Malta was on July 20th, 1943; the 3,340th since June 11th, 1940.

Unexploded Bombs Dealt with by the Royal Engineers

Bomb type	Number of individual unexploded bombs reported					
Year	**1940**	**1941**	**1942**	**1943**	**1944**	**Totals**
High explosive	3	525	1,253	35	14	**1,830**
Anti-personnel	0	459	4,093	530	103	**5,185**
Incendiary	5	281	102	29	1	**418**
Total	**8**	**1,265**	**5,448**	**594**	**118**	**7,433**

The Bombing of Germany

With much of the continent dominated by Nazi Germany, and no hope of opening a European front within the foreseeable future, the only option available to Britain in 1940–1941 was to take the war to the Nazis, bombing their homeland. The RAF had bombed Germany as early as 1939, their raids increasing through the difficult years of 1940–1941. At first they committed to daylight and night raids; experience showed that daylight raiding allowed accuracy in hitting specific targets, but night raids were for area targets. Incendiary bombing at night allowed the creation of uncontrollable fire "conflagrations." For the RAF, a real step-up in capability was the delivery of heavy bombers such as the Short Stirling in 1941 and the Avro Lancaster in 1942. Both were able to carry bomb loads of 14,000 lb (6,350 kg), three times the load of the Vickers Wellington medium bomber they replaced. From 1943 the RAF concentrated on night bombing; daylight raids were taken up by the USAAF, with the arrival of the 8th Air Force in England in 1942.

Percentage of Damage to Cities

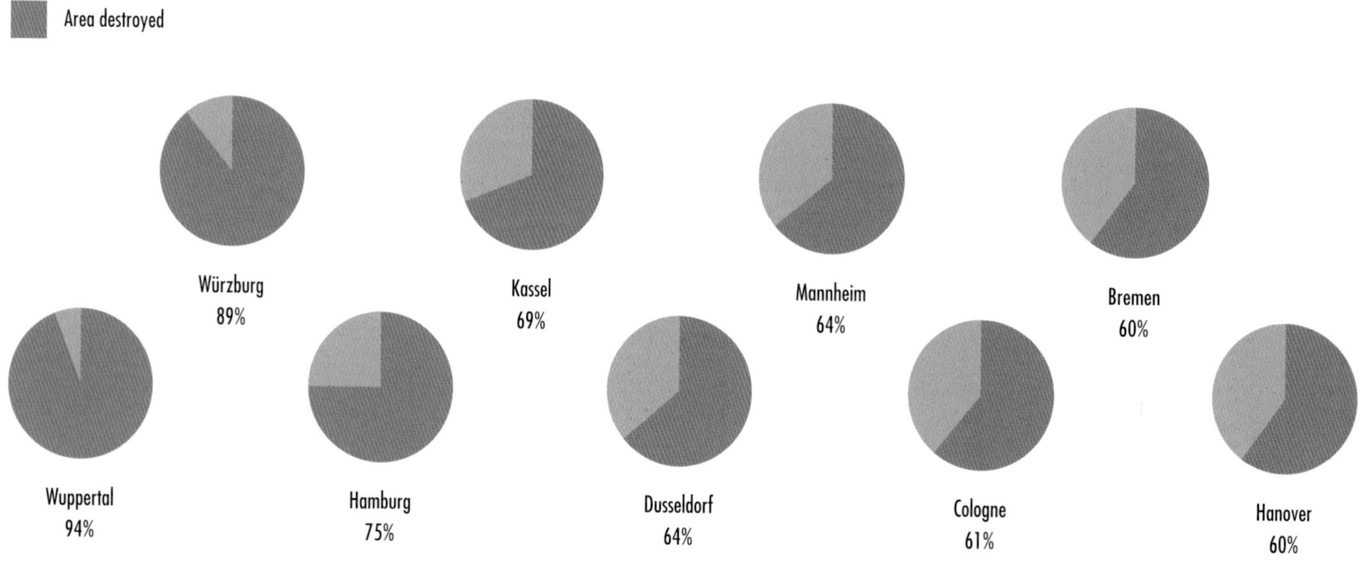

In both the RAF and the United States Army Air Forces (USAAF) there were some who believed that air power could deliver the knockout blow against Germany, but dominant in thinking behind the bombing was preparation for the invasion of the continent in 1944, establishing air superiority, and weakening the enemy's will and capacity to resist. In 1942, the RAF began raids on German urban and industrial centers; on May 30th, 1942, it mounted its first "thousand bomber raid" against Cologne and two nights later struck Essen with almost equal force. On three nights in late July and early August 1943 it struck Hamburg in perhaps the most devastating single city attack of the war—about one-third of the houses of the city were destroyed, and German estimates show 60,000 to 100,000 people killed. No subsequent city raid shook Germany as did that on Hamburg. The RAF proceeded to destroy one major urban center after another, and the tonnage dropped on city areas mounted greatly in 1944–1945.

USAAF strategy was to concentrate on specific industries; and if these targets were to be hit accurately, the attacks had to be made in daylight. But it was not always possible to achieve accuracy under battle conditions, with targets often obscured by clouds, smoke and industrial haze, and bombers had to avoid enemy fighters and flak. Enemy opposition demanded formation flying to get the most from the heavily armed (with 13 .50 caliber Browning machine guns) Boeing Flying Fortress heavy bombers, capable of carrying a bomb load of 8,000 lb (3,628 kg). Though precision was anticipated, the reality was that there was much overspill to surrounding areas. "The target area" became a circle with a radius of 1,000 ft (304 m) around the aiming point of attack, and only about 20% of the bombs aimed at precision targets fell within this target area. A peak accuracy of 70% was reached for the month of February 1945.

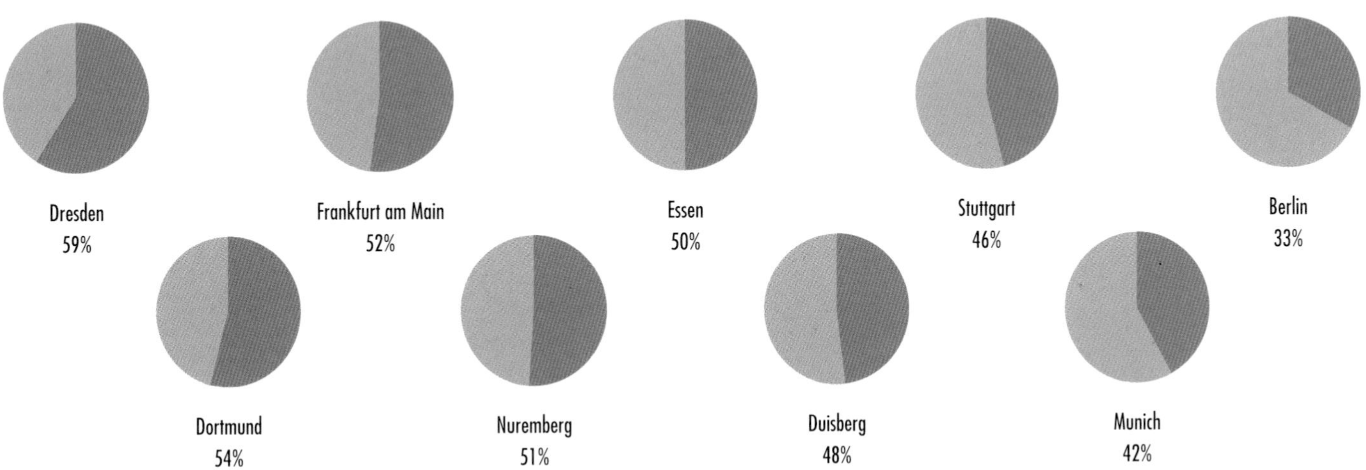

Sorties and Bomb Tonnage Dropped Over Europe

The orange circles on this graphic represent the average bomb tonnage dropped by Bomber Command per sortie. The gray circles represent the average tonnage dropped by USAAF 8th Air Force per sortie.

BOMB TONNAGE DROPPED:

by Bomber Command

by USAAF 8th Air Force

SORTIES FLOWN:

Day sorties (Bomber Command)

Night sorties (Bomber Command)

Sorties (8th Air Force)

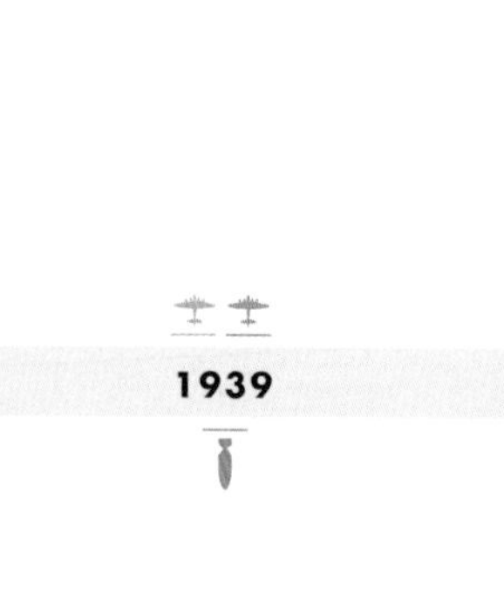

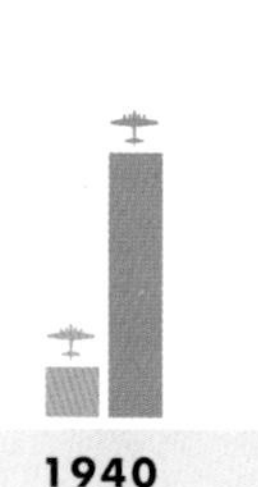

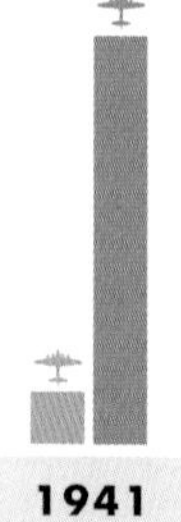

BOMBER COMMAND

Year	Day sorties	Night sorties	Total sorties	Bomb tonnage tons (tonnes)	Average tons (tonnes) per sortie
1939	163	170	333	34 (31)	0.1 (0.1)
1940	3,316	17,513	20,829	14,601 (13,246)	0.6 (0.6)
1941	3,507	27,101	30,608	35,507 (32,212)	1.1 (1.0)
1942	2,313	32,737	35,050	51,028 (46,292)	1.4 (1.3)
1943	1,792	62,736	64,528	176,250 (159,892)	2.6 (2.4)
1944	44,096	113,352	157,448	588,579 (533,950)	3.6 (3.3)
1945	20,664	44,074	64,738	203,548 (184,656)	3.0 (2.8)
Totals	75,851	297,683	373,534	1,069,552 (970,282)	2.7 (2.5)

8TH AIR FORCE

Year	Total sorties	Bomb tonnage tons (tonnes)	Average tons (tonnes) per sortie
1942	1,453	1,579 (1,433)	1.1 (1.0)
1943	27,362	49,487 (44,894)	1.7 (1.6)
1944	210,544	435,816 (395,363)	1.98 (1.8)
1945	93,545	211,201 (191,599)	2.2 (2.0)
Totals	332,904	698,081 (633,289)	2.0 (1.9)

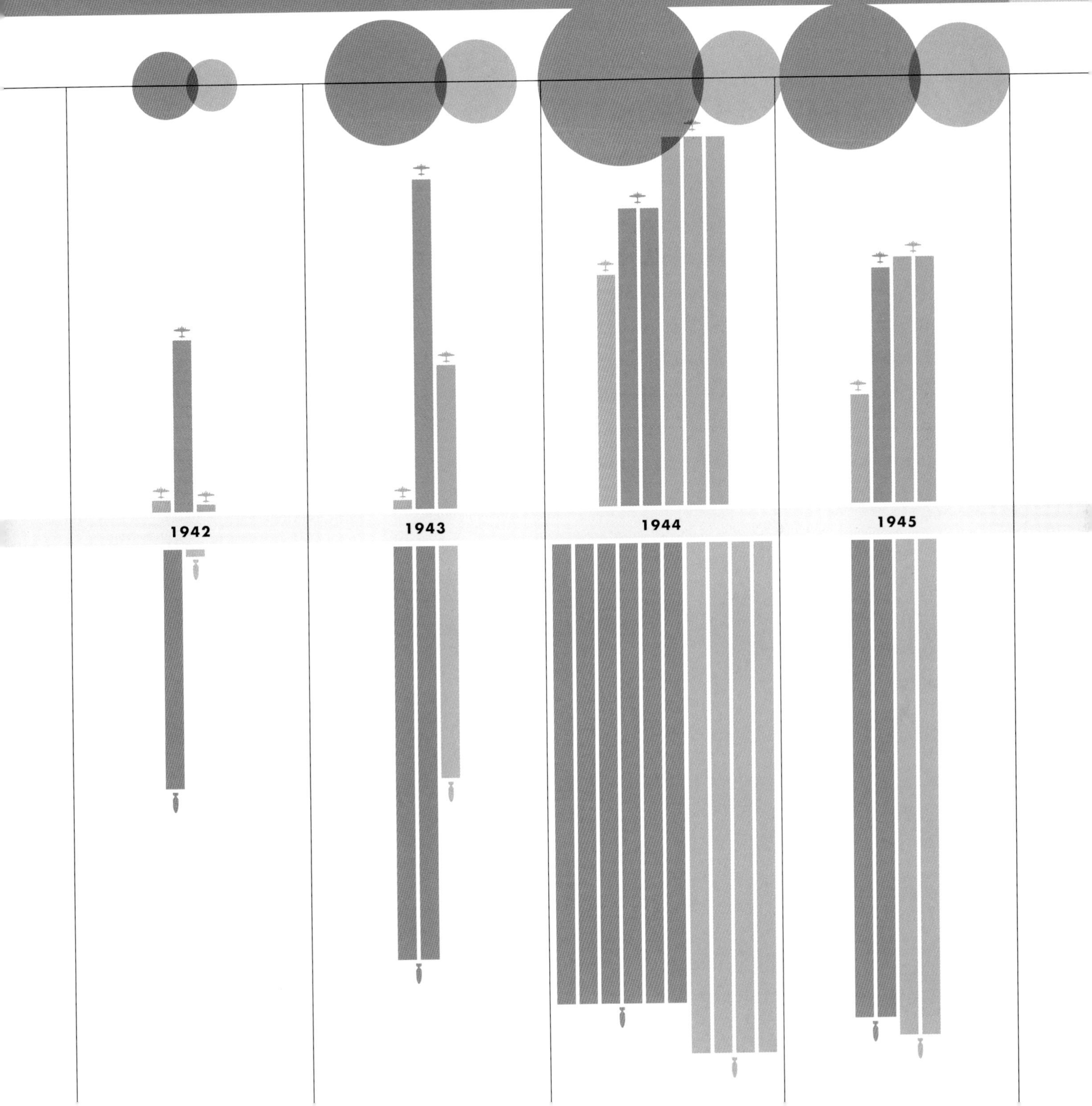

1942

1943

1944

1945

US Bombing of Japanese Mainland
1944–1945

For most people, the dropping of atomic bombs on Hiroshima and Nagasaki in 1945 has largely overshadowed the conventional bombing of Japan by the United States, yet arguably it was the strategic bombing campaign that was the most devastating of the two. Japan was no stranger to aerial bombardment; its forces had systematically targeted Chinese cities to great effect from 1933 onward. But with the Japanese conquest of much of the Pacific region in 1941, there appeared little to fear from Allied bombers—until the audacious Doolittle Raid of early 1942, that is. This raid demonstrated that Japan's mainland was not invulnerable, and with the Allies pushing the boundaries of the Japanese "buffer zone" of island territories, the increase in bombing was bound to happen.

US Air Forces Bombing Japan

Unit / tonnages in tons (tonnes)
(high explosive & incendiary)

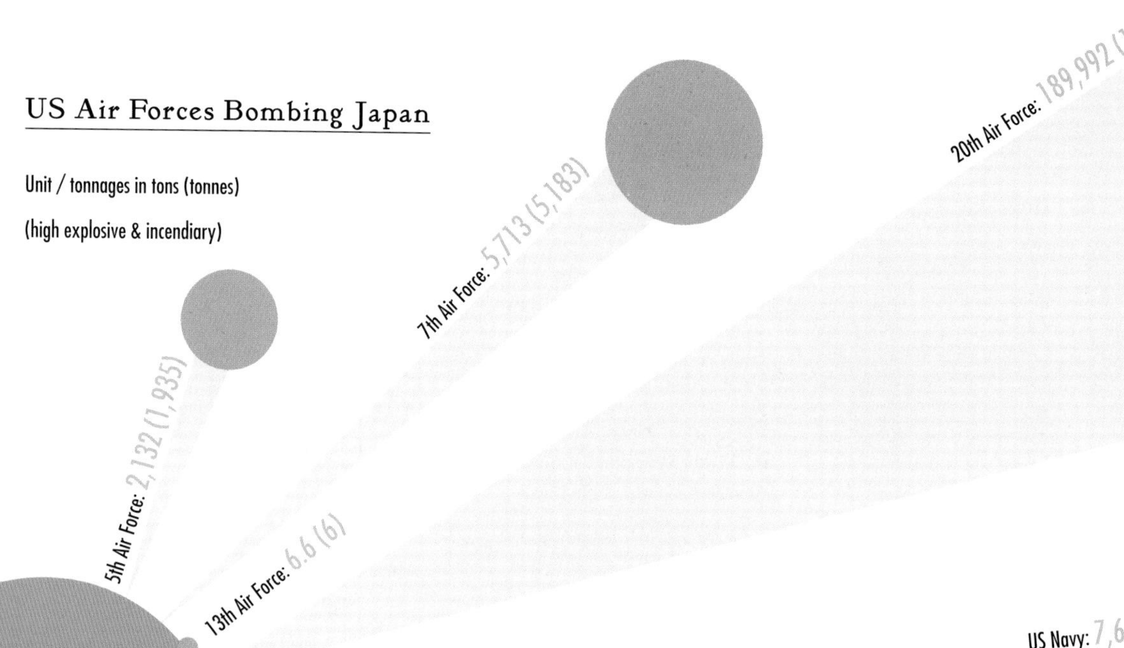

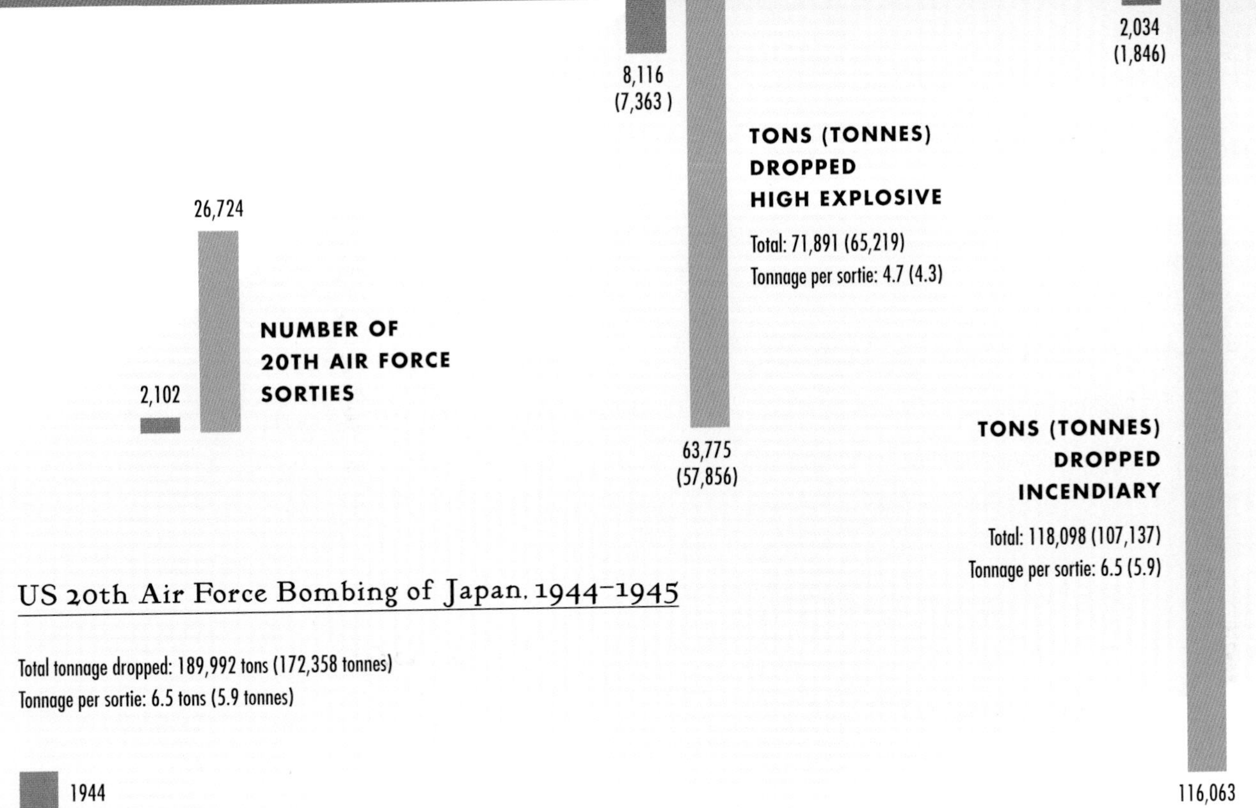

US 20th Air Force Bombing of Japan, 1944–1945

In the early summer of 1944 came the possibility of routine targeting of Japanese targets from China by Boeing B-29 Superfortress bombers, aircraft that were capable of carrying 20,000 lb (9,070 kg) of bombs on what would be a 3,218 km (2,000 mile) round trip. Capture of the Mariana Islands (Guam, Saipan) meant that airbases were even closer. Initially, the US 20th Air Force practiced daylight precision bombing of specific targets, just as it did in the war then being waged against German military targets in Europe. The aim was the same, to "bring overwhelming pressure" on Japan to surrender, or to reduce Japan's "capability of resisting invasion." With limited effectiveness, the B-29 bombers maintained high-altitude flight patterns using general-purpose bombs. With this in mind, General Curtis LeMay, the USAAF new commander in the Pacific, ordered that the B-29 attacks be done at a much lower altitude, and that a policy of area bombing be instigated, with the mostly wooden Japanese buildings targeted with incendiaries. The first attacks took place in February 1945, and on the night of March 9–10th 334 B-29 bombers attacked Tokyo in "Operation Meetinghouse." Some 16 square miles (41 square kilometers) of the city were destroyed, and 100,000 people killed, the most deadly air raid of the war. In this attack, more people died from the immediate effects of the bombing than at either of the two atomic bomb sites of Hiroshima or Nagasaki. Such attacks continued until the end of the war.

Top Five Air Aces in the Two World Wars

The concept of the "Air Ace" derives from World War I, when combat aviators who had scored at least five confirmed "kills" were confirmed as an "ace." The term was originally a French one, derived from the French cavalry school, and was quickly transferred to another elite, the air force, with Adolphe Pégoud being identified as an "ace" by the press.

In the tables, "kills" represent the number of aircraft shot down per fighter pilot; where two pilots have successfully claimed they shot down the same aircraft, they are credited with a "half kill."

Manfred von Richthofen, the German top-scoring ace of World War I.

Air Aces of World War I

Central Powers Allied Powers

GERMANY		KILLS
M. v. Richthofen	Luftstreitkräfte	80
Ernst Udet	Luftstreitkräfte	62
Erich Löwenhardt	Luftstreitkräfte	56
Werner Voss	Luftstreitkräfte	48
Fritz Rumey	Luftstreitkräfte	45

FRANCE		KILLS
René Fonck	French Air Service	75
Georges Guynemer	French Air Service	53
Charles Nungesser	French Air Service	43
Georges Madon	French Air Service	41
Maurice Boyau	French Air Service	35

BRITAIN & COMMONWEALTH		KILLS
Edward Mannock	Royal Flying Corps	73
William Bishop	Royal Flying Corps	72
Raymond Collishaw	Royal Navy Air Service	61
James McCudden	Royal Flying Corps	57
A. Beauchamp-Proctor	Royal Flying Corps	45

UNITED STATES		KILLS
E. Rickenbacker	US Army	26
Frederick Gillet	US Army	20
Wilfred Beaver	US Army	19
Howard Kullberg	US Army	19
William Lambert	US Army	18

The maximum number of kills by air aces in World War I was 80, scored by Manfred von Richthofen. Richthofen was the consummate killer, and perfected his technique against the British observation aircraft that the fighters had been developed to destroy. He himself was brought down and killed by a Canadian aviator—though there is still discussion as to whether ground fire contributed. Allied aviators came close, with scores in the 1970s; US aviators have a smaller score given their relatively short period of operations in 1918.

By contrast, the air aces of World War II have huge kill scores, with the German Luftwaffe having figures measured in hundreds. This compares with tens scored by the Allies, with similar kills being registered by the Allies of Nazi Germany.

There has been much debate why this is the case. Longer operational periods, better aircraft, the poverty of the Soviet air force in the early days of the German invasion, and even accounting procedures have been suggested. Needless to say, the huge disparity indicates that the experience of the German aircrews in aerial combat was second to none in the first part of the war; but by 1943–1944, that tide was turning, and losses of both aircraft and pilots led to the passing of aerial supremacy to the Allies, and the loss of the war to the Nazis.

Air Aces of World War II

Axis Powers Allied Powers

GERMANY		KILLS
Erich Hartman	Luftwaffe	352
Gerhard Barkhorn	Luftwaffe	301
Günther Rall	Luftwaffe	275
Otto Kittel	Luftwaffe	267
Walter Nowotny	Luftwaffe	258
FINLAND		**KILLS**
Ilmari Juutilainen	Finnish Air Force	94
Hans Wind	Finnish Air Force	75
Eino Luukanen	Finnish Air Force	56
Urho Lehtovaara	Finnish Air Force	44.5
Oiva Tuominen	Finnish Air Force	44
JAPAN		**KILLS**
Hiroyoshi Nishizawa	Imperial Japanese Navy	87
Tetsuzo Iwamoto	Imperial Japanese Navy	80
Shigeo Fukumoto	Imperial Japanese Navy	72
Shoichi Sugita	Imperial Japanese Navy	70
Sabur Sakai	Imperial Japanese Navy	64
ROMANIA		**KILLS**
Constantin Cantacuzino	Romanian Air Force	56

CROATIA		KILLS
Mato Dukovac	Croatian Air Force	44
Cvitan Gali	Croatian Air Force	38
Franjo Dzai	Croatian Air Force	16
Ljudevit Benecetic	Croatian Air Force	15
Mato Culinovic	Croatian Air Force	12

SLOVAKIA		KILLS
Ján Režňák	Slovak Air Force	32
Izidor Kovárik	Slovak Air Force	28
Ján Gerthoffer	Slovak Air Force	26
Rudolf Božik	Slovak Air Force	17
František Cyprich	Slovak Air Force	15

HUNGARY		KILLS
Dezső Szentgyőrgyi	Royal Hungarian Air Force	30.5
Lajos Tóth	Royal Hungarian Air Force	26

ITALY		KILLS
Adriano Visconti	Regia Aeronautica	26
Franco Bordoni	Regia Aeronautica	19
Furio Niclot Doglio	Regia Aeronautica	7

BULGARIA		KILLS
Stoyan Stoyanov	Royal Bulgarian Air Force	5

SOVIET UNION		KILLS
Ivan Kozhedub	Soviet Air Force	62
Alexander Ivanovich Pokryhkin	Soviet Air Force	59
Grigoriy Rechkalov	Soviet Air Force	58
Nikolay Dmitrivich Gulayev	Soviet Air Force	57
Kirill Yevstigneyev	Soviet Air Force	53

US		KILLS
Richard I. Bong	US Army Air Force	40
Thomas B. McGuire	US Army Air Force	38
David McCampbell	US Navy	34
Francis Gabreski	US Army Air Force	28
Gregory Boyington	US Marine Corps	28

SOUTH AFRICA		KILLS
Marmaduke Pattle	Royal Air Force	40
Adolph Malan	Royal Air Force	32
John Frost	South African Air Force	15
Basil Gerald Stapleton	Royal Air Force	6.6

CANADA		KILLS
George F. Beurling	Royal Air Force	31
Edward F. Charles	Royal Canadian Air Force	22
Henry W. McLeod	Royal Canadian Air Force	20
William McKnight	Royal Air Force	17
William T. Kiersey	Royal Canadian Air Force	16.5

UNITED KINGDOM		KILLS
James Edgar Johnson	Royal Air Force	38
Brendan E.F. Finucane	Royal Air Force (Irish citizen)	32
William Vale	Royal Air Force	30
Robert Stanford Tuck	Royal Air Force	29
Bob Braham	Royal Air Force	29

FRANCE		KILLS
Pierre Clostermann	Free French Air Force (RAF)	33
Jean Demozay	Royal Air Force	21
Pierre Le Gloan	French Air Force	18
Edmond Marin le Meslée	French Air Force	16

AUSTRALIA		KILLS
Clive Caldwell	Royal Australian Air Force	28.5
Keith Truscott	Royal Australian Air Force	17
Nigel Cullen	Royal Air Force	16.5
Adrian Goldsmith	Royal Australian Air Force	16.25
Les Clisby	Royal Air Force	16

NEW ZEALAND		KILLS
Colin Falkland Gray	Royal Air Force	27.5
Alan Christopher Deere	Royal Air Force	22
Raymond Brown Hesselyn	Royal New Zealand Air Force	21.5
Johnnie Checketts	Royal New Zealand Air Force	14.5
Geoff Fisken	Royal New Zealand Air Force	11

POLAND		KILLS
Stanisław Skalski	Polish Air Force (RAF)	18
Witold Urbanowicz	Polish Air Force (RAF)	18
Bolesław Gładych	Polish Air Force (USAAF)	17
Jan Zumbach	Polish Air Force	13
Henryk Pietrzak	Polish Air Force (RAF)	12.5

CZECHOSLOVAKIA		KILLS
Karel Kuttelwascher	Czech Air Force (RAF)	18
Josef Frantisek	Czech Air Force (RAF)	17
Alois Vasatko	Royal Air Force	17

RHODESIA		KILLS
John I. A. Plagis	Royal Air Force	16

CHINA		KILLS
John Wong Pan-Yan	Chinese Nationalist Air Force	13
Liu Chi-Sheng	Chinese Nationalist Air Force	11.3
Arthur Chin	Chinese Nationalist Air Force	8.5
Liu Chui-Kang	Chinese Nationalist Air Force	7
Le Yi-Chin	Chinese Nationalist Air Force	6

GREECE		KILLS
Steve Pisanos	Royal Air Force/ US Army Air Force	10
Marinos Mitralexis	Greek Air Force	5

BELGIUM		KILLS
Remy Van Lierde	Royal Air Force	6

Brendan "Paddy" Finucane, one of the RAF's World War II flying aces.

Chapter Five

AT SEA

The War at Sea was fought from the start; no lull, no Phoney War: the Battle of the Atlantic was one of the most drawn out and significant battles in history. In the Pacific the Japanese attacked the US base at Pearl Harbor on the "Day of Infamy," December 7th, 1941. But no US aircraft carriers were at harbor; this would haunt the Japanese. The Battle of Midway, June 4th, 1942, fought by carrier aircraft, was a major turning point of the war.

Mers-el-Kebír

The Fall of France in June 1940 was accompanied by armistice conditions that specified that the new French state—Vichy France, under Marshal Pétain—could maintain an armed force of only 100,000 men (the same specified for Germany in the Treaty of Versailles following the Great War), but that its considerable naval force would have to be disarmed under German or Italian supervision.

France was a significant naval power; the possibility that its fleet could fall into enemy hands was a matter of concern for the British. With Britain facing Nazi Germany alone, the addition of French warships to Hitler's growing navy could not be countenanced. Admiral Françoise Darlan was a supporter of Pétain's actions and as Minister for the Navy, he ordered the French fleet to the relative safety of French North Africa. Fearing the worst from the collaborationist, Winston Churchill and the Royal Navy made overtures to Darlan that the ships should instead be handed over to the British, or that they should be removed to the Caribbean. Darlan refused, but gave assurances to Churchill that the French fleet would not fall into German hands. Such assurances were rejected; a British naval task force was dispatched to Algeria with orders to destroy the French fleet if it could not be persuaded to actively join the Allies. Arriving in Algeria, Admiral James Somerville delivered his ultimatum: "we must make sure that the best ships of the French Navy are not used against us... I have the orders from His Majesty's Government to use whatever force may be necessary to prevent your ships from falling into German hands." The negotiations were to break down; with no movement, the British decided to act.

On July 3rd, 1940, the British task force engaged the French fleet as it lay at anchor at Mers-el-Kebír. Bombarding the fleet, the British sunk one battleship and damaged five other naval vessels, and the French suffered almost 1,300 fatalities. The act was controversial, the justification blunt; Britain would be strong in its resolve to fight its enemies.

French sailors attempt to stop the flames caused by British bombardment in 1940.

French Fleet

Ship	Type	Fate	Casualties: Officers	Petty officers	Sailors and marines	Totals
Dunkerque	Battlecruiser	Damaged & run aground	9	32	169	210
Strasbourg	Battlecruiser	Damaged	0	2	3	5
Bretagne	Battleship	Sunk	36	151	825	1,012
Provence	Battleship	Damaged & run aground	1	2	0	3
Commandant Teste	Seaplane tender	Lightly damaged	0	0	0	0
Mogador	Destroyer	Damaged & run aground	0	3	35	38
Volta	Destroyer	Escaped	0	0	0	0
Terrible	Destroyer	Escaped	0	0	0	0
Kersaint	Destroyer	Escaped	0	0	0	0
Lynx	Destroyer	Escaped	0	0	0	0
Tigre	Destroyer	Escaped	0	0	0	0
Terre-Neuve	Patrol boat	Torpedoed & sunk	1	1	6	8
Rigault de Genouily	Gun boat	Sunk	0	3	9	12
Armen	Tug	Sunk	0	3	3	6
Esterel	Tug	Sunk	1	5	0	6
					TOTAL French casualties	**1,300**

British Fleet

Ship	Type
HMS *Hood*	Battlecruiser
HMS *Resolution*	Battleship
HMS *Valiant*	Battleship
HMS *Ark Royal*	Aircraft carrier
HMS *Arethusa*	Light cruiser
HMS *Enterprise*	Light cruiser
HMS *Faulknor*	Destroyer
HMS *Foxhound*	Destroyer
HMS *Fearless*	Destroyer
HMS *Forester*	Destroyer
HMS *Foresight*	Destroyer
HMS *Escort*	Destroyer
HMS *Keppel*	Destroyer
HMS *Active*	Destroyer
HMS *Wrestler*	Destroyer
HMS *Vidette*	Destroyer
HMS *Vortigern*	Destroyer

The Battle of Taranto

The Battle of Taranto holds a significant place in history as the first time that naval aircraft alone had been deployed to destroy naval ships. Taranto was to have a significant influence on the Japanese naval planning when developing the attack at Pearl Harbor, just five months later. Fought by the Royal Navy against the Italian *Regia Marina* at anchor in the harbor at Taranto on November 11–12th, 1940, the attack demonstrated the importance of naval aviation in coming battles—even though the British aircraft were largely obsolete Fairey Swordfish torpedo bombers.

British Forces

HMS Illustrious *at sea in 1944. In November 1940 she was the first aircraft carrier in history to launch an aerial attack at an enemy fleet, at Taranto.*

Length: 36 ft (10.87 m)
Wingspan: 45 ft (13.87 m)
Engine: 1 x Bristol Pegasus radial engine
Max. speed: 139 mph (224 km/h)
Range: 546 miles (879 km)
Ceiling: 19,258 ft (5,870 m)
Armament: 2 x .33 Vickers MG
Bombs: 1 x 1,675 lb (760 kg) torpedo or 1,543 lb (700 kg) mine

FAIREY SWORDFISH

HMS *ILLUSTRIOUS*

Commissioned: 1940
Displacement: 25,759 tons (23,369 tonnes)
Length: 744 ft (226.7 m)
Speed: 30.5 knots
Range: 11,000 nautical miles
Complement: 1,900
Armament: 10 x 320 mm guns
12 x 120 mm guns
8 x 100 mm guns
8 x 37 mm guns
12 x 20 mm guns
Armor: 11 in (280 mm) max

The Italian fleet, consisting of six battleships, seven heavy cruisers, two light cruisers and eight destroyers, was at anchor in the Gulf of Taranto, close to the heel of Italy. With Britain standing alone against Hitler, and Mussolini's impressive navy a distinct threat, it was essential that this navy should be neutralized. Rather than enticing the fleet out to sea for a traditional ship-to-ship fight, it was decided to utilize naval aircraft. The British naval force consisted of the aircraft carrier HMS *Illustrious* equipped with 24 Fairey Swordfish torpedo bombers (some transferred from the older ship, HMS *Eagle*), together with two heavy cruisers, two light cruisers and four destroyers. It was the Swordfish that would deliver the lethal blows, even though the waters were shallow; but the British had modified their torpedoes to operate in much shallower water than normal.

The attack commenced at 21:00 on November 11th, with 11 Swordfish armed with torpedoes, another ten with bombs, attacking in two waves at about an hour apart. The first wave of 12 aircraft attacked at 22:58 and, marked out by flares, the torpedoes were set among the enemy ships. The second wave arrived at around midnight to continue the attack. The torpedo bombers sunk battleship *Conte di Cavour* and left two more, the *Littorio* and *Caio Duilio*, heavily damaged; a heavy cruiser was also badly hit. The Royal Navy lost two Swordfish; the Italian Navy had effectively been halved; there would be 660 casualties to four (two killed, two captured), for the British. The age of the aircraft carrier had well and truly arrived.

Italian Ships Damaged

CONTE CAVOUR	
Commissioned:	1915 (relaunched, 1937)
Displacement:	32,255 tons (29,262 tonnes)
Length:	611 ft (186.4 m)
Speed:	28 knots
Range:	3,100 nautical miles
Complement:	1,236
Armament:	16 x 4.5 in guns
	48 x 2-pounder guns
Aircraft:	15 Fulmar, 18 Swordfish

LITTORIO	
Commissioned:	1940
Displacement:	45,609 tons (41,376 tonnes)
Length:	780 ft (237.76 m)
Speed:	29 knots
Range:	3,920 nautical miles
Complement:	1,802
Armament:	9 x 381 mm guns
	12 x 152 mm guns
	4 x 120 mm guns
	20 x 37 mm guns
	20 x 20 mm guns
	6 x 8 mm guns
Armor:	14 in (350 mm) max

CAIO DULLO	
Commissioned:	1916 (modernized 1937)
Displacement:	29,605 tons (26,858 tonnes)
Length:	554 ft (168.96 m)
Speed:	27 knots
Range:	3,100 nautical miles
Complement:	1,485
Armament:	10 x 320 mm guns
	12 x 135 mm guns
	10 x 90 mm guns
	15 x 37 mm guns
	16 x 20 mm guns
	6 x 8 mm guns
Armor:	11 in (280 mm) max

Pearl Harbor
1941

On Sunday, December 7th, 1941 the Imperial Japanese Navy launched a surprise attack against the US Forces stationed at Pearl Harbor, Hawaii. The Japanese commander attacked at the weekend, in the expectation that US naval activities would be reduced and much of the US Pacific Fleet would be in harbor.

Central to the Japanese plans was the targeting of American aircraft carriers, which were a key component of US naval strength. Fortunately for the Americans, these valuable vessels were all out of the harbor: USS *Enterprise* was returning from Wake Island; USS *Lexington* was ferrying aircraft to Midway; USS *Saratoga* and USS *Colorado* were undergoing repairs. Despite receiving intelligence that the carriers were missing from the fleet, Admiral Nagumo decided to continue the attack. At a range of 230 miles (370 km) north of Oahu, he launched the first wave of a two-wave attack. Beginning at 06:00, his first wave, consisting of 40 Nakajima B5N2 "Kate" torpedo bombers, 51 Aichi D3A1 "Val" divebombers 50 high-altitude bombers and 43 Zeros, struck airfields at Hickam, Kaneohe, and Ewa and the fleet at anchor in Pearl Harbor. The second strike at the same targets consisted of 167 aircraft, and was launched 75 minutes later.

Japanese Forces

AIRCRAFT CARRIERS:

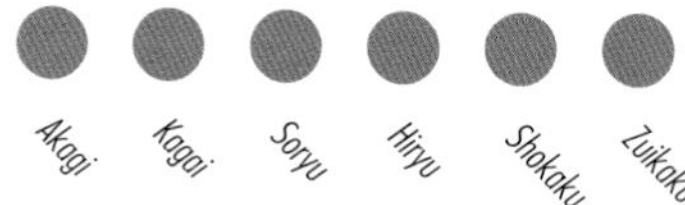

BATTLESHIPS:

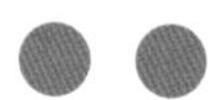

CRUISERS:

DESTROYERS:

TANKERS:

MIDGET SUBMARINE:

SUBMARINES: 213

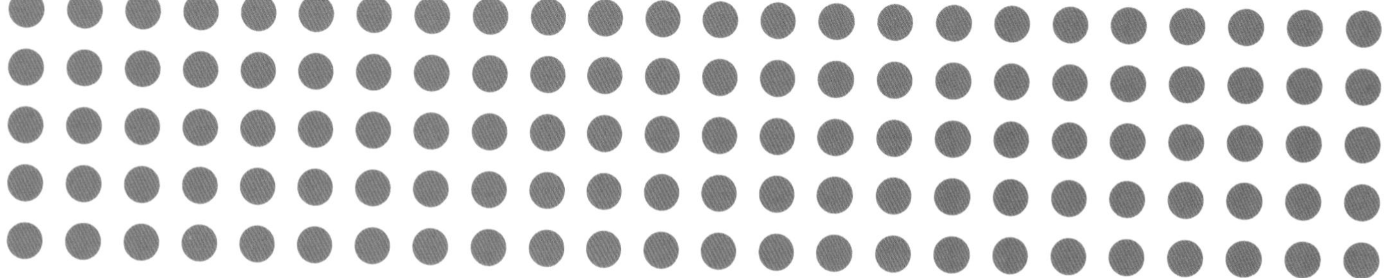

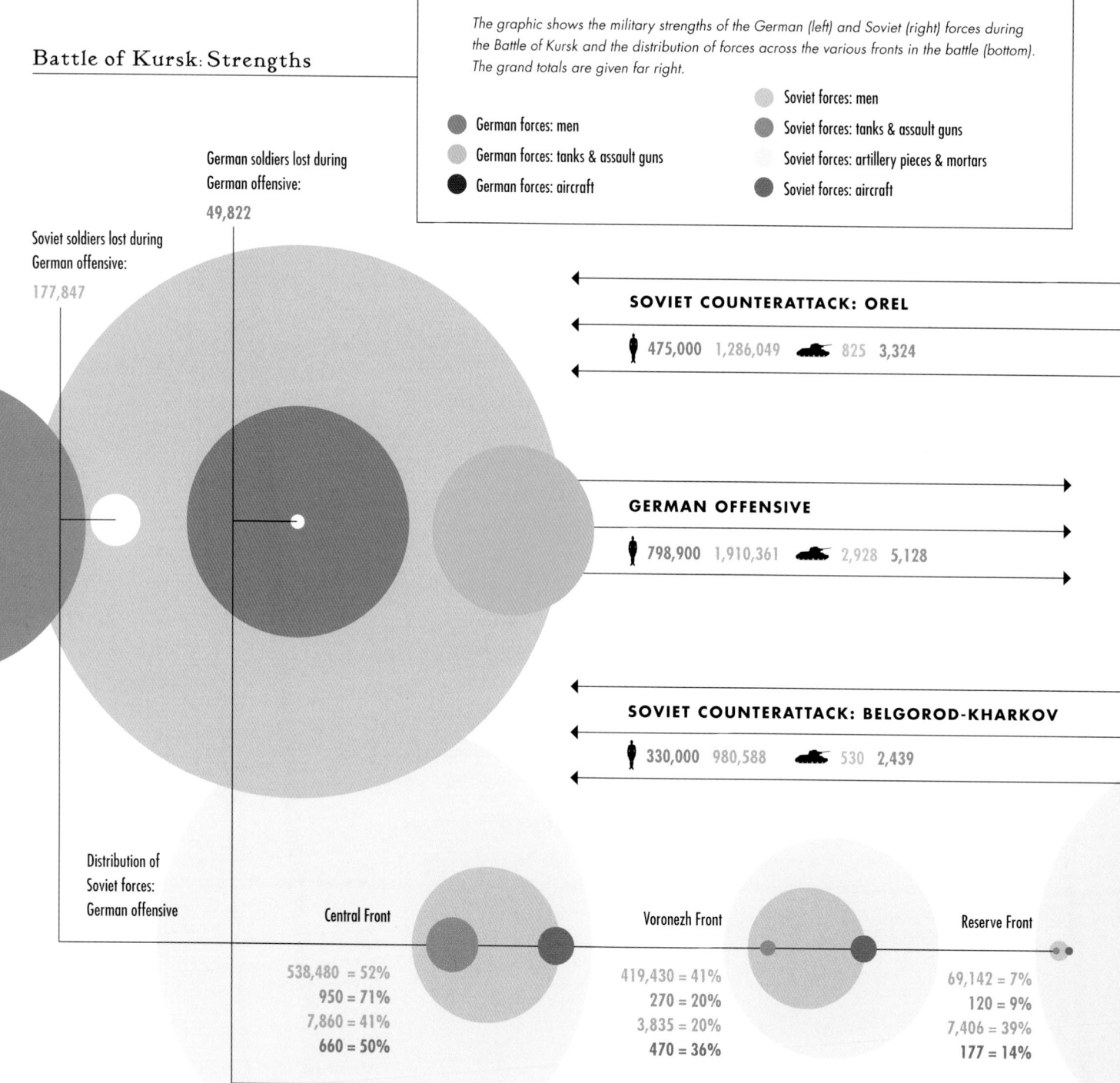

US Forces

BATTLESHIPS:

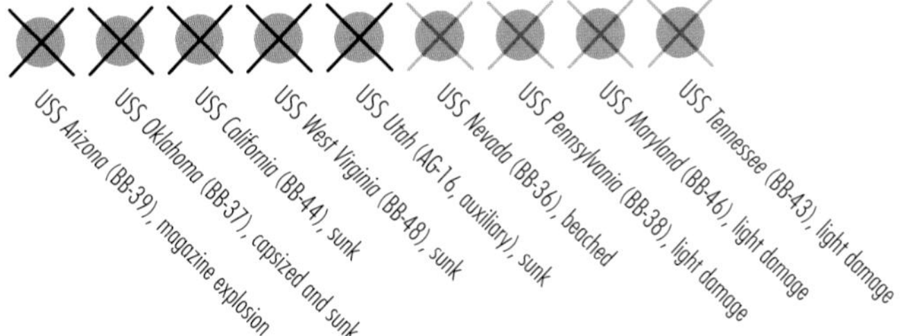

CRUISERS:

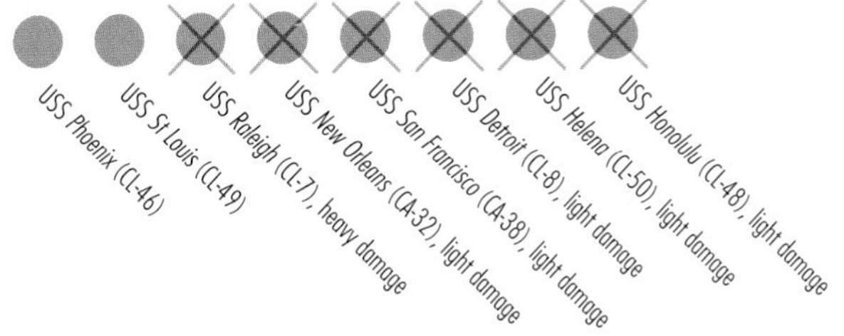

DESTROYERS: 30

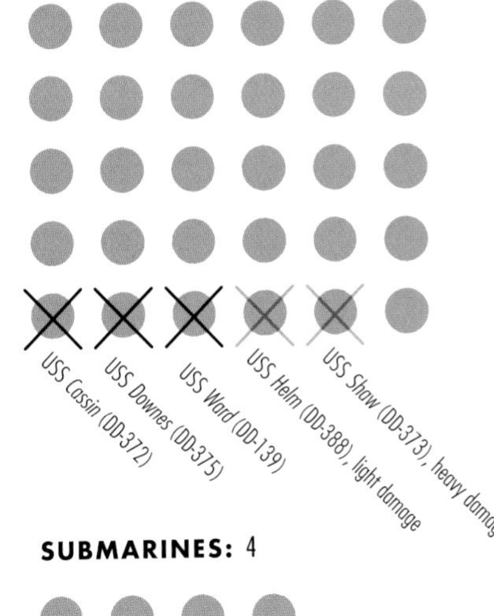

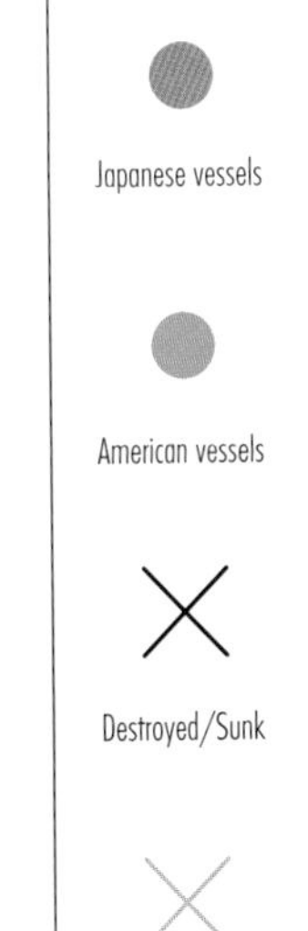

SUBMARINES: 4

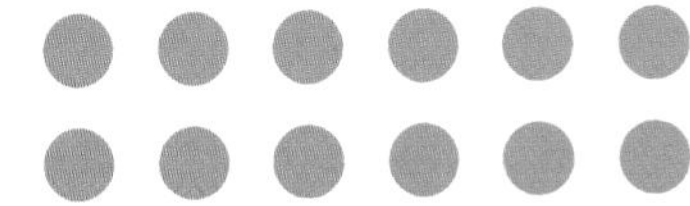

MOTOR TORPEDO (PT) BOATS:

OTHER SHIPS: 68

Pearl Harbor Aircraft Figures

US AIRCRAFT

Total present: 423 Total lost: 328

Present
Unharmed
159 damaged
169 destroyed

USAAF: 223

USMC: 69

USN: 131

JAPANESE AIRCRAFT

Total present: 387 Total lost: 103

Present
Unharmed
74 damaged
29 destroyed

Akagi: 63

Kagai: 72

Soryu: 54

Hiryu: 54

Shokaku: 72

Zuikaku: 72

Casualties

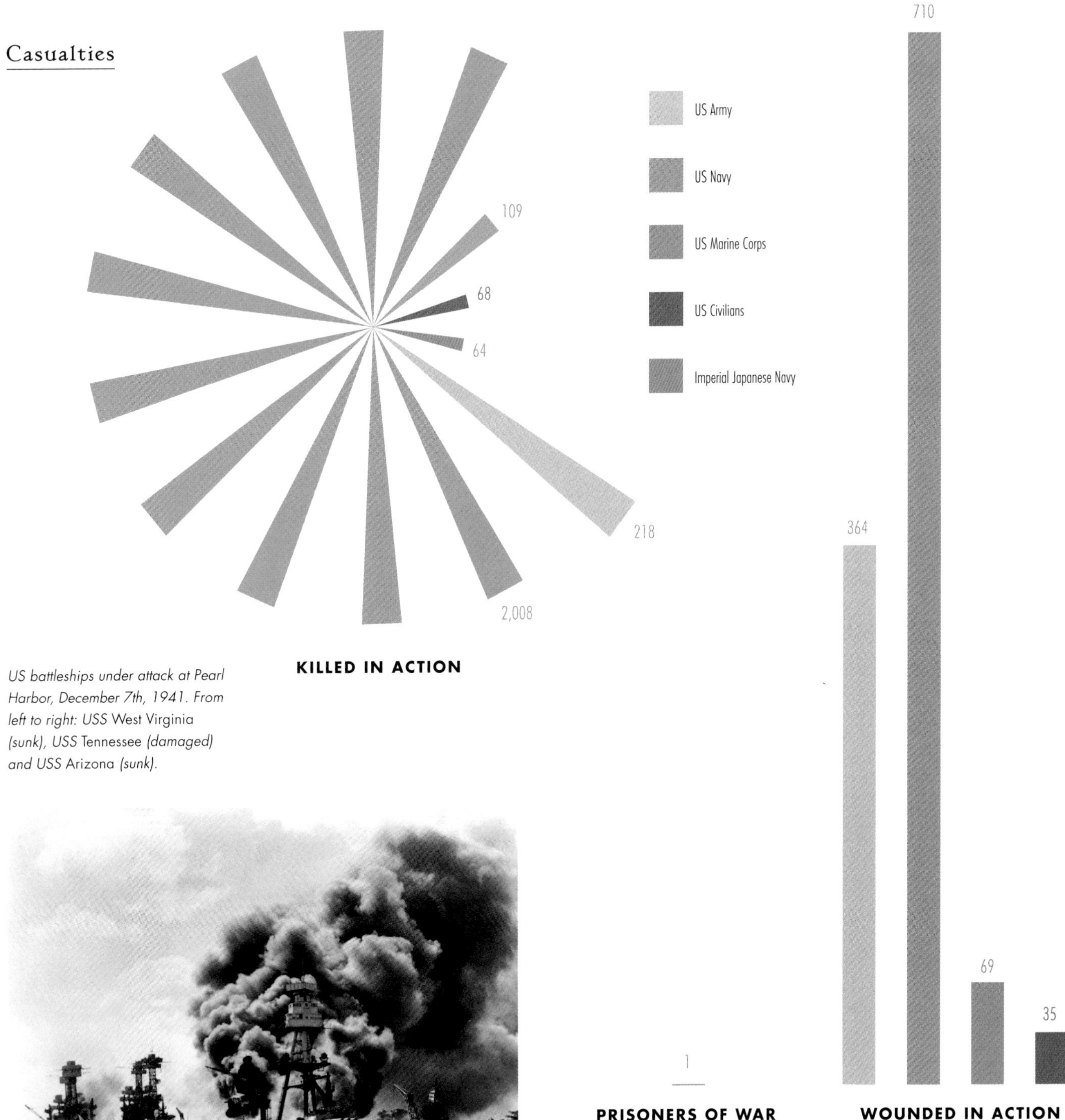

US battleships under attack at Pearl Harbor, December 7th, 1941. From left to right: USS West Virginia *(sunk), USS* Tennessee *(damaged) and USS* Arizona *(sunk).*

The Battle of the Atlantic

The "Phoney War" was the term given to the period of eerie quiet on the Western Front that lasted from the Allies' declaration of war in September 1939 to the German invasion in May 1940. Although there was little active fighting on land, at sea it was another matter.

5,151

2,742

An Allied tanker sinks after being torpedoed during the Battle of the Atlantic, 1942.

With the declaration of war came an immediate response from the Germans, including the first sinking of the conflict—that of the SS *Athenia*—just hours later. What became known as the Battle of the Atlantic would represent the longest-running battle in World War II and would see over 5,150 Allied ships sunk with the loss of more than 30,000 merchant and naval seamen. The campaign would last the full six years of the war.

The purpose of the battle was both to prosecute the Allied intention to blockade Germany and its Allies, and the equally fierce intention from the Axis powers, and specifically Germany, to starve Britain into submission by cutting off its vital supply lines from the US and British

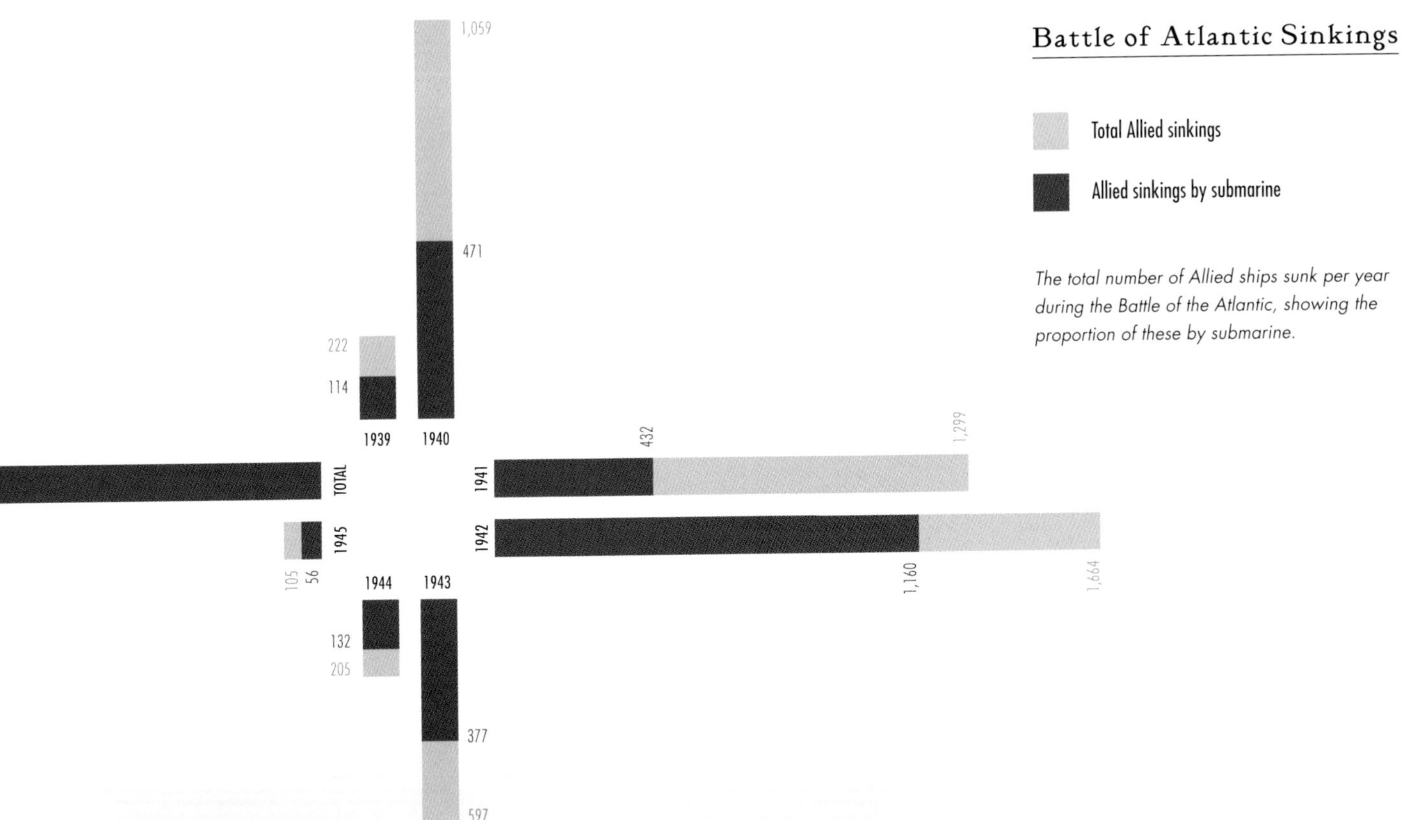

The total number of Allied ships sunk per year during the Battle of the Atlantic, showing the proportion of these by submarine.

Commonwealth. With Britain heavily dependent on imported foodstuffs, and requiring a lifeline to the US to supply military matériel through Lend-Lease, the battle was a highly significant one.

With the German naval fleet comprising mostly U-boats, the war would be largely fought between German submarines and British convoys, together with their British, Canadian, and after 1941, US naval protection vessels. Surface raiders also represented a significant threat to Allied shipping. Convoy battles would be a regular feature of the war—with convoys being targeted by the German raiders—but there would also be many single-ship encounters. The U-boats had their greatest successes in 1940–1941, referred to as the "Happy Time," and over 270 ships were sunk in just a few months in the summer of 1940. U-boats would hunt in packs, known as wolf packs, and would seek out single ships and convoys. But with the entry of the US into the war (and their adoption of the convoy system), the use of coordinated aircraft, and anti-submarine vessels, the Allies gained the upper hand.

First to be beaten were the surface raiders, hunted down and sunk by the Allies by 1942, and in 1943 there was a sharp decline in sinkings by submarine as the new tactics were developed. Though sinkings took place right to the end of the war, after "Black May" in 1943, when the tide turned, the Allies would hold the key to the Atlantic.

Convoy Battles

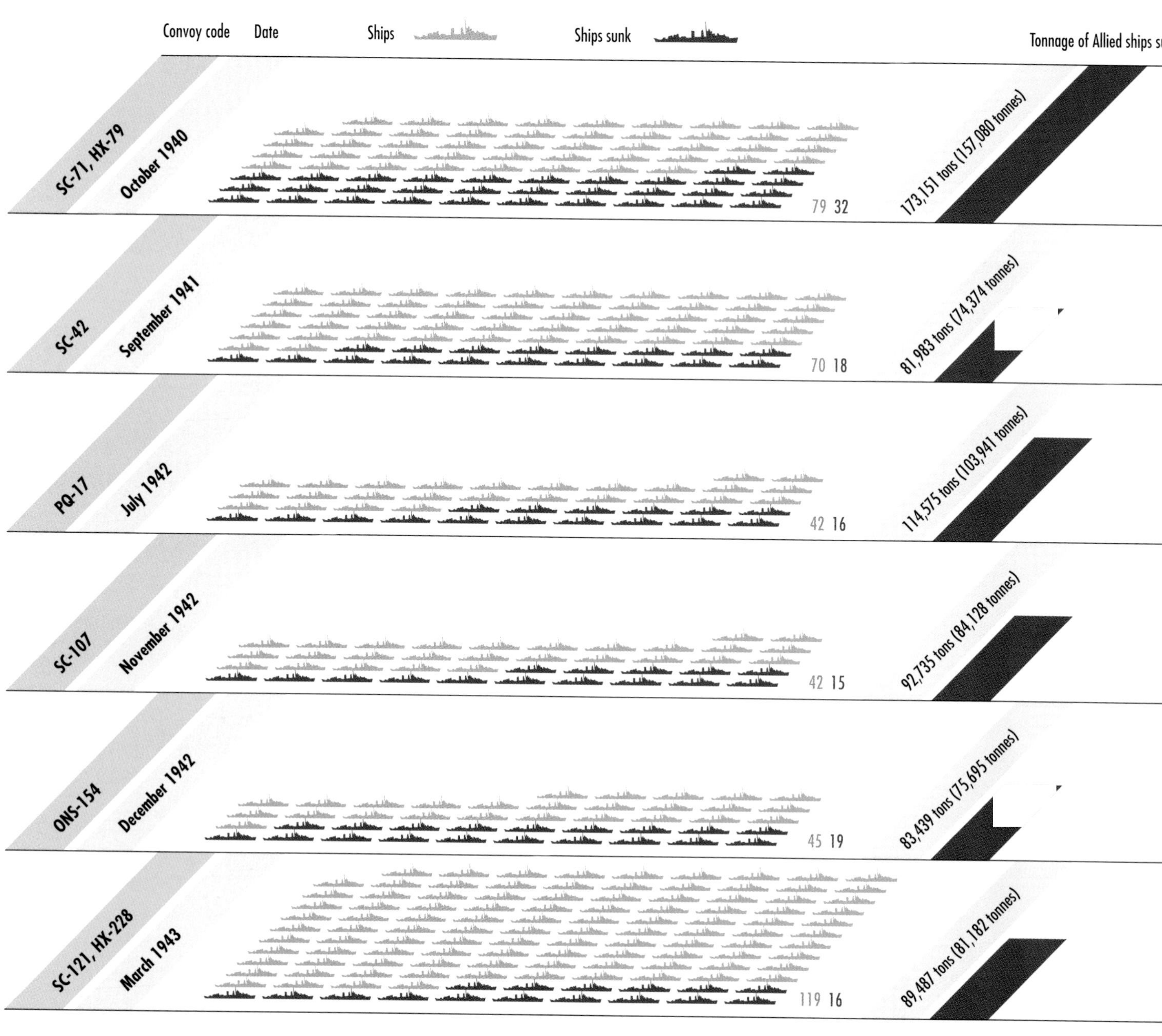
Convoy code
Date
Ships
Ships sunk
Tonnage of Allied ships su
SC-71, HX-79
October 1940
79 32
173,151 tons (157,080 tonnes)
SC-42
September 1941
70 18
81,983 tons (74,374 tonnes)
PQ-17
July 1942
42 16
114,575 tons (103,941 tonnes)
SC-107
November 1942
42 15
92,735 tons (84,128 tonnes)
ONS-154
December 1942
45 19
83,439 tons (75,695 tonnes)
SC-121, HX-228
March 1943
119 16
89,487 tons (81,182 tonnes)

Allied Losses in Convoy Battles, 1940–1943

U-boats | U-boats sunk

12 0

19 2

11 0

18 3

19 1

37 2

CREW LOST

1939	260	495
1940	3,375	5,622
1941	5,632	7,838
1942	8,413	9,736
1943	3,826	4,606
1944	1,163	1,512
1945	229	323

Lost by all enemy causes — Total crew: 30,132 — Total ships: 2,177

Lost by U-boat — Total crew: 22,898 — Total ships: 1,315

SHIPS LOST

1939	50	95
1940	225	511
1941	288	568
1942	452	590
1943	203	266
1944	67	102
1945	30	45

Convoy PQ17: Losses
1942

Convoy PQ17 suffered one of the greatest losses of all convoys during the Battle of the Atlantic. The Battle of the Atlantic was fought from the very beginning of the war; keeping the shipping lanes open to supply the Allies from the US through to the Soviet Union was vital if Nazi Germany was to be crushed.

The convoy system had been developed in World War I as a means of combatting the U-boat menace; introduced in 1917, it allowed merchant ships to sail together and be protected by naval vessels equipped for anti-submarine warfare. In the Great War it had helped decrease the impact of the U-boat dramatically, so it was not surprising

PQ17: Ships Lost

Ships registered in Allied countries as lost during the Luftwaffe and U-boat attack on convoy PQ17, and the causes of their destruction.

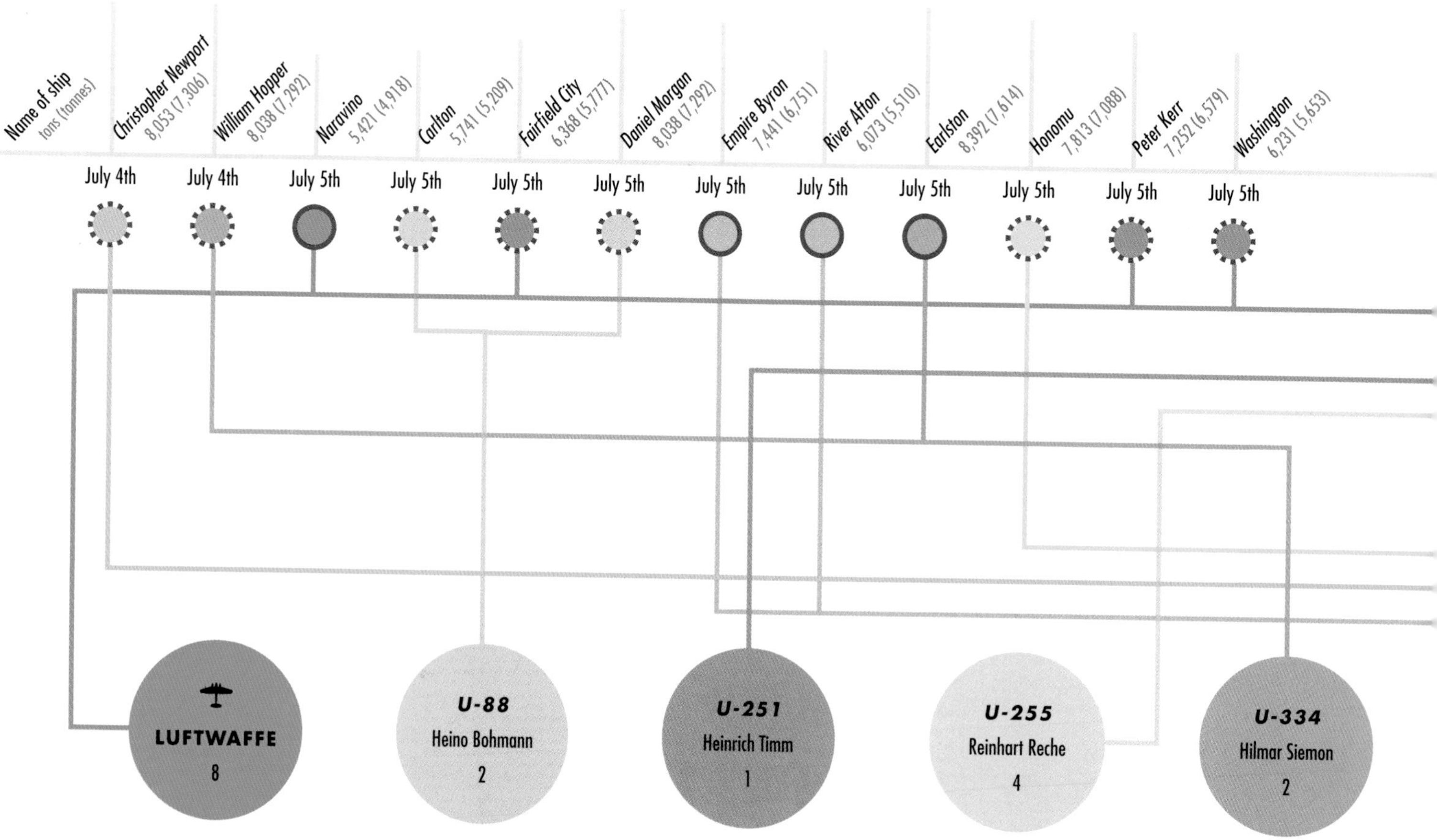

Name of ship	tons (tonnes)	Date
Christopher Newport	8,053 (7,306)	July 4th
William Hopper	8,038 (7,292)	July 4th
Navarino	5,421 (4,918)	July 5th
Carlton	5,741 (5,209)	July 5th
Fairfield City	6,368 (5,777)	July 5th
Daniel Morgan	8,038 (7,292)	July 5th
Empire Byron	7,441 (6,751)	July 5th
River Afton	6,073 (5,510)	July 5th
Earlston	8,392 (7,614)	July 5th
Honomu	7,813 (7,088)	July 5th
Peter Kerr	7,252 (6,579)	July 5th
Washington	6,231 (5,653)	July 5th

LUFTWAFFE
8

U-88
Heino Bohmann
2

U-251
Heinrich Timm
1

U-255
Reinhart Reche
4

U-334
Hilmar Siemon
2

that the system was used again to great effect in World War II.

Despite its overall effectiveness, convoys were still vulnerable. U-boats attacking in packs or alone could stalk vulnerable ships, and there were commerce raiders at large. While tactics were varied during the war to deal with these menaces, there is one convoy above all others that suffered the greatest loss of merchant shipping: PQ17.

On June 27th, 1942 this convoy sailed from Hvalfjord, Iceland, carrying supplies to the Soviet Union intending to dock at Arkhangelsk. Under attack from the start, the convoy was nevertheless well protected by the battleships HMS *Duke of York* and USS *Washington*, the carrier HMS *Illustrious*, six British and American cruisers, 20 destroyers, four corvettes, and a range of other vessels, all serving under British command. The threat of surface raiders was real in 1942, and with information received by the Admiralty that the battleship *Tirpitz* and the cruiser *Hipper* were fuelled and ready to attack, the convoy was ordered to disperse at 21:36 on July 4th, 1942. With this order the escorts departed, and the merchant ships were scattered, vulnerable, and left to their own devices. Only 11 of the original ships would make it into port. For two weeks the largely defenceless merchant ships were attacked repeatedly by U-boats and by Luftwaffe aircraft patrolling in the long summer light of the Arctic. It would be the biggest convoy loss of the entire war.

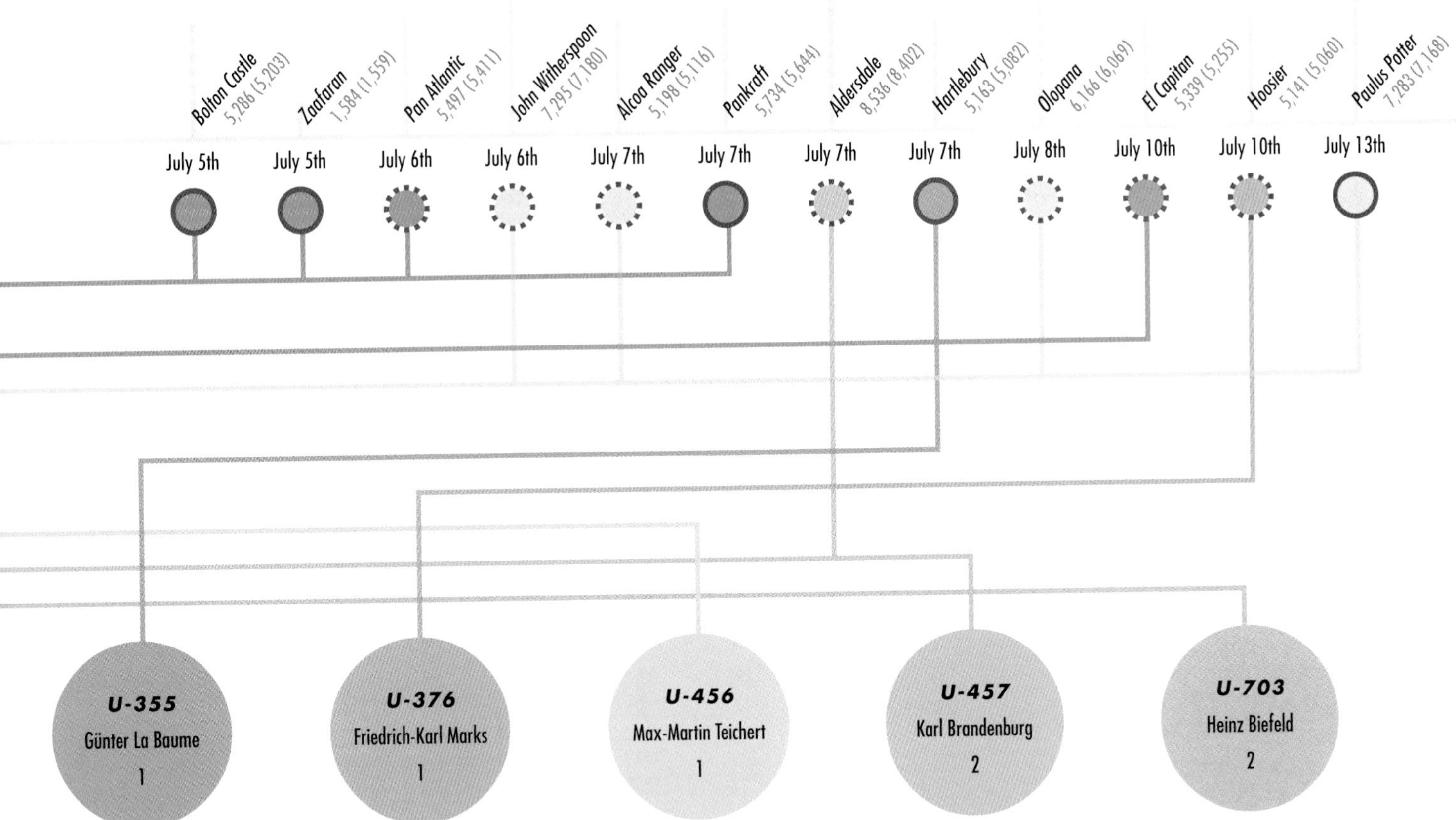

Submarine Losses

The U-boat was the primary weapon of the Kriegsmarine. Though Hitler's battleships were high-profile, the admirals knew that the only effective way for the German Navy to make an impact was to once more attack the merchant shipping that formed the vital supply line between Britain and the US. Admiral Dönitz advocated the use of U-boat packs to seek out convoys and to pick off vulnerable ships while their escorts sought them out. With the fall of France came the opportunity for Dönitz to move his submarine bases to the Atlantic coast, placing his U-boat fleet in closer proximity to the Allied convoys. This was what the U-boat captains called the "Happy Time" with the U-boats sinking large numbers of Allied shipping.

Total Number of Losses Per Year

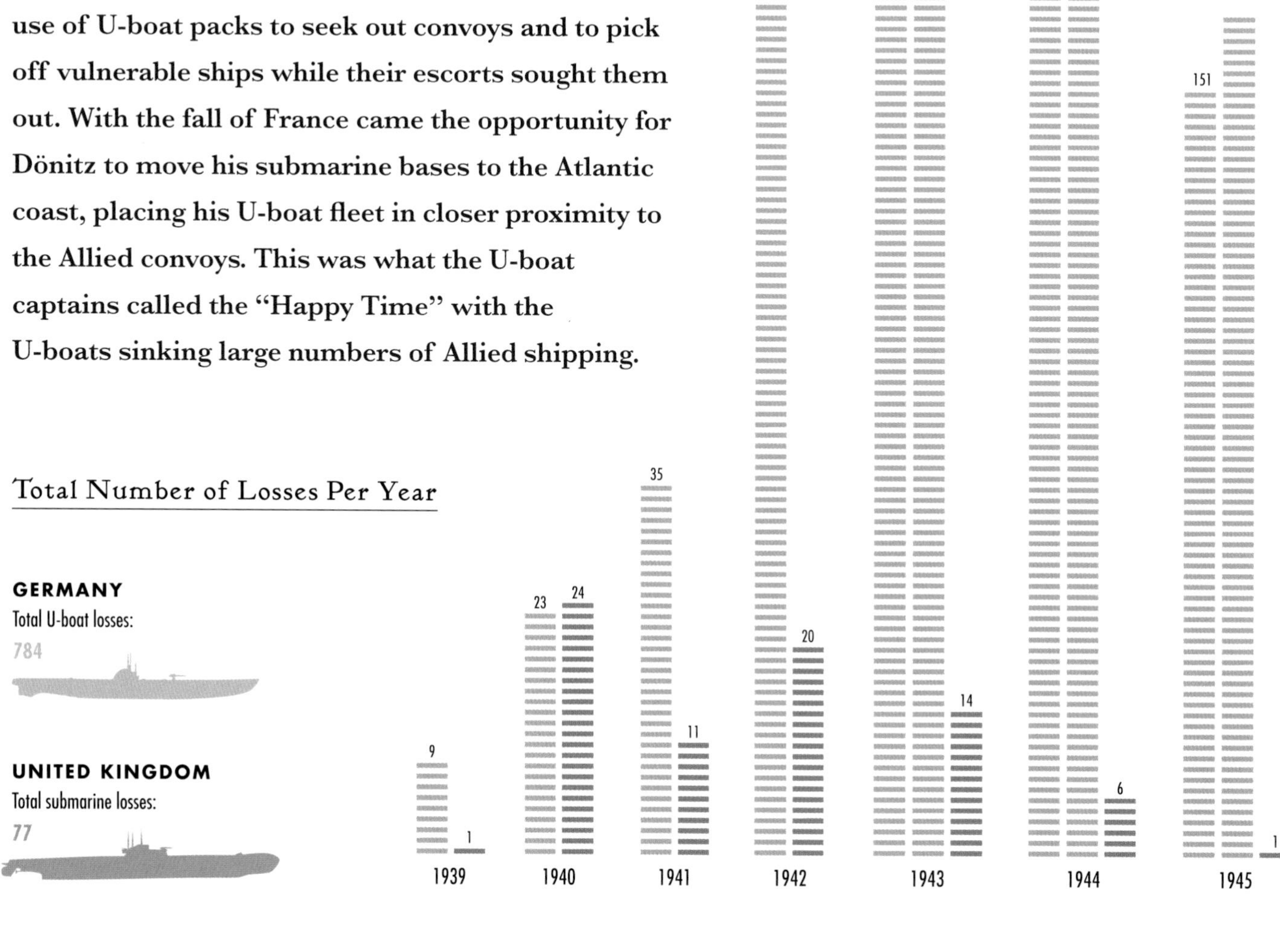

Submarine Losses by Attack Type. 1939–1945

Attacks on British and German submarines for the period 1939–1945. The most effective attacks were made by aircraft at sea, dropping bombs or launching torpedoes; or by naval attacks, such as depth charges when submerged; or gunfire when the submarine had surfaced.

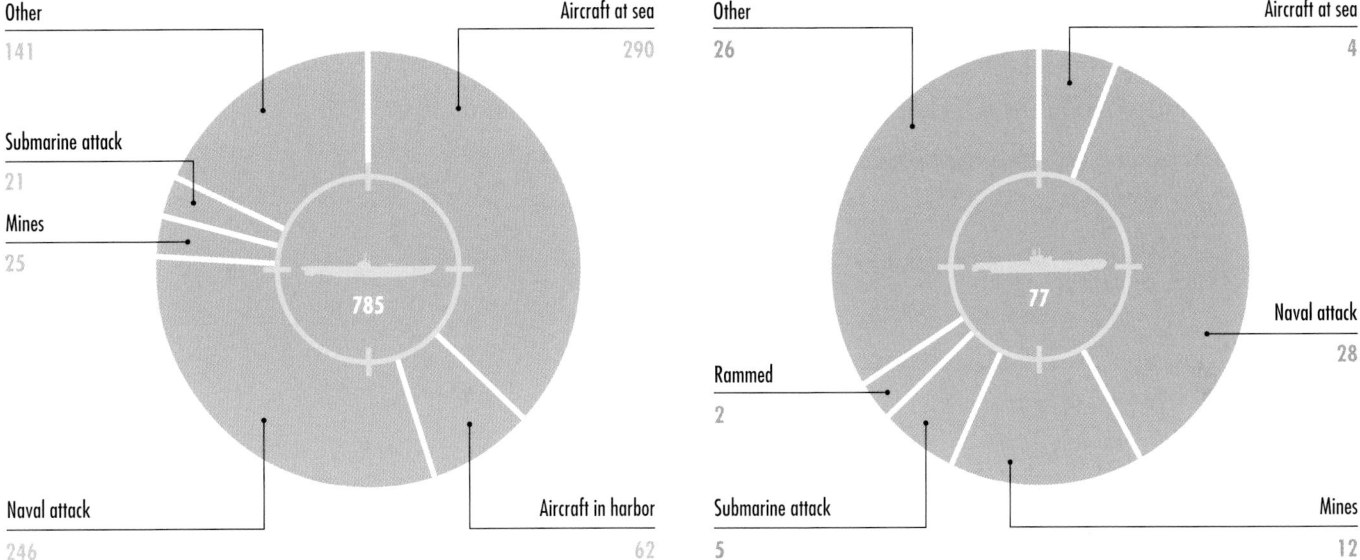

This would last into 1941, when the British improved their tactics, gained new escorts through Lend-Lease, and were more aggressive in searching out the U-boats. But it wasn't until 1942 that the tide began to turn against the Kriegsmarine, when convoy escorts became more numerous, and were tasked with aggressively hunting down the German submarines. For Dönitz, the Battle of the Atlantic became a war of attrition, with more merchant vessels lost than submarines.

In 1943, the Battle of the Atlantic was reaching new heights, and the supply levels in Britain were in a perilous state; but by the spring, the pendulum was starting to swing in the Allies' favor—enhanced by the Allied interception and decoding (through the Enigma machine) of encrypted messages. Critically, the turning point was the successful defence of Convoy SC130, which left Halifax Nova Scotia on May 11th, 1943 with 37 ships; when the convoy docked in Liverpool two weeks later, they had not lost a single ship—yet five U-boats were lost to a combination of defences: Liberator and Hudson aircraft, and the new hedgehog anti-submarine mortar. May 1943 would be dubbed "Black May" with the new tactics and weapons claiming 34 U-boats for the loss of 34 Allied ships. In all, 785 U-boats would be lost in the campaign, some three-quarters of the fleet—and most of these by aircraft. By way of contrast, for the same period, just 77 British submarines would be destroyed, an order of magnitude less.

The Battle of Midway

With the Doolittle Raid on the Japanese home islands in April 1942 came the realization that Japan was not invulnerable to aerial attack. Though mostly a propaganda victory, the audacity of the American aircrews in attacking Honshu was a check to Japanese pride. And with the emperor directly threatened by aerial action, the Japanese were not content to sit back; direct action would be required to make sure this did not happen again.

The Battle of the Coral Sea, fought from May 4–8th, 1942 saw the Imperial Japanese Navy attempting to extend its defensive perimeter to New Guinea and the Solomon Islands—thereby limiting the opportunities for American air raids. A joint US and Australian naval force checked the Japanese, however, and though the Americans lost the carrier *Lexington*, with the *Yorktown* damaged, it was the Japanese who were to suffer the most, their ambitions checked. Their next target, a month later, was the lonely island of Midway, a tiny atoll in the Pacific Ocean that had been US territory since 1867. Some 1,150 miles (1,850 km) north-west of Hawaii and 2,600 miles (4,184 km) from Tokyo, it was nevertheless an important staging post for the US Navy in the Pacific.

On June 4th, 1942, the Japanese fleet sent to attack the atoll was spotted by US naval aircraft; and Midway would become a naval battle that was fought with aircraft almost exclusively. Japanese Zero fighters from the four fleet carriers were quickly engaged and for the most part destroyed; divebombers from the three American carriers (including the *Yorktown*, patched up from her ordeal a month earlier) soon set the three carriers *Akagi*, *Kaga*, and *Soryu* ablaze though with heavy losses. The *Yorktown* would once again be targeted, and heavily damaged, this time by aircraft from the *Hiryu*. The *Hiryu* would soon be destroye by US aircraft; the *Yorktown* would be sunk days later by a Japanese submarine.

The Battle of Midway was a significant turning point in the Pacific war. The Japanese had lost much of their strike force, their valuable aircraft carriers, and the tide had turned in the favor of the Allies. No longer would the Japanese be on the offensive in the Pacific.

► Aircraft

† Men

✷ Ship lost (sunk or damaged)

JAPANESE STRENGTHS AND LOSSES

US STRENGTHS AND LOSSES

JAPANESE AIRCRAFT CARRIERS AND AIRCRAFT LOSSES

AKAGI (sunk)

267 men

24
18
18

KAGA (sunk)

811 men

27
20
27

HIRYU (sunk)

392 men

21
18
18

SORYU (sunk)

711 men

21
16
18

ZUIHO (LIGHT CARRIER)

6
6
12

Japanese carrier planes loss rate: 270/270 (100%)

Aircraft carrier loss rates: 4/4 (100%)

TOTAL JAPANESE AIRCRAFT LOSSES

99 ► Mitsubishi Type 0 fighters
72 ► Aichi Type 99 divebombers
93 ► Nakajima Type 97 torpedo bombers
6 ► Mitsubishi Type 96 attack bombers

✷ Indicates ships damaged or sunk.

JAPANESE CARRIER STRIKING TASK FORCE LOSSES

DESTROYERS

- Akigumo
- Amatsukase
- Arare
- ✷ Arashi (damaged)
- ✷ Arashio (damaged)
- Asagumo
- Ayanami
- Funbuki
- Hagikaze
- Hamakaze
- Harusame
- Hatsukaze
- Hatsuyuki
- Hayashio
- Isokaze
- Isonami
- Kagero
- Kasumi
- ✷ Kazagumo (damaged)
- Kuroshio
- Maikaze
- Makigumo
- Minegumo
- Marazuki
- Murakumo
- Murasame
- Natsugumo
- Nowake
- Oyashio
- Samidaer
- Shikinami
- Shiranuhi
- Shirayuki
- ✷ Tanikase (damaged)
- Tokisukaze
- Urakaze
- Uranami
- Yudachi
- Yukaze
- Yukikaze
- Yura

CRUISERS

- Atago
- Chikuma
- Chokai
- Haguro
- Kumano
- ✷ Mikuma (sunk) +700 men
- ✷ Mogami (badly damaged) +92 men
- Myoko
- Suyuza
- Tone
- Jintsu
- Nagara

BATTLESHIPS

- Haruna
- Hiei
- Kirishima
- Kongo
- Mutsu
- Nagato
- Yamato

Destroyer loss rates: 4/41 (10%)

Cruiser loss rates 2/12: (17%)

Battleship loss rates 0

Total personnel losses: 3,057

Total personnel losses: 307 (92 officers, 215 men)

Destroyer loss rates: 1/15 (7%)

Cruiser loss rates: 0/8 (0%)

CRUISERS

- USS Astoria
- USS Portland
- USS New Orleans
- USS Minneapolis
- USS Vincennes
- USS Northampton
- USS Pensacola
- USS Atlanta

DESTROYERS

- ✷ USS Hammann (sunk)
- USS Hughes
- USS Morris
- USS Anderson
- USS Russell
- USS Gwin
- USS Phelps
- USS Worden
- USS Monaghan
- USS Aylwin
- USS Balch
- USS Conyngham
- USS Benham
- USS Ellet
- USS Maury

US CARRIER STRIKING TASK FORCE LOSSES

US AIRCRAFT CARRIERS AND AIRCRAFT LOSSES

✷ USS *YORKTOWN* (sunk)

10/25 (40%) ►►►►►►►►►►

24/37 (65%) ►►►►►►►►►►►►►►►►►►►►►►►►

12/13 (92%) ►►►►►►►►►►►►

USS *ENTERPRISE*

1/27 (4%) ►

20/38 (53%) ►►►►►►►►►►►►►►►►►►►►

11/14 (79%) ►►►►►►►►►►►

USS *HORNET*

12/27 (81%) ►►►►►►►►►►►►

10/37 (27%) ►►►►►►►►►►

15/15 (100%) ►►►►►►►►►►►►►►►

SHORE-BASED AIRCRAFT

Consolidated PBY Catalina flying boats	1/2	(50%)	►
Brewster F2A Buffalo fighters	13/20	(65%)	►►►►►►►►►►►►►
Grumman F4F Wildcat fighters	2/7	(29%)	►►
Vought SB2U Vindicator divebombers	5/11	(45%)	►►►►►
Douglas SBD Dauntless divebombers	8/16	(50%)	►►►►►►►►
Grumman TBF Avenger torpedo-bombers	5/6	(83%)	►►►►►
Martin B-26 Marauder bombers	2/4	(50%)	►►
Boeing B-17 Flying Fortress bombers	2/19	(11%)	►►

TOTAL US AIRCRAFT LOSSES

25/86 (29%) ► Grumman F4F Wildcat fighter

62/128 (48%) ► Douglas SBD Dauntless divebombers

38/42 (90%) ► Grumman TBD Avenger torpedo-bombers

23/56 (41%) ► Other aircraft

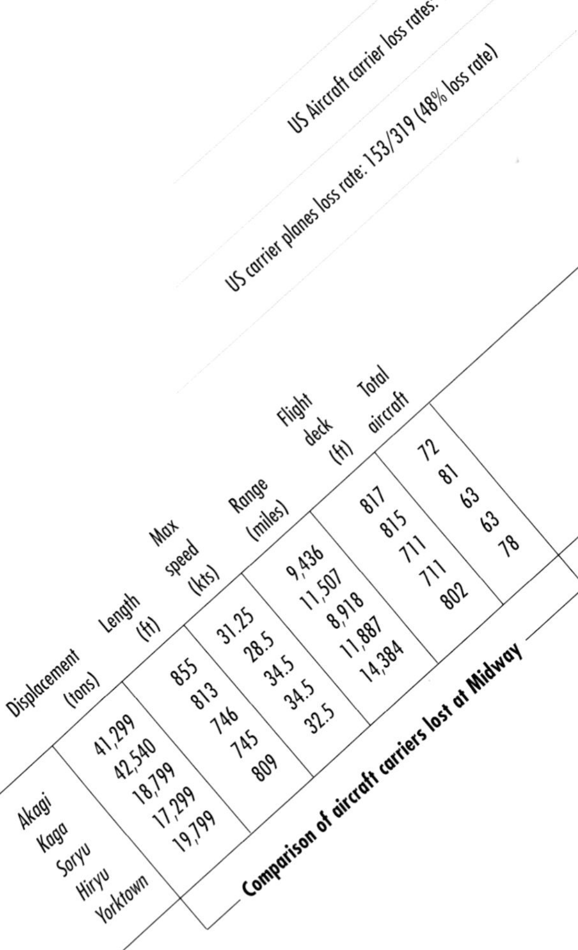

	Displacement (tons)	Length (ft)	Max speed (kts)	Range (miles)	Flight deck (ft)	Total aircraft
Akagi	41,299	855	31.25	9,436	817	72
Kaga	42,540	813	28.5	11,507	815	81
Soryu	18,799	746	34.5	8,918	711	63
Hiryu	17,299	745	34.5	11,887	711	63
Yorktown	19,799	809	32.5	14,384	802	78

Comparison of aircraft carriers lost at Midway

Hunting the *Bismarck*
1941

On May 24th, 1941, the German pocket battleship *Bismarck* sank the British battlecruiser HMS *Hood* in the Battle of the Denmark Strait. The *Bismarck* and the heavy cruiser *Prinz Eugen*, surface raiders, were attempting to move from the Baltic into the North Atlantic to take on the convoys so vital to the Allies, part of Operation Rheinübung. The *Hood* was sunk just ten minutes after first engagement; a shell from the *Bismarck* entered a magazine and sent the ship to the bottom in under three minutes, with the loss of 1,410 lives; only three men survived. Left afloat were the battleship HMS *Prince of Wales*, and cruisers HMS *Suffolk* and HMS *Norfolk*, both of which had engaged the *Prinz Eugen*. With the *Prince of Wales* also damaged, the British broke off the fight; but the *Bismarck* would not be left to escape.

With the *Bismarck* shipping oil, its captain had hoped to call in to Brest for repairs; but not if the British could help it. The "Pride of the British Navy" HMS *Hood* may have been sunk, but now the possibility of a major coup was in their sights, and when a patrolling aircraft observed the *Bismarck* at sea, its reports led to all ships in the area being ordered to seek out the two German warships, and destroy them.

Bismarck Armor

Actual armor thickness (width of bar)

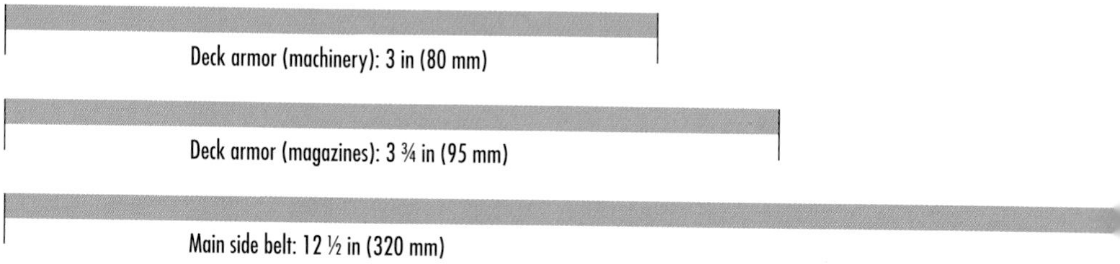

Deck armor (machinery): 3 in (80 mm)

Deck armor (magazines): 3 ¾ in (95 mm)

Main side belt: 12 ½ in (320 mm)

The *Prince of Wales*, still in the company of the *Norfolk* and *Suffolk*, followed the German battleship. HMS *Ramilies* and HMS *Rodney* were both battleships released from escort duties to seek out the *Bismarck*; HMS *King George V* and the aircraft carrier *Victorious*, together with their escorts, were sent down from Scapa Flow. On May 24th, Swordfish torpedo bombers from the *Victorious* scored hits on the *Bismarck*, but with little effect. It was another group, that of the carrier *Ark Royal*, the battleship *Renown*, and the cruiser *Sheffield*, that was to signify the end for the German ship.

On May 26th, at 21:00, another attack from Swordfish torpedo bombers, launched this time from the *Ark Royal*, led to a single torpedo severely damaging the great ship's rudder, causing her to steam directly toward the *King George V* and the *Rodney*, and destroyers kept up torpedo fire at the now stricken ship.

In the early morning of May 27th, 1941, *Rodney* and *King George V* opened fire on the *Bismarck* with a deadly hail of naval artillery fire that would destroy her superstructure and pound her gun turrets with almost 3,000 individual rounds. Within 30 minutes, all of the German ship's guns had been silenced. Low on fuel and ammunition, the two British battleships were withdrawn—even though the German ship showed no sign of surrender. The final blows fell from a lowly destroyer, the *Dorsetshire*, which launched four torpedoes at close range. In a poor state, the ship was abandoned, and orders given for her to be scuttled. The ship sank at 10:39.

With the 22,000-strong Kriegsmarine crew in the water, destroyers *Dorsetshire* and *Maori* attempted a rescue; the presence of a U-boat detected nearby meant that the British ships were forced to leave the Germans to their fate. Only 111 of the *Bismarck*'s crew survived.

British Naval Guns

16 inch	14 inch	8 inch	5.25 inch	6 inch
Weight: 120 tons (109 tonnes)	Weight: 89 tons (81 tonnes)	Weight: 19.5 tons (17.7 tonnes)	Weight: 4.7 tons (4.3 tonnes)	Weight: 8.4 tons (7.6 tonnes)
Barrel length: 60 ft (18.3 m)	Barrel length: 53 ft 6 in (16.31 m)	Barrel length: 33 ft 4 in (10 m)	Barrel length: 21 ft 11 in (6.7 m)	Barrel length: 22 ft 4 in (6.8 m)
Caliber: 16 in	Caliber: 14 in	Caliber: 8 in	Caliber: 5.25 in	Caliber: 6 in
Shell: 2,048 lb (929 kg) armor piercing	Shell: 1,590 lb (721 kg) armor piercing	Shell: 256 lb (116 kg) armor piercing	Shell: 80 lb (36 kg) semi-armor piercing	Shell: 100 lb (45 kg) HE
Maximum range: 39,780 yd (36,375 m)	Maximum range: 36,500 yd (33,400 m)	Maximum range: 30,620 yd (28,000 m)	Maximum range: 24,070 yd (22,010 m)	Maximum range: 14,600 yd (13,400 m)

British Shells Fired at the *Bismarck*, May 27th, 1941

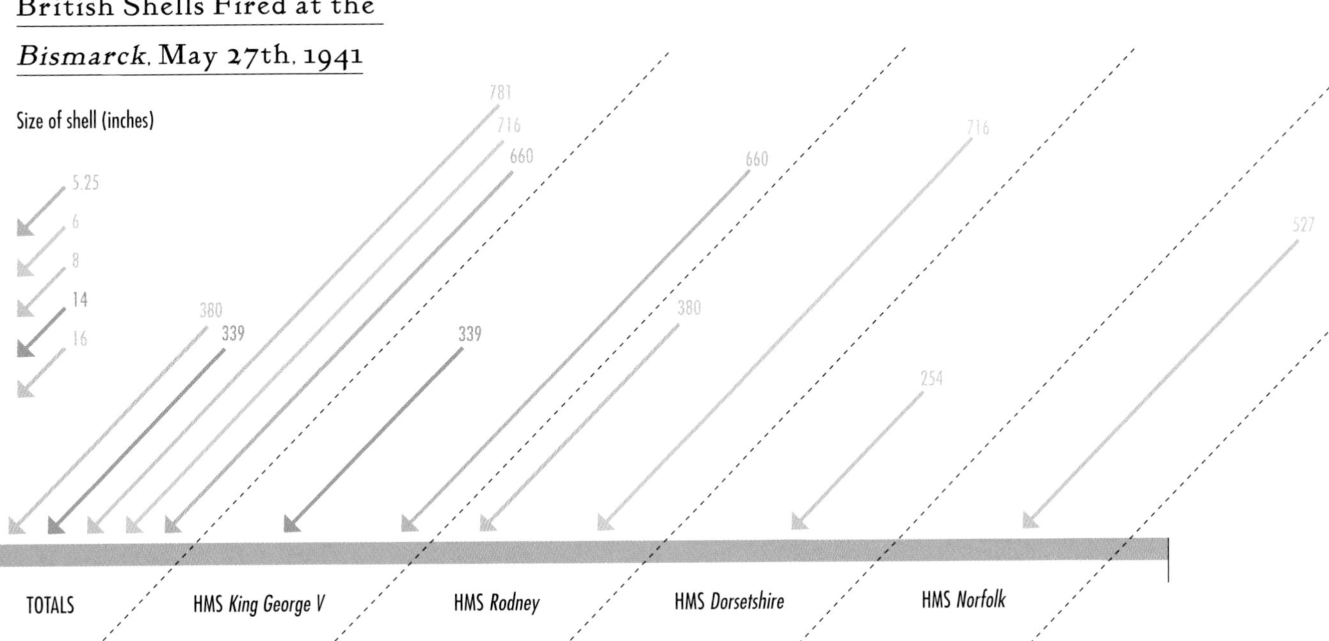

Chapter Six

COSTS

The human suffering of World War II is beyond comprehension. While the loss of combat troops on the Eastern Front and in the Pacific is staggering, it is the systematic destruction of peoples that still has the power to shock. With the largest Jewish population in Europe in 1939, it was Poland that would perhaps suffer the worst under Nazi tyranny. Two out of three Jews would be exterminated. Battle casualties, civilian deaths and the death of prisoners of war (POWs) in captivity, shocking as they are, still pale in comparison.

Prisoners of War

Large numbers of prisoners were captured during World War II. The blitzkrieg of 1939–1940 provided many Allied prisoners; combatants from Poland were first to be incarcerated in POW camps up and down the Reich territory, soon to be joined by Belgian, French and British soldiers after the fall of France in 1940. The tally of Allied soldiers held by the Germans grew steadily throughout the war: captured in the desert campaigns of 1940–1943 (and transferred from captivity in Italy in 1943); in the abortive attempts at stemming the Axis tide in Greece and Crete in 1941; in the Dieppe Raid of 1943 and the invasion of Italy in the same year; following D-Day in Normandy; in Arnhem, and at the Battle of the Bulge in the winter of 1944–1945. In the Pacific, military disasters such as the fall of Singapore in February 1942 led to large numbers of Allied military personnel falling into Japanese captivity; far fewer Japanese surrendered to Allied personnel.

Allied airmen would be captured as their aircraft were shot down or crashed through engine failure and other mechanical fault. With the fall of France, the conclusion of the Battle of Britain, and the German aerial blitz on British cities, came the call for bomber fleets to carry the battle to Germany. Losses were high; for Royal Air Force (RAF) Bomber Command 55,000 aircrew would be killed (40% of the total strength), with only 9,838 (8%) surviving to become prisoners of war. For the United States Army Air Forces (USAAF), in the 8th Air Force alone 26,000 airmen would be killed and 23,000 captured. For the British Royal Navy and Merchant Navy the dominance of U-boat warfare meant that the losses were high; over 3,500 Allied merchant ships sunk, and over 30,000 seamen lost—the majority killed.

In theory, the Third Geneva Convention of 1929 provided universal protection for all prisoners of war. The convention required that prisoners of war should be humanely treated, protected and fed and not subject to maltreatment or derision. Soviet prisoners were notable exceptions, as their government had neither signed nor ratified the treaty; excluded from the care of the Red Cross and the Swiss protecting powers, thousands would be starved and worked to death by the Nazis. Their German counterparts would fare only slightly better, and though many would be repatriated in 1947, the last German military personnel would only be released from captivity as late as 1956. The Japanese were particularly brutal toward their Allied captives; starvation, beatings, overwork and disease were all that Allied prisoners could expect from their captors.

Army (and Marine) Prisoners of War by Theater

Nationality	Confirmed POW	Other casualties (Killed & wounded)	Totals	POW as percentage of casualties
NW Europe				
Britain	14,700	126,950	141,650	10.4%
Canada	2,250	41,650	43,900	5.1%
France	4,730	62,100	66,830	3.5%
Germany	4,209,840	527,890	4,737,730	88.9%
Poland	370	5,000	5,370	6.9%
US	56,630	466,480	523,110	10.8%
Pacific/SE Asia				
Australia	18,130	3,190	21,320	85.0%
Britain	53,230	18,510	71,740	74.2%
India	68,890	31,060	99,950	68.9%
Japan	40,380	599,430	639,810	6.3%
US	30,680	223,540	254,220	12.1%

Estimated Death Rate of Prisoners of War in Captivity

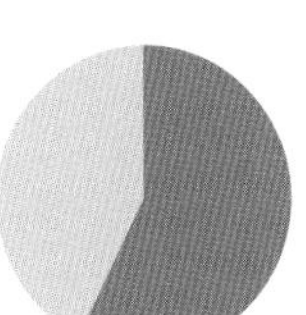

Soviet prisoners in German hands 57.5%

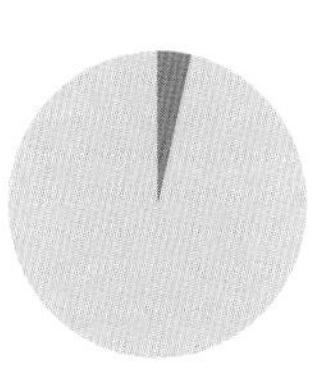

British prisoners in German hands 3.5%

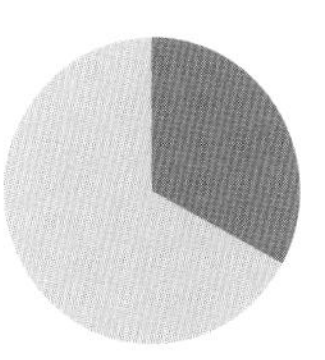

American prisoners in Japanese hands 33.0%

British prisoners in Japanese hands 24.8%

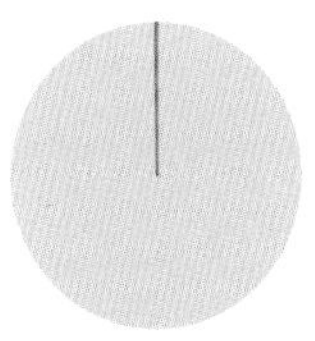

German prisoners in American hands 0.15%

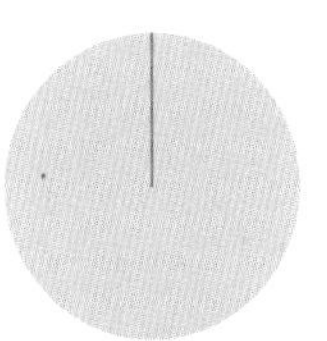

German prisoners in British hands 0.03%

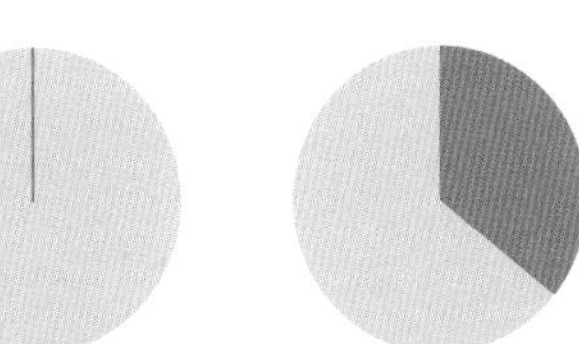

German prisoners in Soviet hands 35.8%

Prisoners

Percentage died

Known Deaths of Soviet POWs in German POW and Concentration Camps

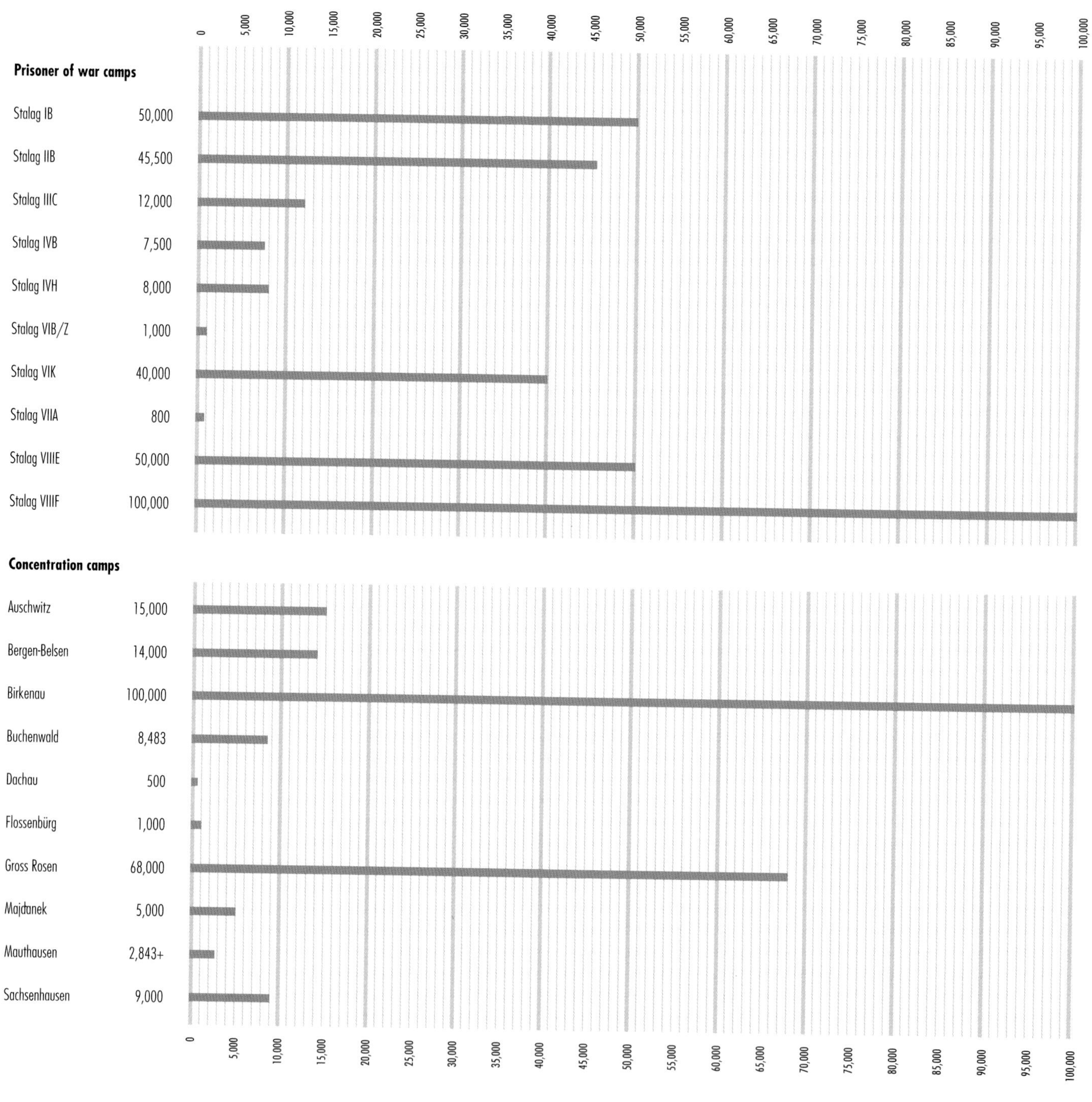

0
5,000
10,000
15,000
20,000
25,000
30,000
35,000
40,000
45,000
50,000
55,000
60,000
65,000
70,000
75,000
80,000
85,000
90,000
95,000
100,000
Prisoner of war camps
Stalag IB 50,000
Stalag IIB 45,500
Stalag IIIC 12,000
Stalag IVB 7,500
Stalag IVH 8,000
Stalag VIB/Z 1,000
Stalag VIK 40,000
Stalag VIIA 800
Stalag VIIIE 50,000
Stalag VIIIF 100,000
Concentration camps
Auschwitz 15,000
Bergen-Belsen 14,000
Birkenau 100,000
Buchenwald 8,483
Dachau 500
Flossenbürg 1,000
Gross Rosen 68,000
Majdanek 5,000
Mauthausen 2,843+
Sachsenhausen 9,000

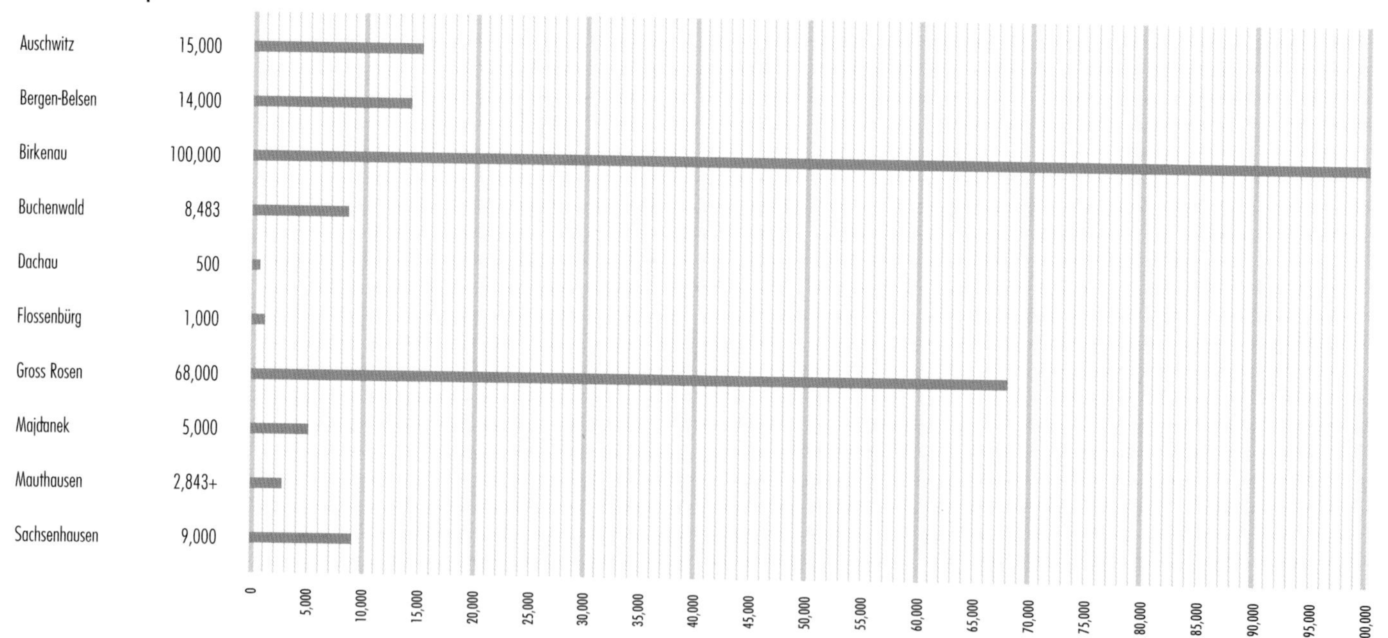

Soviet POWs in Germany

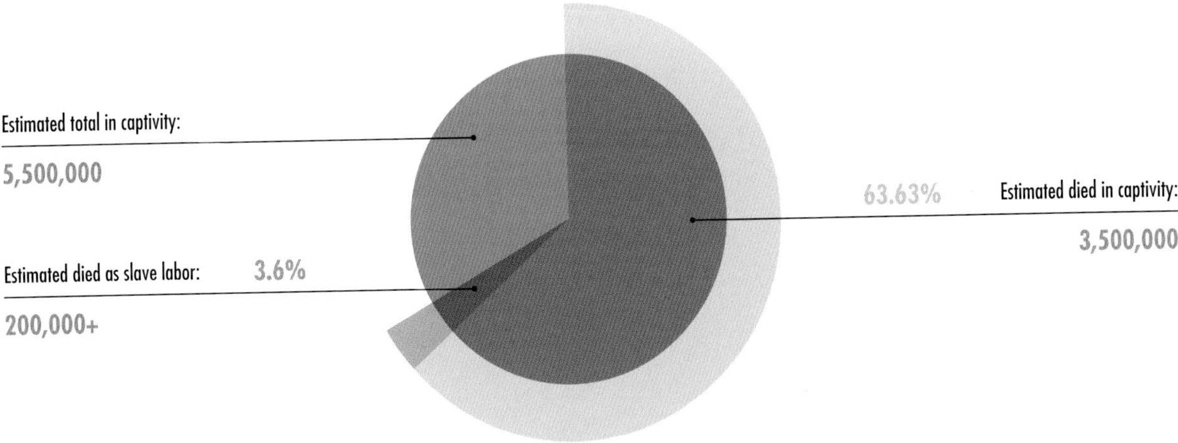

Nationalities of Wehrmacht POWs Still in Soviet Captivity, April 1956

Nationality	POW	Repatriated	Died in captivity	Percentage died
Austria	156,681	14,790	10,891	7.0%
Belgium	2,014	1,833	181	9.0%
Czechoslovakia	69,977	65,954	4,023	5.7%
Denmark	456	421	35	7.7%
France	23,136	21,811	1,325	5.7%
Germany	2,388,443	2,031,743	356,700	14.9%
Luxembourg	1,653	1,560	93	5.6%
Netherlands	4,730	4,530	200	4.2%
Norway	101	83	18	17.8%
Poland	60,277	57,149	3,128	5.2%
Spain	452	382	70	15.5%
Others	3,989	1,062	2,927	73.4%
Totals	**2,711,909**	**2,201,318**	**379,591**	**14.0%**

Battle Wounds and Sickness

In the Great War, it has been estimated that around 60% of all casualties were by artillery fire, and that only 25–30% were the result of small arms; i.e. gun shot wounds to the body (the majority being from the deployment of machine guns, which could deliver a high rate of fire). The remainder was primarily a function of other weapons, such as gas, grenades and bayonet attacks. Gas accounted for some 185,000 wounded, though with the much lower figure of 7,000 fatalities.

Sources of Injury Sustained by British Troops, 1939–1945

Percentage by type of all wounds suffered by British soldiers in all theaters during World War II. The vast majority were blast wounds sustained by artillery fire and aerial bombing (though this includes wounds sustained by mortars and grenades).

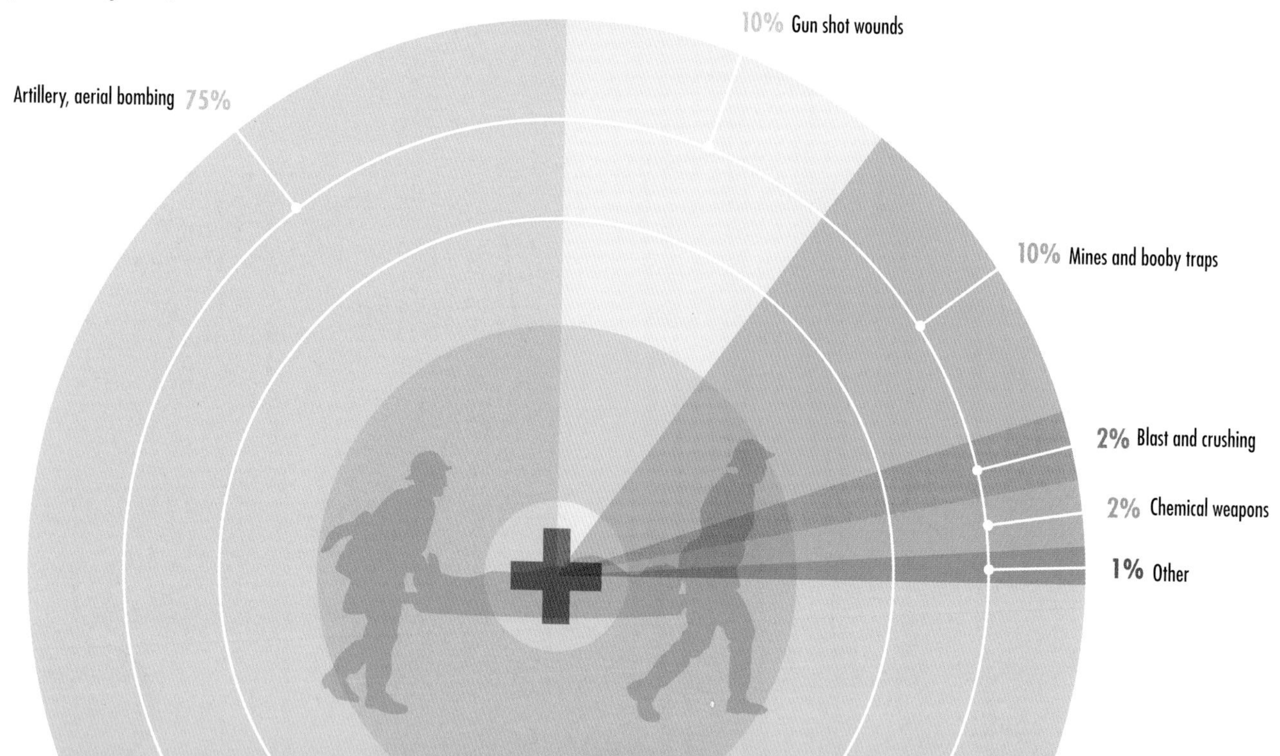

The figures for World War II demonstrate the increased effect of artillery and tank weaponry, as well as the effects of aerial attack and bombardment on the battlefield. Injuries and crushing from heavy weaponry was also a factor. Gas was, however, no longer an issue; its use was proscribed by the Geneva Convention, and the improvement in respirators and their availability meant that the effectiveness of gas as a weapon would be, at best, marginal. Chemical weapons were used, however, specifically the deployment of phosphorous grenades that would burn on impact.

With the war truly global, the fact that most soldiers were removed from the battlezone through sickness comes as no surprise. Operating in the hostile environment of the jungles in the Pacific theater, Allied troops would suffer sickness at rates at least ten times the incidence of battle-related injuries.

Battle Wounds and Sickness in Theater of War (per 1,000)

Hospital admissions per 1,000 soldiers, 1942–1945

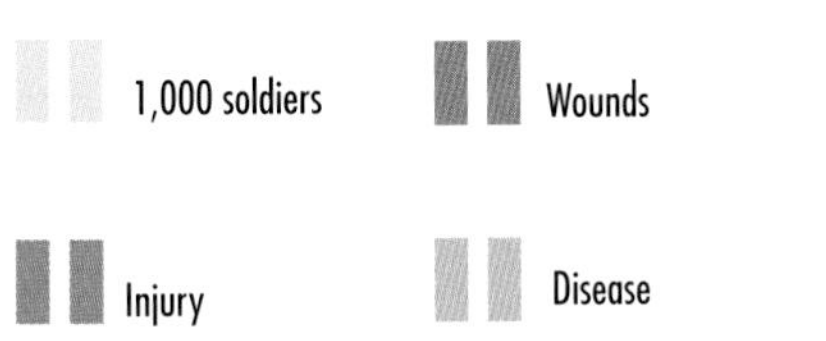

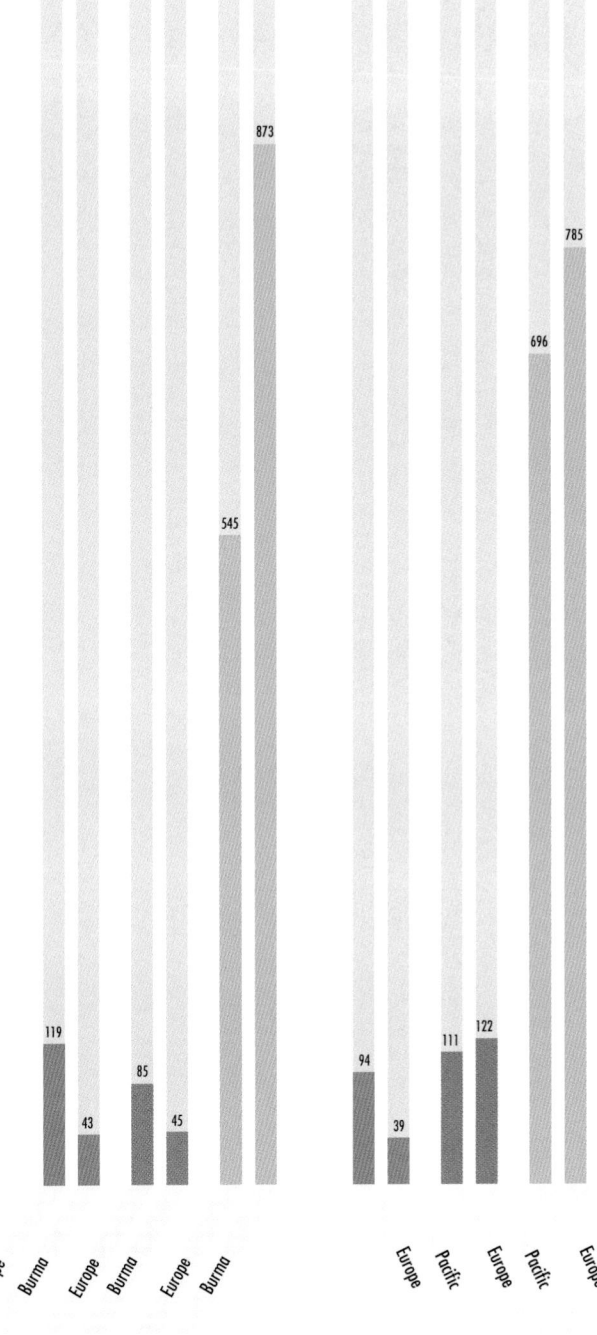

Casualties

World War II saw the greatest loss of life in any conflict, before or since. In World War I there were an estimated 10 million military deaths (either killed in action or died of wounds or disease) and a further 7 million civilian deaths, victims of genocide and starvation. But in the age of total warfare, aerial bombardment, the mass genocide known as the Holocaust and famine, the total number of war-related deaths would increase dramatically. Although the number of military deaths would double from that of World War I, civilian deaths caused by the war would reach catastrophic proportions: at least seven times the number reached in World War I. There would be at least 60 million deaths in total—some 2.5% of the world's population.

Deaths in World War I and II Compared

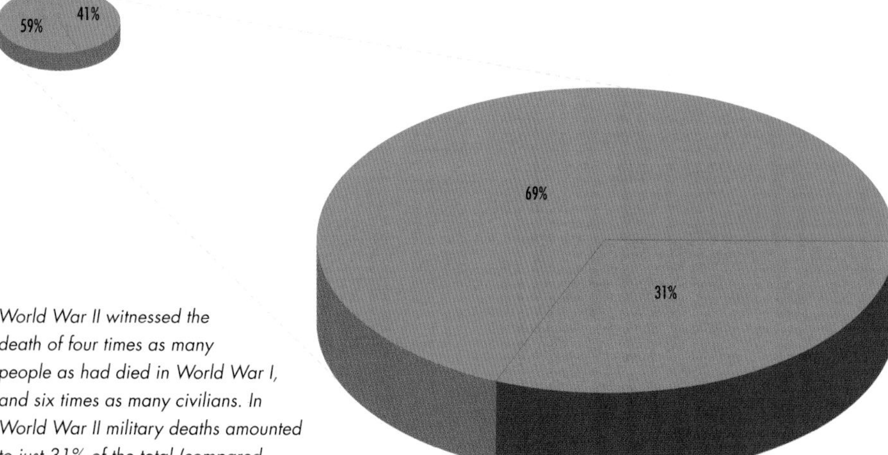

World War II witnessed the death of four times as many people as had died in World War I, and six times as many civilians. In World War II military deaths amounted to just 31% of the total (compared with 59% in World War I).

AXIS POWERS

The Axis powers were to suffer heavily; and no more so than Nazi Germany, whose military machine was not only geared to the successful blitzkrieg offensives against the West in 1939–1940, but also to the invasion of Russia in 1941, in Operation Barbarossa. It would soon be turned to the defensive, with all manpower used to stem the tide of the invading eastern and western armies converging on Berlin.

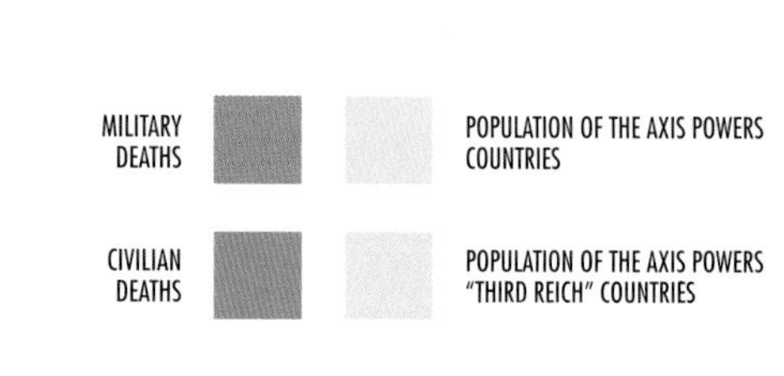

The lines (right) are a logarithmic scale for the graphic on the facing page. The graphic shows total deaths (military and civilian) suffered by the Axis powers in World War II, compared with the total population for each grouping.

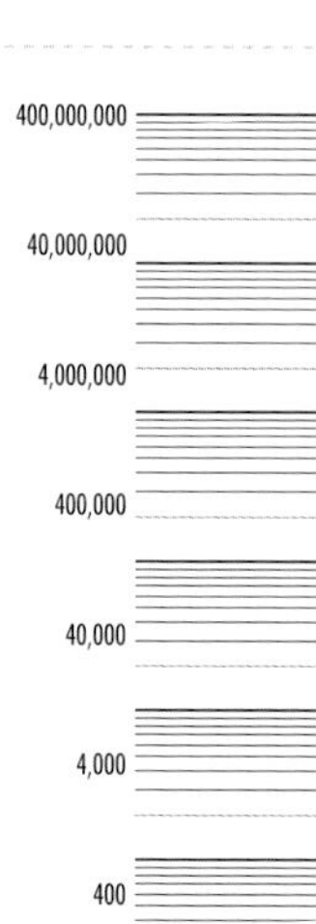

BLITZKRIEG

With the armies of the Third Reich outnumbered by those of the West in the early part of the war, it was the tactical doctrine of blitzkrieg ("lightning war"), of mobile warfare, that was to punish the complacent, defensively-minded Western powers. Though the Allies were armed with almost twice as many tanks as possessed by the Germans, the punishing pace of the Axis armies smashed through the Allied lines, at a cost of some 157,000 casualties; half the total lost by the Allies.

BATTLE FOR BERLIN

In the dying embers of the Third Reich, there would be desperate pitched battles fought among the ruins of what was once Hitler's Imperial City. Old men and boys, and the depleted relics of German divisions sapped by war, grimly held on in the face of the advancing Soviet armies intent on revenge. It would be a decisive victory for the Soviets, and the Germans would lose almost 100,000 military and paramilitary dead, with a further 22,000 civilians.

THE PACIFIC WAR

Japanese imperialist intentions to dominate the Pacific came to a dramatic head on December 7–8th, when the Emporer's forces attacked Thailand, the British-held territories in Malaya, and the US naval base at Pearl Harbor. Intended to be decisive, these battles certainly were shocking in their intensity, and 1941–1942 would be a difficult time for the Allies. The tide would turn in 1944–1945, with the Japanese expelled with heavy losses, their forces pushing back with unrivalled fanaticism.

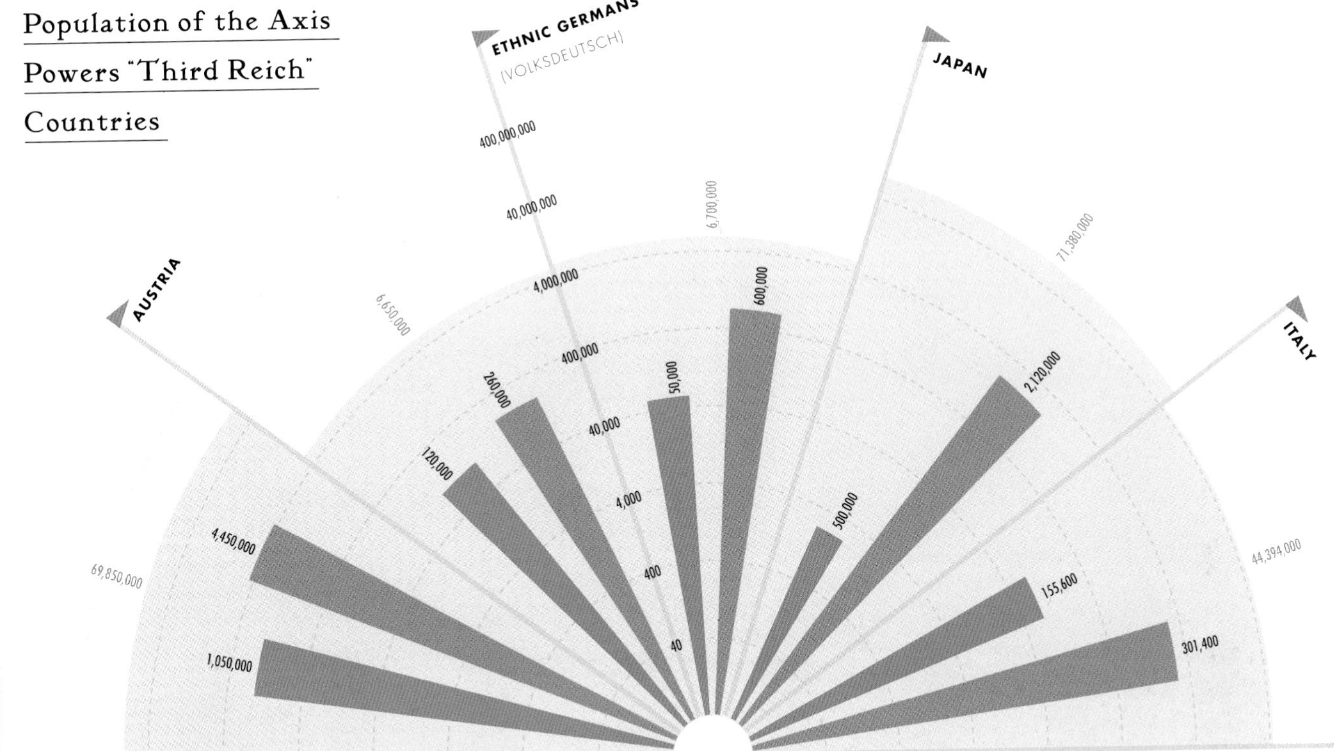

ALLIED POWERS

The invasion of Poland in 1939 brought the Western Allies into the war, but also saw the remarkable cooperation of Nazi and Soviet troops in the crushing of a small but proud nation sandwiched between two giants. The result was inevitable; though the Soviets would lose some 1,475 killed, and the Germans 16,343, the Poles would lose 66,000 military dead—a figure that would escalate as the Poles fought back under occupation. The subjugation of the Polish population by the Nazis would lead to staggering civilian losses, including the transportation and execution of some three million Polish Jews.

British Commonwealth losses would be high, a function of commitments on fronts that ranged from the fighting in Europe in 1940–1941, to the Western Desert in 1940–1942, the campaign in Burma and the Far East, and the eventual invasion of Nazi-occupied Europe in 1944. And, while committed abroad, the British homeland would be targeted with increasingly desperate German bombing and V-weapons campaigns, accounting for some 67,000 civilian deaths.

Hitler's focus well and truly turned eastward when, on June 21st, 1941, 4.3 million men of the Axis armies, organized in 166 divisions along a 1,800-mile (2,900 km) frontage, were focused on the largest invasion in history—that of the Soviet Union. With 600,000 military vehicles, Hitler's drive led him to the gates of the important Soviet cities of Leningrad and Moscow by December 1941. It ultimately resulted in the pivotal battle of Stalingrad, fought from August 1942 to February 1943 at a cost of some 500,000 Axis casualties. The invasion of the USSR would account for some 95% of Nazi casualties in 1941–1944; and 65% of Allied casualties. The Nazi campaign would account for at least three million Soviet prisoners of war; the vast majority would not return home. And some 14 million civilians were killed in, or died of famine in the wake of, the Nazi invasion.

Deaths as Percentage of the Population (1939): Axis Powers

GERMANY	AUSTRIA	VOLKSDEUTSCH	JAPAN	ITALY
5,880,000	380,000	380,000	2,620,000	457,000
7.9%	5.7%	9.7%	3.67%	1.03%

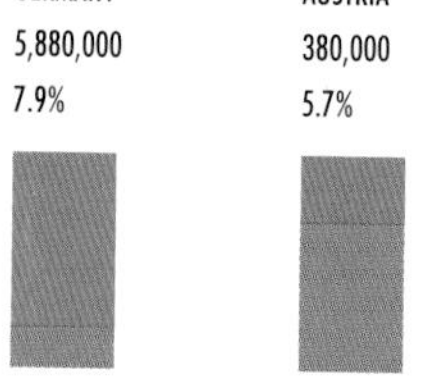
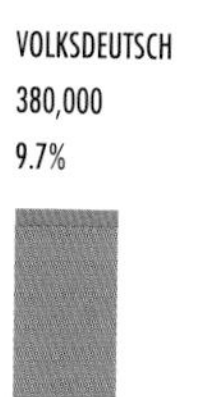
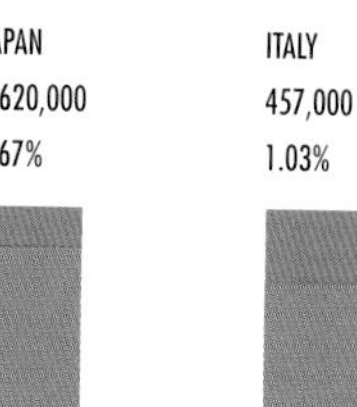

Military and civilian fatalities in Axis and Allied countries. The greatest number of civilian deaths occurred in those countries occupied by Nazi Germany.

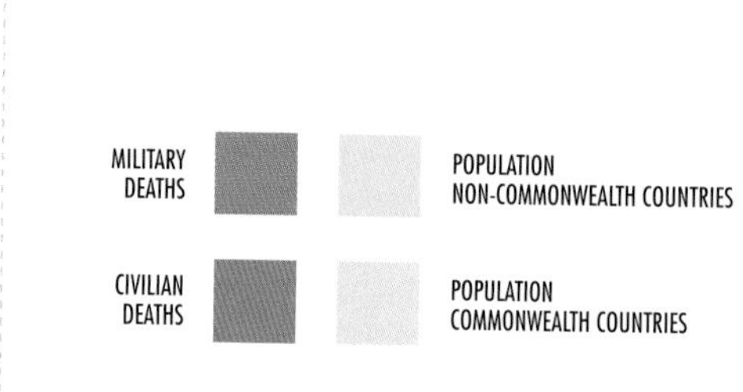

Deaths as Percentage of the Population (1939): Allied Powers

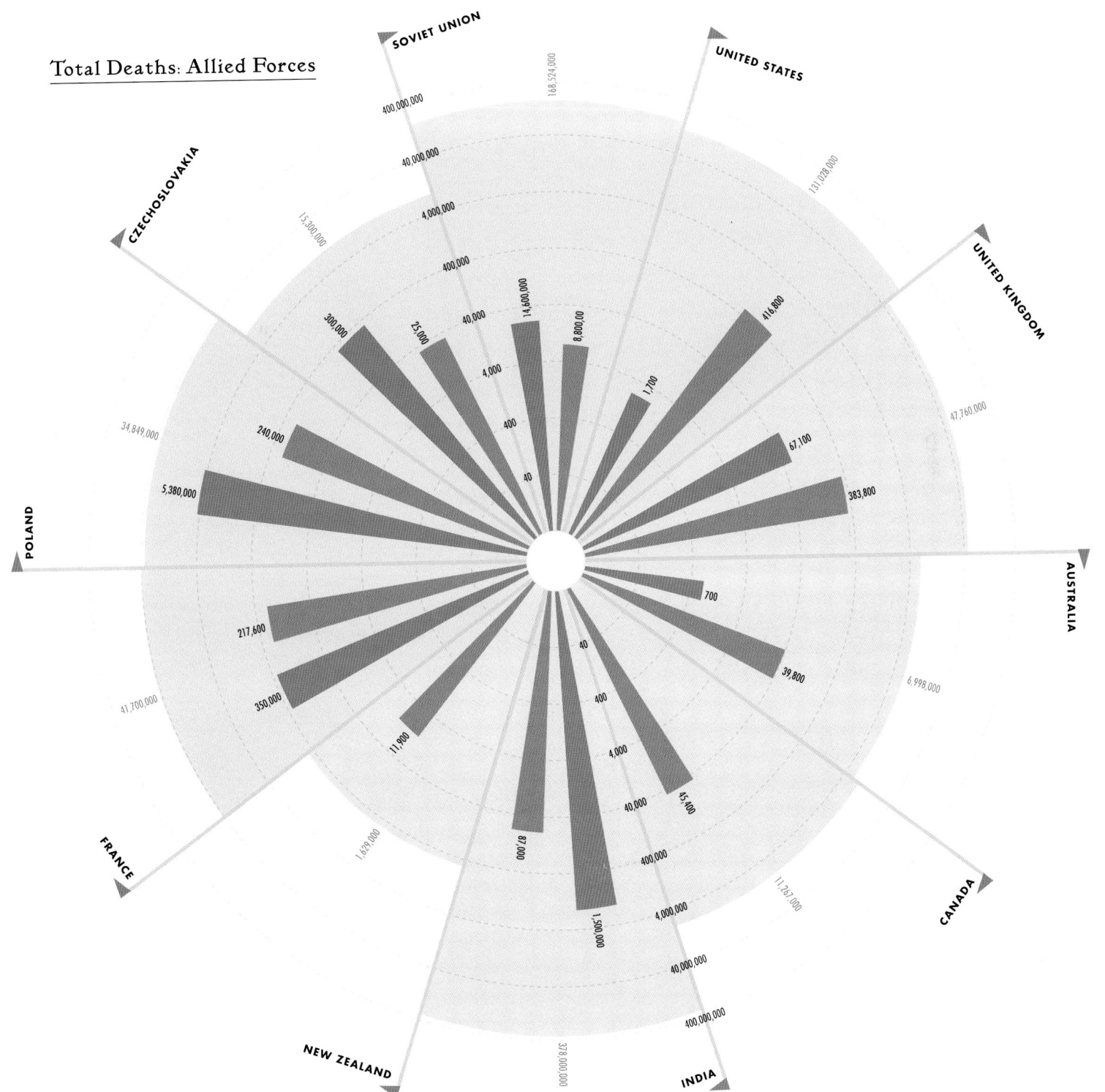

SOVIET UNION	UNITED STATES	UNITED KINGDOM	AUSTRALIA	CANADA	INDIA	NEW ZEALAND	FRANCE	POLAND	CZECHOSLOVAKIA
23,400,000	418,500	450,900	40,500	45,400	1,587,000	11,900	567,600	5,620,000	325,000
9.7%	0.32%	0.94%	0.57%	0.40%	0.42%	0.73%	1.35%	16.1%	2.12%

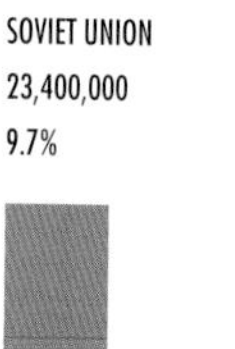

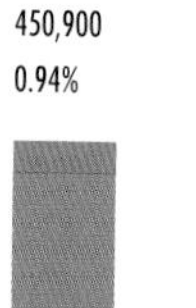

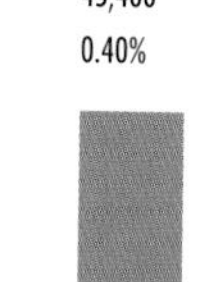

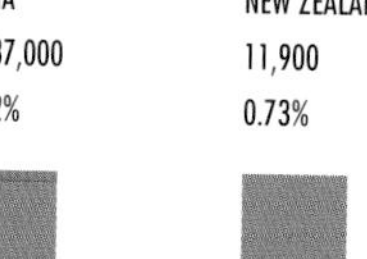
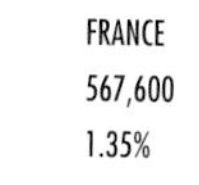

Total Deaths: Allied Forces

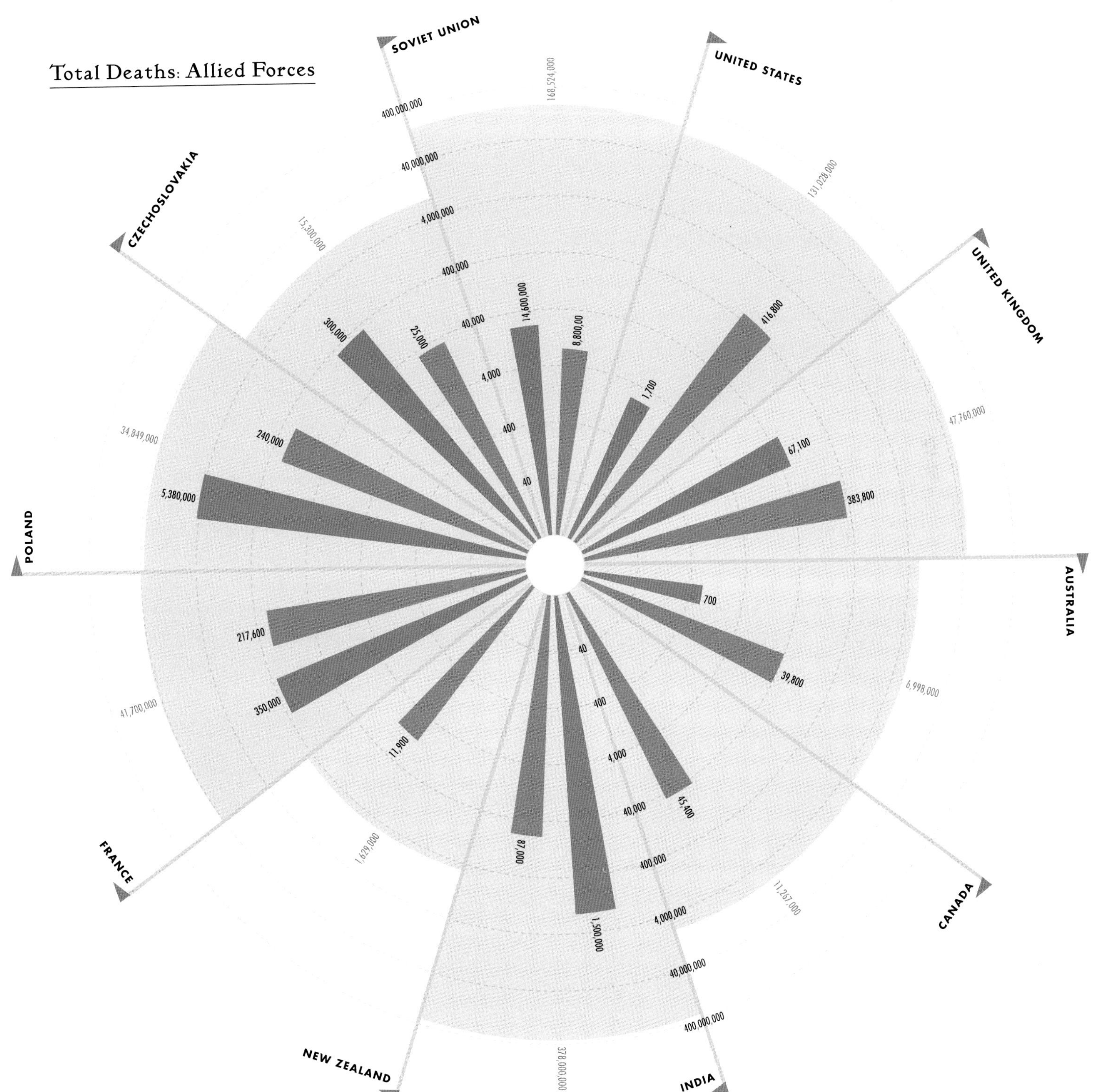

The Volkssturm
1944–1945

The *Deutscher Volkssturm* was a creation of the last days of Nazi Germany. The beginning of the end of the regime came with the penetration of the national borders of the state on August 17th, 1944, when the Soviet Red Army smashed across the border of East Prussia. This was the first time that the Nazi state had been so threatened; no longer was it a battle on the borders of the expanded "Greater Germany," here the Fatherland was under great danger. In 1940, when the homeland of Britain was directly threatened by invasion, the "Home Guard" was created—with Germany now in a similar position came the Volkssturm, its direct equivalent. Comprising old men and boys between the ages of 14 and 60, membership of this force was compulsory, the threat even more real.

The Volkssturm came into being on September 25th, 1944, in the face of increasing pressure from the Soviet forces in the east. The force was a militia, a creation of the Nazi party, but under the local control of the *Gauleiters*, leaders of the 42 regions, or "*Gaue*." Thus locally situated, the Volkssturm from each *Gau* would be best able to deal with challenges in the defence of their local region. Each *Volkssturmmann* was a compulsory recruit, called up under a system of "levies" that graded

The outer ring (below) is a visual representation of the percentage of the German male population for each age group, as broken down into figures in the table (below left). The inner ring shows the percentage of Volkssturm from each age group missing in action.

Ages of Men Liable for Volkssturm Service

Birth years	Ages (in 1944)	National total	% German male population	% Volkssturm MIA
Before 1884	> 60	(not liable)		1.6
1884–1896	48–60	4,890,000	35.96	46.0
1897–1900	44–47	1,823,000	13.30	20.1
1901–1905	39–43	2,104,000	15.35	17.2
1906–1927	17–38	3,092,000	22.56	12.9
1928–1930	14–16	1,796,000	13.10	2.2
Totals		**13,705,000**		

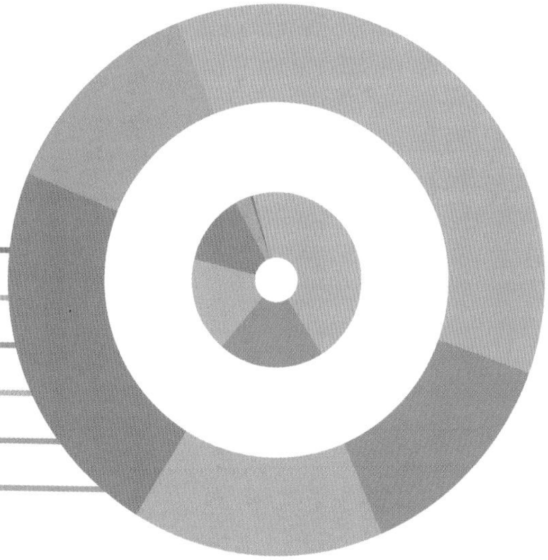

men according to age and health – but was also intended to protect essential industry from a drain in manpower. When Heinrich Himmler announced the creation of the force to the German people on October 18th, 1944, he drew upon links with the *Landsturm*, a historical military militia, in order perhaps to allay fears that their members would not be treated as legal combatants and would be summarily executed—especially as this was the punishment meted out to enemy partisans earlier in the war by the Nazis. As the Germans had rejected the validity of the British Home Guard in 1940, so they sought—and received—assurances from the Western Allies that Volkssturm, many of whom would be simply armed civilians possessing an armband, would be treated as soldiers. Whether they attempted this approach with the Soviets is another matter. The Volkssturm were indifferently trained, shoddily clothed and poorly equipped. Their primary offensive weapon was the deadly panzerfaust, a one-shot weapon that could disable a tank, but that was lethal to the operator if used incorrectly. Though these militiamen were to stand in for more seasoned troops in the west, in the east, they were called upon to stem the tide of the Red invasion, and would join with other determined resistance in the Battle for Berlin. There is no clear idea of the casualties suffered by these men, but estimates suggest Volkssturm units suffered at least 35% killed or wounded, with a further 20% missing in action.

Some idea of the casualty rates can be gleaned from German Red Cross records of Volkssturm men missing in action. Most were older men, men old enough to have seen service in World War I. And most would be men lost on the Eastern Front.

Ceremonial swearing-in of Berliner Volkssturm volunteers in front of Joseph Goebbels, 1945. Most carry panzerfaust, the main weapon of the Volkssturm in the face of the Soviet invasion.

Ages of Volkssturm Men Reported Missing in Action (MIA)

Average ages of Volkssturm missing in action: East, 47; West, 45

MIA West	Birth years	Ages (in 1944)	MIA East
8	Before 1884	>60	380
109	1884–1889	55–60	5,080
248	1890–1894	50–54	6,000
394	1895–1899	45–49	6,855
444	1900–1904	40–44	5,625
190	1905–1909	35–39	2,420
81	1910–1914	30–34	1,000
31	1915–1919	25–29	350
40	1920–1924	20–24	440
50	1925–1931	13–19	940
5	no age specified		100

The Polish Ghettos

The Warsaw ghetto was established between October and November 1940. As the largest of all Jewish ghettos in Nazi-occupied Europe it represents some of the worst scenes of suffering and privation associated with the Nazi regime.

The principle behind the ghetto was simple; the Polish capital was home to a large Jewish population, and by building a ghetto, it was possible to physically separate Jews from the remainder of the Polish population, and from the occupying Germans. They were rounded up and forced to live in cramped and

Indicates number of Jews incarcerated

Table shows Polish ghettos with populations of 10,000 or more; there were many others in smaller towns across Nazi-occupied Poland. Orange lines indicate the number of Jews incarcerated in each ghetto. Warsaw was the largest by far.

Name	Number of Jews incarcerated	Created	Liquidated	Extermination camp
Będzin	7,000–28,000	July 1940	August 1943	Auschwitz
Dąbrowa Górnicza	4,000–10,000	1940	June 1943	Auschwitz
Działoszyce	c.15,000	April 1940	October 1942	Kraków-Płaszów & Bełżec
Kozienice	13,000	January 1940	September 1942	Treblinka
Łódź	200,000	February 1940	August 1942	Auschwitz & Chełmno
Otwock	12,000–15,000	December 1939	August 1942	Treblinka & Auschwitz
Radomsko	18,000–20,000	1939–January 1940	July 1943	Treblinka
Tomaszów Mazowiecki	16,000–20,000	December 1940	November 1942	Treblinka
Warsaw	450,000	October–November 1940	September 1942	Treblinka & Majdanek
Zduńska Wola	8,300–10,000	1940	August 1942	Chełmno
Białystok	40,000–50,000	July 1941	October 1942	Majdanek, Treblinka
Bochnia	14,000–15,000	March 1941	September 1942	Bełżec & Auschwitz
Brześciu nad Bugiem	18,000	December 1941	October 1942	Executed locally
Chełm	8,000–12,000	June 1941	1942	Sobibor
Chmielnik	10,000–14,000	April 1941	November 1942	Treblinka
Częstochowa	48,000	April 1941	September–October 1942	Treblinka
Hrubieszów	6,800–10,000	June 1941–May 1942	May–November 1943	Sobibor & Budzyn
Izbica	12,000–22,700	1941	November 1942	Bełżec & Sobibor
Kielce	27,000	1941	August 1942	Treblinka
Końskie	10,000	1941	January 1943	Treblinka

unsanitary conditions. To contain them, high walls were constructed, and passage into the ghetto was strictly controlled. Inside these *Jüdischer Wohnbezirk* or *Wohngebiet der Juden*, food was extremely limited. The weak and the vulnerable were often left dying on the streets by the Nazis and their collaborators, and disease such as typhus was rife. Persecution was an everyday occurrence.

The ghettos were very evident and physical reminders of the Nazi's policy toward Jews, and toward anyone else they considered undesirable, for that matter. From the ghettos, Jews and other people deemed undesirable were transported to the death camps.

Although the Warsaw ghetto is perhaps the most notorious, there were many others across Poland. The system was initiated almost as soon as the Germans invaded the country. From October 1939 to July 1942 the ghetto system was instigated to hold the nation's 3.5 million Jews. Ghettos were established in most cities. In some cases they held just hundreds, but in the major cities they would contain tens of thousands in indescribable conditions. With Operation Barbarossa, the Nazis occupied the remainder of Poland, and new ghettos were established across the rest of the country. Others were established in the wake of the Wannsee Conference, held on January 20th, 1942.

Name	Number of Jews incarcerated	Created	Liquidated	Extermination camp
Lublin	30,000–40,000	March 1941	November 1942	Bełżec & Majdanek
Łomźa	9,000–11,000	June 1941	November 1942	Auschwitz
Łuków	10,000	1941	October–November 1942	Treblinka
Opatów	10,000	1941	July 1942	Executed locally
Ostrowiec Świętokrzyski	16,000	April 1941	October 1942	Treblinka
Opole Lubelskie	8,000–10,000	1941	October 1942	Sobibor
Radom	30,000–32,000	March 1941	August 1942	Treblinka
Słonim	22,000	July 1941	July 1942	Executed locally
Tarnopol	25,000	July–August 1941	June 1943	Bełżec
Wilno	30,000–80,000	September 1941	September 1942	Executed locally
Zwoleń	6,500–10,000	1941	September 1942	Treblinka
Żelechów	5,500–13,000	1941	September 1942	Treblinka
Drohobych	10,000	March 1942	June 1943	Bełżec
Kowel	17,000	May 1942	October 1942	Executed locally
Międzyrzec Podlaski	20,000	August 1942	July 1943	Treblinka
Przemyśl	22,000–24,000	July 1942	September 1943	Bełżec, Auschwitz & Janowska
Sosnowiec	12,000	October 1942	August 1943	Auschwitz
Starachowice	13,000	1942	1942	Treblinka
Stryj	4,000–12,000	1942	June 1943	Executed locally

The Holocaust

The scale of the Holocaust—the systematic persecution and mass murder of the Jews of Nazi-occupied Europe—is simply overwhelming. Two-thirds of the standing population of some 9 million Jews were executed in extermination camps, summary executions and through death squads. Nazi racial beliefs condemned all Jews as inferior, so-called *untermenschen*, and Germans as racially superior, and attacks on Jews and the Jewish way of life commenced early on in the establishment of the Nazi state in 1933. With the Nazis triumphant in their march across Europe, their hatred toward those deemed inferior increased. The extent of their racial beliefs meant that other groups were targeted as undesirable: Slavs (Poles and Russians), Roma Gypsies, disabled persons, homosexuals, political dissidents, and other beliefs and creeds, such as Jehovah's Witnesses.

Methods of Extermination

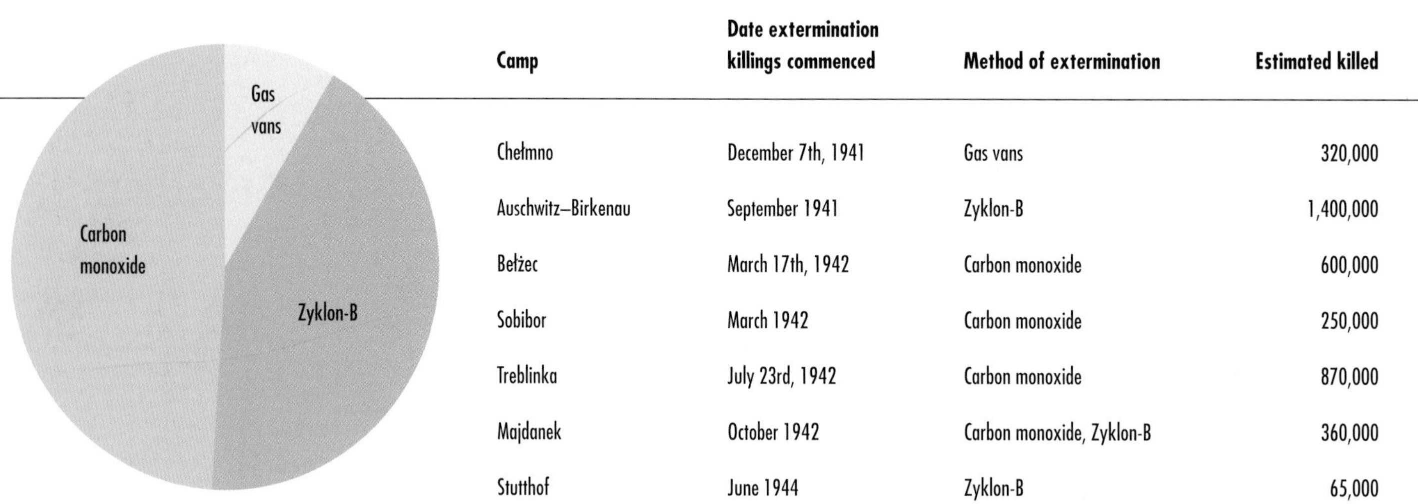

Camp	Date extermination killings commenced	Method of extermination	Estimated killed
Chełmno	December 7th, 1941	Gas vans	320,000
Auschwitz–Birkenau	September 1941	Zyklon-B	1,400,000
Bełżec	March 17th, 1942	Carbon monoxide	600,000
Sobibor	March 1942	Carbon monoxide	250,000
Treblinka	July 23rd, 1942	Carbon monoxide	870,000
Majdanek	October 1942	Carbon monoxide, Zyklon-B	360,000
Stutthof	June 1944	Zyklon-B	65,000

Concentration Camp Distinguishing Marks

Group		Estimated killed
Ukrainians	Red triangle with "R"	5.5 million +
Soviet POWs	Red triangle with "R"	3.3 million +
Poles	Red triangle with "P"	3 million +
Soviet civilians	Red triangle with "R"	2 million +
Yugoslavians	Red triangle with "J"	1.5 million +
Gypsies	Black, later brown, triangle	200,000–500,000
Disabled	Black triangle	70,000–250,000
Homosexuals	Pink triangle	Tens of thousands
Spanish Republicans	Red triangle with "S"	Tens of thousands
Jehovah's Winesses	Purple triangle	2,500–5,000
* Political prisoners	Red triangle	Unknown
Criminals	Green triangle	Unknown
** "Asocial elements"	Black triangle	Unknown

* Political prisoners, liberals, communists, resistance fighters, socialists, social democrats, trade unionists, Freemasons

** "Asocial elements," including alcoholics, vagrants, pacifists, prostitutes, drug addicts

Across occupied Europe, the Nazis developed concentration camps. In Poland, with its huge Jewish population, Jews were segregated into "ghettos" that were walled in, sealed off from the rest of the townspeople. In these ghettos, disease and starvation was rife, and Jews were rounded up and transported to death camps for extermination. From 1941–1944, millions of people were transported to death camps in order to enact the "final solution," the systematic execution of the Jews. Gassing was seen as an "efficient" means of dealing with the large numbers of people concerned, and in camps located in Greater Germany and Poland, carbon monoxide or the poison gas Zyklon-B were pumped into gas chambers to kill these helpless people.

For non-Jewish prisoners, forced labor camps were the alternative; here the SS authorities were keen to mark out each prisoner with a badge that might in itself promote a pecking order and create dissent and unrest. In other cases, and particularly in the occupied Soviet Union, roving murder squads, *Einsatzgruppen*, would deal with any group deemed undesirable. As a lasting legacy of the war, the Holocaust serves as a remembrance of how low the human race can stoop.

The Final Solution: Percentage of Jewish Population Killed in Occupied Countries

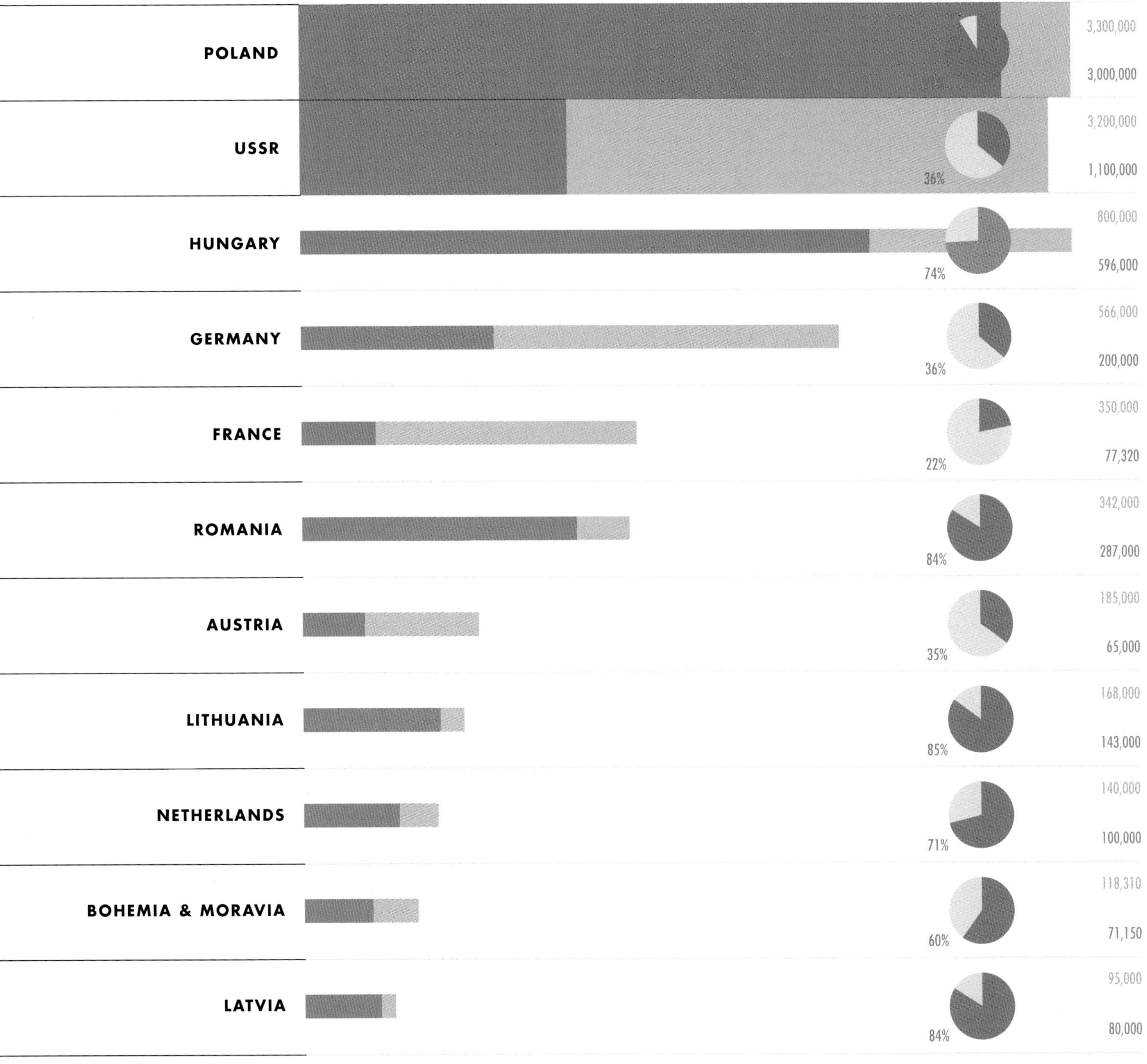

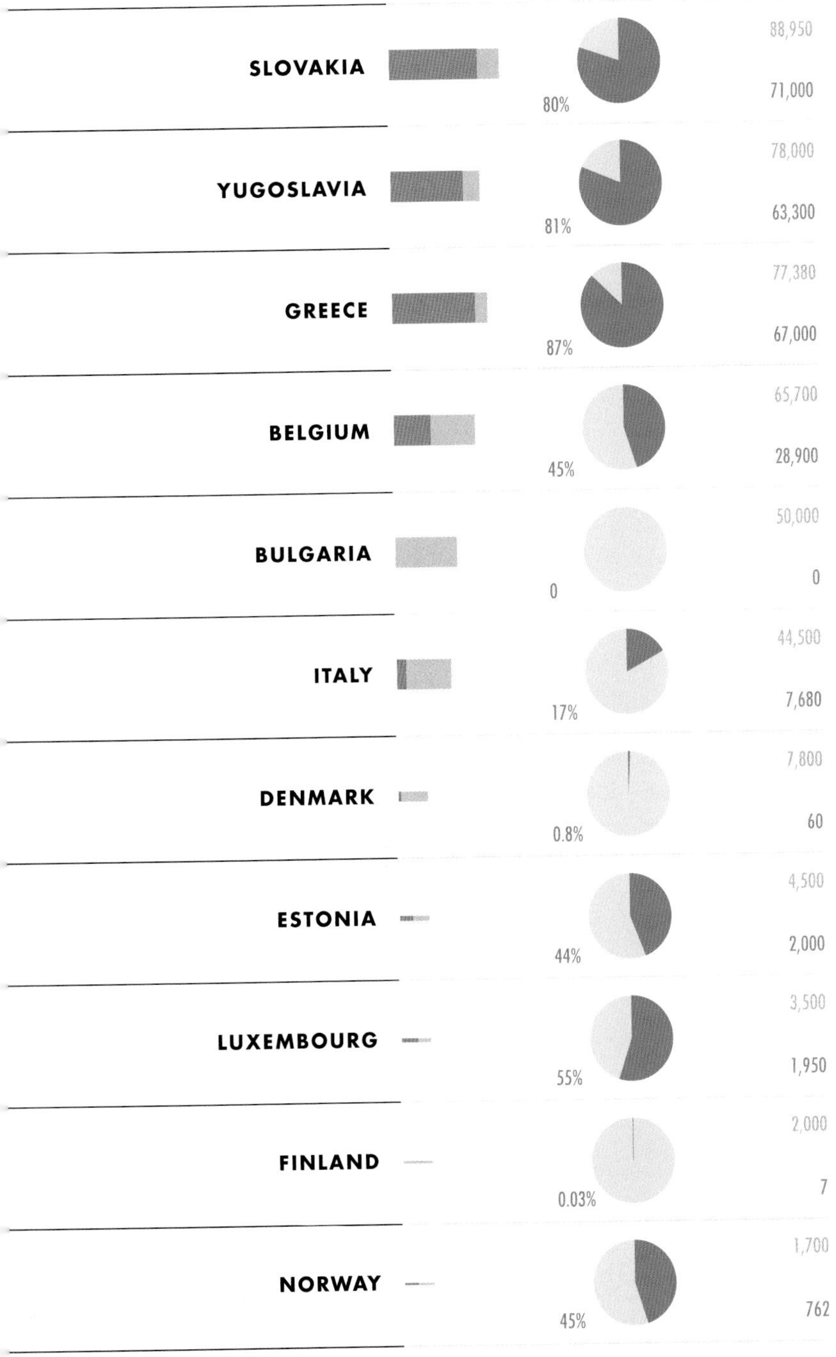

Country	Percentage of the Jewish population killed	Initial Jewish population	Estimated killed
SLOVAKIA	80%	88,950	71,000
YUGOSLAVIA	81%	78,000	63,300
GREECE	87%	77,380	67,000
BELGIUM	45%	65,700	28,900
BULGARIA	0	50,000	0
ITALY	17%	44,500	7,680
DENMARK	0.8%	7,800	60
ESTONIA	44%	4,500	2,000
LUXEMBOURG	55%	3,500	1,950
FINLAND	0.03%	2,000	7
NORWAY	45%	1,700	762

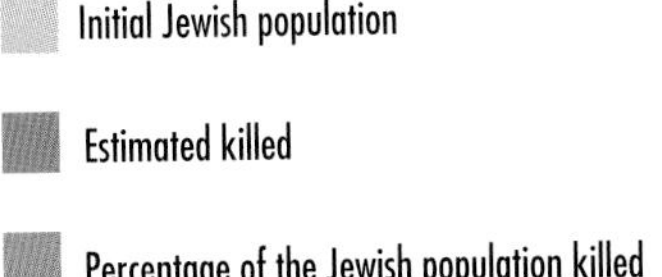

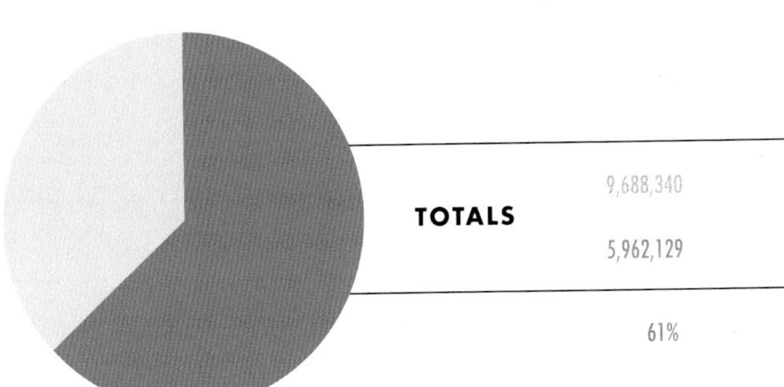

Percentage of the Jewish population killed in occupied countries during enactment of the "final solution," the Nazis' plan to exterminate Jews and other groups it considered "undesirable." With the population of the Nazi-controlled or occupied countries initially standing at over 9.5 million people, almost two-thirds were exterminated. In Poland, of its pre-war Jewish population of 3.3 million people, only 300,000 survived, a death rate of around 91%.

Selected Sources and Further Reading

Askey, N. 2008. *Operation Barbarossa: the Complete Organisational and Statistical Analysis.* http://operationbarbarossa.net

Badsey, S. 1993. *Arnhem* 1944. Osprey Publishing.

Bell, P.M.H. 2011. *Twelve Turning Points of the Second World War.* Yale University Press.

Bishop, P. 2008. *The Battle of Britain.* Quercus Books.

Chamberlain, P. & Doyle, H. 2004. *Encyclopedia of German Tanks of World War Two.* Silverdale Books.

Chamberlain, P. & Ellis, C. 2004. *British and American Tanks of World War Two.* Silverdale Books.

Collier, B. 1957. *The Defence of the United Kingdom.* Imperial War Museum.

Ellis, J. 1993. *The World War II Data Book.* Aurum Press.

Forty, G. 1995. *US Army Handbook 1939–45.* Sutton Publishing.

Forty, G. 2002. *The Desert War.* Sutton Publishing.

Gazarke, W.H. & Dulin, R.O. 1991. *The* Bismarck *Encounter.* Chesapeake Section, Society of Naval Architects & Engineers.

Gilbert, M. 2008. *The Routledge Atlas of the Second World War.* Routledge.

Glantz, D.M. 1986. *CSI Report No 11.* Combat Studies Institute, US Army Command & General Staff College.

Goldsmith, R.W. 1946. 'The power of victory: munitions output in World War II'. *Military Affairs*, 10, pp.69–80.

Gray, E. 1992. *Hitler's Battleships.* Leo Cooper.

Gruhl, W. 2006. *Imperial Japan's World War Two: 1931–1945.* http://www.japanww2.com

Harrison, M. 1988. Resource mobilization for World War II: the USA, UK, USSR and Germany 1938–1945. *Economic History Review*, 42, pp.171–192.

Haskew, M.E. 2009. *Order of Battle: Western Allied Forces of WWII.* Amber Books.

Hayward, N.S. 1998. *Stopped at Stalingrad: The Luftwaffe and Hitler's Defeat in the East 1942–43.* University of Kansas Press.

Healy, M. 2008. *Zitadelle: The German Offensive Against the Kursk Salient.* Spellmount.

Heaton, C.D. & Lewis, A-M. 2012. *The Me262 Stormbird.* Zenith Press.

Higgins, W.J. *et al.* 1985. *CSI Battlebook 10-C Imphal–Kohima.* Combat Studies Institute, Fort Leavenworth, Kansas.

Hudson, S.A.M. 2010. *UXB Malta.* History Press.

International Branch, Headquarters Army Service Forces. 1945. *International Aid Statistics World War II.* http://www.archives.gov/research/guide-fed-records/groups/169.html

Kwiatkowski, B. 1949, *Sabotaż i Dywersja*, Bellona, London, vol. I, p.21.

Lehmann, D. *Number of AFVs on 10th May 1940.* http://www.tarrif.net/wwii/pdf

Leland, A. & Oboroceanu, M-J. 2010. *American War and Military Operations Casualties: Lists and Statistics.* Congressional Research Service Report for Congress 7-750.

McNab, C. 2009, *The Third Reich 1933–45.* Amber Books.

Rossignoli, G. 1989. *The Allied Forces in Italy 1943–45.* David & Charles.

Silverstrim, K. *Overlooked Millions: Non-Jewish Victims of the Holocaust.* University of Central Arkansas. www.ukemonde.com/holocaust/victims.html

Wesolowski, Z.P. *The Polish Monte Cassino Cross.* www.virtuti.com/order/articles/cassino.html

Willmott, H.P., Cross, R. & Messenger, C. 2004. *World War II.* Dorling Kindersley.

Wright, M. (ed.) 1989. *The World at Arms.* Reader's Digest.

Yelton, D.K. 2002. *Hitler's Volksstrum: The Nazi Militia and the Fall of Germany 1944–45.* Kansas University Press.

Zaloga, S.J. 2005. *D-Day Fortifications in Normandy.* Osprey Publishing.

Zaloga, S.J. 2011. *Kamikaze: Japanese Special Attack Weapons 1944–45.* Osprey Publishing.

Zetterling, N. & Frankson, A. 2000. *Kursk 1943: A Statistical Analysis.* Frank Cass Publishers.

WEB RESOURCES

www.angelfire.com/ct/ww2europe/stats.html

www.angelfire.com/wi2/foto/ww2/proh/page4.html

www.archives.gov/research/guide-fed-records/groups/169.html

www.bismarck-class.dk

www.century-of-flight.net

http://cz-raf.hyperlink.cz/first.html

www.ddaymuseum.co.uk

www.doolittleraider.com/80_brave_men.htm

www.feldgrau.com

www.german-navy.de/kriegsmarine/ships/index.html

www.history.army.mil/documents/mobpam.htm

www.history.navy.mil/faqs

www.historyofwar.org/articles/operation_dynamo.html

www.japanww2.com

www.microworks.net/pacific/orders_of_battle/midway_usa.htm

www.midway1942.org/specs.shtml

www.militaryeducation.org

www.militaryhistoryonline.com/wwii/articles/polishcavalry.aspx

www.history.navy.mil/branches/teach/pearl/aftermath/facts.htm

http://necrometrics.com/battles.htm

www.nzhistory.net.nz/war/the-battle-for-crete

operationbarbarossa.net

www.polamjournal.com/Library/APHistory/Cavalry_Myth/cavalry_myth.html

www.populstat.info

www.raf.mod.uk/history/aircraft.cfm

www.secondworldwarhistory.com

http://stalingrad.net

www.statisticbrain.com/holocaust-statistics/

www.ukemonde.com/holocaust/victims.html

www.ushmm.org/research/library/

www.virtuti.com/order/articles/cassino.html

www.warhistoryonline.com/featured-article/facts-and-figures-of-d-day.html

www.warsawuprising.com

http://world.guns.ru/grenade/de/panzerfaust-e.html

www.worldwar2facts.org

www.worldwar2facts.org/battle-of-crete.html

http://ww2db.com

Index

Credits

p8 © Roger Viollet/Getty Images
p10 © Getty Images
p21 © Getty Images
p33 © IWM via Getty images
p47 © Hohum | Creative Commons, © baku13 | Creative Commons, © Hohum | Creative Commons
p54 © Arthur Conry | Creative Commons
p56 © Creative Commons
p68 © Creative Commons (Image of Erwin Rommel)
p76 © Wittke | Creative Commons, Image of Polish cemetery © Creative Commons
p77 © Jacek Gralak | Creative Commons
p82 © Koll | Creative Commons
p86 © Time & Life Pictures/Getty Images
p87 © Getty Images, © Time & Life Pictures/Getty Images
p108 © Getty Images
p110 © Getty Images
p114 © Time & Life Pictures/Getty Images
p118 © AFP/Getty Images
p119 © De Agostini/Getty Images
p134 © Popperfoto/Getty Images
p143 © Getty Images
p146 © Popperfoto/Getty Images
p149 © Getty Images
p154 © Roger Viollet/Getty Images
p161 © Time & Life Pictures/Getty Images
p163 © Roger Viollet/Getty Images
p174 © Petrified Collection
p176 © Getty Images
p198 © Time & Life Pictures/Getty Images
p211 © Creative Commons